An
Essential
Grace

An Essential Grace

Funding Canada's Health Care,
Education, Welfare,
Religion and Culture

BY SAMUEL A. MARTIN

McCLELLAND AND STEWART
TORONTO

McClelland and Stewart Limited
The Canadian Publishers
25 Hollinger Road
Toronto, Ontario
M4B 3G2

Canadian cataloguing in publication data

Martin, Samuel, A.
  An essential grace

Includes index.
ISBN 0-7710-5803-9

1.Charities — Canada. 2. Endowments — Canada. 3. Art
patronage — Canada. 4. Humanitarianism. I. Title.

HV 105.M37 1985 361.7   C85-098004-6

Printed and bound in Canada by
T.H. Best Printing Company Limited,
Don Mills, Ontario

For Helen

Contents

Introduction by
Peter C. Newman

Back in the late 1950s, when Billy Graham was still a prime newsmaker, he launched one of his "Crusades" in Canada. For reasons that now escape me, I was assigned to cover his Toronto visit for the American edition of *Time*. Being even the temporary representative of a major U.S. newsmagazine allowed me access to the Graham entourage, and I well remember dropping in backstage after the first night's activities were over.

The Canadian National Exhibition Coliseum, which had been turned into a makeshift place of community worship for the occasion, was still reverberating with the echoes of that slick salvation-machine's performance; backstage, the mood of the Billy team was one of annoyed puzzlement. The crowd response had been so much better than they had expected for a first night. That wasn't the trouble. Encouraged by local churchmen who were cooperating with Graham, more than a thousand Canadian "converts" had stepped forward to ask for Billy's blessing, displaying the familiar symptoms of evangelical ecstasy. The problem was that when it came around to collection time, the crowd had responded with nickels and dimes instead of the more substantial contributions the Graham people had always received at stateside revivals.

"What can we do?" Bev Shea asked me, because I happened to be the only Canadian behind the curtains with the Graham operatives.

"Simple," I remember answering, "just make it clear that you'll issue tax receipts."

"Bless you, brother," he mumbled and, next evening, the appropriate announcement preceded the passing of the collection baskets. Hallelujah, how the money rolled in.

In its way, that small incident serves as a relevant introduction to this valuable book: altruism surely is *the* "Essential Grace"—yet Canadians have always held their generous impulses in check, making absolutely sure they were deductible.

Professor Samuel Martin's book is not only important because it examines the sources that finance the quality of Canadian life, but timely because it is being published just as governments at all levels have become unusually parsimonious. "Social welfare is perhaps the most controversial topic in Canada today," Martin writes. "Payments expand annually as the rolls of legitimate participants swell. Governments strain to meet the financial demands with increased taxes and borrowings. A wary, and weary, public decries the tax squeeze, denounces fiscal mismanagement and alludes to gross abuses in the welfare system. Social agencies are not immune to the backlash. Their direct appeals to the public for gifts are frequently rejected because 'my taxes are already too high' or 'the funds will be poorly managed.'"

In this context, it is more essential than ever to determine what motivates Canadians to donate money to charitable organizations—and why philanthropy is in such sad decline. Professor Martin tackles the political, social and economic factors that influence altruism in this country and manages to extract some fascinating new answers to the question: what, precisely, goads citizens' collective and individual tender consciences? With the deft touch of a computer designer, he follows the circuits of "kinship" within the Canadian Establishment that are the most compelling force in private donation decisions. He is not fooled by his subjects' power and glory, recognizing that even at this level, fund raising really consists of a fair exchange of favors. He calls it "the only acceptable form of influence peddling," and ventures into the once-sacrosanct precincts of how honorary university degrees are marketed. He concludes: "For the man who has everything but the privilege of calling himself doctor, an LL.D. holds a certain attraction. . . ."

Professor Martin's main conclusion can probably be summarized as a *cri-de-coeur* against the egoistic society he believes we have evolved in Canada. "Preoccupation with self-interest may advance some individuals," he writes, "but it weakens the community, the nation. Surely Canada will regress in stature if Canadians lose sight of our larger personal duty. If training in morality and ethics no longer is acquired through the conventional socializing institutions—the church, the home—then it must be taught in the schools. Psychologists have shown that altruism can be learned, not through a three-day seminar for top management held in some exclusive training centre but through disciplined, repetitive, intelligent instruction begun in early years and reinforced throughout adolescence.''

Canadians have always had genuine difficulty being open and generous— with themselves as well as with others. Yet one cannot help but be touched by a remark attributed to Edmund Charles Bovey, the private sector's most enlightened and successful fund raiser, who once complained that ''it is very difficult to be generous in this country.''

Part of the prevailing dilemma is that most professional careers are consummated inside large corporations, mainly multinationals, and not within definable geographic communities. This tends to scatter personal loyalties so that humanistic endeavors that were the priority of a previous generation do not count for nearly as much as before. Another problem is the incredible secrecy surrounding the act of giving. Professor Martin points out that, among the annual reports of 168 leading Canadian companies, only two (the Bank of Montreal and John Labatt Limited) revealed the dollar amounts of their annual donations (0.5 per cent of pre-tax income for Canada's first bank and 1.7 per cent for the beer company). ''If corporations are taciturn about their donation activities,'' he complains, ''Canadian foundations are downright clandestine.'' His letter politely requesting basic financial facts from the country's top 50 foundations brought precisely one reply that contained the requested financial statements—from the Richard Ivey Foundation in London, Ont. There are approximately a thousand foundations in this country, controlling assets worth at least $1 billion and enjoying many tax concessions, yet they retain an attitude of privacy which the good professor brands as ''an attitude that borders on arrogant concealment.''

One of the book's more interesting statistics is that foreign-owned corporations have a higher tendency to make charitable donations than their domestic counterparts. Almost half of the outside-owned firms donated something, compared with a Canadian participation rate of nine per cent.

In my own continuing studies of how the private sector reacts to funding appeals, I have detected a strong tendency towards ritualistic response. (''Let's find out how much Charlie got out of the Royal for the United Way and prorate ourselves at 10 per cent . . . I must remember to nail him when I get into that damn Heart Fund drive this fall . . .'')

There are exceptions to the pattern of not-giving—the Koerners in Vancouver; the Harvies in Calgary; the Richardsons in Winnipeg; the Chalmers in Toronto; the McConnells in Montreal, among others. And every once in a while a real event stirs Canadians' subdued generosity: the Terry Fox run raised $23 million within a week of his poignant capitulation. But each year's commemorative marathon raises less, and the whole exercise may soon be dropped.

It seems to be self-indulgence rather than altruism that currently dominates the Canadian ethic. If that depressing state of affairs is to be changed, we must first understand how the philanthropic impulse works, how large the gap it must fill is going to be and what alternate funding sources exist. The answers to these and many other questions are documented in the pages that follow. It is a worthy story, well told.

But it still bothers me that I gave away the secret route to Canadians' pocketbooks that long-ago night at the CNE. What if Billy tells God?

Peter C. Newman

Preface

The theme of *An Essential Grace*—allocating resources to humanistic service—is hardly in the mainstream of contemporary economic thought. Fashionable today is a formula for producing more with less, tips on harnessing the microchip, advice on coping with robotics. Production. Efficiency. Industrial strategy. Not that such activity is misdirected. More than 1.3 million unemployed Canadians depend on a strong and sustained recovery to open jobs for their talents.

Ironically, most of the newly minted openings will demand skills vastly different from those possessed by the pool of unemployed. And so, many shall remain out of the workforce, casualties of the third industrial wave, dependent on state agencies or private welfare organizations for economic sustenance and moral support or on a community college to train them for re-entry.

Canadians are fortunate. We face the apprehensive eighties with a sophisticated infrastructure dedicated to serving our humanistic needs: a health-care system ensuring every Canadian, regardless of circumstances, of first-class treatment; schools and universities of respectable quality, accessible to all who possess the capacity to learn and the desire to grow; churches and synagogues to cultivate our conscience, to sustain our moral and spiritual values; theatres, art galleries, museums that create and articulate a culture unmistakably Canadian. And a welfare net that catches those who drop, or are pushed, out of the productive mainstream.

This intricate system of social organizations is a legacy from the days of the British conquest which emphasized private responsibility but has developed to its pervasive level largely over the last generation. Unique among highly industrialized countries, Canada's humanistic sector is a political and organizational anomaly. By long tradition, humanistic institutions are privately, voluntarily governed and controlled, yet today they derive almost all their revenue from the state. In fact, they are neither private nor public bodies. They are Canadian—an obfuscated compromise which Mackenzie King, were he alive, likely would explain away as "State interference if necessary, but not necessarily state interference."

Its quasi-independence and segregation by specialties leave the humanistic sector without a collective voice to observe its progress, to identify its problems, to conceive policies that integrate it smoothly into the dynamics of the public and private sector. The problems are legion. Demand for humanistic service appears insatiable, brought on by past availability which seemed limitless and future economic expectations which portend increased demand for human support. Governments suddenly have become parsimonious, largely from necessity, and are constricting funds to the humanistic sector. Volunteers, who once supplied significant personal and financial resources, have become indifferent, unwilling or unable to supplant the lost revenues.

This book addresses some of the issues confronting humanistic institutions in the eighties. It examines how Canadians supply the resources for that sector of the economy which is concerned not with the quantity of possession, but the quality of our living. Its thrust is not towards the creation of material wealth but to its constructive distribution. Not about expanded production but civilized consumption. Not on making money quickly but spending it thoughtfully. Its message complements, not contradicts, the nation's preoccupation with the means of economic renewal. Both build on the best attributes of the Canadian character.

My task was neither modest in scope nor simple in execution. Canada has close to 50,000 humanistic organizations; they handle nearly one-third of the country's national income, but their published financial statistics are sketchy and discontinuous, often unreliable, and sometimes non-existent. Mine was as much a task of data gathering as it was analysis and evaluation.

Significantly, the impetus for this inquiry came from the private sector. More than a decade ago, executives at John Labatt Limited encouraged The University of Western Ontario to study the question of corporate responsibility for charitable donations by offering seed money for research. Their initiative culminated in the publication of *Financing Humanistic Service* in 1975. Labatt again in 1981 was first to endorse the present inquiry and to provide the lead research grant. John Labatt Limited has a proud tradition of responsible, thoughtful management, concerned as much with quality of community as with integrity of product. I acknowledge with gratitude the confidence that John Labatt President Peter N.T. Widdrington and his colleagues demonstrated in this undertaking through their generous financial support, patience and understanding.

Union Gas Limited also made an early and significant contribution. It, too, is a corporation with a management acutely aware of its larger responsibilities to society. I recognize the generous support of Union Gas and the genuine interest of J.E. Mahoney, chairman, and members of Union Gas' Donation Committee, in the issues we addressed. The project received a substantial allocation from the Associates' Fund for Excellence in the School of Business Administration at The University of Western Ontario. As dean of the Business School, and its chief fund raiser, C.B. Johnston insisted on assuming responsibility for funding the project, freeing the research team to concentrate on its essential task. I thank my university and the Associates of the Business School, in particular, for making it possible for me to devote the considerable resources necessary to generate the intellectual capital emanating from this study.

It is equally important to record the conditions under which these grants were made. Apart from a vigorous scrutiny of the integrity of the research proposal, and a healthy interest in progress, the sponsors made no attempt to interfere or influence the study or its results.

Many others contributed. John W. Adams, James W. Burns, John B. Cronyn, Michael M. Koerner and John H. Moore constituted a senior advisory panel for the research team. Messrs. Adams, Cronyn and Moore, based in London, read the original proposal and made constructive suggestions, met regularly with the project team to assess progress, and offered experienced insights. Messrs. Burns and Koerner always were available by telephone for introductions, advice and counsel. The research team imposed considerably on their time, knowledge and goodwill. But it would be impossible in Canada to find better role models for the 20th-century equivalent of Cardinal Newman's gracious gentlemen. I salute their contribution.

My research team was extraordinary. Its anchor was Deborah Vuylsteke, history major, encyclopedia, interviewer, data processor, devil's advocate, patient and tactful colleague. For 30 months Miss Vuylsteke shared the highs and lows of long-term project research. But she maintained a single standard: uncompromising intellectual integrity. Steven Cox, Rosamond Ivey and Brian Crombie became involved in the inquiry first as senior students, joined the project as research assistants for the summer of 1981, then when the budget was exhausted continued an active extra-curricular contribution as volunteers for the next 12 months. Mr. Cox assembled the research material on corporations and performed the exhaustive statistical analysis reported throughout Book Two. Mr. Crombie prepared a thoughtful analysis of the United Way movement in Canada presented in Chapter IX. Miss Ivey's painstaking research and fundamental knowledge of Canadian foundations provided much of the background for Chapter XI. Their energy, probing intelligence, idealism, good humor—and irreverence—turned an otherwise routine task into an unforgettable experience. Their influence on the content of this book is substantial and I thank them warmly.

To name others is to overlook many who were helpful but I must acknowledge the abundant, yet constructive, criticism of many of my Western colleagues, including historian John Gwynne-Timothy, psychologist D. Carlton Williams, statisticians Thomas Wonnacott and Peter Bell, and philosopher A. Brandon Conron. In crossing disciplines one tends to simplify, often to the point of irrelevance. If I have avoided this snare, it is because of their patient counsel. If not, the fault lies in my own shortcomings.

Hundreds, indeed more than a thousand, of other individuals contributed. Corporations, large and small, opened their records for scrutiny and their top executives participated in interviews or completed exhaustive questionnaires. Foundation officers supplied hitherto confidential data. Bureaucrats patiently unravelled the complex maze of government finances. Fund raisers—volunteers and mercenaries—shared intimate, sensitive experiences. Officials and volunteers throughout the humanistic sector responded generously to every call for assistance. And the heads of more than 1,000 Canadian families (and another 100 in the United States) took time to answer an array of highly personal questions on their financial affairs and donation motives. Many are acknowledged throughout the text. Most are not. Let me say simply that without their contribution, there would have been no study.

Phyllis Jackson requires a special word. As my secretary for nine years, Mrs. Jackson managed an office as diversified as it is demanding. I grew to assume she understood that a frustrated twitch of the left hand requested the instant retrieval of an obscure telex received from Tokyo in 1980. Her stability, prodigious capacity, saintly patience, undeviating loyalty—and magic smile—have earned her my profound respect and inadequate gratitude.

John and Isobel Burke-Gaffney edited the manuscript with care that extended far beyond a professional contract. But, without the generous support and sensitive encouragement of Peter F. Bronfman, it would not have been published.

While I have received help in abundant measure, I alone accept responsibility for the quality of this book.

S.A.M.

"Llyndinshire"
Hyde Park, Ontario
October 1984

Prologue

T he rain in Toronto had not stopped by noon on Monday, November 16, 1981. It was dull and cold as the small group began to arrive by car and cab at the York Club on St. George Street for a private luncheon, an opportunity to plan strategy for their 3.30 p.m. meeting with Ontario Premier William G. Davis. The six were hospital board chairmen and spokesmen for OCATH,[1] an association formed with optimism in 1967 to unite and advance the interests of Ontario's 19 teaching hospitals. They came from Kingston, London, Ottawa and Toronto.[2] Luncheon host and chairman of the *ad hoc* group was Fraser M. Fell, Q.C., chairman of the board of Toronto Western Hospital.

---

[1] The Ontario Council of Administrators of Teaching Hospitals. The association operates out of Women's College Hospital, Toronto, with a full-time staff of three researchers and a budget of $150,000 levied equally on the 19 members. Chairman for 1982-83 was Peter Carruthers, CEO for Ottawa Civic Hospital.

[2] The board chairmen, their real-life occupations and hospital responsibilities were: Thomas J. Bell (CEO, Abitibi Paper Limited) Toronto General Hospital, 950 beds, 1982 budget of $97 million, projected deficit $11.4 million; Lillian Vine (homemaker) Hamilton Civic Hospital, 991 beds, $68 million ($3 million); Fraser M. Fell (partner, Fasken Calvin) Toronto Western Hospital, 668 beds, $56 million ($7 million); Samuel A. Martin (professor, University of Western Ontario) St. Joseph's Hospital, London, 534 beds, $44 million ($2.9 million); Wayne Gay (partner, Sand Pattenden Gay and Kemp) Kingston General Hospital, 518 beds, $42 million ($3.5 million); Betsie Rymes (homemaker) Children's Hospital of Eastern Ontario, 272 beds, $22 million ($2 million).

They shared one common, urgent problem—each of their hospitals was spending more money than the Ontario Ministry of Health was committed to provide. The impending deficits were large, even by inflated standards: $30 million for the six hospitals represented in the room; $81 million for all 19. Some had borrowed heavily from their banks to cover the shortfall, others were drawing down reserves. As trustees, legally responsible and publicly accountable[3] for the management of their institutions, the board chairmen had considerable personal incentive to press their case vigorously for more operating funds from the province.

The financial crunch, for that is what it felt like to those responsible, had been building since the late 1970s. Ontario teaching hospital deficits totalled $4 million in 1979-80; $20 million in 1980-81; now, in November, with five months until year end, deficits were projected to exceed $80 million for 1982. That gap represented spending beyond the annual budget increase of 13 per cent authorized by the province at the start of the year. Most of it was being used to pay for added costs tied to existing activities or increased volume. OCATH was of the view that the deficit was a provincial responsibility. Up to now the province had always come through at the eleventh hour.

Luncheon was pleasant. But, perhaps predictably, not much was accomplished in the strategy caucus: "We should lay it on the line...either they give us more money or they take responsibility for the consequences...but we're the ones on the bank notes, not the province...better to appear cooperative than confrontative...."

By two-thirty the rain had stopped and half the delegation walked the few blocks to Queen's Park. When they reassembled in the reception lounge in Room 281 of the Premier's office it was barely three o'clock so some climbed to the visitors' gallery to watch and listen to question period. The Exolon court case for environmental pollution...prison overcrowding...gas furnace valves...liquid waste disposal.

---

[3]Responsibility and accountability derived from at least two separate statutes. First were the general legal obligations of trustees (directors) for non-profit corporations chartered by the Province of Ontario. Second were the specific responsibilities and obligations delineated in the *Public Hospitals Act*: "A hospital shall be governed and managed by a board...." Public accountability could be formal and intermittent such as the provincial inquiry into the management and internal affairs of Toronto East General Hospital in June 1981 or achieved through lawsuits for negligence or malpractice. Or it could be informal and ongoing through media coverage, patient complaints, and so on.

At precisely three-thirty, Edward E. Stewart, the Premier's deputy minister, opened the door to Office No. 2,[4] settled the delegates around the northern end of the Regency dining table and introduced the bureaucrats attending from the Health Ministry. Two minutes later Provincial Treasurer Frank Miller and Health Minister Dennis Timbrell arrived with aides. More introductions and place settings, the Treasurer on the southeast; the Minister of Health on the southwest. Three more minutes and the Premier entered through his private passage directly into Office No. 2. The entrance was vintage Davis: the totally engaging and disarming smile; warm handshake; a personal word to all; an intimate recollection to many; confident; upbeat; fluid.

Few preliminaries. The Premier had obviously read the OCATH brief. Fell underscored the tensions mounting in the hospital community without hysteria or hyperbole. The meeting opened for discussion.

The Health Minister swiftly demonstrated an impressive grasp of each hospital's affairs. To one: if your board can't live within its budget, you should be prepared to use your reserves...(But those reserves are for capital.) To another: I'm not satisfied that all is being done to contain your costs...(But our cost overruns result from provincially negotiated salary settlements which we don't control.)

The Treasurer's turn: Can you tell me when this is going to stop? Dennis told me how much he needed to run the hospitals at the start of the year and I put that in the budget. Three months later he asked for another $50 million, now another $80. If you get this, can you promise you won't be back?
No.

---

[4]The Prime Minister of the Province of Ontario occupies a suite of offices located in the southeast corner of the second floor of Queen's Park. Public access to the Premier's private corner office—office No. 1—is gained through a door (Room 281) off the main corridor, protected by OPP Detective-Sergeant Guay on November 16. Mrs. Margaret Aikins receives visitors and delegations in a long, narrow reception lounge comfortably appointed with sofas, chairs and reading tables. The anteroom to the Premier's suite is at the south end of the reception area, watched over by a copper bust of Sir John A. Macdonald. Office No. 2, adjacent to and immediately west of the private office, is large enough, 400 square feet, to seat 15 or 20 comfortably, 10 of whom could occupy matching chairs around an exquisite Regency walnut dining table. Folklore around Queen's Park holds that the gold-inlaid table, 10 chairs, buffet and writing desk that furnish Office No. 2 were sold to the province by Dr. Sigmund Samuel along with his residence on 104 Forest Hill Road in 1956 for $2 during Premier Leslie Frost's government. A magnificent seven-foot Victorian grandfather clock "Ja. Gray, Edin." commands attention on the north wall. Large and small paintings from the Art Gallery of Ontario grace the other three walls, including the yard-square *Untitled Oil on Canvas, 1963* by Gerald Gladstone, one of the Premier's favorites. Tasteful, comfortable.

The Premier said little throughout the discussion[5] but clearly absorbed its tone and substance. At five past four Ed Stewart quietly entered the boardroom and discreetly passed the Premier a note. I'm told there is somewhat of an emergency on the floor of the House and I must get there quickly. Dennis, how quickly can you have a recommendation to Cabinet? Two or three weeks, Premier. Let's say then that I get back to you with a decision in a month's time. But regardless,[6] it really will only be an interim measure. I hope we could count on this group to cooperate with us in finding a lasting solution.

The rain hadn't resumed as the delegation broke up. But neither was the sun shining.

The autumn of 1981 had been equally disquieting for David Lloyd Johnston,[7] principal and vice-chancellor of McGill University in Montreal. Last year had ended in May with reason for optimism in many quarters: healthy enrolments; expected high-quality applicants; continued personal popularity with the student body. McGill's finances were troublesome, but after four years of fiscal restraint an anticipated cash deficit for 1981 of $2.6 million on a spending base of $200 million somehow would be manageable. Anyway, the deficit was comfortably below the ceiling of five per cent of operating revenue that the Ministry of Education had placed on Quebec universities.[8] Even the demand by the Ministry for McGill to submit a financial

[5] The Premier had had an exhausting November. He had played an important role in the gruelling First Ministers' Constitutional Conference which had concluded successfully in Ottawa barely a week earlier. His schedule today had been relatively light: a half-hour with John Latimer at 10:30 a.m.; an hour with W.D. McKeough; luncheon in Office No. 2 with Dr. Brian Segal; a 15-minute legislative briefing; question period in the House. Tomorrow morning was Cabinet, that night he flew to Boston to address the Boston Economic Club at luncheon on Wednesday.... .

[6] The Premier kept the promise. His speech to the annual meeting of the Ontario Hospital Association on November 30 contained the following reference: "I will assure you right now there will be additional funding from the provincial treasury to assist hospitals with cash overruns. Now, while this may not total the $100 million that I have been reading about and hearing about all morning in and on the media, the amount will be substantial."

[7] Vice-Chancellor Johnston, appointed the 14th principal of McGill in 1979, was born in Sudbury, Ont., June 28, 1941. He attended secondary school in Sault Ste. Marie, and university at Harvard (A.B. 1963), Cambridge (LL.B. 1965), and Queen's (LL.B. 1966), trailing a long list of distinctions, honors, fellowships and scholarships (e.g., Harvard University Scholarship, 1959-63, All American Hockey Team 1962 and 1963, Doctor of Laws, *Honoris Causa*, Law Society of Upper Canada, 1980). He taught at Queen's and the University of Toronto before becoming dean and professor, Faculty of Law, University of Western Ontario, 1974. Easygoing David and Sharon Johnston have produced five daughters and much goodwill in their various locations.

[8] The threatened penalty for universities accumulating deficits exceeding five per cent was to be placed into virtual receivership by the Province.

plan demonstrating how it would achieve a balanced budget by the 1984-85 year could be handled as soon as the government provided information on the operating grants McGill could expect through to 1985.

The Quebec grant news, when it came on September 14, stunned Johnston and his colleagues. All Quebec universities were told that operating grants would be cut in real terms by more than six per cent in 1982-83 and five per cent in each of the two subsequent years. For McGill, this meant slicing $19 million from its current spending level. After 1985? It was unlikely universities would enjoy high priority for government funds. By then the university-age population would have shrunk considerably and accessibility to university could be expected to become a less-urgent political preoccupation. At best McGill should expect that grants would thereafter increase only at the rate of growth in government spending.

What about the federal government? Ottawa provided $3.5 billion for university education and research but virtually all of it flowed through the provinces under Established Programs Financing, bulk funding for health care, social services and education. EPF was being renegotiated but many believed education was the most vulnerable of the three if the new agreement specified reduced funding levels.

Student fees? Only seven per cent of McGill's budget and they had been frozen by the Quebec government since 1970. Fees for foreign students could be raised again but the increased revenues would be deducted from provincial operating grants. And the foreign student fee premium already in place in Quebec even now threatened to lower enrolment from other countries.

Reduced expenditures? Expenditure cuts of this magnitude inevitably meant lost jobs or reduced salaries since salaries consumed 80 per cent of the university budget. Neither alternative was particularly attractive. Since 1976, McGill's faculty had shrunk by 77 full-time positions, 42 of these in 1980-81 alone. Course offerings were being denied students. At some stage academic quality would most certainly be compromised, a prospect of horrendous consequence to a proud university acknowledged to be among the best several dozen universities in the world. In any event, there was a limit to terminations because tenure agreements protected faculty positions.

Sustaining academic excellence meant attracting new faculty and keeping the best. But McGill had been able to give her faculty a salary increase of less than 10 per cent in 1981 while non-university public service employees in Quebec had settled for 17 per cent.

While costs most certainly would have to be trimmed, the cornerstone of McGill's strategy for economic survival in the 1980s was increased funding from private sources. McGill counted on three separate flows of private sector revenue—endowment income, current gifts and allocations from the Development Campaign Fund.

McGill's endowment was valued at $150 million in 1981, making her by far the "richest" university in Canada. In fact, her investment portfolio was second in size only to the McConnell/Griffith Foundation as the largest pool of private funds dedicated for charitable purposes in existence in the country. McGill's assets had grown handsomely over 160 years. In 1821 the Honorable James McGill had bequeathed "Burnside," his 46-acre estate "near the City of Montreal," plus the sum of £10,000, to the Royal Institute for the Advancement of Learning for the establishment of a university.[9] Now managed by three different investment counsellors, the fund had generated an average annual return of 14 per cent in recent years. Eight per cent was reinvested to protect the capital value of the fund and just over six per cent was made available to augment operating and research funds.

Current gifts from private sources, mainly from McGill's alumni/ae and friends, amounted to $13 million in 1980-81, a level that had been more or less constant over the past few years. All but 10 per cent were designated gifts ("donors wish to see where their gift makes a difference") leaving little flexibility in the deployment of these funds. Typically the level of current gifts increased noticeably during the period of a McGill Development Campaign and maintained a higher plateau thereafter.

McGill had launched four development campaigns since the end of the war, one a decade, and had raised more than $50 million in gifts to enhance the quality of her teaching and research programs. The most recent campaign for the decade of the seventies raised a total of $38 million. McGill's board of governors had approved in principle a development campaign for the eighties with the monetary target to be struck in 1983. It would be based on three principles: the proceeds would not cover deficits; amounts received would not result in the reduction, in any form, of government grants; the development funds would be devoted to reinforcing and augmenting high quality in teaching and research.

But those plans were longer range. McGill's immediate problem was to reach 1985 in a debt-free state. By November the most feasible plan produced by a budget task force called for severe cuts in expenditures, deficit spending totalling $11.5 million through 1984 and a balanced budget in

---

[9]The will contained one important condition: "That one of the colleges...shall be named and perpetually be known and distinguished by the app [appellation] McGill College."

1985. Unrestricted endowment funds would cover $7 million of the deficit, leaving $4 million unfunded. The task force recommended a careful review of other endowed funds to see if the capital could be encroached on and urged an immediate inventory of saleable assets such as redundant buildings and artistic works.

Even if the cash were found, the university would face serious problems by cutting expenditures seven per cent each year for three consecutive years. A negative trend could trigger pessimism and discontent and become self-reinforcing. Financial duress would severely test the strength of collegial government, a proud tradition at McGill. The Principal knew that it would be much harder to foster excellence in a situation of financial retrenchment than it had been in years of prosperity. McGill's stature was clearly at stake.

These were the harsh facts foremost in David Johnston's mind as he conferred in his office with John Armour, vice-principal Administration and Finance, on the afternoon of November 16. The Budget Task Force Report placed McGill's financial problems in sharp focus, carefully, honestly, dispassionately, professionally; problems that had posed an unrelenting challenge to Johnston ever since he had assumed office two years earlier. But in the month since the report had been released he had begun to conceive a clearer vision of McGill's future. He and his colleagues would simply learn how to do better with less, learn how to improve existing programs, develop new ones, ensure that professors had time and facilities for research, the precious ingredient that would keep McGill in respected academic ranks.

Planning was the answer. Governments did it, corporations did it, organizations did it. McGill would do it, and with style. Not planning for people, that worked badly, but planning by people. Each unit would be involved; it would identify where it was headed, where it wanted to go, and how to marshall its resources. Unit plans would fit into faculty goals which would be merged into an overall university plan. The board would establish priorities, specify and articulate the unique service McGill offered the community. McGill wouldn't attempt to do everything, but what it did it would do well! McGill's standards would remain as high as those of the dozen or two best universities in the world. McGill would not dissipate capital. The money would come—external research funding, money from governments, foundations and industry. It would come because people who command the resources respect excellence and reward those who are uncompromising in her pursuit.

As Johnston pondered the implications of various financial strategies, he was conscious that he was not the first Principal beset with difficult choices who had occupied the spacious corner office on the fifth floor of the Cyril James Building. They had been inspiring men, all of them, leading an institution into a position of world-class prominence. Now it was Johnston's and his colleagues' turn to display the same inspiring leadership. For the talented and competitive, problems were exciting opportunities.

Twelve of 14 campaign cabinet members made it for buffet breakfast on November 16 in the Oak Room of Vancouver's trendy Four Seasons Hotel. The volunteers had begun meeting intermittently in January, then regularly for breakfast since early summer, to direct the fund-raising campaign of the United Way of the Lower Mainland, 18 communities that sprawled from Vancouver south to the U.S. border.

George Fierheller,[10] campaign chairman, dropped the news almost casually. Receipts to date were just under $7 million, about the same as last year and almost a million shy of the objective. It was now clear that the campaign would not reach its goal by November 30.

Tough news for a team that had set out enthusiastically to raise 16 per cent more money than the previous year despite an iffy economy and a public attitude of growing indifference to the annual United Way Campaign. This meeting would mark the 130th hour that each member had already invested in the project. All but one, who was retired, were business or professional people responsible for managing companies that were themselves facing stiffening competition and eroding profits.

The reaction was interesting. No pessimism. They would extend the deadline to December 5 and begin a three-week blitz to get in the money that was in the pipeline and form a special telephone committee to make the calls. They would ask the 60 loaned representatives to stay on to tidy up the work not followed through by 3,400 volunteers. There would be a one-day media blitz. Fierheller would appear on a series of talk shows starting with Jack Webster, Vancouver's disputatious TV personality. He would tell the people of the Lower Mainland that the campaign was well on its way but would fall short of its goal. This meant that 83 social service agencies depending on United Way funds for most or part of their operating funds would have to

[10]George Fierheller was born in Toronto in 1933, attended the University of Toronto Schools, and was graduated Bachelor of Arts from U of T's Trinity College in 1955. Fierheller levered a successful career with IBM into a major equity interest and position as founding president of Systems Dimensions Ltd. in Ottawa. He sold out that interest to Crown Life Insurance Co. in 1979 and moved to Vancouver to head Premier Cablesystems Ltd. A natural leader, Fierheller has always participated actively in community affairs where he invariably becomes chairman of the board.

scale back. Yes, unemployment was up considerably from a year ago but didn't that make the need more urgent? They would keep the books open to December 31. By God, they could still make the whole thing!

Fierheller had grown accustomed to the enthusiasm. These were good people to work with, professionals who worked hard and well on whatever they undertook. They didn't like to lose, and neither did George Fierheller.

How and why did he become involved in the United Way? Fierheller moved to Vancouver from Ottawa in April 1979 to become president and CEO of Premier Cablesystems. A veteran fund raiser, he had been slated to head the 1982 campaign but advanced a year when the 1981 chairman was transferred out of town in November 1979.

Fierheller was an agnostic. He believed the volunteer approach was a sensible and practical one for the community: "If volunteer giving disappeared then voluntary donation of time to serve agencies would likely also disappear. The proportion of volunteer-time to volunteer-dollars-raised is about 5:1. This loss would be a serious drawback to the community. Almost no one volunteers to work for the government."

Heading the campaign would be a good way to get to know more about the community and it would provide a high profile for the company which had not always enjoyed the best of public relations. Fierheller's board of directors at Premier felt it would be a good investment from the company's standpoint.[11]

Fierheller reflected on the campaign as he drove back to his office. The size of the goal had seemed reasonable when the committee struck it in April. The 83 participating health and welfare agencies had tabled budgets totalling $53 million for their community work in 1982. Penetrating budget reviews had failed to establish waste or duplication. In fact, with larger numbers unemployed many welfare organizations clearly would be strained to meet the inevitable surge in requests for food, clothing and shelter. While governments would supply the agencies with 85 per cent of their revenue needs, the United Way component was crucial to their survival. It was discretionary income that gave the organizations flexibility to react quickly and to tailor their services to the ever-changing needs of society.

---

[11]Premier Cablesystems estimated the cost of Fierheller's involvement to be $60,000, likely a conservative figure since they valued time on the basis of actual cost without reckoning the cost of lost opportunities. Time (value): 20 per cent of Fierheller's plus benefits ($30,000); secretary ($6,000); v-p marketing and public relations director ($10,000); other employees ($4,000). Expenses (actual cost): supplies ($3,000); lunches and breakfasts ($4,000); thank-you gifts ($800); thank-you advertisements ($2,200).

The outlook had remained optimistic until the summer months. By fall the B.C. economy—which is really the pulp and paper, mining and fishing industries—began to fall apart as markets weakened around the world. Corporations, upon which the United Way depended for half its goal, began experiencing sharp profit declines. Some had to withdraw or cut back on charitable donations, many were able only to maintain last year's level of giving, a few managed to increase their commitment.

Fierheller swung the campaign emphasis away from corporations towards the individual: "one day's pay a year to the United Way." The strategy had worked well. Roughly 100,000 individuals, one out of five potential donors, had contributed to the campaign, a sizable dollar and proportional increase. "Most who did not give were not asked, or were very poorly canvassed."

It had been a good experience, more fun than his last campaign in Ottawa in 1972. Ottawa was the federal civil service and once that sector was organized the campaign became routine. The size, complexity and diversity of the southern British Columbia region posed a much more challenging organizational problem, with more opportunities for imaginative action. The team,[12] his team, because Fierheller had recruited them all, had been splendid. Morale had been high throughout the campaign and report meetings such as the one that morning were always lively, fun affairs. Regardless of the final total, Fierheller relished the personal satisfaction of having done a big job as well as could be reasonably expected given the state of the economy.

Would he do it again? Yes, but not for another decade.

Canada's humanistic organizations, the 47,000 corporations, institutions and agencies that deliver health care, education, welfare and cultural services, are clearly in financial difficulties. Understandable, perhaps, in the economic malaise that has settled over the country. But their troubles began

[12]All first-stringers: D.E. (Ed) McGeachan, president, Bank of British Columbia, in charge of major corporations; Hugh Magee, chairman, Great West Steel Industries Limited, manufacturing corporations; George C. Reifel, vice-president, Daon Development Corporation, trade and finance corporations; Allan R. McKenzie, general manager, Toronto-Dominion Bank, general business; Marion Jones, C.A., individual gifts; R. Beverly (Bev) Harrison, senior partner, Arthur Andersen Co., professional; David S. Catton, v-p and director, Ian Roberts Inc., public service; J.B. (Jim) Flett, president, Vancouver General Hospital, health, education and welfare; S.J. (John) Hatchett, B.C. Tel., training; R.W. Bonner, chairman, B.C. Hydro, loaned representatives; Frank Palmer, Palmer Jarvis Associates Advertising Ltd., public relations; Art Kube, Canadian Labor Congress, labor; Howard Nephtali, executive director, United Way of the Lower Mainland.

well before the onslaught of the recession of 1982 which cut deeply into the economic fibre and self-confidence of all sectors of society. The problems are not unique to Canada of course. But because no other country reflects the same diversity of regional interests and heritage, our solution must be unique.

Nowhere are the problems more visible and compelling than in health services. For 22 years, almost a full generation, every Canadian requiring hospitalization has received this care with little or no direct personal cash outlay. Since 1971, medical care—the services of both general practitioners and specialists, for accidents and the treatment of virtually all acute or chronic illnesses—has also been universally accessible.

Not only have health services been universal, accessible and comprehensive, their quality has been good. Many of Canada's hospitals are new and contain the world's most sophisticated diagnostic equipment. Canadian medicine is respected for its clinical effectiveness and its scientific contributions. A handful of Canadian physicians and surgeons have gained world-wide preeminence: Banting, Best, Drake.

Canadians have grown accustomed to first-class health care. And because it is "free" (even though most suspect that lunches never are free) we don't often think about how much it costs and who eventually pays the bills. We do react with apprehension to headlines proclaiming "Waiting lists threaten patients' lives" and with anger to charges of hospital mismanagement, both in their financial and operating affairs. But for the most part the problems are remote, someone else's responsibility.

Whose? The original version of Canada's constitution, the British North America Act, placed the responsibility for public health care under provincial jurisdiction. The obligation was of little consequence at the time. Hospitals, such as they were, were privately owned, mostly by religious orders. The medical profession was proudly entrepreneurial while following the Hippocratic tradition of service before personal gain. Payment for service was a private matter between the cared for and the caring.

Today that innocent obligation is far from trivial for both the provinces and the federal government. Doctors bargain with health ministers, not patients, for fees.[13] Hospitals still are managed by independent, autonomous

---

[13]Canada's 45,000 medical doctors are organized along provincial lines to match provincial government responsibility and regulation. Medical education and degree-granting at the undergraduate level is the responsibility of medical schools located within universities. Provincial Colleges of Physicians
(Cont'd)

boards,[14] but they, too, negotiate 97 per cent of their revenues from provincial governments. The small balance derives from fees for upscale accommodation, services to non-resident patients, and from charitable gifts from foundations, corporations and individuals.

This financial squeeze results from the confluence of many pressures. Almost all health service employees belong to unions, powerful monolithic bargaining units that have won and are keeping increases in the salaries of nurses, housekeepers and maintenance staff above national norms.[15] Diagnostic and life-support equipment is staggeringly expensive. And the capital cost is the tip of a financial iceberg; a million-dollar CAT Scanner adds a quarter-of-a-million dollars to a hospital's operating budget into perpetuity.

Hospital budgets, typically prepared by hospital administrators on the advice of medical and support staff, have increasingly projected a deficit on operations based on the funding level in prospect from provincial governments. In a business setting, such a result would initiate a gruelling process of matching expenses to revenues. Rarely would a corporate board give approval to an operating plan that budgeted an excess of expenditures over anticipated income. Yet, hospital boards often have tacitly, even explicitly, approved a deficit budget and authorized expenditures without first tying down the funding.

That board action then triggers the following sequence of steps. First, the hospital appeals its allocation with the Health Ministry citing extraordinary costs, increased volumes or expanded services. The appeal sometimes is made "public" to engage community support through the media. Second, the hospital negotiates a bank loan to support the deficit spending, or draws down reserves. Third, it steps up its private fund-raising activities if it engages in ongoing appeals, or engages a development officer[16] to investigate the potential of private funding. Finally, and reluctantly, it might direct a

---

and Surgeons regulate entrance standards, issue licenses to practice medicine, and discipline members. Medical specialties have nation-wide standards and are controlled by the Royal College of Physicians and Surgeons. Provincial medical associations concern themselves with the economic well-being of the medical profession, negotiating fee schedules with provincial health ministries and providing courses and seminars for the continuing education of members.

[14]More than 1,300 teaching, general and special hospitals in Canada contain 185,000 beds, one for every 130 Canadians.

[15]Settlements negotiated in late 1981 in Alberta, Nova Scotia and Quebec could increase hospital salary costs by 40 per cent over the following two years.

[16]Euphemism for fund raiser.

serious examination of proposals to cut staff or reduce services.

The last step is understandably painful and unpopular. Health care is an issue charged with emotion and its delivery is an immensely complicated process. Laymen, even intelligent laymen, in fact don't understand medicine despite the efforts of Dr. Spock, W. Gifford-Jones, M.D., Ann Landers and *Time* magazine. Faced with a request to expand, re-equip and restaff the Intensive Care Unit because "inaction may endanger lives," a board dominated by laymen must rely heavily on expert medical advice to assess the scope and urgency of the expenditures.

Little wonder then that hospital deficits have been a way of life in Ontario, Quebec and the Atlantic provinces where provincial governments have restricted per capita health care spending to below the median of the five Canadian regions. And little wonder it costs the burgeoning western provinces up to 56 per cent more than median expenditures to expand and service their health care delivery systems.[17]

Education also is a provincial exclusive. But unlike their role in delivering health care, the provinces have a long tradition of direct participation in educational administration and financing, an involvement that pre-dates Confederation. The federal government, as well, has become indirectly involved by injecting significant financial support for education, prompted by the educational explosion of the post-war years.

The educational delivery system divides roughly into three categories—public elementary and secondary schools, public post-secondary institutions, and private schools. Each has problems that reflect its peculiar role and responsibilities.

Grade school attendance is compulsory for about 10 years with a minimum leaving age of 15 or 16. Provincial control is decentralized into school boards, elected for each municipal jurisdiction. The burden of financing elementary-secondary education has evolved from almost exclusive reliance on real estate taxes levied by municipal governments to heavy (almost 80 per cent) dependence on provincial revenues. Federal funds, which are channeled through the provinces, are not a major factor at the elementary-secondary level.

There are more than 60 degree-granting institutions in Canada—universities, liberal arts colleges, theological colleges and specialized colleges of art,

---

[17]Per-capita health care expenditures by provincial governments in 1980-81 were as follows: Atlantic Provinces, $511; Quebec, $602; Ontario, $572; Prairie Provinces, $870; British Columbia, $685; Canada, $604.

engineering or education. Just over 12 per cent of the population aged 18-24 attended universities in 1981, 400,000 full-time students. Since the middle sixties, non-degree or diploma-type post-secondary training has emerged as the alternative to university education for growing numbers of young Canadians.

Community colleges (or CEGEPs[18] in Quebec) now number 200 with an enrolment of 250,000 full-time students. Colleges offer university transfer programs or semi-professional career programs lasting at least a year, usually two or three, and at most four years. While a number operate privately, most are provincially controlled and all receive provincial funding.

Technical and trades training for those wishing to acquire career skills is available through separate divisions of community colleges or specialized institutions. More than 400,000 full-time students are enrolled in these programs which last from a few weeks to as long as four years.

Up to four per cent of elementary-secondary students attend private schools: French-instruction schools, the Montessori system, Hebrew schools, Lower Canada College, Branksome Hall, St. John's Ravenscourt, Brentwood and the like. These are primarily or wholly financed through student fees and private charitable donations,[19] but operate on a non-profit basis. A larger proportion of the students studying technical and trades subjects attend private schools. Many such institutions, particularly those offering business, engineering and mechanical career programs, operate as profit-making business enterprises and are therefore financed entirely through student fees plus government subsidies where available.

Three fundamental forces complicate the financial affairs of education today.

The first relates to population demographics, problems familiarly associated with the post-war baby boom that peaked in 1961. As this population cohort moved its way through the elementary system in the late sixties, the secondary schools in the seventies and now through the universities and colleges, it required large resources in teaching manpower and space. Post-peak enrolments in the system have shrunk faster than educational governing boards have been willing, or able, to cut back on fixed costs such as teachers' salaries and maintenance of redundant plant.

[18]An acronym from the French designation *Collèges d'Enseignement Général et Professionnel*.

[19]Donations are not totally a personal financial sacrifice. As we shall examine later, income tax deductibility for individual and corporate charitable donations effectively shifts part of the cost of the gift from the donor to other taxpayers.

Second, government attitudes towards funding schools and colleges have cooled considerably over the past decade. Other problems are now more urgent and compelling and are competing more successfully for government revenues, which themselves reflect the sluggish growth of a sluggish economy.

Third, those institutions depending on donations from private sources have found the population often fickle and increasingly parsimonious. If they were to be successful in 1982, fund-raising appeals required significantly more effort than even a decade earlier.

Canadian welfare services have roots in the charitable organizations of old Quebec, in Anglo-Saxon traditions, and in evolving mores of social justice. While Canadians have grown accustomed to equate social welfare with government support programs, the voluntary sector is still very much a part of the welfare delivery system.

Well over half the 47,000 charitable organizations registered in Canada could be classified as welfare related. The list is endless: Salvation Army mission houses, meals on wheels, drug abuse and addiction centres, child care agencies, crippled and disabled persons treatment centres and vocational rehabilitation programs. Services for the young, the old, the troubled, the troublesome—the casualties accumulated by any fast-moving society. Those who cannot cope successfully because of luck, accident or circumstances beyond their control. And those who will not try.

Every nation has its lowest population quintile. No matter how prosperous a country becomes, how high its per capita productivity, some members participate less in the fruits of production. It has been and always will be thus. Yet, notwithstanding the inevitability of income disparity, mankind is attracted to the elusive ideal of human equality. All three levels of government in Canada participate aggressively in public social-security programs to provide income protection, health care and a range of social services for Canadians who need them and, increasingly, for those who don't.

The provision of welfare services, like health care and education, is primarily a provincial responsibility under the BNA Act. Municipalities[20] and their local voluntary agencies generally provide most direct services to the public. Initially these were confined to modest income-support programs for single parent families and injured workers, and direct relief payments to

---

[20]Municipalities are creatures of provincial governments. They are neither specified nor even recognized in the British North America Act.

the poor. Today, the scope of social security is greatly expanded with funding provided by both federal and provincial governments. The federal government is itself the largest welfare agency in the country, transferring income back and forth to every Canadian family—old age pensions, family allowances, unemployment insurance payments and so on.

Social welfare is perhaps the most controversial topic in Canada today. Payments expand annually as the rolls of legitimate participants swell. Governments strain to meet the financial demands with increased taxes and borrowings. A wary, and weary, public decries the tax squeeze, denounces fiscal mismanagement and alludes to gross abuses in the welfare system. Social agencies are not immune to the backlash. Their direct appeals to the public for gifts are frequently rejected because "my taxes are already too high" or "the funds will be poorly managed."

Perhaps it was Expo '67 that gave Canadians pride in our national heritage, curiosity about our identity and confidence in our artistic creativity. Clearly Canada has enjoyed an upsurge in cultural activity in the last two decades: theatre, music, dance and opera; painting, sculpture and crafts; libraries, museums and art galleries. The quantitative growth is measurable, and undeniable. Judgment is less unanimous on artistic quality since the talent of a performer, a writer or an artist is appraised subjectively by a public with multi-dimensional taste. But if the bottom line is measured in attendance statistics, Canadians are applauding our artists as at no other time in history.

The number of cultural organizations fluctuates constantly. Groups spawn, struggle, survive or succumb. Canada supports more than 100 significant theatre companies, 34 orchestras, 16 dance companies and six opera companies—a small fraction of the total number when one adds the amateur groups active in most communities across the land. There are 150 large art galleries, museums, restoration sites, planetaria and public archives. And there are close to 1,000 public libraries containing over 40 million volumes.

Performing arts groups are invariably structured as private, non-profit organizations. They earn close to half their total income from box office receipts and sales of programs and beverages at performances. The balance is subsidized—four-fifths from the three levels of government and the balance from gifts by foundations, corporations and individuals.

But cultural organizations, too, are seriously short of funds. Consider these headlines selected at random from newspapers across the country: "BC Symphony Battles Deficit"—"$50,000 Needed Today to Save Stratford Show"—"Dal Art Gallery Could be Closed."

This book examines carefully how the humanistic sector[21] in Canada raises funds to render its services to society. Its emphasis is on funds from the private sector, charitable donations, even though this source accounts for the smallest share and is in decline. The focus is understandable. Some believe that private-sector funding of humanistic service is anachronistic, that governments exclusively offer the only rational, equitable mechanism for raising the massive revenues required to sustain such a sophisticated system. Some are concerned whether taxpayers ever will be willing or indeed able to provide enough money to meet the expectations of universities,[22] hospitals, welfare agencies and cultural institutions. They argue for more reliance on the private sector. Some, no most, Canadians give the matter very little thought.

What motivates Canadians to donate money to charitable organizations? Why are voluntary contributions in relative decline? What is our capacity, as individuals and corporations, to increase our annual donations? Whose responsibility is it to raise funds for humanistic service?

Before we address these questions, crucial questions for those responsible for balancing budgets in the humanistic sector, we must understand a great deal about the nature of humanistic service and something about human nature as it applies to giving and receiving. We begin by examining what services qualify for inclusion, why they exist and how much of them we require or desire.

---

[21]The neutral territory between the private (for profit) sector and the public (government) sector. Also referred to as the Third Sector in the economy, the Non-Profit Voluntary Sector, etc. A debate is now emerging as to how this sector should be defined: by who contributes the service, the Volunteer Sector, or by what service is contributed, the Humanistic Sector.

[22]Hon. Bette Stephenson, minister of Colleges and Universities on May 8, 1981: "I feel strongly that everyone who has had the privilege of attending university has an added responsibility beyond that of the taxpayers. (Each graduate) should be prepared to give at least $10 per year to the university from which we...graduated." If Canada's 1.5 million university graduates responded unanimously the $15 million would scarcely provide enough money to keep the University of Toronto in funds for three weeks. Perhaps understandably, Dr. Stephenson upped the ante to $25 in December.

Book One

To whom much is given...

I

What, why and how much humanistic service?

Humanistic service? Humanistic sector? The phrases are hardly household expressions. They need to be explored but their nature and scope must be fixed to limit the range of discussion. Otherwise, as with any discourse on economic or social activities, this examination could become so all-embracing and so generalized it could quickly lose relevance. The boundary lines drawn for this discussion may include or exclude topics at the margin but the reader will understand the arbitrary nature of fences.

Humanistic service, in the context of this thesis, embraces activities generally recognized as ''good works'' in the community, services centring upon ''distinctively human interests and ideals'' as opposed to those activities contributing less directly to the enhancement of these intimate human values, the means of personal growth.

The segregation is subjective and descriptive classification a matter of judgment. Two categories—health care and education—are widely comprehended and by tradition qualify as humanistic services. The notion of welfare services, too, is broadly understood but has expanded considerably in recent years to embrace a variety of social welfare programs for the benefit of the whole population (universality) rather than being confined to services for the disadvantaged minority.

In choosing the term ''culture'' as the designation to describe all the services not classified under the three previous headings, we are drawing on the broadest classical definition of the term: "the concepts, habits, skills, art, instruments, institutions, etc., of a given people in a given period; civilization." Such a definition makes it possible, for example, to group the work of religious organizations with that of museums and art galleries.

The common bond of all such organizations is their dedication to the enhancement of our civilization which, according to Edith Hamilton, "stands for a high matter quite apart from telephones and electric lights...it is a matter of imponderables, of delight in the things of the mind, of love and beauty, of honor, of grace, courtesy, delicate feeling." Those who engage in these types of activities are said to be serving their fellow man, hence the notion of humanistic[1] service. The group of vehicles or institutions through which the services are carried out comprise the humanistic sector.

Health services embrace hospitals, hospital schools, health and medical research institutions, and generally those organizations that provide health treatment by qualified medical, dental or nursing staff, rather than those that provide the prolonged care of the aged, which are classified under welfare.

Educational service includes nursery, primary and secondary schools, post-secondary institutions, private schools and government training and retraining programs.

Welfare service embraces the total range of programs for the unemployed, aged, disabled and under-privileged, as well as general social welfare programs, such as family allowances, Canada and Quebec pension plans, whether provided by public or private organizations.

Culture includes services provided by all humanistic organizations not classified under the three previous headings but which reflect a particular aspect of our "civilization." Included here, for example, would be religious organizations, athletic and community organizations, performing arts

---

[1]Not to be confused with Humanism, often regarded as the characteristic attitude of the Renaissance. *Studia humanitatis*, from which the Humanists derive their name, was a comprehensive discipline including grammar, rhetoric, history, poetry and moral philosophy based on the study of relevant Greek and Roman texts—original manuscripts, not translated copies. Humanism developed ideas such as the importance and potential of man as an individual, belief in the power of learning and science to produce the complete man, the desire to enlarge the bounds of learning and knowledge, and the growth of skepticism and free thinking—a return to the freer intellectual spirit of classical times. In northern Europe, Humanism is also associated with the Reformation and criticism of the medieval church. (See *Encyclopedia Britannica*.)

organizations (theatre, music, dance), fine arts organizations (painting, sculpture), and organizations dedicated to the preservation of the environment. Cultural service for this discussion excludes the activities of many organizations engaged in artistic or cultural expression on a profit-making basis: movie making, publishing, theatre, sports and so on. The distinction is widely understood and generally accepted as appropriate.

Why has society made the segregation? Why are humanistic services regarded as higher values, worthy of community prestige and esteem? What common characteristics bind the activities of the humanistic sector together? First, humanistic services are intensely personal, labor-intensive activities—people reacting with other people directly and intimately. Second, they engage our deepest emotions: fear (for our health); desire (for our intellectual enlightenment); compassion (for the welfare of others); joy (in touching artistic expression). Third, they are highly specialized, demanding activities. Those who serve possess talents and training not shared by the majority of the population. Humanistic service once was a calling, now more often a profession, demanding a high order of intellectual capacity and personal dedication.

Perhaps the most distinguishing characteristic of humanistic service is the tradition of service before personal gain. Men and women were drawn into the healing arts to relieve suffering, not to make a living. Teachers taught to share their knowledge, not increase their net worth. Artists painted to release feelings and reflect a view of the world that was theirs alone; if they sold, it was a bonus. Romanticised as that view may appear today, the expectation of service before gain remains in the minds of many who are dependent on the services of specialists in the humanistic sector.

In return for sublimated economic gain, society elevated humanistic service to the highest levels of prestige, respect and social status. What it did not pay in cash was given in psychic income. High salaries were traded off against job security. The not-for-profit motive attracted gifts beyond fees for service to further the good works. Governments encouraged this private philanthropy by allowing charitable donations to be deducted from income in calculating the amount of income tax payable by the donor to the state.

Humanistic services taken together constitute the ingredients necessary for the good life, the hallmark of a civilized society. In man's hierarchy of needs, the giving and receiving of humanistic service spans every category from survival to self-actualization—physiological needs (food, water, shelter), safety (avoidance of pain and discomfort), belonging (love and intimacy) and esteem (acceptance).[2]

Consider health care. In its primary form, health services by doctors and nurses were largely confined to responses to urgent demands by those requiring care—victims of illness, disease, accidents. As the medical arts advanced, and as society prospered, care was expanded to embrace chronic illnesses and elective procedures—treatment beyond that previously considered essential. The next stage was preventive medicine, anticipating diseases and treating healthy people before they were stricken. Today health care has entered the era of technological medicine, harnessing the most sophisticated electronic equipment to aid in diagnosis, treatment, patient care and convalescence.

Man's concept of education, too, has evolved from its early concentration on the rudimentary skills needed to survive and function in an industrial society which demanded literacy, but little else. With some education man observed that knowledge was often the source of advancement and power, economic, technical, intellectual, social. Larger numbers of people pursued higher levels of education, some motivated by pragmatism, others because the pursuit of knowledge itself became an illusive, intoxicating, infinite attraction.

Cultural pursuits are an extension of education. They offer a means of unique expression, the pleasure of deep feelings, refinement, dignity, harmony. Cultural activities are as varied as they are complex. Because they are art forms, not susceptible to objective evaluation, they are enjoyed by some,

---

[2]Actualization psychologists such as Abraham H. Maslow (1908-1970) believed that humans have a tendency toward self-actualization, a desire to realize one's potential. These theorists placed emphasis on cognition (present experiences, as opposed to Freud who stressed the past), personal thought and perception. They stressed the positive forces of personality and regarded love as one of those positive forces. They proposed that humans required mutual acceptance, intimacy, openness and trust. This brand of psychology is regarded as humanistic because it sees humans as thinking and perceiving of what happens around them. Its premise is optimistic and emphasizes man's potential for good. Its opposite in the world of psychology is behavioralism, a belief that humans simply react to stimuli received from the surrounding environment. Maslow categorized two broad areas of human motives: growth motives and deprivation motives. Growth motives pushed one toward an actualization of inherent potentialities, while deprivation motives were required only for the maintenance of life, not its enhancement. These motives (needs) were classified into an hierarchy. The first needs were the physiological (food, water, etc.); the second, safety (the avoidance of pain and discomfort). When these needs were satisfied, the need for belonging (love and intimacy) became significant. In turn, these needs were superseded by the need for esteem (acceptance). Only when the survival needs were satisfied could actualization tendencies be expressed strongly. (See Mussen, Paul, Rosenweiz et al.; *Psychology: An Introduction* (Toronto:D.C.Heath, 1973).

despised by others. They share one common requirement—the luxury of leisure time for both participant and observer. That is why culture and recreation have long been associated with the leisure class and why post-war affluence has made their pleasures accessible to large numbers of Canadians.

Welfare services differ from the previous categories. They are not so much a type of service as an action prompted by compassion or concern for some person or group less fortunate. Welfare delivery can take the form of money or time or physical necessities such as food, clothing and shelter. It can provide health care (public clinics), education (scholarships) and even culture (support for a talented but impoverished artist). Private expenditures for welfare are outgoing acts to benefit someone else, not acts of self-improvement or self-indulgence. When one thinks of an act of charity, one associates the term with a transfer from the "haves" to the "have-nots"—welfare.

The term, of course, has a broader meaning: general well-being and prosperity, social welfare. As a nation prospers, average incomes rise. Even though income distribution remains unequal, the lowest incomes still rise. Where is the line drawn to separate the poor from the rest of the population? In a practical sense, the floor tends to elevate as society adjusts its notion of necessities and luxuries. As the state expands its involvement in welfare services, it tends to adopt an ever-broadening definition—generalized welfare—to put supports under the entire population, not only those in need. Thus are spawned "universal" welfare programs that transfer incomes through the tax system into the hands of all members of the population regardless of their current level of income or wealth.

If one examines the evolution of the delivery of humanistic service in a single nation over time and repeats the analysis for other societies in the western world, a common pattern of change emerges that can be described in four stages of interaction and financing: individual to individual; individual to institution; collected individuals to institutions; the state to institutions.

Each of the four classes of humanistic service moves through the four stages of delivery at different speeds. The movement is not always to the next-higher level since circumstances may cause a reversion from a higher to a lower stage of evolution. And it follows that at any given time a particular country could have a humanistic delivery system in which each type of service was at a different stage of evolution. Or, indeed, that one particular service had elements of all four stages present simultaneously.

This classification scheme describes a central tendency only and, while imperfect, has proved to be a helpful—indeed, essential—device to organize an overwhelming quantity of historical detail.

The Stage I society is characterized by a high degree of personal involvement, interaction and responsibility for the delivery and receipt of humanistic service. Its parameters are the personal covenant between doctor and
patient, the teacher and family, the patron and the artist, personal assistance to a neighbor weakened by accident or misfortune. If money changes
hands, the payment is direct, fees from recipient to the provider of services,
gifts from donor to donee. A Stage I society has as an integral element the
concept of personal service, the giving of self. It is also characterized by a
large investment of time on the part of the benefactor, who receives immediate and personal rewards. The personal involvement heightens one's
awareness of social problems and opportunities. But it is voluntary. One
could choose *not* to participate in either side of the transaction.

Stage II evolved out of necessity. Urbanization concentrated the population and forced the deliverers of humanistic service to institutionalize: to
form hospitals, medical clinics, schools, soup kitchens, museums. Yet the
responsibility for funding the service still rested with individuals, or tight
groups of individuals, sharing a common bond. The members of a religious
denomination operated a hospital, a neighborhood built a school, the Salvation Army organized a hostel and so on. Interaction lost some of its intimacy in a Stage II environment since the providers of the resources and the
providers of care often were separated by a layer of administrators. Notwithstanding, there still existed a strong personal involvement—and commitment—by individuals in the affairs of humanistic organizations as well
as a deep sense of responsibility for the financial well-being of *their*
institutions.

Stage III evolved more out of convenience than conviction. As humanistic organizations proliferated in number, nature and quality, the alignment
of individuals with institutions became complex. Involved, prosperous individuals qualified as patrons for an ever-expanding group of organizations
as their affiliations broadened and diffused. Demand for humanistic service
increased, causing organizations to step up appeals for operating funds, first
by separate intensified campaigns to individuals, next by federated (or
group) appeals to individuals and corporations, then tentatively, reluctantly, to governments. Stage III recognized the limitations of balancing
widespread demand for humanistic service with voluntary supply of the financial resources necessary to sustain the humanistic infrastructure. Individuals continued to support, manage and operate hospitals, schools and
social institutions. But they acknowledged the role of public financial support in meeting their obligation of service.

To many people, Stage IV is the logical, inevitable, and ultimate human-istic delivery system. In this terminal stage, society as a whole decrees that all its members shall be provided with an appropriate level of health care, education, cultural enjoyment and general social well-being. These shall become public not private goods. The allocation of society's resources for the attainment of the good life shall be skimmed off the top of the national wealth in the only fair and equitable way yet devised by mankind: through a tax system imposed by a democratic government. Charity—a word with demeaning connotations—would cease to exist. Each citizen would accept humanistic service from public institutions as his or her right. Their sole obligation and responsibility would be to the state, to pay their fair share of the tax burden needed to sustain the system. The state would decide how much humanistic service and who pays. Efficient, professional, dignified, equitable, ideal.

How does Canada's humanistic evolution fit that descriptive model? While Chapter III addresses this question more fully, it is appropriate to es-tablish fundamental facts and broad relationships at the outset of the dis-cussion—benchmarks to provide perspective and a sense of proportion to a plethora of unavoidable detail.

Reliable national data that are comparable over time begin in 1937 when the Dominion Bureau of Statistics undertook its first comprehensive survey of family income and expenditures.[3] That exercise, repeated every decade since, enlisted the cooperation of a large sample of Canadian families, rep-resentative of all regions of the country. Each kept a meticulous record of all its income and expenditures, segregated into minute categories, over a pe-riod of a year. Canadians by then had survived seven years of economic depression and had yet to feel the economic stimulation provided by the Second World War. Jobs were scarce, public relief a necessity for many families. National income[4] was small by today's standards. Most family in-come was spent on the basic necessities of life. That year, the nation as a whole allocated 17 per cent of its income for humanistic expenditures, 6.3

---

[3]The family income and expenditure series provided only part of the data for the humanistic matrix summarized in this discussion. A citation of sources is listed with the tables presented in Appendices A, B and C.

[4]The national income is the sum of all incomes from productive activity, representing the earnings of the factors of production: land, labor, capital and entrepreneurship. The concept is less embracing than the widely quoted Gross National Product measure, since it does not include depreciation and indirect taxes. It is, however, more representative of incomes in the conventional sense of the term.

per cent on social welfare, 5.1 per cent on health care, 4.3 per cent on education, and 1.7 per cent on culture, recreation and religion.

When the next survey was taken a decade later, Canada had survived the war and was well launched into post-war prosperity. Prime Minister Mackenzie King was completing the longest term of office of any Canadian prime minister. Society needed the infrastructure to supply the goods and services denied Canadians for almost two decades of depression and war. Resources were invested heavily in roads, communications, housing, capital works and suppressed consumption. The allocation to humanistic service declined proportionately to 13 per cent of national income. The largest share, 4.7 per cent, still went to social welfare; health care and education drew closer together at 3.7 per cent and 3.4 per cent respectively; the allocation to culture, recreation and religion dropped slightly to 1.4 per cent.

Rt. Hon. Louis St. Laurent presided as prime minister over the next decade, perhaps one of the most prosperous and tranquil economic periods in Canadian history. By 1957 the total national allocation for humanistic service had once again regained its late-depression high of 17 per cent. The major gains went to health care, back to 5.1 per cent, and education, to 4.6 per cent of national income. Cultural expenditures remained in the same proportion as 20 years earlier.

Canada was 102 years old in 1969 and a vigorous, provocative prime minister, scarcely two years in power, had already placed his imprimatur on Canadian lifestyles and the humanistic sector. Rt. Hon. Pierre Elliott Trudeau proclaimed his commitment to continue, and advance, the social programs initiated by his predecessors, King, St. Laurent and Pearson. Medical legislation would be enacted immediately, hard on the heels of a gargantuan spending binge on education launched by the provincial premiers—with federal prodding—earlier in the decade.

As the sixties closed, Canadians had upped their expenditures for humanistic service to 24 per cent of national income. Education now stood first at 10.1 per cent, more than twice the level of a decade earlier. Welfare was next at 7.2 per cent of income, also a sharp advance. Health-care expenditures had dropped slightly to 4.9 per cent of national income, not yet feeling the impact of expenditures for universal medical coverage. Cultural expenditures rose to 1.8 per cent of income, evidence of a new interest spawned by the artistic creativity demonstrated during the year of our centennial celebrations.

The humanistic sector blossomed in the seventies and by 1978 consumed nearly 32 per cent of national income. All segments had grown: social welfare to 11.8 per cent, reflecting the broad-gauged universal support programs initiated in earlier years; education and health each to nearly 9 per cent of national income; cultural expenditures to 2.2 per cent, continuing their accelerated expansion.

Today, nearly one out of three dollars of national income is spent on the four humanistic services.

EXPENDITURES ON HUMANISTIC SERVICE
EXPRESSED AS A PROPORTION OF NATIONAL INCOME

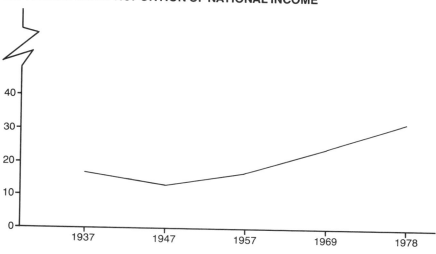

Clearly, Canadians' choices in allocating resources have followed the pattern described earlier: an expanding appetite for the ingredients of the good life as the general level of prosperity increased and basic needs were satisfied. Were Canadians pulled along by a paternalistic government or did they push for the changes? A moot question. Its answer may indeed become relevant in the future but at this point it can only be addressed obliquely by examining how the expansion of the humanistic sector was financed.

The base year is again 1937. Despite depressed family incomes, extraordinary government support for the unemployed and a well-entrenched public commitment to universal primary and secondary education, the cost of providing humanistic services that year was split almost equally between individuals and governments. Most of the private-sector share—seven out of eight percentage points—resulted from expenditures by individuals for personal health-care services, educational costs beyond the public school subsidy, private social welfare and cultural expenditures. The remaining percentage point (1.2 per cent to be precise) was contributed by individuals and corporations voluntarily through charitable donations to humanistic organizations.

The significance of that one per cent may not be readily apparent. It amounted to $43 million, roughly $10 per family, at a time when yearly family income averaged little more than $1,000. A gift of that size, out of an income hardly large enough to cover essentials, surely must have represented a sacrifice to many donors. Private corporate donations totalled $4 million, not an insignificant sum considering that the economy in 1937 could hardly be described as robust.

As already noted, humanistic expenditures had dropped proportionately by 1947 yet it was not the public sector but the private sector that cut back its allocation. Individuals reduced their level of expenditures on humanistic services by more than two percentage points to just over three per cent of national income. They also allocated less to charitable gifts, a withdrawal that was partially offset by a surge in corporate generosity. Donations from the private sector had now dropped to 1.0 per cent of national income—0.8 per cent from individuals and 0.1 per cent from corporations. The ratio now was 60:40 in favor of governments.

A further realignment in 1957. Individual allocations rebounded slightly to 5.3 per cent of national income but the private sector was overtaken by further sharp advances in government funding of all four services. The ratio now stood at 2:1 for governments.

The pattern became familiar over the next two decades: sharp advances in humanistic expenditures by governments, from 11 per cent to 19 per cent to 28 per cent of national income; proportional withdrawal by the private sector; dwindling direct personal expenditures, from 4.3 per cent to 4.2 per cent to 3.1 per cent; finally, an ever-sharper decline in charitable giving. Private-sector donations dropped from 1.0 per cent in 1957 to 0.7 per cent in 1978. Both individuals and corporations withdrew relative support, but the shrinkage in individual giving was the most severe. By 1978, individual donations had dropped to 0.6 per cent of national income and corporate contributions to 0.09 per cent, a lower level than early post-war years but almost precisely the contribution they had maintained in 1937.

The flow of decennial comparable national data terminated in 1978 with the publication of the latest family income and expenditure survey. Statistics for the year 1980, drawn from a much more comprehensive data base,

FINANCING THE HUMANISTIC SECTOR

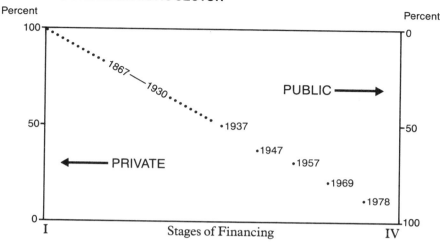

confirm the trend and provide startling new insights. Since the numbers for 1980 are reliable[5] and constitute the foundation for much of the ensuing discussion, they are valuable in fixing magnitudes and relationships firmly at the outset.

More than $70 billion flowed through the humanistic sector in 1980, 31 per cent of the country's national income. Nearly a third of it, $25 billion, was transferred directly by the federal and provincial governments to individual Canadians in the form of old age pensions, unemployment insurance benefits, welfare assistance, medical billings, and the like. Most, $45 billion, was handled by humanistic organizations: hospitals, universities, school boards, family-service agencies, churches, theatres, fraternal societies.

The humanistic sector employed more people—and higher-priced people—than were on the direct payroll of all governments combined. Its

---

[5]Government expenditures on humanistic service are available in various annual publications by Statistics Canada. The statistics on charitable donations for 1980 are drawn from *Selected Financial Statistics of Charitable Organizations*, Catalogue 61-59, Statistics Canada. We are indebted to Jacques Beauchamp of the Special Projects Branch for providing valuable background and interpretation of the data. This was the first comprehensive compilation of charitable donation receipts by the humanistic sector ever undertaken in Canada. While the accuracy of the statistics is challenged in some informed quarters, we have accepted them as a reliable base for the present discussion.

size and labor intensity made its impact on total economic performance both important and immediate. Its influence on a specific community could be decisive or devastating.[6] Those who managed large humanistic organizations possessed economic power and influence vastly exceeding that of most corporate executives. By 1980 the humanistic sector had indeed become big business.

Just how big is not widely comprehended. The social welfare sub-sector alone siphoned off 12 per cent of national income, one dollar in every eight earned, the health-care sector another nine per cent, education eight per cent, and culture two per cent. And dollars tell only part of the story. The humanistic sector employed a large share of the best-educated, most creative and articulate members of society, most of the so-called "professional" class. They moved in, or had access to, the power centres of government and business.

Who wields the ultimate power in the humanistic sector? When in doubt about such questions, ask who puts up the most money. On that criterion alone, the answer is indisputable: governments contributed more than six times as much to humanistic service as did individual Canadians in 1980. In the fields of education and welfare, state responsibilities by long tradition, the dominance was decisive: 13:1 in favor of public-sector funding. The field of health care, funded almost exclusively by the private sector in 1937 and still private-sector dominated in the early sixties, had also adapted to the modern financial profile by 1980: the ratio of government funds to private-sector funds was 4:1 in 1980. Even culture, which by our grouping embraces recreation and religion as well as the arts, was dominated by public spending, a ratio of 1.2 public dollars for every private dollar.

The private sector spent $9 billion on humanistic service in 1980. Two-thirds of this, a total of $6.6 billion, was derived from private expenditures by individuals directly for goods and services received. For example, medical and health-care needs—drugs, extra medical billings, health insurance premiums, dental work and so on—totalled $3.4 billion. Private monetary assistance for the welfare of persons living inside or outside Canada totalled $1.6 billion. Tuition fees for full-time and part-time courses, books, supplies and other educational expenses cost $1 billion. And expenditures for admission to cultural events totalled $650 million.

---

[6]Visualize Kingston, Ont., without Queen's University and Stratford, Ont., without the Shakespearean Festival.

The balance supplied by the private sector—$2.3 billion—came in the form of charitable donations and gifts of all kinds and from all sources. Voluntary donations made by individuals directly to humanistic organizations totalled $1.88 billion, 80 per cent of the total.

That is a comprehensive figure. It includes every conceivable gift and donation, from the loose change dropped into the crippled kids cash box at the Brewers' Retail to payroll deductions for the United Way, envelope offerings on Sunday, cash gifts to one's alma mater, the tariff for opening-night festivities to launch the theatre season. Deceased individuals bequeathed an additional $55 million to humanistic causes, amounts specified in wills or other directions payable from estates. The total take from individuals in voluntary donations in 1980 therefore was probably close to $2 billion, a level many times larger than previous estimates. Business and corporate cash gifts and contributions totalled $260 million in 1980, roughly one-tenth the amount donated by individuals. Foundations and endowments accounted for the remaining $100 million.

The gifts went to all four categories of humanistic service. But religious organizations received by far the largest share, $1.35 billion, about 60 per cent of the total. All categories of donors made gifts to religious organizations, from a relatively small proportion of business gifts to one-third of all bequests made in 1980. Welfare organizations were the next largest recipients: $290 million representing 13 per cent of the total. Hospitals and health-related institutions received $240 million, 10 per cent of all donations. All education including schools, universities, teaching institutions and various institutions of learning received a total of $250 million, 11 per cent of the total. The remaining seven per cent, some $160 million, went in support of a wide variety of cultural and community causes from promotion of the arts to libraries, to conservation and preservation, recreation, playgrounds and vocation camps, temperance groups and so on.

Private charitable donations represent a significant pool of funds in the Canadian economy. Yet the flow of those funds has not kept pace with the expanded needs of humanistic organizations nor with the expanded incomes from which donations are made.

Why? Does prosperity inhibit generosity? Is the shrinkage inevitable and permanent? Have people's fundamental values and natures changed over time? Do political, social and economic structures influence altruism? To help answer these questions we must turn first to history to trace the evolving patterns of responsibility for the provision of humanistic service.

CHAPTER **II**

History is philosophy
learned from examples...*

As we examine the historical record for insights into the delivery of humanistic service in earlier civilizations, we are struck by how its provision and financing, its quantity and quality, become entangled with personal philanthropy, benevolence and altruism, and how those in turn relate to morals, religion and eventually to politics. We also observe how the provision of humanistic service moves back and forth among the four stages from individual to state responsibility. Clearly a brief review cannot do justice to the topic, a rarely explored theme of human history.

This chapter distills the essence from a year's research notes—facts, anecdotes, observations—on the evolution of humanistic service in a dozen different civilizations reaching back to the very cradle of humanistic philosophy. It samples beliefs and behavior in earlier societies as our story moves westward: Ancient China, India and Japan, Classical Greece, the East European states, France, Great Britain and Sweden, and finally North America.

The next chapter focuses mainly on the development of humanistic thought and service in Canada from the first settlements at the beginning of the 17th century to the present time. The illustrations are for comparison and contrast, to recognize the similarities, to ponder and analyze the differences. If history is philosophy learned from examples, our roots will expose the very foundations of our attitudes and actions towards responsibility for

---

*Dionysius of Halicarnassus c. 54-7 B.C. *Ars Rhetorica XI*, 2.

providing the ingredients of the good life. The focus is narrow. Humanistic service is extracted from the complex themes of history in order to show how societies evolve from the simple family-oriented responsibility of Stage I to the sophisticated, bureaucratized delivery system characterized by Stage IV.

The ancient Chinese concept of humanistic service and responsibility was deeply rooted in their predominant philosophy and world view. Humanism was an integral part of their man-centred philosophy. The *shih* (Chinese intellectuals) concerned themselves with the study of human welfare, considering man the worthiest topic of all learning. Man was the measure of all things but the Chinese focused on man as a social being, not man as an individual in the Western sense. In China, the well-being of the group, the centre of which was the family, preceded that of the individual. One sacrificed individual needs for the welfare of the group. Submission and conformity dominated Chinese daily life.

In this milieu, the philosopher Confucius (born 551 B.C.) had the most profound influence on Chinese thought and attitudes. Confucius defined what was good and prescribed action necessary to achieve the state of virtue. Improvement of individual character served the betterment of society as a whole, so Confucius developed a code of ethics for individuals. Confucius said that man was an ethical being, unique among animals since he needed no inducement to be good. His code provided guidelines for human behavior and observance of these ethics came from no other consideration than that man, being a social animal, had to live by certain rules.

The teachings of Confucius did not form the basis of a religion but rather established principles of virtue enabling society to function in a state of respect, peace and harmony.

The Confucian code of ethics revolved around two underlying virtues, *jen* and *li*. *Jen* embodied a variety of interpretations including love for all men, goodness and benevolence. "*Jen* is self-sufficient, it comes from your inner self, it requires no outside help."[1] Goodness coming from within the self was most revered and admired. "If man performed good deeds for ulterior purposes, whether they be fame or wealth, his motives were not pure and there

---

[1] Source material for this chapter is many and varied, embracing a wide variety of classical and established works. For the convenience of the reader, references are not footnoted although direct quotes are indicated. The following authors in particular have been cited in this chapter: (China), Will Durant, J Gernet, Dun Li.; (India), P.N. Chopra, J.E. Padfield, S. Radhakrishan and C. Moore, G.H. Sasaki.; (Japan), Japanese National Commission for UNESCO, G.B. Sansom, P.H. Varley; (Greece), Edith Hamilton, M.L.W. Laistner, X.L. Messinsi; (Europe), I. Barta, Sir Sidney Caine, H.A.L. Fisher, W. Friedlander, B.K. Gray, C. Hallendorff and A. Shuck, B. Nightengale, H.E. Raynes, K. de Scheinitz, I. Scobbie, F.D. Scott, K. Woodroofe, *Encyclopedia Britannica*.

was little goodness in his deeds.'' To Confucius, motives were more important than results. *Jen* expressed man's innate goodness, the source, and *li*,
the second virtue, demonstrated that goodness. *Li* embodied the conventional rules of personal behavior which governed relations among men.

Confucianism provided the Chinese with standards of conduct and rules
by which he could attain virtue. Once he reached this status he became a
chun-tzu or morally superior man. The ethical code had no religious ties until the fifth century A.D. when Buddhism was introduced to China. The
new religion was quickly adopted by the people and it provided the spiritual
substance for Confucian values. The religion and the philosophy in Chinese
society were compatible and the two immediately became meshed in
Chinese life. Like Confucianism, Buddhism emphasized humane thought
and action. The Buddhists' doctrine stressed compassion and love, and encouraged acts of charity.

Love for fellow man was espoused in Chinese religion and philosophy.
Humane ideals were studied by intellectuals and advocated by monks and
priests. Were the ideals widely implemented in daily action?

The basic social unit in China was the family and the Chinese looked there
for the fulfillment of their basic needs. Adhering strictly to custom and tradition, the family assumed responsibility for all its members, and the
Chinese family was large and extended. A distant relative could go to a family for aid and expect the family to offer what it could to satisfy his needs.
When that proved impossible, individuals were forced to look to different
sources for help. The most common alternatives were friends and private
sources since one could appeal to their ''virtuous state'' and ''innate goodness.'' The heavy reliance on individual goodness to care for the needs of the
people pre-empted an abundance of government involvement in the daily
life of society including responsibility for the four humanistic services. Ancient China was a classic example of a Stage I society.

Although Confucianism and Buddhism flourished in ancient China, the
Hindus dominated in India, ironically the land of Buddha's origin. India
was, and remains, a land of disparity, incongruity and colorful variety. Differing geographic regions allowed for the development of diverse groups of
people—Hindu, Buddhist, Moslem—yet the Hindu religion came to represent the Indian way of life.

The Hindus did not view the individual as a distinct entity with needs,
desires and wants seeking fulfillment but as a ''link in the chain of life, a page
in the chronicle of the soul, a part of nature neither its centre nor its master.'' Hindu religion compelled members to become contemplative and in-

trospective in manner, forever turning toward the inner life, concentrating their efforts on following the path of the soul. Life on earth was a passing phase in one's journey through time and space. Spiritual concerns were revered and continually pondered. Thoughts and ideas regarding man's existence and salvation were intertwined with the quest for knowledge and the ultimate realization of truth.

The acquisition of knowledge and the attainment of truth could be achieved only through study, good works and experience. One lifetime was too short in which to reach this goal, therefore the Hindus believed in rebirth and the transmigration of the soul: "If a man does justice and kindness without sin his reward cannot come in one mortal span, it is stretched into other lives which if his virtue persists he will be reborn into a loftier place."

Rebirth was the method by which the moral order of the universe was worked out in the life of man. It was the instrument by which man could become morally and spiritually perfected. Only by reaching moral and spiritual perfection could one cease the process of rebirth and soul transmigration and achieve salvation.

As a Hindu soul passed through the stages of its existence it was embodied in man and born into one of the four main Hindu divisions or castes. The castes were roughly based on occupational and religious divisions. In descending order of honor, esteem and prestige, the castes were: Brahmin (teacher, priest), Ksatriya (kings, political and military leaders), Vaisya (merchants) and Sudra (laborers). The first three castes were called the twice-born, meaning they were religiously initiated Hindus, unlike the Sudras who were not so accepted.

The caste system became a way of life for the Hindus and was entrenched in every aspect of their society. It had a seminal influence on Hindu attitudes towards humanistic services, as did the spiritual nature of the Hindu religion. Rules of caste and morality were written and followed. A good life, a life full of merit, could be obtained by obeying the *dharma* (laws) which basically held the principle that neither pleasure nor wealth was to be procured by violating the rules of morality.

Giving to the poor and providing for the needy were considered good works and added to one's stockpile of merit. It was the custom in many houses to set aside a certain portion of grain each morning to be distributed to beggars who might come that day. The wealthy reserved a portion of their income, usually four per cent, for donations to the poor. Impoverished travellers were almost always assured a meal when arriving at a new village for it was binding upon those who could do so to give food to the needy regardless of caste or condition. To send a supplicant away hungry was considered a sin which would have repercussions in the next life. Beyond the village level, humanism was channeled by tradition, custom and caste. "A gift to one not a Brahmin produces fruit of middle standard, to...a Brahmin, double, to a well-read Brahmin, a hundred-thousand fold...."

Each caste established its own schools, financed by fees or services from the students' families or gifts from well-to-do members of the caste, in return for instruction and board. Health care in ancient India was highly advanced and scientific when compared to its contemporaries. A person wishing to become a doctor had to be a member of one of the twice-born castes and must belong to a good family. Payment for medical services was equivalent to the deed performed and doctors in the employ of kings and nobles were prosperous and highly respected. Art schools were established and supported by royal and noble patronage. Donations towards these projects were considered acts worthy of merit and even the Sudras contributed what they could to the production of works of art.

Humanistic behavior in ancient India, as in China, remained at Stage I for many centuries, but individual responsibility was rigidly circumscribed within castes. If it seems unfair to 20th-century North Americans that Brahmins because of their birth should be the most exalted recipients of humanistic service while Sudras and others could not as easily reap the benefits of generous-minded people, we must remember that the souls of Sudras, should they lead good and honest lives, move up the caste scale and one day, as they near goodness and truth, receive the honor awarded to Brahmins.

It is a rare Occidental who, having spent a decent length of time in Japan, is not intellectually disarmed and emotionally captivated by the Japanese people. Like a Bach fugue, cultural impressions flow endlessly, each revealing but a glimpse of a sophisticated, intricate, underlying design. Outward expressions are obvious: Japanese industry, composure, grace, manners, cleanliness, refinement, proportion. Inner sensibilities are more subtle. Trevanian describes them in terms of "spiritual tranquility...elegant simplicity...articulate brevity...modesty without prudency...."[2]

---

[2] Japan, like the blind man's elephant, depends where and how it is sensed by visitors from the West. This description, probably highly romanticized, is based on the author's impressions from a short visit and extensive historical reading. Those who know Japan emphasize different features of the Japanese character, especially the interpretation of *bushido* and *giri*. Indeed, Allan Jones, who served at the Canadian Embassy in Tokyo, 1979-1982, read this section and has reservations with the emphasis. I acknowledge his superior knowledge of Japan and Japanese culture. Trevanian's phrases are taken from his *Shibumi* (Toronto: Random House of Canada Ltd., 1979).

The group is everything in Japan. And there is a group for every conceivable activity: the family group, the work group, the religious group, the sports group, the social group, the literary group—the list is endless. Decisions are not made without careful, fastidious group consultation and consensus. But when the group has decided to act, the problem will be resolved if it is humanly possible.

Japan is admired today as one of the world's most technologically advanced and highly developed countries. Yet in the delivery of humanistic service, Japan remains essentially a Stage I-II society where individuals still react to and with other individuals, with few bureaucratic intermediaries. The process of meeting human needs, humanistic exchanges, resembles transactions motivated not so much by altruism as by two feudal principles which have established guidelines for human interaction.

The code of *giri* (moral duty) and the concept of *bushido* (the chivalrous ways of warrior nobles in daily life as in vocation) have directed the course of humanistic services throughout Japanese history and remain important factors in contemporary Japanese attitudes toward the funding of those services.

Feudalism dominated the Japanese historical scene for eight centuries, exerting a tremendous impact on Japanese thought and action. The codes of acceptable human behavior developed during the early stages of this era (c. A.D. 1000) continued through the years with little modification. Respect, duty, loyalty, piety: all of these qualities reflect the nature of the Japanese people, all were ingrained and refined during the feudal era. Lord and vassal, master and servant, *samurai* (warrior) and peasant. These were the accepted positions in life, the natural order in this formerly agrarian society.

Class lines were distinct and clearly drawn in descending order: *samurai*, peasant, artisan, merchant. Birth was the only entrance to high rank; ability and achievement counted for little in the eyes of the nobility. Relations among the classes were transactions, established so that society could function in a reasonable manner. Protection and places to work and live were offered to peasants by *samurai* in return for service and loyalty. The bond between *samurai* and peasant and among *samurai* found expression in the concept of *bushido*, a code of honor, loyalty and morality.

Thus, early in the development of Japanese society, the notion of responsibility for those entrusted to one, or in one's employ, grew strong. The complement to the idea of *bushido* was *giri*, a moral code which basically called for "the return of anything that was given, not only in matters of money and presents, but also of labor." So powerful was this code that those who did not adhere to it faced ostracism from the community.

Duty/loyalty was an exchange for the mutual benefit of the people involved. One cares for one's own. In return one is guaranteed allegiance. This
was the traditional feudal concept, similar throughout the world. However,
in Japan the concept was not allowed to die even after Japan industrialized
during the latter part of the 19th century. Instead, the Japanese adapted it
to meet the needs of changing society.

As the nation modernized the tradition was extended into the shops and
businesses. Today, the Japanese family business has diminished and large
corporations dominate the economic scene but concern for responsibility for
employees has not. Many companies provide substantial fringe benefits and
bonuses. For example, employee benefits routinely provided by Japanese
companies include family allowances, position allowances, housing allowances, transportation allowances, salesmen's allowances and luncheon subsidies. In return, employees pledge lifetime loyalty and allegiance to the
company. The caring group has now become enlarged.

What role, if any, did religion play? Barring artistic inspiration and the
construction of the great temples, religious influence on humanistic behavior appears to have been minor. Shinto, the indigenous religion of Japan,
Buddhism and Confucian philosophy all played important roles in the development of other aspects of Japanese society but with regard to charity
they appear to have had little impact.

Buddhism was imported from China and adopted as the official religion
of the court and upper classes. In China, Buddhists promoted charity and
good works. In Japan, Buddhism became more practical. For the Japanese
Buddhist, meritorious service more likely found expression in the building
of a temple or the donation of a Buddhist image.

The four humanistic services in Japan to this day remain substantially in
the private sector. The state provides public education but private schools
and colleges thrive; private hospitals and clinics offer care and treatment for
those who prefer that alternative. Freedom of choice in humanistic service
is still very much the condition.

The East held a fascination for our European forefathers, enticing the great
explorers, merchants and missionaries to undertake dangerous treks in
search of adventure, new lands, new wealth and new souls. In the 17th century, when Europeans began to make lasting inroads into the far East, they
became aware that theirs was not the only civilized culture on this earth. To
their surprise they discovered ancient and highly developed civilizations
with a charitable ethos not inferior to Europe's and not animated by the
Christian disposition.

Then began the modern comparative study of world religions and societies. No doubt, the Orient and India have had negligible impact on Canadian
attitudes towards humanistic service.[3] Yet the discovery of like ideals and
the elevation of similar noble human attributes in civilizations totally separated from one another is at once exciting and perplexing.

But occidentals *are* different. As H.A.L. Fisher points out:

> We Europeans are the children of Hellas. Our civilization, which has its
> roots in the brilliant city life of the Aegean, has never lost traces of its or-
> igin and stamps us with a character by which we are distinguished from
> the other great civilizations of the human family, from the Chinese, the
> Hindus, the Persians, and the Semites.... There is an European civili-
> zation [and] our civilization...is distinct: it is also all-pervading and pre-
> ponderant...the kind of civilization which we specifically designate as
> European reposes not upon a foundation of race but on an inheritance of
> thought and achievement and religious aspirations.[4]

Greece's Golden Age. It spanned the century that began 500 years before the
birth of Christ. And it probably had as much influence on intellectual and
cultural development in the west as Christianity has had on its spiritual and
moral development. Greek literature and drama remain the standards by
which contemporary works are judged; Greek philosophy, ethics in particular, has shaped the thinking of intellectuals for 2,500 years. Western democracy began in the Council of 500. In medicine, Greece gave us the
Hippocratic oath, that noble ethic that established the standard of public
service, not only for physicians but for all men who presume to regard themselves as professionals.

Greece had a highly developed humanistic sector, not surprising when one
considers the Greek preoccupation with human nature in general and individual nurture in particular. The principles underlying that system are

---

[3]This may well be changing. In 1980 more than 70,000 Asians migrated to Canada, half the total number of immigrants that year, no doubt reflecting the influx of boat people from Vietnam. The dilution
of Anglo-Saxon blood in Canada is strikingly apparent at citizenship ceremonies held weekly in most
Courts of Canadian Citizenship across the land. At the special Christmas citizenship ceremony held
in the London, Ont., court on December 16, 1982, for example, 24 new Canadians swore the Oath of
Citizenship ("'that I will faithfully observe the laws of Canada and fulfill my duties as a Canadian citizen...'"). They came from 15 different countries including Poland, Germany, Lebanon, Ireland and
Guyana, with four members of the Tran family from South Vietnam. Clerk of the Court Ann Hurley
conceded that the ethnic mix was more heterogeneous than average in recognition of the special
occasion.

[4]H.A.L. Fisher, *A History of Europe from the Earliest Times to 1713* (London: Eyre and Spottiswood,
1935).

worthy of careful examination since many endure to this day as the fundamental values underlying humanistic behavior in western civilizations.

Religion played a highly significant role in formulating cultural habits
with regard to art, literature and theatre. Greek religion was characterized
by marked secular qualities, lacking a theology of hard and fast dogmas.
Worship of the gods was part of the Greeks' daily life. If the gods were ap-
peased with prayer and sacrificial offerings, then the supernatural might
reasonably be expected to do their part in helping and protecting their human petitioners. Worship of the gods was practiced among the rank and file.
It was expected of those who held official positions.

Religious festivals took on a national or Panhellenic character. As an imperial state, Athens requested contributions by her dependencies and while
the rest of the Greek world was not obligated to patronize Athenian festivals, they did so. With this support, Pericles built temples to hold the musical contests of the day, which more than ever brought religion into the realm
of culture. The exploits of the gods, with their human foibles of treachery
and bribery, inspired the imaginations of poets and writers in literary and
dramatic works. Competitive spirits inspired the Olympic Games.

It was later, in the fourth century, that followers of Sophocles encouraged
open criticism of the established religion. Worship of the Olympian gods
declined, though their rituals survived, and they were still depicted in literary works. In its place emerged a new spirituality based on man as a social
being.

The emergence of the *polis* or city-state, which was a government by democratic means, was strongly linked to the new spiritual world of the Greeks
while the common sharing of political authority also had a decisive influence on the participation in culture and the evolution of ideas. Free discussion and reasoned debate became a way of life. Never has there been a
community in which the ordinary citizen had his critical faculties so highly
developed for the appreciation of culture. Participation in festivals and attendance at the theatre were opportunities open to all citizens.

In his writings, Plato concentrates on his conception of the "ideal man."
He was an Athenian who regarded his membership in the *polis* above his existence as an individual. Because every citizen participated in the management of the *polis* at some time, the citizens felt themselves much more a part
of the city than a part of the family. The family was but one element of their
civic duty, since it was their responsibility to produce fit and respectable
citizens.

The system of public finance relied chiefly on voluntary contributions
from wealthy and ambitious citizens to equip the navy, to mount theatre

productions and for other public works. Taxation was imposed only as a last resort. Wealthy Athenians felt it was their pleasure as well as their duty to support the state. Failing that, peer pressure exerted a compelling force for compliance with the code.

One of the civic duties or "liturgies" of the rich was the financing of the production of a drama or comedy. Wealthy citizens were assigned entrants vying for the prize winner's crown (in a competitive structure similar to the Olympic Games). They not only had to pay for the actors but also for the maintenance of the chorus during training. The performance was judged by audience response and a prize brought a thrill to the cast and glory to the patron. Theatre performances were religious in their roots and under the control of the state. The attendance fee for the public was two *obol* but Pericles arranged that those who could not well afford even this should have the tickets at the expense of the state. Eventually he made the tickets free to all and used any entrance money for the maintenance of the theatre. Art flourished under such patronage. In Athens patrons such as Peisistratos, Hipparchos and his brother Hippias, Kleisthenes and Pericles became prominent figures, respected, admired, recognized.

The common man with his cultural awareness was an important factor as well. There was a wide range of literary and artistic activity during the fifth century. While poets depended on individual patronage, historians and philosophers received little or no pecuniary rewards. The other arts, such as sculpture and architecture, were subject to public favor. The Greek musician also received honors and rewards from his community, which initially included a comfortable seat in the centre of the hall and a choice cut from the meat of sacrifice but which later became more bountiful when tours from city to city became popular. The rhapsodist made his living by reciting Homeric poems at the great festivals and rendered a priceless service to literature, in an age when complete copies of Homer were scarce, as custodians of the text.

Homeric poems became part of the curriculum of elementary education along with those of Hesiod, Theognis, and other poets. The essence of Greek nature and the basis of Greek conduct were present in these works and instilled in all boys from seven to 14 years. Unlike Sparta, which controlled its educational system, Athens and other city-states left the provision and financing of elementary education in the hands of individuals, except for the sons of citizens who had been killed in battle, who were educated at public expense.

Training of the body ranked no less important than other subjects and was carried on concurrently with intellectual studies. Classes began with lessons in deportment and graduated to wrestling, sprinting, jumping and boxing. The standard of instruction varied greatly due to the private undertakings but the state appointed certain boards whose duty it was to see that there were no offences against tradition or morality.

At age 13-14, the sons of the poorer citizens and resident aliens ended their formal education. They went on to their father's farm or were apprenticed to a trade. Higher education, primarily science and philosophy, became established by the Sophists in the last quarter of the fifth century. It entailed considerable expense, so only the wealthier members of the community could afford to send their boys.

Within the ideal city, which Plato and Aristotle held in such high regard in their writings, education was the business of the state to organize and control. Aristotle wrote, ''It is difficult to get from youth up a right training for virtue if one has not been brought up under the right laws; for to live temperately and hardily is not pleasant to most people, especially when they are young. For this reason their nurture and occupations should be fixed by Law, for they will not be painful when they have become customary.'' Ironically, this philosophy was never fully realized in Aristotle's day. But it has remained an enduring principle in the value system governing education throughout history.

Health care in the Greek world was a shared responsibility. The community chose and paid for public physicians who treated poor citizens. The state also supported and embellished the temples of Epidaurus, which were shrines for healing comparable to Lourdes.

In both cases, however, the rich could secure alternative services. The healing shrines at Asclepian, for instance, developed into a form of health spa where the sick or convalescent with money could repair for rest, relaxation and proper diet. There were also private physicians devoted exclusively to caring for those who could afford their services. They either visited their patients or gave them advice in their own homes which contained consulting, bathing and operating rooms. Some of these doctors took on slave doctors as assistants who treated those who were unable to afford a high fee.

Despite the segregation of care, it is doubtful if treatment was denied those in real need. The spirit of the physician's practice is enunciated in the Hippocratic oath, which is still taken to this day and contains high ethical and professional standards.

A social welfare scheme as we know it did not exist, although the welfare of each citizen was considered important to all. The aged were greatly respected and cared for by their families. Generally, assistance to the needy was in the hands of the tribe who governed the city. It was first a personal responsibility to provide for one's health, education and old age. For the few who were not self-sufficient for cause, there was aid from the state, welfare without shame, because the community knew that genuine misfortune struck its victims randomly.[5]

One will recognize elements of all four stages of humanistic service in the Golden Age. The good life was *the* way of life for the Greek citizen. He was the complete man who accepted excellence as the only worthy standard of performance; who accepted the responsibility for his community as a personal obligation; who derived joy (and reaped honor) in benevolent acts. Industrious, enlightened, honorable.

Humanistic Nirvana? Yes, if one wasn't a woman or a slave.

Greece's intellectual preeminence in Europe gave way to the physical dominance of the Roman Empire. In due course, Roman legions occupied the entire continent, as far north as Britain, a remarkable feat considering the immaturity of transportation and communications.

But Europe 2,000 years ago was sparsely populated, mainly agrarian and largely illiterate. All roads led to Rome—for about five centuries. Slavery was a dominant feature of Roman society, as it had been for the Greeks. Roman legions enslaved the citizens of Greece, but never really captured the essence of Hellas. Romans admired and emulated Greek humanistic qualities, adopting the Greek educational pattern: fine arts, poetry, philosophy. They even added oratory and eloquence to the curriculum. But at best, the Romans acquired but a cultural veneer—a preoccupation with form, not substance.

For instance, formal education did not extend to religion, history and nature. Consequently nothing equipped the Romans to perceive the grave social and economic calamity which eventually surrounded and destroyed them.

After the decline of the Roman Empire, events and trends in Europe were slow to emerge when judged by today's standards, yet once begun they frequently radiated their influence throughout the continent.

Such was certainly the case in attitudes towards the delivery of humanistic services. Stories of charity, charitable institutions and social services were often comparable and parallel, north and south, east and west, a fact

---

[5]Thucydides expressed Greek welfare philosophy eloquently in the *Funeral Oration of Pericles* "...and poverty we think it no disgrace to acknowledge but a real degradation to make no effort to overcome."

that enables us to glance at Europe as an entity, concentrating on those countries that supplied Canada with its founding populations: France, Britain, Germany, Italy and, to a lesser extent, Eastern Europe and Sweden.

With few exceptions, humanistic service in Europe remained at Stage I or Stage II until the end of the 19th century. Individuals or private institutions administered health care, educated the population and cared for the needy. One either provided for oneself or turned to benevolent individuals and religious philanthropies. Neither the financing nor the distribution of services was particularly equitable.

Yet each of the great periods of European history—feudalism, the Renaissance, monarchies, revolution, democracy, war, recovery—moulded perceptible changes in the humanistic delivery system. Gradually, often painfully, Europe was propelled inexorably through the stages and deposited by degrees at Stage IV in the aftermath of the Second World War.

When the Roman Empire disintegrated in the fifth century, it removed monolithic control over the welfare of Europe's sparse population. For long centuries thereafter the west languished through the Dark Ages, a period characterized by widespread oppression, intellectual and physical poverty, inhumanity and stagnation. This was the era of feudalism when local lords ruled over manors, large land areas populated by serfs or peasants, a system which became the basis of economic and social life: a European country-state in which the many produced wealth for the few and in return were provided food, shelter and the comforts of life and granted protection from aliens. *Bushido*. Chivalry.

Charlemagne, the most celebrated and eulogized warrior-king who united a great part of western Europe in the ninth century, decreed the minimum standard of humanistic service that should be provided: all lords should care for the poor on their manors and provide food for the destitute.

Alas, it was largely a romantic ideal. For the most part the lord provided the poor peasants with few health or welfare services and no education or cultural opportunities. This vacuum in humanistic care was filled by the Christian church.

The ethical essence of Christianity permeated European thought and provided the standard for social behavior—purity of heart, generosity of behavior, the dignity of the weak, empathy, compassion, altruism. How logical for the church to evolve from preaching humanistic doctrine to performing humanistic service. And how fortuitous, since no one else seemed to be doing it.

Would the church have become so awesomely powerful in the Middle Ages without its undisputed control over education? (Teaching Latin to the few scholars training to become clergy, lawyers or physicians.)[6] Health care? (Hospitals often fell under the patronage of a monastery, religious order or bishop.) Welfare? (Following Christ's teachings and example, the church took responsibility for administering to the poor and sick.) Artistic inspiration? (Witness the architecture, sculptures and paintings of the great cathedrals and monasteries.)

No matter, the church *was* powerful and it succored an impoverished population. Its resources, funds from the flock: tithing, voluntary donations and subscriptions, gifts of works of art from wealthy parishioners. It most certainly controlled the dominant share of Europe's gross national product during the Middle Ages. The bishops decreed that the parishes dedicate anywhere from one-quarter to one-third of their revenue to feed and clothe the poor. If one classifies the medieval church as the state, then humanistic service was largely at Stage IV during this period.

As church authority and obligations expanded, other more aggressive fund-raising techniques began to be employed. While lucrative, some, such as the sale of indulgences,[7] were thought by many to be abuses of the church's position and prestige. In 1517 Martin Luther, an angry German monk, documented the grievances of the people in 95 theses which outlined the abusive practices of the clergy. Luther confronted the pope's envoy in public debate, refused to recant his allegations, was excommunicated, then led a vanguard of reformers in asserting a purified Christian church, independent of Vatican authority.

Thus was launched the Reformation, the establishment of the Protestant church and the end of Roman Catholic monopoly of the Christian religion in Europe. But even before Martin Luther's dramatic break, a cultural movement known as the Renaissance emerged in Italy and quickly spread its enlightened philosophy throughout Europe. It was the "rebirth" of the

---

[6]The first universities in Europe were established by religious orders to train candidates for the three traditional professions.

[7]Indulgences began as the relaxing of punishment imposed by the church for violation of the commandments. Originally they were given by the popes to the Crusaders going off to fight the infidel. Over the centuries, indulgences were extended to include financial gifts for worthy causes, e.g., the financing of cathedrals, monasteries, hospitals. In that age of superstition and doubt, people came to believe that through indulgences they could buy relief from the punishment of after-life, e.g., a donation to a cathedral building fund netted one a specified number of 'parole' days from Purgatory. This practice was open to abuse and eventually degenerated into outright cash sales of indulgences. Martin Luther's argument was not so much concerned with these selling practices as with their theological implications. He did not believe that the pope had the power to remit punishment from God. Luther became incensed when the indulgence seller came to Wittenburg in 1517, thus sparking his tirade against the church.

classical emphasis on secular rather than religious activities, a turn to worldliness rather than otherworldliness, the freeing of man's imagination to create, produce, thrive and grow in the contemporary, secular sphere.

The output, especially in the arts, was prodigious. During the 15th and 16th centuries, Italy was once again *the* cradle of intellectual thought and culture. Artists, poets and philosophers from all over Europe flocked to the cities of Florence, Venice and Rome hoping to absorb the aura, the excitement and the elegance of Italian civilization. Renaissance Italy, however, was not a single entity. Rather it was divided into a collection of states and principalities, a lack of cohesion that later left her open to a series of foreign invasions following the Renaissance period, a decay of Renaissance ideals, and the sacking of Italy's great cultural treasures.[8]

The cachet of the Renaissance is, of course, its legacy of art, the famous works of Raphael, Da Vinci, Michelangelo, *et al*. Their patrons, the Medici, the Duke of Milan, and a host of Europe's royalty, enjoyed the work more for its intrinsic beauty, its harmony and its exquisite proportion, and less for its religious value. Painting and sculpture were elevated from crafts to art forms.

The Renaissance also stimulated free thinking and intellectual curiosity, which led in turn to a skepticism that challenged the established order. The Reformation seriously undermined the power and influence of the traditional church and led to new initiatives in humanistic service. In Sweden, for instance, Gustav Vasa, king from 1523-1560, expunged the Roman Catholic Church from Sweden and established the new Lutheran Church as the state church. It continued with the administration of charitable services, but the state assumed fiscal responsibility.

As time passed, each successive Swedish king cut more and more deeply into the church's former areas of authority. Sweden's most illustrious king, Gustavus Adolphus, who reigned from 1611-1632, granted state support for the *gymnasia*, a type of secondary school formerly operated by the church. King Gustav II endowed the University of Uppsala, which had faced financial difficulties since its founding in 1477, with practically all the land belonging to the House of Vasa. This endowment has ever since provided the

---

[8]It was not until 1870 that Italy became a politically unified nation-state. For humanistic service, the consequence of these centuries of confusion was a strong retention of, and reliance upon, Stages I and II with almost no government involvement in these areas until the end of the Second World War. The Roman Catholic Church remained the dominant humanistic organization in Italy. Other non-religious charitable organizations also thrived leaving it with a strong tradition of private charity.

chief source of income for the university. In England Henry VIII confiscated all property and monasteries belonging to the Roman Catholic Church and turned them over to the state or to other humanistic organizations. This included many hospitals, orphanages and alms houses.

With the traditional position of the church seriously weakened or destroyed in many countries, the provision of humanistic service—the former prerogative of the religious—was correspondingly diminished. Poverty, of course, continued, and many poor beggars and vagabonds, denied the traditional source of relief, wandered the countryside. In response, the royal governments in France and England called forth the community spirit and decreed a renewal of local responsibility. Thus were written the poor laws to provide relief and maintain some semblance of social stability. The Royal Edict of Moulins in 1566 and the Elizabethan Poor Laws of 1572 established the principle of municipal taxation to finance welfare services. It was the first formal entry of governments into the area of welfare, and set precedents for further government action. The poor laws deserve further examination.

In England, the parish, the smallest unit of local government, was the jurisdiction for the administration of the poor laws and the collection and distribution of the Poor Law tax. The local justice appointed an overseer to assess the tax base and levy a poor-rate on all householders. It was a position hardly coveted. Failure to comply with one's appointment resulted in imprisonment.

The poor laws required those who supported indigents on relief to find some useful work for them to perform in return. The motive was sound: permit the poor the dignity of working for their support, and train them to become self-sufficient, productive members of society.[9] Its execution was a disaster. The poor were usually herded into work houses where conditions, physical and administrative, often deteriorated into unbelievable depths of degradation and wretchedness.

It took 160 years before reform measures were instituted. The new philosophy was based on the following logic: present laws had the potential of turning otherwise able-bodied poor into indolent vagrants and beggars; if the hardy were segregated into well-regulated work houses, and if the working conditions in the houses were strict and miserable, they would be given

---

[9]The notion behind the poor laws has re-emerged from time to time over the centuries. Its most recent incarnation in Canada was the suggestion of Work Fare, promoted by Hon. Gordon Walker, MPP, and others in Ontario, c. 1980.

the incentive to leave and find productive work outside. These were the conditions so poignantly described by Charles Dickens in his 19th century classic, *Hard Times.* It was to be another 50 years, until the extension of the franchise in 1884, before serious reform measures began in England.

Meanwhile, a century earlier, another social movement was taking shape throughout Europe, one that would fundamentally alter people's attitudes towards responsibility for humanistic service.

The class system—segregation of the population into separate, easily distinguishable social classes—was a pervasive aspect of European society. Each person was a member of a distinctive estate: the clergy, the nobility, the peasantry and, later, the middle class (people with some wealth or professionals such as lawyers, doctors, shopkeepers, small landowners, etc.). Power and wealth were still concentrated in the hands of the few.

In the latter part of the Middle Ages, representatives of these classes began to meet in national assemblies,[10] such as Riksdag, Reichstag, Dumas, etc., that came into being in most of the European kingdoms. The classes most often represented were the first estate (clergy), the second estate (nobles), and the third estate (other privileged classes such as the middle class). The voice of the peasant was rarely, if ever, heard.

The wealth created by the industrial revolution spread itself beyond the ranks of the upper-tier estates and into a rapidly rising, vocal and aggressive middle class that demanded social, political and economic reform. Humanistic services were often focal points of the reform movements. People began to view health care, education and human welfare as fundamental human rights, not privileges or benevolences bestowed on them by the class above. Sometimes the forces for reform were peaceful and confined within the established political process. Sadly, too often they were violent and revolutionary.

The French Revolution, 1789, characterizes the upheaval. The wealthy nobles and expanding bourgeoisie were effectively excluded from political decision-making power although they were taxed for public services. The peasants, too, were restive under the remaining vestiges of feudalism, an institution still very much alive in France, yet effectively superseded in England. A new breed of powerful, compelling moral philosophers—Voltaire, Rousseau and Montesquieu—were proselytizing a new political order in

---

[10]National assemblies were the forerunners of modern parliaments.

which the state would guarantee its citizens personal freedom and dignity and assume responsibility for the support of the destitute. The new order—the birth of the French Republic—did come. But at the cost of the execution of the king and his family, and the indignity of a bloody revolution.

The first National Assembly promptly enacted measures which reformed the delivery of some humanistic services. French society as a whole would become responsible for relief of the poor and sick. A few of the programs were:

- Poor relief is a national debt, so hospitals, foundations and endowments for the poor shall be sold for the profit of the nation;
- Society has to provide maintenance for destitute citizens at the place of their residence, either by employment or by granting the means of support for those unable to work;
- Medical care for the population shall be secured by a licenced physician serving in each cantonal district;
- Parents who are financially unable to support their children shall receive public aid from the nation.[11]

The thrust of the French Revolution was political, not social. Yet its aftermath, these actions and decrees, planted firmly the seeds of a Stage IV society.

In Eastern Europe, the Age of Enlightenment did not lead to revolution but it did broaden the perspectives of those interested in education and committed to progress. As in Western Europe during the Middle Ages, the church had controlled education. With the dissolution of the Jesuit order in 1773, Poland moved to state direction of this humanistic service and established its first ministry of education. The great properties of the Jesuits were used to finance a new era of teaching, more secular in philosophy and encompassing the scientific progress of the West. In Hungary, the most influential circles of the court came to believe that education was a state affair, and pressed for the *Ratio Educationis* of 1777 which gave the state responsibility for organizing schools at all levels, as well as financing them through taxation.

The 19th-century period of democratization gradually placed more and more responsibility for humanistic services in the hands of governments. As

[11]See Walter Friedlander, *Individualism and Social Welfare* (New York: The Free Press of Glencoe Inc., 1962).

they came to be viewed, human rights, health, welfare and education ceased to be controlled by the wealthy or the responsibility of a select religious group.

Education in particular noted the change. For example, in Sweden during the 1830s and 1840s, Crown Prince Oscar argued for the free election of school boards and the establishment of universal education. The Swedish state, while supporting primary and secondary school systems, promoted equality in education. The result was close to universal literacy. All levels of society attended public schools and, although they were not illegal, there were few prestigious private secondary and preparatory schools established in Sweden.

While Sweden, France and Prussia experimented with state-supported elementary education, England demurred. For the British, it was an agonizing process to switch responsibility for education from the private to the public domain. Public finance of education began in 1833 when the British Parliament voted the sum of £20,000 to be set aside as building grants for voluntary schools.[12]

Over the next half-century the nature and scope of the grants slowly changed so that by the end of the 19th and beginning of the 20th centuries elementary education in England was universal and state supported. By the end of the First World War, money for the maintenance and development of British universities was still derived from private sources: benefactions, endowments and student fees.

The support for the students was also private, with individuals relying on themselves and families to pay their way, although some scholarships were awarded to outstanding students with limited financial means of support. From 1919 on, the system of state grants to universities grew to such an extent that they now overshadow all private sources of funding. Although now almost entirely financed by the state, British universities remain independent and self-governing.

---

[12]What North Americans call private schools, the British term public schools. Winchester and Eton, two of England's most prestigious, began as partial charity schools. Winchester, for example, allowed 10 sons of nobles to attend on a fee-for-service basis and 10 poor boys to attend free. The schools eventually became the domain of the gentry and the rich middle and upper classes who believed that graduation from the best public schools favored one's entry into Oxford and Cambridge, and ultimately into national politics. Today there are 30 to 40 top public schools and a larger body of lesser ones projecting an image of exclusivity and competitive advantage to Britons still conscious of class distinction. Apparently with great success, public schools in Britain have enjoyed unprecedented prosperity since the Second World War.

At the turn of the 19th century, Europe was becoming a patchwork of all stages of humanistic service, from Stage I to Stage IV. The coming of the Industrial Revolution, with its restructuring of the old economic, social and political orders, brought about monumental changes in the delivery of humanistic services and attitudes toward them.

Industrial capitalism altered associations between men and women. For "the old relations based on custom and...sweetened by sentiment...has now substituted the cash nexus between master and man." The ideals of *laissez-faire*, and of Adam Smith, may have benefited the burgeoning capitalists; their reality often wrought havoc on the lives of the laboring classes.

Accompanying rapid industrialization and urbanization was the growth of slum areas with all of their well-known and documented vices: alcoholism, prostitution, child abuse, murder, and so on, not to mention the poor and dangerous working conditions in the factories.

Concerned citizens spoke out against these abuses. For example, Lord Shaftesbury, the English philanthropist who became a leading proponent of factory reform, agitated throughout the 19th century for improved working conditions, more humane lunatic asylums, and a higher standard of public health. The appalling conditions inspired liberal politicians such as John Stuart Mill to work for more humane reforms through the parliamentary system and more radical political writers such as Karl Marx to call for proletarian revolution.

While politicians and writers debated the best method of coping with the greater need and demand for health, welfare and education, private groups attempted to deliver them. Private and religious philanthropies, including remnants of feudalism in Eastern Europe, were thriving all over the continent. In some countries, there was such a proliferation of charitable activity that it led to the formation of yet additional voluntary organizations to systematize their efforts.

The social, economic and cruel climatic conditions of 1860-61 aroused the sympathies of many citizens and brought forth a flow of charitable donations which soon became a flood. High unemployment and a business depression encouraged those with resources to contribute, and private relief agencies literally sprang up everywhere. Interest and activity was kept alive by dedicated, visible and articulate humanitarians. Edward Denison, Frederick Denison Maurice and Octavia Hill were some who dedicated themselves to working among the poor, and promoting social reform.

The proliferation of charitable societies led to a growing concern over wasted resources and duplicated effort. This anxiety led to the establishment of the Charity Organization Society in the latter half of the 19th century, a movement dedicated to the coordination of philanthropic endeavors to ensure a more equitable distribution of funds and the prevention of overlapping and competitive activity: Stage III.

And on the horizon of this milieu loomed Stage IV. At the end of the 19th century, the French government enlarged the existing welfare bureau and expanded its network of public relief agencies. In 1893 France passed the National Law for Free Medical Assistance. Under this statute, the first of its kind in Europe, the French who could not pay the fees were provided with free medical treatment and hospitalization.

Social legislation spread rapidly throughout Europe. In 1908 Lloyd George, who would later become Prime Minister of England, toured Germany to study the system of social security initiated by Bismarck in 1880. England enacted a non-contributory old-age pension scheme in 1908 and the National Health Insurance and Unemployment Insurance Acts in 1911. The French, who had resisted a full-blown national insurance scheme, succumbed in 1919 when they reacquired Alsace Lorraine from the Germans, a population grown accustomed to the rather liberal social-welfare insurance program.

By the time the economic depression of the 1930s gripped Europe, most European states had experimented with national programs of humanistic service—the leading edges of Stage IV. Following the Great Depression and the Second World War, many of them took the plunge into full-scale socialized humanistic service: health, welfare, education and, for some, cultural services. In Sweden, the depression increased the demand for more government-supported relief, and the freely elected Social Democratic government responded by expanding unemployment insurance and old-age pensions and adding motherhood benefits, marital loans, grants to widows and subsidies for school lunches.

Nor did they ignore art and culture. In 1937 the Swedish Riksdag allocated a minimum of one per cent of state construction expenditures to the acquisition of art for public buildings, and assigned part of the profits of the state lottery to the arts.[13] In 1946 the Riksdag legislated free, universal health services and state subsidies to cover the cost of medicine and sickness ben-

[13]Irene Scobbie describes how, following the Second World War, artists began to call themselves "cultural workers" and demanded the same rights as other workers, thereby fully democratizing the arts in Sweden. Irene Scobbie, *Sweden* (New York: Praeger Publishers, 1972).

efits. By 1950 the structure of the welfare state had been completed; Sweden had reached Stage IV.[14]

Other European countries followed the Swedish model. In Great Britain, a government white paper released in 1942 was to become the blueprint for state control of health and welfare. The Beveridge Report, written by a man who had worked closely with Winston Churchill in establishing the unemployment section of the National Insurance Program in 1911, recommended a system of child allowances and a comprehensive program of health, rehabilitation and unemployment insurance. By 1946 Britain had the Family Allowances Act and the National Insurance Act, which provided universal health services including dental care.[15]

Following the Second World War, the Eastern Bloc countries, then under Soviet influence, converted smartly to Stage IV humanistic service. Today, while private philanthropy and generosity of spirit most assuredly must live in the hearts and minds of individual citizens, these do not find scope for institutional expression through voluntary involvement and individual responsibility for humanistic service in the communist states.

Although its format varies, Europe, the homeland of our forefathers, has responded emphatically and uniformly to the powerful and expanding demand for humanistic service—with Stage IV delivery.

---

[14]So complete is the loop closed over Stage IV in Sweden that even the church is financed by tax revenues. Swedes are assessed a separate income tax levy ranging from one-half to one per cent of income to support the state (Lutheran) church. As we shall see in a later chapter, however, philanthropy is far from dead in Sweden.

[15]State-financed dental care has provided irrepressible British comedians with more material than perhaps any other single topic. Who can suppress at least a smile at the vision of a set of clacking dentures protruding from the mouth of some hapless, oblivious dustman in a BBC sit-com?

CHAPTER **III**

Towards Stage IV

It was this Europe that sent her adventurers westward to populate North America, generally in the 17th century. And it was France— in the person of Samuel de Champlain—who first settled the Canadian soil claimed by Cartier as her western colony. For 150 years, from the founding of Quebec in 1608 to the British conquest, Canada such as it was *was* French in language, custom, culture, heritage, habit and emotion. No subsequent event will ever alter the reality of that fact.

The population base was small, barely 65,000 people when New France fell to the British in 1758, but so long as Canada remains united, that intrepid core shall forever remain our French-Canadian cultural and ethnic fountainhead. Our French-Canadian forefathers re-shaped and adapted Old World methods and institutions to meet the needs of the new and harsh environment. Yet they would always revere their past and honor their traditions.

This adaptation permeated every aspect of daily life from religion to economics to the delivery of humanistic service. The colonists depended on France to supply an army to defend them, and as a place to dispose of their New World goods. As the settlement grew, this dependence also grew and moved beyond the realm of defence and economics, into the areas of health, education and welfare. In the area of humanistic services, the new colony perhaps not surprisingly began at Stage IV, not the state dependence of modern-day Sweden, nevertheless an aristocratic welfare state.[1]

New France was settled at the peak of one of France's greatest ages. Louis XIV, who could well have proclaimed *L'Etat, c'est moi!* (I am the State), guided the French colonial regime with a strong and paternalistic hand. The French court generally believed that the state must safeguard the legitimate interest of all ranks in society: "The rich must nourish the poor." The goal of the king and his court was to establish a prosperous and thriving colony in the New World. Therefore, to ensure its survival, the "general good" assumed priority over the individual and the crown decided *what* was to become the general good. Humanistic services were basically financed and administered from New France.

The basic unit of colonial society was the family, not the individual, and everyone was expected to care for his own. However, disease and poverty were widespread, notably among those who had just arrived, making it difficult for families to survive as a unit. Begging became endemic, so the state established a Bureau of the Poor in 1685 whose aim was to solve a social problem as well as to provide an outlet for Christian charity. Its members, one of whom was the parish priest, were charged with responsibility to identify the "unfortunate and miserable poor." The three main objectives of the Poor Board were to see that no person starved, to find useful work for those capable of working, and to put an end to the public annoyance created by beggars.

Funds for the Bureau came from a variety of sources. In each town two women were appointed to go door to door collecting alms. They were instructed not to press people for donations but "to allow all to contribute according to their means and dictates of conscience." Fines from felonies and misdemeanors were also paid to the Bureau. However, the main source of revenue (6,000 *livres* per annum)[2] came from crown subsidies.

---

[1] See W.J. Eccles, *Canadian Society During the French Regime*, E.R. Adair Memorial Lectures (Montreal: Harvest House, 1968). Other works from the following authors were employed in the compilation of this chapter: J.H. Archer, A. Artibise, A.A. Chiel, S.D. Clark, P. Collins, S. Crean, J.C. Falardeau, J. Fingard, R. Fulford, G.P.T. Glazebrook, M. Horn, H.F. Johnson, H. McDermot, H. Morgan, H.B. Neatby, B. Ostry, C.E. Phillips, J. Porter, M. Ross, S. Ryerson, J. Schull, L. Sclater, H. Shillington, Goldwin Smith, R. Splane, M. Kirkpatrick-Strong, J.C. Turner and F.J. Turner, M. Wade, E. Watkins, H.H. Walsh.

[2] The monetary system during the period of the French regime was based on the *livre tournois*. W.J. Eccles of the University of Toronto, one of the leading modern students of French Canada, estimates that the *livre* had the buying power of roughly two 1968 Canadian dollars (Eccles, *The Canadian Frontier 1534-1760*). That would place its value at about $6.50 in 1984.

By the end of the 17th century the crown had established alms houses for the aged, crippled and orphaned. In 1736 the crown accepted responsibility for the care of foundlings and the local crown prosecutor was charged with the task of obtaining a wet nurse for abandoned infants, and finding an ''honest'' home later to adopt the children.

While the state was involved in providing for the welfare of its inhabitants (Stage IV), examples of individual altruism were also present. The pioneer ethic of helping a neighbor in trouble was much in evidence. Disasters were common. When one struck, the pioneer depended on the aid of his neighbors to pull through.

The Roman Catholic Church, a manifestation of Stage II, was an integral factor in the dispensing and financing of humanistic services. Besides performing religious duties, the priests and members of religious orders,[3] the only educated people in the parish, also taught school.

And true to its Christian tradition, the church offered relief to the poor. However, the church in the colony often relied on the state for financial support. The official income of the *curé* (parish priest) was *la dime* (tithe), set at 1/26 of the harvest. Unfortunately for the priests, this did not yield an adequate income so the responsibility to finance the priests and their churches fell once again on the royal treasury. The first churches were made possible with grants from the seminaries at Quebec and Montreal which, in turn, were supplemented by royal grants. Parishioners contributed material and labor for the construction of the edifices.

Although the state supported the churches in the colony, the settlers were encouraged to make their parishes financially self-sufficient. The crown offered reward and recognition for major contributors to church construction. A royal edict in 1769 proclaimed that a *seigneur* who donated the total cost of construction of a new church would have the right to be considered the patron founder, with the right to propose a new *curé* in case of a vacancy. Considering the importance of the priest in the parish, the right of selection afforded the patron a great deal of potential power.

But most of the inhabitants, including *seigneurs*, were cash poor. They could donate the land, but could not finance the church construction. For

---

[3]Marguerite Bourgeouys, co-founder of the Congregation of Notre Dame, the first religious order to originate in Canada, and Marie Guyart, who helped bring the Ursuline Convent to Canada, both established schools to teach the native Indians and the French. The Jesuits, Récollets, Capuchins and other Roman Catholic religious orders also worked to further education in New France. In addition to their educational causes, the fathers and the sisters aided the sick and poor.

such a gift, donors received their own pew in the new building.

Educational opportunities were sparse. The schools that were established initially were based on the classical model and managed by religious orders. But by 1722 the king allocated 3,000 *livres* annually to support eight school masters. The subsidy was paid to the general hospital established in Montreal and stipulated that the schools should be free "without anything being required by the parents of the young boys whom they wish to instruct." Free, yes, but the wise monarch could not resist a commercial: "His Majesty does not, however, intend to restrict the charities that the inhabitants of Canada would wish to make to the said hospital for the instruction of their children."

Health care for many years remained primitive in New France. Canada's first hospital was established at Quebec in 1639, a gift from the Duchess D'Aiguillon, a niece of Cardinal Richelieu, the cardinal-minister who dominated France between 1624-42. Doctors were imported from France to care for the medical needs of the colony. Care was on a fee-for-service basis for those who could afford the tariff. Some imaginative physicians even offered a pre-paid health insurance plan. For a fee of five *livres* per family per year, Dr. Etienne Bouchard of Montreal agreed to care for all ailments excluding plague, small pox, leprosy, epilepsy and cutting-for-the-stone.[4]

State or crown involvement in humanistic services in Quebec continued until the conquest when, with the coming of the British, financing humanistic services reverted to Stages I and II.

British rule brought abrupt changes in responsibility for providing humanistic services. The umbilical cord to the French treasury was, of course, severed. Now inhabitants assumed personal responsibility for their own welfare—the British colonial tradition. Failing that, they could turn to the church, which was not to expect the same level of financial aid from the British crown as it had from the French. Over the next hundred years the shape of Canada's humanistic sector gradually took form. Hospital care would remain at Stage II, medicine at Stage I. However, education would move from Stages I and II directly into Stage IV, post-secondary education would emerge in both Stage II and Stage IV forms. Welfare would remain largely at Stages I and II, although the Maritimes began experimenting with local public welfare aid. And what cultural activities existed were provided and financed by individuals or the church.

---

[4]According to W.J. Eccles, several families (approximately 200 individuals) signed for the service.

It must have been a wrenching adjustment. The official historical record is thin on anecdotes which illustrate response to human needs, but accounts that do exist paint a picture of unbelievable hardships endured by the French colonists, matched with spontaneous acts of benevolence and charity by some of the more prosperous newcomers. One observer wrote "the merchants and officers have made a collection of five hundred pounds Halifax currency and the Soldiers insist on giving one day's provision in a month for the support of the indigent, without these aids many might have perished and I still fear (in spite of all we can do) a famine...."[5]

In order to overcome the vastness of the wilderness, the loneliness and the adversity, early settlers for the most part depended on family and neighbors. The spirit of working together to combat the elements yielded such traditional events as house and barn-raising bees, quilting bees and the like. This type of "helping" relationship within the settlements implied what R.L. Tivers, an altruism theorist, termed reciprocal altruism whereby people under similar conditions and circumstances willingly pull together to help one another, with the realization that someday the "helpers" could themselves require assistance from neighbors and friends.[6] Viewed in this manner, mutual aid became a form of disaster insurance with the premiums payable in labor rather than cash.

Old World institutions relieved the settlers of some of their humanistic duties. In Lower Canada, the Roman Catholic Church continued its function of administering to the poor and sick. But with reduced financial support from France, the church was forced to seek new sources of revenue, an especially difficult task since there were continual political and constitutional changes. It was 40 years after the conquest before the state reassumed limited financial responsibility for church-administered welfare. In 1801 the provincial legislature appropriated £1,000 per annum for three years for "support of such religious communities as receive and administer relief to sick and infirm persons and foundlings."

Increased demand, due to heavy immigration and settlement growth, stretched private finances and services to the limit. What was needed was a source of funds more reliable and much larger than the inhabitants could,

---

[5]The French endured. Over the next decade they would record the highest birth rate ever achieved by a white population.

[6]R.L.Tivers is mentioned in J. Philippe Rushton's *Altruism, Socialization and Society* (Englewood Cliffs: Prentice Hall, Inc., 1980). This theorist also says that a reciprocal altruism may be a function of biology.

or would, voluntarily provide. What was needed, claimed a number of settlers, was government revenue.

Slowly, the colonial governments began to subsidize private welfare organizations on a regular basis. The unpalatable alternative was instability in the colony. Yet, make no mistake, although these governments subsidized private charity from the public treasury they wanted *no* part in administering these organizations, or even inspecting them. That was to come many years later.

Among the colonial governments, there were subtle yet very important differences in the dispensing of the allotted funds. For example, in Lower Canada grants were given *only* to religious communities organized for philanthropic work while in Upper Canada the public hospitals and houses of industry receiving government support were managed by independent boards.[7]

Typical of the organizations managed by private groups in the Atlantic colonies was the Halifax Poor Man's Friend Society, a benevolent club whose object was to relieve the distress of the poor with a supply of wood and potatoes during the winter. Membership was voluntary and the group was formed "solely for benevolent purposes, none of its members shall receive the least remuneration for their services, and each subscriber shall at any time be at liberty to withdraw his name...." These organizations frequently were under religious auspices and, in other instances, the members were inspired largely by patriotic motives and worked solely for persons of their own country of origin.

Unlike Upper and Lower Canada, the Atlantic colonies initiated a system of state poor-relief to combat urban poverty. Government involvement took the form of locally enacted poor-laws which provided for municipal assessments in Nova Scotia and New Brunswick, and executive initiative for appropriating colonial revenue for the poor in Newfoundland.

However, "goaded by tender consciences" and a regard for benevolence as a Christian duty, the eastern colonists played a vital role in the relief of indigent sick and poor when city and province were reluctant to undertake

---

[7]This difference may provide some insight as to why Quebec's modern-day donation habits are so remarkably different from the rest of Canada. The Roman Catholic Church took *so* much responsibility for humanistic services that the general public had less chance to become involved (unless a nun, monk or priest). Quebecois were *passively* involved, whereas in Upper Canada more people had the opportunity to become *actively* involved in charitable work. Upper Canadians, by direct participation, experienced the problems of administering charities and therefore were able to make personal appeals to friends and neighbors with conviction and insight.

large-scale programs. Throughout the mid-19th century, charitable organizations to aid the poor sprang up by the dozens. These new societies "fulfilled a basic middle-class instinct" for collective efforts as well as providing
communities with experience in social investigation, organization and fund
raising.

Unfortunately, there were some undesirable side-effects. By mid-century
"every church and every ethnic and interest group had its own charitable
society or charitable foundation," fragmenting, even balkanizing, voluntary effort. Charitable organizations in the Atlantic colonies, as well as in the
Canadas, divided along religious and ethnic lines with each catering exclusively to members of its own group. This continued to occur despite attempts throughout the period by "the most public-spirited citizens to
promote comprehensive, non-partisan relief."

The financing and administering of hospital and medical care in British
North America followed much the same pattern as welfare services. In
Lower Canada, the religious auxiliaries of the church coordinated what little health care there was. In Upper Canada, the early public hospitals began
as military installations converted for civilian use.

In 1813, the Loyal and Patriotic Society of Upper Canada set up support
for a hospital in the town of York subsequent to the evacuation of the place
by the commander-in-chief of the army. Their method of financing this
hospital is interesting to note. Following the War of 1812-1814, the Society
decided to reward with gold medals those who had demonstrated outstanding courage and patriotism during the war. The issue as to who was the most
deserving defied resolution, so a decision was made to melt down the medals and sell them at their intrinsic value. The money made, together with
substantial funds already in their hands, was used for various benevolent
purposes, and in 1818 when a movement began to build York General Hospital, the society furnished the bulk of the money required for the project.

The first provincial operating grant to a hospital in Upper Canada was
voted to York General in 1830. It amounted to £100 and became an annual
allotment. A capital grant of £3,000 was made to help erect a hospital in
Kingston in 1832.

The generosity and efforts of a few individuals towards the founding of
hospitals should be noted for the record. Early in the 19th century the citizens of Montreal appealed, unsuccessfully, to the government and governor-general for funds to establish a new hospital, the Montreal General
Hospital. Undaunted, the citizens regrouped and with public subscriptions
and charitable donations raised enough to buy a house which would serve

in the interim. The board of directors then published the names of donors and amounts of all subscriptions in the local newspaper while continuing their fund-raising efforts. By the summer of 1821 they had raised enough to begin construction of a new building but before it was completed costs had escalated to twice the original estimate. (So what's new?)

Yet within two years the debt was extinguished through the generosity of an anonymous benefactor—generally recognized to be John Richardson, president of the hospital's board of directors. Upon his death, the board named a new wing in his honor noting "when hospital funds were low or totally expended a sum of money was frequently given as from a friend by the hand of this respected individual, but it has been well ascertained that that friend was no other than our now-lamented president." The Montreal General continued to rely on private support, mainly gifts from the Montreal establishment: John Richardson, Samuel Gerrard and John Molson. Poorboxes were located throughout the city. Those who could contributed, but those who could not afford the cash often gave donations in kind, e.g., food, clothing, a barrel of meal, etc.

Public education has been a divisive factor throughout Canadian history. The issue has never failed to spark heated debate and animosity, splitting the population on ethnic, religious and economic lines. Throughout the pre-Confederation era, Canadians were influenced greatly by American thought and democratic theories. Yet, the notion that education for all children should be provided and controlled by the people was still a revolutionary concept in the early 19th century and it was not suddenly accepted and applied.

At that time the only institutions recognized as having responsibility for education, apart from the family, were church and philanthropic or charitable organizations, usually affiliated with a religious group. The government in England, as well as the colonies, recognized the weight of responsibility assumed by these organizations and offered grants-in-aid to supplement other sources of revenue. This assistance was confined largely to the so-called grammar school, schools that prepared the future governing class for university.

Common schools, the pre-Confederation equivalent of today's public schools, taught rudimentary subjects to others. These monitorial schools were strict, and sometimes cruel, institutions where children were taught by the rote method. In English-speaking Canada, the monitorial school movement was the last important attempt by philanthropic minorities—often benevolent societies—to provide schools for the people as a benefaction or charity. Common schools would eventually become the basic unit of the provincial education system. But prior to 1840 they were administered by churches and philanthropic organizations and financed by subscriptions, limited government grants and fees. There was no local taxation.

As time passed the public view of education became more egalitarian. Education, at least elementary education, became viewed as a right for all citizens, and those supporting democratic ideals strove for the attainment of universal elementary schooling. One such person was Egerton Ryerson,[8] superintendent of education from 1844 to 1876. Upon his appointment to this position, Ryerson studied the school systems of four foreign countries in an effort to design a new system for Canada. His recommendation favored the principle of local autonomy under supervision and inspection by the government. In 1846, he introduced the School Bill which proposed that *all* property owners (not simply parents) be taxed. Perhaps understandably, the parents of children who attended private schools were unimpressed by the suggestion. ("We do not wish to be compelled to educate all the brats in the neighborhood.") The property tax was not fully implemented until 1871. Despite the opposition, property taxation was an idea whose time had arrived. This marked the beginning of Stage IV financing of Canadian education. From this point forward, governments would supervise and inspect schools, and fund them through taxation.

A discussion of the history of public education would be incomplete without reference to the issue of the Clergy Reserves of Upper Canada. The statutes that allocated one-seventh of public lands to endow the Church of England were the subject of "overwhelming grievance." Non-Anglicans in Canada West assailed the reserved lands as an unjust monopoly of a privileged minority. In Upper Canada, the Assembly demanded that instead of subsidizing an Anglican state-church, the Clergy Reserves should be used to finance a system of common schools.

In 1831, 10,000 persons petitioned in support of this notion, and for the separation of church and state. Yet it was not until 1854, a generation after the rebellion in Upper Canada that challenged the so-called Family Compact, that the provincial legislature settled the question. Proceeds from the sale of Clergy Reserves—some $1.6 million—were paid to municipalities for educational purposes. Unfortunately the windfall was wiped out during the depression of 1857.

---

[8]Ryerson was born in 1802 near Vittoria, Norfolk County, Ont. He was a powerful Methodist leader and first principal of the Methodist Victoria College in Cobourg, Ont.

Canada's first English university was chartered by King George III in 1802—the University of King's College in Windsor, N. S. It grew out of a classical college established by the Church of England in 1787 through the vigorous efforts of the Right Reverend Charles Inglis, D.D., first Anglican bishop in Canada.

Its financing provides an important insight into the delicate blending of state, church and private funds which would characterize higher education in Canada throughout our history. The seed money—£400—was appropriated by the Nova Scotia House of Assembly. It was considered a legitimate public expense since it was feared that without an indigenous college Canada's future leaders would attend universities in the United States where they would be taught republican ideals—an unacceptable, even pernicious, philosophy to the United Empire Loyalists. The British crown agreed. The Imperial Parliament granted the college £4,000 in 1790. But state support for denominational universities remained a bitter issue until after Confederation, when grants to denominational colleges were withdrawn.

Universities in Upper Canada were exclusively denominational until the Hinck's University Act of 1853 established University College as the non-sectarian teaching arm of the University of Toronto. It named the University as the examining and diploma-granting body, and provided for affiliation agreements with religious colleges. That model—a non-denominational parent with religious affiliates—set the pattern for Canadian higher education.

In Lower Canada, the School Act of 1846 established the structure of Quebec education for the next century. The act decreed the union of religion and education and provided for two state-aided school systems, Catholic and Protestant. The role of the state was chiefly that of providing finances and establishing lists of text books for selection. The power of the church remained pervasive in French-Canadian education and much of the teaching was done by members of religious teaching orders.

They also maintained a number of residential schools and colleges outside the public system. Of these, the *collèges classiques* were particularly important in providing secondary education for the wealthier classes, preserving the French tradition of classical humanistic learning. McGill, as noted earlier, was founded in 1821 as an Anglican college. Thirty-one years later a royal charter was obtained for Laval University, which emerged from the ancient *Seminaire de Québec* founded in 1663.

Frontier living exerted unrelenting pressure on the pioneer. Much energy was consumed in supplying the means for survival, leaving little surplus for growth and self-actualization. Cultural diversions were rare and judging from the record, not always totally enriching: "The drama often amounted to indiscriminate offerings of wild farce and crude melodrama by threadbare touring groups; the art might be limited to florid French church ornamentation or stiff portraiture of English merchant worthies...." In the more established centres of Toronto and Montreal patrons supported the Royal Lyceum Theatre and Theatre Royal respectively. Several painters including Paul Kane and Cornelius Krieghoff made significant and lasting contributions to Canadian art during this era. There appears to have been no state support for cultural activities.

Such was the humanistic milieu when Sir John A. Macdonald became Canada's first prime minister in 1867. While there was precedent for modest government subsidies to humanistic organizations deemed necessary for life support and social stability, humanistic needs were essentially private concerns and at that time were not considered elements in the making or breaking of governments. Giving the provinces responsibility for health and welfare implied relinquishing little real federal power. Education remained a thorny issue but was delegated to the provinces as a concession to the French majority in Quebec. Culture—art, literature, theatre, dance—these were luxuries for those with time and money and not a priority of elected officials.

Indeed, not much changed in a fundamental way during the first 60 years of Confederation. Predominant opinion held that humanistic service should be held at the early stages of evolution. The era saw the flowering of Canadian philanthropy. Personal service and altruism were elevated to the highest levels of social esteem. Some called it Philanthropy's Golden Age. Stage III, the federation of humanistic organizations for private fund-raising, emerged with the establishment of the Community Chest. State aid, when it came, was supplied largely by local governments, those nearer the people. Upper-tier governments expressed little enthusiasm for invading the private domain of the humanistic sector.

As governments did enter the field, questions inevitably arose over responsibility and accountability. If governments supplied public funds, did they not likewise assume responsibility for the service? Should private citizens have the power to dispense public money? How could these individuals be held accountable? None were answered definitively. The humanistic sector was to remain a loose combination of public and private input until the Great Depression forced a fundamental realignment.

Industrialization and urbanization in the late 19th and early 20th centuries had a deplorable impact on laborers and their families living in Canadian cities. The middle class accepted responsibility for care of the poor with some ambivalence. It was, of course, one's Christian duty to help, and pragmatically it was risky to permit too much poverty for fear of social revolution.

Yet as the *Toronto Globe* declared, "Promiscuous alms-giving is fatal.... A poor-law is a legislative machine for the manufacture of pauperism. It is true mercy to say that it would be better that a few individuals should die of starvation than that a pauper class should be raised up with thousands devoted to crime and the victims of misery."

Canadians were admonished to provide for their own welfare and that of their families. For the destitute there were houses of "industry" or "refuge" under religious or private management. Funds were provided from the provinces, principal municipalities, rental income, payments from inmates and subscriptions and donations. The proportions varied—some homes relied mainly on government funds, others were self-sufficient. The Ontario Charity Aid Act of 1874 pinned down the province's right to inspect social welfare institutions and formalized the linkage between resources and control.

The YMCA at this time was deeply involved in social welfare programs. Y leaders were expected to raise funds but were cautioned not to indulge the organization. "If he (the president) is a man of means, others will be influenced by his example to give time and money, but he should be careful to avoid any ostentation of giving or the impression that he can be relied on to make up deficiencies in expenses." Countless benevolent institutions were chartered: for the sick, the poor, for destitute children and neglected animals. Each required an organization of volunteers, often the rich and socially prominent who gave of their time and money. *Noblesse oblige.*

Were the rich in fact generous? No statistics are extant and one must rely on anecdotal evidence to form an impression. There are enough university, hospital and community buildings standing from coast to coast, still bearing the names of their benefactors, to attest to many individual acts of large-scale turn-of-the-century philanthropy: Massey Hall, McMaster University, Percival Molson Memorial Stadium. Serious dollars were often raised with dizzying speed.

Goldwin Smith, a social and political gadfly of some consequence in that era, relates the following humorous but revealing anecdote in his memoirs.

I received an invitation to a "conference" about a charity specially patronized by a peeress who, with her husband the Governor-General, had honored Toronto with a visit. I went expecting what an invitation to a conference implied. Instead of this, I found myself in a large room

full, not of authorities on questions of charity, but of the wealthy mag-
nates of Toronto. Her ladyship made a speech and left the room. Then
instead of a conference about her charity, there was a call, evidently pre-
arranged, for a subscription, and in a quarter of an hour or little more
there was drawn, in some cases visibly wrung, from the lords-of-the-
dollar a sum of which local charity could hardly have coaxed out of
them in a year.

Predictably there are accounts of parsimony, even stinginess, on the part
of wealthy Canadians. Hansard in 1917 contains this illuminating insight by
William A. Buchanan, the Member of Parliament for Lethbridge. The debate was over the equity of permitting deductions for charitable donations
from income before the calculation of the new income tax.

> It has been my experience during patriotic fund campaigns in the
> southern part of Alberta to find some of the greatest shirkers with re-
> gard to patriotic giving to be the men of the very greatest wealth.... The
> only way they can be reached is by a form of income taxation. In the city
> of Calgary it was almost impossible to reach one of the wealthiest prop-
> erty owners for the first two years of the patriotic fund campaign or to
> get a cent from him for any patriotic purpose. That man was not being
> reached by the taxation of this government as he should have been
> reached.

And later in the debate, Sir Herbert Ames:

> It must be remembered that there are in every community a certain
> number of extremely stingy men, who have not given a dollar to any-
> thing since the war began, who have dulled the edge of every campaign
> committee we have had, who have been the obstacle in every attempt
> we have made to make money. Other people would say: "There is
> Jones with a big income, he has not given a red cent for war purposes;
> if he won't give, why should we give?" We have frequently found two
> of three men in a community with big incomes who had contributed
> absolutely nothing, and I would like to have these men feel that they
> could not escape the 1917 tax by being stingy.

Smith claimed that it was the people of small or moderate means "whose
souls were not enslaved by money," not Toronto wealth, that provided most
of the support for charitable causes. The reason? "(Unlike) the wealth of the
United States...the colonist who is making money looks, perhaps uncon-
sciously, for social recognition and gratitude, not so much to the colony in
which his money is made as to the Imperial Country in which he may end
his days, possibly with a title."

Regardless of where the money came from, or how evenly the sacrifice was distributed, charitable causes abounded. As settlement moved west, institutions adapted to local circumstances. Many benevolent societies were established for the aid of a single ethnic immigrant group. In Winnipeg, for instance, Jewish immigrants established the Hebrew Benevolent Society in 1887 to provide relief, assistance to general community causes, relief for Jewish farmers, railway fares for families seeking re-settlement, and job placement for new immigrants. Funds were raised through local projects, individual contributions, dances, social picnics, etc. Every charitable group apparently had the same idea: "Hardly a day passed without a banquet, bazaar, tag day, or door-to-door solicitation."

It was an environment that led logically to a more rational approach to raising funds for charities, a cooperative, not competitive, canvassing effort, a community appeal that would fill a chest with funds to be divided equitably among the many worthy causes. The Community Chest (now the United Way movement) was launched in Toronto in 1918 as the Toronto Federation for Community Services to offer a practical solution to the proliferation of charities and public appeals. Borrowing from the Charity Organization Society movement in Great Britain, the Chest would scrutinize the activities of its members, put its good-housekeeping seal on the authenticity of their budgets, and launch one annual federated appeal for funds. No irritation. Efficient. It marked the arrival of Stage III financing for humanistic services in Canada.[9]

Financing of health care and education continued as before: large private gifts for buildings or endowment funds; donations, contributions and subscriptions to assist in ongoing operations. Corporations, too, entered the field of private philanthropy. In 1881, Bell Telephone installed a telephone free of charge in the Montreal General Hospital in order to convey messages on behalf of the sick. Private, volunteer work for hospitals was admired and encouraged by the provincial governments which were willing to partly finance, but not to manage, the charitable organizations: "No more laudable or praiseworthy effort can be entered upon than that which presents itself in the Hospital work of the Province...." Furthermore, the private sector could do the job better! According to one member of the Ontario Legislature, "It was well known that establishments supported by voluntary con-

[9]In 1922, the Hebrew Benevolent Society joined the Winnipeg Community Chest. It remained a member for three years, then withdrew because the Jewish board believed they could do better with a direct appeal to Jewish residents.

tribution were invariably more efficient than those assisted by Government grants."[10]

A record of personal service was obligatory for federal politicians, many of whom continued their involvement during their term in the House of Commons and Senate. For instance, of the 298 members of the Eighth Parliament of Canada,[11] serving under Prime Minister Sir Wilfrid Laurier, 24 members proudly claimed ongoing community involvement.

Their interests were diverse: Hon. William Stevens Fielding, Minister of Finance, Liberal, Halifax, "a governor of Dalhousie University and president of the St. George's Society;" Hon. G.W. Allan, Senator, Conservative, York, "honorary president of Ontario Society of Artists and president of Upper Canada Bible Society;" B.M. Britton, M.P., Liberal, Kingston, "chairman, Kingston Public School Board, and governor, Kingston General Hospital;" G.E. Foster, M.P., Liberal/Conservative, Ottawa, "connected with the highest positions in the Temperance Movement in Canada and the United States of America."

Education remained on the road to universality and continued to be supported through local taxation. Secondary education became a public good, accessible to all. The era also saw the development of provincial boards of education, trained teachers, inspection, and curricula development.

Fortunately for the arts in Canada, some wealthy Canadians followed the lead of their British counterparts and, as time and money permitted, developed an avid interest in cultural expressions. Theatre and dance troupes grew numerically, literary and poetry societies flourished, and opera and orchestral music became accessible in Canadian cities. Hart Massey, founder of the farm implement company that bears his name, donated a music hall to the City of Toronto. Massey Hall, built in 1892 at a cost to the Massey family of $152,000, was erected as a remembrance of Hart's eldest son who died suddenly in the prime of his life. For many years Massey Hall fulfilled its primary function of providing high-calibre entertainment for the broad masses of citizens at a minimal charge. A new era of popular entertainment had begun.

Such appears not to have been the case in Quebec as the arts truly struggled to survive. According to Bernard Ostry, "One reason for the lack of continuity of patronage of the arts in Quebec stemmed from the absence

---

[10]Mr. Beatty, *Ontario Legislature Debates*, December 19, 1868.

[11]Elected June 23, 1896.

there, outside the church, of the English tradition of volunteerism and, of course, of a strong middle class. It is not that there were no voluntary associations; there was the influential *Société Saint-Jean-Baptiste* and the *Institut Canadien*, first in Montreal and later in Quebec (1842). But they were of less consequence when compared with the proliferation of voluntary societies in other parts of Canada, with their mushrooming cultural activities and the influence they were able to bring to bear on government and the rich.''

This cultural parturition was nurtured exclusively through individual initiative, personal patronage and voluntary gifts. Culture was still regarded as a luxury, and governments refrained from providing financial support.

It was a time of building, of excitement, of dreams fulfilled. Laurier proclaimed, ''The 20th century belongs to Canada.'' And a self-confident Canada believed him. Industry, population, cities, western boundaries, all swelled to heights never before imagined. Humanistic services were pulled along in this expansion. As Canada matured, resources and time became available and were devoted to the service of others. The issue of who should take responsibility for these services was raised but never answered. Individuals with greater freedom of action than governments were able to mobilize faster and respond to circumstances requiring humanistic services. Unfortunately they were reluctant to surrender the resources necessary to sustain an expanding commitment to the various charities. Governments possessed the resources, but expressed little inclination to become involved.

Throughout this period Canadians worked in the grey area of shared public and private responsibility with a degree of success. In the decade following, the worst economic disaster in Canadian history would necessitate a change in the formula.

The economic collapse of the 1930s, resulting in the disaster known as ''The Great Depression,'' had a profound impact on the Canadian psyche. Years of hardship and travail changed attitudes, which led to political changes which, in time, led to the implementation of ''revolutionary'' methods of coping with the needs of humanity.

Throughout ''The Dirty Thirties'' many fell short of their basic needs and depended on private charity for survival. Limited government programs were introduced to alleviate some of the Depression's worst symptoms, but unfortunately they were usually too little, too late. Following the Second World War and a return to prosperity, those bearing the economic, social and psychological scars of the previous decade needed assurances that a catastrophe of that magnitude would not recur.

The result: unparalleled public-sector intervention in the areas of welfare, education, health and, later, culture. The face of humanistic service, its administration, delivery and financing in Canada, was forever changed.

The "crash" of the stock market in 1929 signalled the beginning of a decade of adversity and frustration. The afflictions of the poor, the unemployed and the prairie farmers, who in addition to being subjected to falling prices for goods and services endured a seven-year drought, have been well documented. The tales of the "Dust Bowl" are well known: its ceaseless winds sweeping dust storms across the barren prairie, the scorching heat of the summers, the fierce cold of the winters, the plagues of grasshoppers, the desolation, the hunger, the fear and the anxiety. Survival. How to provide for self and family on a day-to-day basis dominated the thoughts of men and women on the prairie, and across Canada.

Desperate men and women seeking immediate relief from their plight looked to the political arena for solutions. Canadians, particularly in the west and Quebec, turned from the traditional political parties and began to listen to, and support, more radical groups. In 1933 the Cooperative Commonwealth Federation (forerunner of the present-day New Democratic Party) was created under the guidance of one of Canada's most respected politicians, J.S. Woodsworth.[12]

The CCF spoke of a new social order, of substituting economic planning for the capitalist system and of replacing the profit motive with Christian charity. It strongly bore the mark of its leader who believed charity, love and brotherhood meant that everyone was responsible for his neighbor. In the federal election of 1935, the CCF received just under 400,000 votes and elected seven of its members to Parliament. Woodsworth and his party, though small in number, were effectively vocal and played a key role in the creation of a Canadian social-welfare policy.

In Alberta, farmers hard-hit by the Depression turned to a different political phenomenon—Social Credit. Under the leadership of the dynamic

---

[12]J.S.Woodsworth, M.P., Winnipeg North, a sensitive and dedicated Christian, had long been an advocate of the social gospel. His commitment to the social outcasts of north Winnipeg led him into politics. In 1939, Prime Minister Mackenzie King said of him, "There are few men in this Parliament for whom, in some particulars, I have greater respect than the leader of the CCF. I admire him in my heart because, time and again, he has had the courage to say what lay on his conscience regardless of what the world might think of him. A man of that calibre is an ornament of any Parliament." H.B.Neatby, *The Politics of Chaos* (Toronto: Macmillan, 1972), p.90.

radio evangelist, William "Bible Bill" Aberhart, the Social Credit party was swept into power in Alberta in 1935.[13] Unfortunately for Premier Aberhart, many of his Social Credit schemes were declared unconstitutional by the Supreme Court.

Quebec elected Maurice Duplessis, leader of the *Union Nationale*, as premier in 1936. This uncompromising politician advocated and promoted a return to the era of *l'habitant* when family and church were pre-eminent. In this "natural" world, people would return to the soil and become self-reliant. There would be no need for public intervention in health and welfare since in this rural society each would be able to care for his own. The return to the rural society did not materialize, of course, but Duplessis remained popular as a defender of Quebec's provincial rights and as a protector of its distinctive cultural mystique.

As the factories closed, and the drought continued, people were left penniless and homeless, lacking both nourishing food and proper clothing. Churches and private charities such as the Canadian Red Cross collected and distributed trainloads of food and clothing for those needing relief. Railways waived freight charges as another charitable gesture. Distribution of these gifts and donations in Saskatchewan was coordinated through the Saskatchewan Voluntary Relief Committee. This group developed a voucher system to prevent abuse of the free gifts, and managed to apportion the needed articles to areas in greatest need.

For those on relief, the humiliation was often times unbearable. Most people found it degrading, dehumanizing, to apply for "the dole." "There was a deep-rooted feeling that to accept charity, especially charity from the state, was a confession of failure." A lag remained between the attitude that an individual was completely responsible for his or her own position in life and a realization that the complexities of industrialized society rendered such dogma anachronistic.

Of course, when faced with the prospect of starvation there was little alternative but to accept the charity and donations offered. As a result, private social agencies were literally swamped with requests. Municipalities, traditionally charged with the responsibility of administering local relief, went bankrupt under the strain of the costs. During the Depression years,

[13] William Aberhart was a former high-school principal turned evangelist. He managed to combine God and Major Douglas (creator of Social Credit theory) into political success in Alberta.

15 to 20 per cent of the population was dependent on municipal aid.

In desperation everyone, including the provinces, turned to the federal government for help. The people evicted the Liberal government of Prime Minister Mackenzie King on August 7, 1930, and looked to Prime Minister R.B. Bennett, leader of the Conservative government, for fresh, decisive, effective action.

Bennett immediately set aside $20 million for relief purposes, unprecedented federal action because prior to this the government had shown little interest in social welfare programs.[14] Relief camps were established and they provided a place for single, unemployed men to stay, at the expense of the government. Unfortunately, these camps were later to evolve into hotbeds of social unrest, sometimes erupting in violence. Other solutions were tried. But sadly, government initiatives were impotent against the stagnation and social distress that enveloped the world.

Prime Minister Bennett was a wealthy corporate lawyer and Canadians were well aware of this fact. Many, out of desperation, wrote pitiful letters to the prime minister begging him for personal help. Bennett answered many of them, often granting them their small requests—a winter coat for a young mother, $10 to send a child to a medical specialist. The private donations given by the prime minister must have been numerous although there is no formal account of them and Bennett told no one "save those who have a need to know."[15]

Notwithstanding his personal generosity, Bennett lost the confidence of the people and was defeated in the federal election of 1935. William Lyon Mackenzie King was returned to office, after a five-year absence, with the largest parliamentary majority in Canadian history up to that time. In his younger days, under the tutelage of Sir Wilfrid Laurier, Mackenzie King was considered a social reformer and an advocate of improvements for labor. He was regarded as progressive and liberal. However:

> Beneath the jargon of this liberalism there was a belief in the virtue of public service, and of service especially to the less fortunate members of society. For King, charity was the cardinal Christian virtue. Charity was somehow dissociated from Christian humility and even Christian

---

[14]The first entry of the federal government into the realm of social welfare was in 1927 when Prime Minister Mackenzie King's Liberal government passed the Old Age Pensions Act.

[15]Ernest Watkins, Bennett's biographer, describes him as the kind of man "who has a strong attachment to what he owns particularly if he has won it by his own efforts, and yet who believes that it is his duty to share these with others.... He was never quixotic about money...(but considered it) a duty...to put it to work for others as well as himself."

love. It had been transmitted into humanitarianism, although it is still an article of faith. The pattern of King's early life—the Sick Children's Hospital, Hull House, the report on sweated labor, the Industrial Relations Foundation—was a pattern traced out by this humanitarian ideal. The ideal seems overshadowed by the exigencies of politics in his years as prime minister, but it does not disappear.

King's public record on social welfare, like the rest of his policies, was one of shrewd compromise and conciliation. ''King was always reluctant to enact definite measures, waiting until he was convinced that the majority of the people wanted them and supported them, or until his political survival hung in the balance.'' Social welfare measures had the people's support.

Following the Depression, Canadians yearned for security, and there was general agreement that the best way to attain that security was to provide insurance against unemployment. In 1940, the King government passed the Unemployment Insurance Act which provided for a compulsory contributory unemployment insurance program, and the establishment of a national employment service. This was followed by legislation in 1944 to authorize both a national family-allowance scheme (The Family Allowances Act) and a federal Department of Health and Welfare. During the decades following the war, the federal government added piecemeal to this legislation, entrenching the notion of guaranteed universal social welfare benefits firmly in the minds of all Canadians.

The impact of the Depression on humanistic services was to remove them from private-sector dominance and to place them with the public to administer and finance. The transition of health care is the most dramatic example. At the height of the Depression, many people, and especially those on the prairies, could not afford the services of a medical doctor. In Saskatchewan, for instance, the situation was so bad that doctors were often in the same economic position as their clients—on relief. The Saskatchewan government paid doctors a salary to entice them to remain in the areas hard hit by the drought and Depression.

There were many attempts to reform the system. A British Columbia health commission recommended a comprehensive government health-insurance scheme in 1932. A bill providing for means-tested medicare was introduced in the B.C. Legislature in 1935 and passed in 1936. The new act covered people earning less than $2,400 a year, and left the doctors free to charge as they wished above that income level.

The Medical Association was vehemently opposed. They refused to accept the legislation, and they were successful in having it withdrawn in 1937. A more serious confrontation developed in Saskatchewan. T.C. ''Tommy''

Douglas (CCF) was elected premier of that province in 1944 on the promise that he would make medical, dental and hospital services universally available "without counting the ability of the individual to pay." His first action was to declare cancer treatment free for all, just as tuberculosis care had been since 1929. Medical, hospital and dental care was added for "blue card" pensioners and indigent people in 1945. Then mental and polio treatment.

An experimental health unit was established at Swift Current,[16] where 40 doctors served a population of over 50,000. The scheme was financed by a family payment of $48 a year and a land tax. The doctors received remuneration on a fee-for-service basis. In 1947, Saskatchewan began a hospital insurance plan, with initial premiums being $5 per person, $10 per family. There was some scattered opposition from hospitals, as officials feared too much government interference in the day-to-day running of the institutions. Premier Douglas assured them that he and his government had too many other things to worry about and that the hospitals would be basically left alone.

Despite misgivings, the plan was well received, for the premiums and a sales tax on certain retail items helped to finance and keep hospitals out of debt. In 1957, Ottawa introduced a federal-provincial hospital insurance program and, after 10 years of going it alone, Saskatchewan was able to share part of the cost of its hospital scheme with the federal government.

Hospital insurance programs were introduced with relative ease when compared to the trauma of introducing medical insurance. Premier Douglas announced a medicare plan in 1959 based on five principles: pre-payment, universal coverage, high quality of service, administration by a public body responsible to the Legislature, and a form acceptable to those providing and receiving the service. The medical profession refused to accept the plan and attacked the government politically by urging the people of Saskatchewan not to vote CCF in the 1960 provincial elections.

The CCF won that election and the doctors went on strike in the summer of 1962. Throughout that summer there was a "sense of civil war" as the province divided either for or against the doctors. The government broke the strike largely by importing British doctors. But bitterness remained long after the strike ended. Other confrontations in other provinces would follow.

---

[16]The experiment in Swift Current was praised by Justice Emmett Hall in the Hall Report, The Royal Commission on Health Services.

Province by province, there was no standard of medical payment. Some provinces were introducing medicare schemes, while others attempted to combine public and private insurance schemes, and still others left payment for medical services much the same as it had been 100 years earlier. In 1961, Prime Minister John Diefenbaker appointed a Saskatchewan jurist, Mr. Justice G. Emmett Hall, to head a royal commission to study health services across the country. Justice Hall took three years to report, then made 200 specific recommendations covering the whole range of health services: education, facilities, manpower, financing, development of a medical insurance system, etc.

The core recommendation was the introduction of a universal health-care plan to cover all Canadian residents for all medical services. Most public reaction was favorable, but many cautioned the government to proceed slowly. At a federal-provincial conference one year later, Prime Minister Lester B. Pearson shocked those in attendance by announcing his decision to go ahead with a federal medicare scheme.

Medicare was to meet four general criteria: cover all doctors' services, be universal, be publicly administered by the provincial governments and, considering the mobility of Canadians, ensure transferability of benefits. On July 12, 1966, Bill C-227 (federal medicare) was introduced to Parliament and received its first reading.

By mid-1967 it was bogged down in an atmosphere of uncertainty.[17] Inflation and taxes were both on the rise, and people were having second thoughts about medicare. Finance Minister Mitchell Sharp estimated that medicare would cost $1 billion in its first year and would require a tax increase equalling 12 per cent of personal income tax.

Prime Minister Pearson retired on April 20, 1968. His successor, Pierre Elliott Trudeau, announced that medicare, as it stood, would become law effective July 1, 1968. For most practical purposes health-care delivery had now reached Stage IV.

The advancement of public education in the 1930s was severely retarded by the economy of the time. School boards knew that financing public education almost entirely by real-property taxes made them potentially vul-

---

[17]While C-227 languished on the order paper, Canadians were being infected with the largest case of national pride since Confederation. Canada's Centenary celebration, EXPO 67, opened in Montreal on July 1, 1967.

nerable if this income source were ever threatened. The property tax base was, of course, virtually devastated after 1930, especially in the West. The average annual salary received by rural Saskatchewan teachers dropped by more than one-half between 1930 and 1935, from $1,067 to $465 a year. Hard cash was scarce, and teachers often took salaries in kind. Urban teachers generally had higher incomes, as tax collections were better in cities and towns. Teachers were best paid in urban Ontario and were often regarded as the "plutocracy" of the profession, since their average salaries showed little decline and stayed above $2,400 even during the worst years.

As family incomes declined sharply, university education was a luxury few could afford. As a result, expansion at universities was arrested, budgets were slashed, research curtailed, salaries cut, and teaching loads increased. Throughout these dismal years, only one new college was founded, tiny St. Thomas College, in Chatham, N.B. The Second World War provided relief for the universities as the Canadian government pumped money into them for defence research and for officer training. Between 1942 and 1944 the heads of universities foresaw the influx of returning veterans eager to receive an education and they agreed that federal financial support would be essential if their institutions were to provide it. It was a major concession to their financial independence.

Returning war veterans were offered federal financial assistance to attend colleges and other educational institutions, provided they undertook to forsake all other tasks on "civvie street." For each veteran, the federal government contributed $150 plus fees to the university. When the number of veterans entering college declined sharply in 1948, the universities, which had undertaken expansion schemes to accommodate the veterans, remained dependent on federal aid.

Then came the prosperous fifties and sixties. Provincial governments had revenues, education was a provincial responsibility, the post-war babies now demanded a college education, so universities undertook frenzied building programs. Capital expenditures for new buildings and facilities rose from $12 million in 1954-55 to $200 million 10 years later.

In 1965, universities and colleges received revenue from four sources: provincial, 40 per cent; federal, 22 per cent; fees, 25 per cent; gifts and other, 13 per cent. From 1965 onwards, federal direct aid to universities would be replaced with block financing to provincial governments which would distribute the funds through their own ministries. Today universities in Canada depend on governments to the extent of roughly 80 per cent of their operating budgets. Student fees pay for roughly 15 per cent of the costs and all other sources, including charitable donations and gifts, supply the balance.

Culture—the arts and letters—was the last of the four humanistic services to forge a liaison with the state. Understandably. Dependence breeds conformity which stifles creativity and inhibits free expression. The intelligent artist senses the undeniable link between money and power and hesitates to accept the former if it means surrendering the latter. Above all else, the artist survives on freedom.

But artists of every description—novelists, composers, actors, painters—were not surviving on what Canada paid them. To whom then could the artist turn? Patronage of the courts, the kind offered by King Ludwig II to Richard Wagner, was, of course, unavailable to Canadians with no aristocratic leisure class. Despite its progress over 300 years, Canada was still economically immature at the end of the Second World War. General prosperity had yet to reach levels where large numbers had the interest and resources to indulge in cultural enrichment. A handful of well-to-do Canadians, some of those who had prospered in the new land, had made generous gifts to support cultural causes, but the voluntary flow was intermittent and, compared to the parched cultural landscape, amounted to barely a trickle.

Three great Canadians were to combine their considerable talents to conceive, choreograph and stage-manage a new art form that would provide a reliable, sustaining, untainted cash flow for creative Canadians. The collaborators were Rt. Hon. Louis St. Laurent, Rt. Hon. Vincent Massey and Most Rev. Georges-Henri Levesque. Their vehicle? The Canada Council.

St. Laurent was chosen by Mackenzie King to succeed Ernest Lapointe as Quebec leader of the Liberal Party in 1941, and was hand-picked again to succeed King as prime minister in November 1948. The choice may well have been King's greatest act of public service to the people of Canada.

One need only examine a portrait of St. Laurent to understand why he was simply and affectionately dubbed "Uncle Louis"—warm, intelligent, comfortable brown eyes counterpoised by a precise mouth beneath a neatly trimmed Guard's moustache. A modest, gentle, reliable countenance. But Uncle Louis was also chairman of the board, an immensely successful corporate lawyer who attracted the brightest and best to his Cabinet, and demanded—and received—excellence from all his ministers.

It was St. Laurent who was sensitive to the cultural dilemma facing the country and who appointed two other brilliant Canadians—Vincent Massey and Georges-Henri Levesque—to advise the government on a desirable course of action.

Massey was the son of a rich Canadian manufacturing family with an honorable record of personal service and philanthropy to Canada. Born in 1887, educated at the University of Toronto and Oxford, Massey served as Canadian minister to Washington and high commissioner in London for the decade which spanned the Second World War. His appointment as head of the Royal Commission on National Development in the Arts, Letters and Sciences gave him the opportunity to share his considerable experience, knowledge, sensitivity and wisdom with the people of Canada.

Levesque, a Dominican priest and dean of social sciences at Laval, was the French-Canadian power on the commission. The Massey-Levesque Commission Report must rank among Canada's finest works of art. Its perceptions of the country, its elegant prose, its understated but undeniable conclusions touched the hearts and emotions of all who read it. It also touched the Government of Canada for $100 million[18] as seed money to establish the Canada Council on January 8, 1957.

The council (Can Cow as it became affectionately known) immediately distributed half its endowment to help finance the building boom in Canadian universities and invested the balance as a perpetual endowment "to foster and promote the study and enjoyment of, and the production of works in, the arts, humanities and social sciences."

Over its 25 years, the council has distributed half a billion dollars fulfilling its mandate and now receives 80 per cent of its annual budget from federal tax appropriations. It has spawned the establishment of provincial arts councils[19] in all but the Atlantic Provinces. Today, the public, through governments, has become the number one patron of the arts in Canada.

But the diffidence towards state dominance lingers despite assurances by former Prime Minister Pierre Trudeau that "we do not propose to tell a dancer through what hoops he should jump...."[20] Peter Dwyer, former chairman of the council, replies with poetic simplicity: "Like Janus we face two ways, up the footpath of the spirit and along the autobahn of efficiency."

---

[18]In reality, the touch was on the estates of two wealthy tycoons, Isaac Walton Killam of Royal Securities and Sir James Dunn of Algoma Steel, who had died and left estates that would yield the federal treasury $100 million in death duties—an act of involuntary philanthropy that may well have denied them a place in cultural posterity.

[19]The largest provincial council, Province of Ontario Council for the Arts (POCA), distributed $12 million to 3,300 individuals and artistic groups during its 18th year in 1981.

[20]"I do not think that modern society, nor the artist as a member of that society, need fear a generous policy of subsidy to the arts from governments as long as those governments have the courage to permit free expression and experimentation—and, for that matter, to take it in good part if the mirror held up to their nature is not always a flattering one." Pierre Elliott Trudeau, "An Essential Grace," in *A Special Number on Canada and the Arts* (New York: Associated Council of the Arts, 1969).

That enduring ambivalence has encouraged cultural groups in Canada to cultivate strong liaisons to strengthen their independence—financial, artistic and administrative. The Niagara Institute in the east and the Banff Centre in the west have initiated seminars, workshops and conferences focused on the needs of executives, decision-makers and policy planners working in cultural organizations in Canada.

But perhaps the most sustained, concentrated and effective voice for arts independence and integrity is The Council for Business and the Arts in Canada which grew out of a conference on corporate support of the arts held in Ottawa in 1974. Chief executive officers from 50 of Canada's major corporations and observers from 20 others attended the conference.[21] It was agreed there that a central resource for business's involvement in the arts should be established. Forty businesses became founding members; today the number exceeds 100.

The geniuses behind that movement were Edmund Charles Bovey and Arnold Edinborough. Bovey, board chairman of Norcen Energy Resources Ltd. and in the inner circle of corporate activity in the country, has long been an indefatigable champion of the arts in Canada and in the United States.[22] Bovey chaired the Ottawa Conference, was first chairman of the CBAC[23] and is credited with providing the strength and leadership that has more than doubled corporate gifts to cultural causes over a six-year span.

Edinborough is the council's president and CEO, a post he has held since its inception. British-born and Cambridge-educated, he exudes what one might expect from a cultured, intelligent, dedicated arts protagonist. He travels, lectures, confers, promotes and writes at a breathtaking pace. Perhaps his most grueling labor is the column he writes regularly for *The Financial Post*—1,000 words a week covering a wide range of cultural topics ranging from philosophy to economics. For more than a decade Edinborough's column has added a touch of elegance to a publication dedicated to pragmatic business reporting, and has enriched Canadians' understanding of the diversity and quality of artistic expression in their country.

---

[21]The conference was sponsored by the Canada Council and concluded with a banquet at Government House, hosted by the late Governor-General Jules Leger—one of the last public functions before His Excellency's crippling stroke on Saturday, June 8, 1974.

[22]He served as a member of the International Council of the Museum of Modern Art in New York.

[23]Bovey retired as chairman in October 1982. His successor, John H. Devlin, chairman, Rothmans of Pall Mall Canada Limited, promises leadership of the same high quality.

As Canada completes almost four centuries of development, it is interesting that it has come almost full circle in the delivery of humanistic service. During the first 150 years, the aristocratic welfare state of New France, with its sparse population, of necessity was ultimately dependent on the French crown for resources to sustain what must have been a modest level of health care, education and welfare. Individuals, Stage I, and the church, Stage II, did what they could, but Canada was largely at Stage IV, state dominance, during its early historical period.

During the second era, the pre-Confederation years from the British conquest to 1867, Canada set in place the foundations of its humanistic delivery system. During those 11 decades, the church and individual initiative conceived, created and financed the schools, hospitals, welfare and cultural organizations that would serve an expanding population. A benign government provided moral support but, apart from the field of basic education, offered little financial support. For humanistic service, those foundation years were most decidedly Stages I and II.

Canada's first 60 years as a nation were marked by a blossoming of philanthropy and personal service, The Golden Age of Philanthropy. Charitable activity in the form of both dollars and time was most certainly an important element in the lives of many Canadians in all walks of life. It was the accepted and expected norm of behavior. People were involved in all four classes of humanistic service. But demand began to exceed the supply of resources provided voluntarily. People grouped together to raise funds jointly and approaches were increasingly made to local governments for supplementary financial support. However, there was no doubt that the humanistic sector was still controlled by individuals. Stage III.

In the years since the beginning of the Great Depression, Canada has moved steadily towards Stage IV delivery. First by necessity, then by choice, governments have provided more and more of the funds for education at all levels, for health care, for specific and general welfare, and increasingly for cultural expression. Humanistic institutions—hospitals, universities, welfare and cultural organizations—are still nominally controlled by individuals following the tradition of the foundation years. But increasingly, governments, who control the flow of funds, are sharing the decision-making process. In all but the field of culture, government funds overwhelm the share provided voluntarily from the private sector.

Is culture in Canada at Stage IV? If one looks only at finances the conclusion is "almost." But the future is ambiguous. Canadian culture has lost a sensitive and sympathetic advocate with the retirement of Prime Minister

Pierre Trudeau who governed on the assumption that ''arts, which are an essential grace in the life of civilized people, should be available in full measure to those who want them.'' Little is known yet of Prime Minister Brian Mulroney's personal taste and philosophy—economic, political, cultural. Are the arts a sacred trust? Or a dispensable luxury?

Canadians have changed in their attitudes and behavior towards responsibility for the provision of humanistic service. How and why?

CHAPTER **IV**

The Canadian collage, circa 1980

The previous chapters describe the evolution of humanistic thought and action, its scope and nature and the various stages of its development in Canada. We have paid sparse attention to the nature of the people who demanded, delivered and financed those services, yet the composition, make-up and characteristics of a population determine its attitudes towards humanistic service in general and its financing in particular.

How one views responsibilities is a function of how one was bred and brought up. Attitudes and behavior are also influenced by a complex array of social, economic and demographic forces—family status, education, religion, mobility, and so on—each with the potential to alter the capacity and willingness to provide humanistic service, and to affect the form that contribution will take.

This chapter addresses that deficiency by focusing briefly on the anatomy of the Canadian population, its fundamental characteristics, composition and make-up. The discussion highlights aspects of our background and nature which may have an influence on our propensity for caring, for humaneness—for giving. It is the one dimension remaining before we attempt to postulate a comprehensive theory to explain why people donate money for humanistic service.

Canada today is a nation of almost 25 million people spread across the country roughly in the shape of a normal curve with its centre in Ontario; 10 per cent of the population in each of the two coastal regions, 17 per cent on the prairies, 27 per cent in Quebec, and 36 per cent in Ontario. It took

Canada 150 years, the entire era of New France, to attract 65,000 people; the next hundred-odd years, the foundation era of pre-Confederation, added 3.4 million; the first 60 years of Confederation, philanthropy's Golden Age, attracted 7.5 million more; in the 50 years since the Great Depression, as she moved towards Stage IV, Canada has added another 15 million people.

Where have these people come from and how well have they merged and blended together to form a distinctive Canadian character? Since the native population was sparse, immigration has played an important role in the growth and development of Canada. As Hon. James Fleming, former minister of state for multiculturalism, reminds us, "We're all boat people—except for those native Canadians who got here by foot. The only difference is some of us caught an earlier boat."

In the beginning, the boats brought men and women to settle and farm the land; later, to build the canals and railroads, to turn the sod, to tame the wilderness and to open the northwest. Traditionally, Canadian immigration policy has aimed at filling the void, whether this void was on virgin soil, in the factories or in the professions. But immigration policies determine the type of cultural baggage the new settlers bring. A person's original culture affects him deeply, often lasting over several generations. Customs become firmly rooted in man's actions and very being.

Reflect briefly on Canada's ethnic heritage. For 150 years we were exclusively French—a small homogeneous population in a new, sometimes hostile, environment but sharing a common set of moral, religious, educational, social and economic values. Then suddenly we were also British—with a ruling core who possessed a totally different set of traditions in religion, custom, humanistic duty. For the next 150 years, to the turn of the 20th century, the two streams advanced in parallel, each acknowledging, if not always entirely accepting, the other's right to pursue a different lifestyle, to revere and honor a different heritage. Two solitudes.

Before 1900, much of Canada's population growth resulted from natural increases[1] from these two ethnic streams. Even as the first significant wave of European immigrants began to arrive after 1901, the population was 90 per cent French or British. The population grew one-third in the first decade of the 20th century alone—1.8 million new Canadians, almost half of whom were new immigrants.[2] The inflow continued until the Depression

---

[1]Indeed, in each of the decades from 1861 to 1901 the ratio of natural increase to total population growth exceeded 100 per cent.

[2]In fact, immigration reached 1.5 million during that decade, its highest level ever. But half that number emigrated, leaving Canada with 800,000 net immigrants over the decade—44 per cent of the total population growth.

with more than one million immigrants arriving in each of the next two decades. Although Canada did not retain them all, the ethnic mix was becoming noticeably altered. By 1930, almost two million of Canada's 10 million people claimed ethnic extraction other than the two founding cultures.

Immigration was not a significant factor for the next two decades, but after 1951 net migration accounted for roughly 25 per cent of the growth of Canada's population. And from that point on, there has been a sharp decline in the proportion of British immigrants entering Canada. Economic growth after the Second World War demanded an increase in immigration in order to fill the demand for skilled and unskilled labor. During the 1950s, for example, the total number of immigrant professionals was equal to roughly one-half of the total supply from Canadian universities. Furthermore, half the new skilled jobs created by industrial development were filled by immigrants.

They came from north, south and east-Europe and from Commonwealth countries—India, Pakistan, the West Indies. Each wave added color, religious diversity and philosophical enrichment to the communities in which they settled. Asians became a significant segment of the population on the west coast; Ukrainians, Scandinavians and Poles, in the Prairie Provinces; and virtually every ethnic group, 70 different cultures, settled in Toronto (by 1961 more than 40 per cent of Toronto residents were *not* born in Canada). Only Quebec and the Atlantic Provinces have remained largely French or British. Today, one in four Canadians traces his or her ethnic roots to other than the two founding cultures.[3] In Toronto, and other large urban centres, no single linguistic group now forms a majority of the population.

What we may not fully comprehend today is that Canada ceased to be a nation of two solitudes more than 50 years ago. The 20th century inflow of immigrants from all over the world has irrevocably altered our collective ethnicity. The Canadian gene no longer is a one or a zero. Our inheritance is now polygenic.[4]

The impact of multiculturalism on private philanthropy in Canada is ambiguous. Because many recent immigrants came from countries well into Stage IV in their delivery of humanistic service, they brought little experi-

---

[3]In 1981, Canada's ethnic distribution was as follows: British, 40 per cent; French, 27 per cent; Northern European, 10 per cent; Eastern European, three per cent; Southern European, five per cent; Asian and African, three per cent; all others, 12 per cent.

[4]According to the law of genetics, polygenes act together in such a way that their effects on a particular trait become additive or cumulative or complementary—the so-called "nicking effect." This gives Canada the potential for producing the most vigorous, progressive, civilized strain of humanity the world has known.

ence with voluntary associations and little sympathy for personal philanthropy. In the homeland, the state had provided health care, education and welfare services; the family, the kin group and the church were the focus for social, religious and cultural diversions.

Those who settled in the rural areas of Canada saw little reason, and were given little incentive, to expand their notion of community involvement. But those who settled in the towns and cities tended to establish ethnic associations to fill old wants or to meet new needs created by migration, wants and needs that new Canadians could share with their ethnic fellows but not with the community at large.

The organizations were of many types: mutual-aid or benefit associations, designed to give assistance in crises such as unemployment, illness, accident or death; philanthropic or social-welfare associations, through which the more successful and established members of the group could assist the less prosperous newcomers; associations with political aims, either in the homeland or the new country; social and recreational associations; schools; cultural groups.

Often the new organizations were short-lived. Mutual-benefit organizations, for example, have tended to decline in recent years. Immigrants have become increasingly sophisticated in education and training, the expanding economy provided prosperous opportunity (until recently) for newcomers, and Canada's expanding universal-welfare programs have rendered the ethnic self-help association redundant.

Others have thrived. Churches, for instance, often sponsored ethnic organizations which in turn established private schools to transmit and perpetuate language and cultural heritage.[5] Often these were part-time efforts designed to supplement the no-name-brand education in the public school system. Some were serious, full-time establishments.

Perhaps the strongest, most firmly entrenched, ethnic private schools are the Jewish or Hebrew schools, established and maintained in major centres by local congregations or lay bodies. There were 26 Jewish elementary schools in Canada in 1969 with an enrolment of 4,500 students, 13 located in Montreal, the balance in other urban centres with concentrated Jewish populations. Ethnic schools, like other private schools, are financed through fees paid by students or parents, subsidies from sponsoring organizations, or by gifts and donations. They appear to have chronic financial difficulties.

---

[5]The Report of the Royal Commission on Bilingualism and Biculturalism listed a total of 507 part-time ethnic schools operating in Canada in 1965 with a total of 40,000 students. Enrolment in the German, Ukrainian and Jewish schools contributed about 65 per cent of the total.

The existence of these private, ethnic schools—full or part-time—is largely unknown to many Canadians. They have been the object of little research, yet they play an important role in preserving and maintaining the languages and cultures of the non-British, non-French segment of our population. Indeed, they are etching an enduring mark on the contemporary Canadian countenance.

Since the Second World War, many of the newer ethnic associations have been concerned with fostering arts, letters and crafts among members of their cultural group. Some organizations devote most of their efforts to fund raising—foundations offering small scholarships and rewards to deserving students who usually share the donor's cultural background. Others are voluntary associations of like-minded individuals of a single ethnic strain, groups pursuing a wide range of interests—literary, musical, drama, university clubs, book clubs, research institutes, and so on.

Invariably, the success of both types of organization depends to a large extent on the generosity and financial strength of sponsoring groups. Their methods of financing include endowments, special fund-raising campaigns and regular subsidies. Rarely is money raised from outside the ethnic group. And an important corollary—one offered tentatively now, but explored intensively in Book Two—rarely do *new* Canadians donate to causes beyond those identified with their cultural group. That wider sense of responsibility comes with full assimilation into the Canadian way.

Ethnic origin and immigration patterns are closely related and intricately linked to religion, one of mankind's strongest social forces. Whether one belongs to an organized church, or chooses a less-structured format, religion (or non-religion) plays an important role in shaping moral philosophy, beliefs, values, behavior, social conscience—indeed, all aspects of day-to-day living. In times past, religion has been a unifying theme or a divisive force. It has always exerted a powerful influence on the humanistic delivery system.

As in most Western countries, the Judeo-Christian religion clearly dominates Canadian thought and action. Our laws are based on Judeo-Christian laws. The vast majority of the population belongs to churches espousing Judeo-Christian thought, teachings and values.[6]

Judaism or the Hebrew religion pre-dates Christianity and, according to

---

[6]In 1971, only four per cent of the population claimed No Religion (930,000 Canadians) or affiliation with non-Judeo-Christian denominations. The latter included 16,000 Buddhists, 2,000 Confucianists, and 21,000 Unitarians. The 1981 census reported a sharp increase in those claiming no religion, almost eight per cent of all Canadians.

the Old Testament, originated with Abraham who preached the ideals of monotheism—the belief in *one* God, the creator of all things, including man, the crowning glory of His creation. Such theology may not appear bold and revolutionary today but some 4,000 years ago when men prudently diversified their spiritual commitments, Abraham could not be considered entirely in the mainstream.

These ideals were transmitted to Isaac, to Jacob, and eventually to Moses, a man with a strong, dominating personality. Moses refined the original notions of Hebrew doctrine based on the Ten Commandments, was struck by a series of divine revelations, synthesized them into a book of laws governing doctrine, practice and morals called the *Torah*, gathered the children of Israel together and formed a nation which he claimed had a covenant with God to bear and protect this belief. Jews were the chosen people, bound in all actions to the God of Israel with His claims and promises to the people of Israel, together with privileges and expectations.

The Jewish religion has remained almost exclusively the property of one people—the Jews. Judaism is complex and comprehensive since it embraces religion, social, political, ethnic and historical elements.[7] Perhaps its fundamental feature is the strict merging of morality and the worship of the deity which are inextricably meshed in the Jewish belief. The Jewish population in Canada is small in numbers, yet profoundly influential in the important spheres of activity—economic, artistic, scientific and political.

Christianity grew out of the life, works and beliefs of one man, Jesus of Nazareth (c. 4 B.C.—c. A.D. 29), who spoke with authority as the son of God. A Christian is one who believes in Christ, Jesus, the individual who personified God. The term was first used to describe the disciples of Christ but later expanded to include those who exhibited qualities considered appropriate for association with Him (e.g., Christian acts, Christian character, etc.). The personal ethics of Christians embrace the moral essence of Old Testament precepts but replace the austerity of the Old Testament, with its emphasis on law and fear, with a New Testament ethic of love, love of God and neighbor.

Christ preached the concept of neighborly love and elevated love to the ultimate order of grace. He broadened the definition of neighbor to embrace all mankind—universal love. No exceptions. To be truly Christian,

---

[7]Is Judaism a racial origin or a religion? The census of 1871 listed 125 citizens claiming Jewish racial origin and 1,115 claiming Jewish as their religious denomination; by 1901 the numbers were roughly equal at 16,000; by 1971, 297,000 claimed Jewish racial origin and 276,000 adherence to the Jewish religion.

one must love even one's enemies, a formidable screen. Luke also warned Christians that "...unto whomsoever much is given, of him shall be much required." We shall examine later how influential Luke's doctrine has been in shaping man's attitudes towards sharing and giving for human needs.

Christianity, with its gentle, compelling ideals, conquered Europe. It became institutionalized in the Roman Catholic Church which claims to be the one legitimate continuation of the apostolic community established by Jesus. At the earthly summit is the pope or Roman pontiff, a successor of St. Peter to whom Christ delegated leadership. Below the pope is a hierarchy of cardinals, bishops, priests and a host of religious orders. Roman Catholics equate tradition and scripture. Form and ritual are essential ingredients of worship. Salvation in the eyes of God can be attained only by combining Roman Catholic faith with merit which is accumulated by doing good works.

Roman Catholics attain grace through participation in the seven sacraments: baptism, confirmation, holy eucharist, penance, extreme unction, holy orders, matrimony. The sacraments can be received *only* through an intermediary of the church, usually a priest. Worship is confined to a prescribed liturgy and the eucharist is central to the celebration of the Mass. The Roman Catholic Church is firmly dogmatic, strict and cautious. It plays an important role in the daily lives of its members, taking stands on current issues such as divorce, abortion, birth control and political action when they infringe on morality or freedom.

The Roman Catholic Church has always claimed the largest single membership in Canada and its 1981 standing—47 per cent of the population—is the highest proportion ever in Canadian history, a four-point increase over the 1951 census.

The Reformation of the 16th century broke the Roman Catholic monopoly over western Christianity. Martin Luther in Germany, John Calvin in Geneva, Henry VIII in Britain, and a host of other participants initiated actions which swiftly diverted a sizable tributary away from the mainstream—Protestantism. The name is derived from the protestation of German princes and cities at the Diet of Speyer in 1529, organized by the nobility to protest the re-entrenchment of the Roman Catholic Church in their territories and the laws against evangelical sects. Protestant[8] was to be-

---

[8]The verb *protestari*, from which Protestant derives, means not simply to protest in the sense of raise an objection, but also to avow, witness or confess.

come the generic term describing many individual religious brands which were to follow.

Protestant churches had two characteristics in common. First, the appeal to scripture and the historical interpretation of the apostolic age—not tradition derived from the accumulated heritage of the subsequent centuries—was the supreme authority. Second, only the two dominical sacraments were essential: baptism and the Lord's Supper (eucharist).

Protestants resurrected another ethical concept that is germane to this inquiry, the renewed emphasis on personal stewardship. Invoking New Testament passages (such as Luke and 1 Corinthians 4.12, 9.17), Protestants declared that man must live as the faithful trustee of what he has received from God and must render an account. Stewardship was not confined to material possessions which found expression in tithing[9] to support the church, but extended to possessions of time and talent.[10] Stewardship is recognized as a powerful philosophical justification for the accumulation (and disbursement) of great wealth, a theme that will reappear in a later discussion.

In England, the Protestant Church emerged as the Church of England or Anglican communion. Its genesis is well known. An adamant pope refused to grant King Henry VIII a divorce from his barren wife, Catherine of Aragon. Determined to marry Anne Boleyn in the hopes of producing a male heir, the willful king annulled the pope's authority in England through the Act of Supremacy in 1533, removed the obstacle to the divorce, legalized his marriage to Anne and opened the way for an indigenous church—or, more precisely, the catholic church in England.

The Church of England retained much of the form and tradition of the Roman church—many of the sacraments such as the orders of bishops, priests and deacons, a common liturgy but written in English in the Book of Common Prayer,[11] and some of the ritual and physical accoutrements. But

---

[9]Literally to tax to the amount of a tenth. In practice, any small part or proportion.

[10]In *The Protestant Ethic and the Spirit of Capitalism*, Max Weber (1864-1920), a German sociologist and political economist, advanced the theory that the doctrinal revision of the Reformation gave capitalists divine sanction for their way of life—i.e., self-discipline and hard work were regarded as a sign of grace; initiative and acquisition were acceptable provided wealth was not diverted to human pleasure; and so on. Weber's work-ethic theories have since become controversial.

[11]Few books of English prose can equal the Prayer Book for sheer beauty of writing. Pithy yet poetic, dogmatic yet democratic, comprehensive yet concise, the Book of Common Prayer remains the focal point of faith and worship for millions of Anglicans around the world. So beloved are the comfortable

(Cont'd)

it relaxed (some say purified) much of the rigid dogma and monolithic authority of the Roman Church. Anglicans adopted a "non-confessional" attitude, retaining only those Christian statements and creeds essential to church life, and permitting wider latitude for opinion and judgment on religious issues. Elizabeth I, who ruled during the church's formative years, remained conservative in religious matters, preferring not to have "a window into men's souls." Considering the turbulent political and religious milieu, the queen's policy undoubtedly was sound.

It was the Anglican religion that British immigrants brought with them when they settled Canada in the 18th century. The first primate of the Church of England in Canada, Bishop McCrae of Rupert's Land, was elected in 1893. In 1955, the name was changed to the Anglican Church of Canada, the first use of Anglican in such a manner. Today, one in 10 Canadians claims membership in the Anglican Church.

Ironically, the largest of the Protestant bodies in western Christendom traces its origin to Martin Luther, who intended not to found a new church but rather to purify the old. Like the Anglican communion, the Lutheran Church considers itself catholic (universal) in its affirmations. A central doctrine of Lutheran belief is "justification by faith." The bridge between God and man is faith alone. If man is to be saved from eternal damnation, he must put absolute trust in Jesus Christ as his saviour. That faith, alone, would qualify him for a place in paradise. Trust and faith, not fear and good works, were the keys to Christian living.

Lutherans practice baptism and communion, sacraments administered by a "priesthood of believers." Lutheran ministers are respected for their education and scholarship, not for their exclusive connection or linkage with God. Roughly three per cent of Canadians claim Lutheran as their religion, many of whom brought it with them from their native Germany and other northern European countries.

Meanwhile, a French theologian by the name of John Calvin was postulating yet another variation of Protestantism. Calvinism, which found expression in the Presbyterian faith, developed the theme that man belongs to God, that it is man's duty to sacrifice himself to God and through such sacrifice achieve union with Him. Calvinists were obliged to set an example of obedience through their struggle against sin. Life on earth was hard, one needed to lead a disciplined life because there is constant tension between

---

words that the church faces a serious conflict between those who would modernize the form of worship to the Alternate Rites, now used on an optional basis in Anglican parishes, and those who prefer—no, insist—that the church maintain the traditional rites.

human nature and God's wishes. No rest, man must always act through hard work. One's conscience was the direct link with God. A clear conscience signalled election to God's grace. But even that was not certain....

Presbyterianism, though oligarchic, was the most democratic principle of the Protestant theologies. It viewed the church as a community with Christ as its only head and all others equal under him. The ministry was given to each unit of the church and from there was shared among all elected officers. Worship was not confined to a fixed liturgy, and a sermon by an ordained minister occupied a central place in the service. Both the service and the church itself were characterized by austere simplicity. Presbyterians stressed the two dominical sacraments—baptism and the Lord's Supper. There were more than 1.4 million Presbyterians in Canada in 1921 at the close of the Golden Age of Philanthropy, second in number only to Roman Catholics.

The Methodists, who sprang from the Anglicans, were closely related to Presbyterians in their zeal for inward religion, a religion of the heart, and their emphasis on a life of regimented, methodical study and conduct. The movement traces its origins to the early 18th century when John and Charles Wesley were students at Oxford. The brothers experienced awakenings in Christ, committed themselves to prepare for the priesthood of the Church of England, then visited the United States where they made a great local impression. Then John Wesley had a revelation from Christ on Aldersgate Street in London and founded a religious society. After his death, the Methodists broke away from the Church of England and the movement spread throughout Wales, Ireland and the wider world. Methodists numbered more than one million adherents in the 1921 census of Canada.

Such was the fragmentation of the Christian community in Canada by the 1920s that three of the Protestant faiths—many Presbyterians, most Methodists and all Congregationalists[12]—merged their interests into one United Church of Canada in 1925. It was the first major union of differing traditions within Protestantism.[13]

The United Church retained a Protestant concern for simplicity in worship with emphasis on reading and exposition of scripture. The Bible was acknowledged as the supreme authority, although the Book of Common

---

[12]Another of the Reformed Churches which desired freedom from binding creed and ecclesiastical control. It was never a large movement in Canada, reaching a peak of 34,000 members in the 1911 census.

[13]A strong minority of Presbyterians, one-third of the membership, opposed union on any terms. They split from their brethren and continued as an independent congregation.

Order was adopted in 1932 as a guide for conduct of worship. A regular service included hymns, prayer, scripture and meditation. Adherents recognized the two sacraments of baptism and the Lord's Supper, and vested authority in a hierarchy of courts, rather than individual office-holders. The United Church claimed 16 per cent of the population as members in 1981, a proportion second only to Roman Catholics.

Not all sects that shared the idea of local autonomy and strong individualism joined in the union of 1925. The Baptists placed strong emphasis on the necessity of personal commitment to Christ and the personal experience of his grace or favor. Baptism was reserved for believers only—infants were ineligible—and membership accorded to persons mature enough to give credible testimony of conversion. Baptist services tend to be simple and informal, and worship largely non-liturgical, with emphasis on preaching and hymn singing. Baptists are the largest Protestant denomination in the United States. In Canada, their determined individualism may have fragmented their influence. Baptists represented three per cent of the population in 1981, down from four per cent a generation earlier.

The Evangelical sects place even greater emphasis on personal commitment and open profession of their faith in Jesus Christ. An evangelist is literally one who proclaims the Gospel, and Evangelical Christians are marked by their devotion to the ''sure word of the Bible.'' The Evangelical sects, and there are at least half-a-dozen active in Canada today, often with American support, place major emphasis on personal salvation. They stress personal religious experiences and the need for decisive, even dramatic, individual conversion—the occasion when, by God's initiating grace, man responds to the Saviour's invitation and enters the Kingdom of the Church. Converts in turn are expected to proclaim the good news of God in the fellowship of their church and in the vocations of their personal lives.

It is difficult to determine just how large the Evangelical movement is in Canada, since adherents may not be classified as such in official statistics. Certainly, evangelists have long played a highly visible and influential role in the United States. And with the advent of the electronic church, whose congregation is not constrained by physical or national boundaries, the movement may be gaining momentum in Canada as well. The most authoritative estimate places affiliation at three per cent of the population in the eight major Evangelical denominations in 1981.[14]

---

[14]Adventist, Brethren in Christ, Christian and Missionary Alliance, Church of God, Church of the Nazarene, Evangelical Free Church, Pentecostal, Evangelical Free Methodist.

These 15 Judeo-Christian denominations account for about 86 per cent of the Canadian population. Add another seven per cent for those Canadians who adhere to a variety of smaller Christian and non-Christian religious sects, and there remains about seven or eight per cent of the population claiming no religion. A rather small proportion, but many times larger than the 17,000 Canadians (0.15 per cent of the population) who claimed no specific religious affiliation in the 1941 census.

To summarize for easy future reference, the denominations divide out into the following proportions:

	Percentage
Roman Catholic	47
United	16
Anglican	10
Presbyterian	3
Lutheran	3
Baptist	3
Evangelical sects	3
Jewish	1
Other	7
No religion	7
	100

Source: Census of Canada 1981

If religion prompts the heart to monitor man's morals, education conditions the mind to absorb new knowledge, to reason dispassionately, to be stimulated by fresh and novel ideas. Education challenges people's ways of thinking and acting and is the primal force of change in our society. Education has played a major role in shaping attitudes towards the demand for and supply and funding of humanistic service.

Levels of educational attainment in Canada have increased dramatically since the Second World War. At the beginning of the post-war economic boom, Canada had a rather poorly educated work force when compared with other technologically advanced countries. For instance, the 1951 census showed that 55 per cent of men in the work force had elementary grade-school education only. The crash program of the sixties compensated swiftly, not only for the new crop of post-war babies but for all levels of educational attainment.

During 1961-1971, school attendance rates for both the male and female population ages 15-19 showed remarkable and steady improvement.[15] University attendance trebled and at the post-graduate level attendance quadrupled. Ontario, Alberta and British Columbia reported the highest proportions of population with secondary and university-level education. Canada has also attracted highly educated immigrants. For example, during the decade of the sixties, four per cent of the incoming population had advanced university degrees compared with less than one per cent for the population as a whole.

Today Canada's educational profile is as follows:

	Percentage
Elementary grade school or less	26
Full or partial secondary education	44
Some post-secondary education	12
Post-secondary diploma or certificate	10
University degree (of which 20 per cent are advanced degrees)	8
	100

Source: Statistics Canada 1976

Much has been written in recent years about the "alarming" rate at which the Canadian population is aging. Indeed, Canadians age no more or less rapidly than other nationalities, nor has the rate of physical maturity increased over past generations. But like other countries in the western world, our birth rate (live births per 1,000 total population) has declined sharply from 28 during the fifties to a record low of 15 in the seventies and eighties.[16] When that fact is coupled with the knowledge that life expectancy has increased steadily over the last 40 years,[17] then it follows that the weighted average age of the population will tend to increase.

The alarm-bells ring when futurists extrapolate trend lines that assume a continuation of both tendencies and imply difficulty or even inability to cope

---

[15]It is interesting to note that the attendance rates were higher for girls than boys in 1921, 1931 and 1941, but beginning with the 1951 census and continuing for each subsequent decennial census higher attendance rates were reported for boys.

[16]A far cry from the 45 recorded in the 1850s. Even during the Great Depression, the rate was in the 20s.

[17]A 50-year-old male can now expect to live another 25 years, a female 30 years.

with required levels of economic production, and so on. The changing age composition does, of course, pose important consequences for the future demand, nature and financing of humanistic service. This thesis will make no attempt to explore those implications fully. Rather, it accepts the realities of an aging population and will consider in due course the possible effects of accepted demographic projections on financing humanistic service in the years ahead.

As a benchmark for future reference the reader will find it useful to know the broad age distribution of the Canadian population in 1981.

	Percentage
Pre-school (under age 5)	7
Elementary-school age (5-14)	15
Secondary-school age (15-19)	10
Post-secondary school age (20-24)	10
Demanding years (25-44)	29
Established years (45-64)	19
Senior years	10
	100

Source: Census of Canada 1981

Ethnicity, religion, education, and age: these are four fundamental characteristics that shape and influence man's humanistic behavior. More subtle, but perhaps equally important, are actions and patterns rooted in how man chooses (or is ordained) to organize his life and occupy his days—lifestyle. Family size, composition and stability, occupation, vocation or profession, place of residence, income class, social class: each of these exerts authority on how man views the world, his or her world, and how he accepts humanistic duty.

How to describe the lifestyle of eight million Canadian families? The unit itself is amorphous. Perhaps more appropriate today is the notion of household, which describes a living arrangement rather than kinship. Whatever definition is used, the size of the unit is decreasing. In 1966, there were 3.9 persons in each family, in 1976 there were 3.5, today that number is smaller yet, reflecting among other factors the lower birth rates of the past decade.

It is shrinking also because there are now more single-parent families—the proportion increased from eight per cent to 10 per cent of all families over the decade ended in 1976. In 1981, 637,000 Canadian households were headed by single parents. Many couples choose not to marry. And more marriages today end in divorce—54,000 in 1976 alone.

Divorce is an institution confined almost exclusively to this generation of Canadians. In 1946, there were only 7,600 divorces granted in all of Canada. And from Confederation to the turn of the century—during the Golden Age of Philanthropy—there were fewer than 20 divorces per year in each of the 33 years. The divorce rate is now 2.4 per thousand of population; the duration of dissolved marriages was 10.8 years in 1976, down from 12.6 years in 1971.

Family income, too, defies comprehensive description. Averages are confusing and the numbers change so frequently that what is reported today is obsolete by the time it is read. More helpful, perhaps, are a few relative relationships over time, across geographic regions and across income class. As a point of reference, the mean (average) income of all Canadian families in 1981 was $29,900. In 1961, the figure was $5,300, so the increase was 460 per cent over the 20-year period. But those are nominal dollars. In constant dollars, adjusting for inflation, the increase over the two decades was 80 per cent.

Incomes, of course, are not distributed equally across geographic regions, nor across families within regions. Since British Columbia has reported the highest family incomes in recent years, let it assume the standard of measurement for the rest of Canada with a level of 100. Ontario is next at 97; the Prairie Provinces, 91; Quebec, 87; the Atlantic Provinces, 73. Those indices refer to gross incomes, unadjusted for taxes and differences in cost of living.

Of more interest to an individual family is its disposable income after taxes, and perhaps even more intriguing than the amount is the comparison of one's family income with other families.

Family-income comparison is most conveniently shown by grouping families into income classes. And the most concise and informative reporting format is the quintile analysis. A quintile represents one-fifth of the population. If all eight million Canadian families were arranged in ascending order of family income—from lowest to highest—the first quintile would include the lowest 1.6 million families, the fifth quintile the highest 1.6 million, and so on. If the total income of all 1.6 million families in the quintile was aggregated, and a mean income calculated, that number would represent the average family income in that quintile. Imperfect perhaps, but concise and informative.

The distribution of Canadian family income, as shown by quintile analysis, has varied little over the post-war period. The 1978 distribution is typical.

FAMILY (HOUSEHOLD) DISPOSABLE INCOME (AFTER TAX)

	Canadian Total Income	Quintile One (Lowest)	Quintile Two (——	Quintile Three Middle	Quintile Four ——)	Quintile Five (Highest)
Proportion of Disposable Income Received	100	6.9	13.2	18.6	24.5	36.6

Letting quintile five, the highest income earners, represent the reference class with an index of 100, the lowest class would have an index of 19.[18] Expressed another way, the discrepancy in income between the upper and lower class is greater than five times. The index for the middle class is about 50.

The distribution of wealth is similarly concentrated. Its index of distribution ranges from 19 in quintile one to 34 in quintile three to 100 in quintile five. The extent to which Canadian families move up (and down) the economic classes is a subject that has fascinated observers and participants throughout our history. The topic will have relevance later in this inquiry.

Incomes are linked closely to occupations. As Canada has matured industrially, the proportion of the work force engaged in upscale occupational classifications has increased, shrinking the proportion in the labor categories. Today about 20 per cent of the work force is engaged in management or professional pursuits, and the remainder is split almost equally between white-collar and blue-collar classifications.

Apart from financial flexibility, Canadians have demonstrated a propensity to physical mobility. Over the long term, the population has become highly urbanized. The population was predominantly rural from our very earliest days until the Great Depression when the proportion of urban res-

---

[18]The sum of 6.9 divided by 36.6 multiplied by 100. Our U.S. neighbors have an income distribution that is even more skewed; in 1973 the lowest quintile had an average family income scarcely 10 per cent of the upper quintile.

idents first exceeded the rural group. Today more than three Canadians out of four live in an urban centre. And even the rural classification could be misleading, if equated with farming. Many Canadians who pursue careers in an urban environment now make their home in the country.

Mobility is demonstrated by 1976 census data. That year 10 million Canadians, almost half of the population, reported that their place of residence then was different from their residence five years earlier. And more than half of the movers migrated beyond the boundaries of the census district within which they resided; almost one million moved to a different province in that five-year span.

Many terms have been used to describe the distinctive Canadian ambiance. Mosaic[19] is perhaps the most colorful simile. Not surprisingly, it was coined first in 1922 by a U.S visitor to describe the diversity of church architecture, reflecting the range of European cultures represented on the Prairie Provinces. To Victoria Hayward, Canada was affectionately "a mosaic of vast dimensions and great breadth...."

This theme of an harmonious, horizontal, cultural mosaic was developed extensively by John Gibbon in *Canadian Mosaic*, published in 1938. It gained a new dimension, and widespread usage, after 1965 when John Porter published *The Vertical Mosaic*, which depicted Canada as a society rigidly stratified into classes, each with its elite. Porter identified political elites, social elites, economic elites, intellectual elites and (God forbid) religious elites. He postulated that one does not necessarily need to belong to all groups in order to be considered elite, but demonstrated that there is a high degree of inter-relatedness. According to Porter, there has been little crossover by non-elites into the exclusive ranks.

Porter's thesis, combined with the succinct historical and cross-sectional description contained in this chapter, portrays an intriguing comparison.

Do the many dimensions of the Canadian character truly blend harmoniously into one pattern or picture?

Do the 70 different ethnic strains in Canada subordinate (not disavow) their native heritage to the pre-emptive love of and loyalty to one Canada?

Have the different Christian denominations (which numbered 18 in 1951 and 65 in 1981) shown increasing tolerance, initiative and willingness to merge their interests into a common moral, if not theological, mission?

---

[19]A surface decoration made by inlaying small pieces of variously colored material to form patterns and pictures.

Have higher levels of educational attainment promoted greater under-standing and interaction across different educational levels?

Do the various population age groups live and interact harmoniously?

Is there much social intercourse across the income classes? Between ur-ban and rural residents?

If one answers no to these questions, then the Canadian mosaic is but a romantic metaphor. Such an observer might more accurately describe Canada in terms of a collage—"a surrealist pictorial composition in which figures from engravings, photographs and printed illustrations are shown in an incongruous environment."

But similes and metaphors must not divert the flow of this discussion. We are now equipped with sufficient background to address the central theme of this thesis.

CHAPTER V

A rationale for donation behavior

T he giving of gifts has always impressed mankind as singularly noble. Something we value highly we give to another, enriching both the giver and the receiver. Thought and empathy precede our action. We know the need and sensitivities of the receiver and offer just the correct present. The gift should cost the giver something, yet it should be viewed as an investment rather than an expenditure. Because it is an intimate gesture, its sentiments live and continue to bring pleasure long after the act itself. To qualify, a gift must be unexpected, capricious, undeserved, occasional. Giving a gift is an act of absolute freedom, mankind's most cherished value. Giving is the supreme altruistic expression.

Such gifts are rare, particularly in a society approaching Stage IV. More often, we make a monetary donation, subscription or pledge, a gift surrogate which is more flexible, less time-consuming, more suited to our complex society in which institutions and bureaucrats intervene between benefactor and beneficiary. Spontaneity has given way to solicitation. We are asked for donations by people we do not know, and for causes that often are but vaguely familiar. Yet we recognize that they *are* humanistic causes, that the work is worthy, that the need is great, that we have some responsibility for their welfare. And so we contribute to one, some or all. Anyway, the donation is tax-deductible!

Their range, form and variety is comprehensive: a request to subscribe through a newspaper or television appeal, a telephone solicitation, an invi-

tation to lunch followed by the personal touch. And letters!
us in our homes and in our offices, mimeographed and hand
letters and personal messages, rubber-stamped and signed, lo
businesslike and emotional, with and without enclosures, d
pathetic, compelling, poignant.

Let me share a small sample of the letters of solicitation mailed to me over
the past number of months. The list will be familiar and will assist our sub-
sequent discussion: Amnesty International, from Margaret Atwood;
Canadian Blind Mission International; Harvard Business School, Class of
1958; The Cancer Research Society, Inc., Montreal; The United Way of
Greater London; Canadian Cancer Society, London-Middlesex Unit;
Canadian Diabetes Association, London—Birthplace of Insulin; Rotary
Club of London in partnership with the Easter Seal Society; Stratford
Shakespearean Festival Foundation of Canada; Canadian Civil Liberties
Association—from Pierre Berton *et al.*; The Canadian Save the Children
Fund; Dr. J.P. Metras Memorial Fund; Ontario Heart Foundation—Lon-
don and Area Chapter; Independence House New York—from Clem Has-
tie HBS '58; Mental Health/Elgin—invitation to Art Auction; The McGill
Parents Association; Unicef Canada; Museum of Indian Archaeology....

What factors cause us to contribute to some appeals, to reject others? To
respond with alacrity or delay interminably? To give generously or at the
minimum acceptable level? Few decisions are embedded in such a complex
array of motivating forces: biological, cultural, economic, environmental,
social, psychological, philosophical. Our research and intuition have identified 16 separate factors associated with the financial generosity of individuals. There may be more, or fewer, but our notion is that these are the major
forces which determine the quantity and quality of individual charitable
donations certainly in Canada and probably in North America today.

The factors group logically and conveniently into three distinct clusters—
a set of enabling circumstances which provide the ability or capacity to give,
and two distinct groups of forces that stimulate a positive donation decision.

THE DONATION MODEL

Ability

A—1   Income
A—2   Wealth
A—3   Taxation

MOTIVATING INFLUENCES

Level Two		Level One	
II—1	Ethnicity	I—1	*Noblesse oblige*
II—2	Transaction	I—2	Tradition
II—3	Leverage	I—3	Power
II—4	Recognition	I—4	Philosophy*
II—5	Education	I—5	Freedom
II—6	Social mobility	I—6	Altruism
II—7	Social acceptance		

*Moral philosophy, religion, humanism

No gift or donation is possible unless the donor first possesses the economic means to be generous—capacity, ability. People must *perceive* themselves as holding a surplus beyond their own needs. Charity begins at home. One cares for one's own. Only then does one extend care to others. *Ego ante alter*. Not an altogether unhealthy philosophy for fostering an independent society. Ability has three dimensions in this discussion: income, wealth and taxation.

One may have the capacity to give, but not feel inclined to do so. A positive donation decision requires an effective stimulant, a motivating influence to prompt action. The dozen-odd animating factors separate almost equally into two groups, each with recognizably different characteristics.

Level Two influences originate from circumstances or actions outside the individual: biological, environmental or social forces strong enough to impel a positive decision to contribute. Each individual is born with a genetic, biological legacy that influences the emotions and actions: a group of business clients adopts a worthy cause and invites participation; an attractive upscale social group encourages patronage of a cultural function. Level Two donation decisions contain a strong element of self-interest—*quid pro quo*. Such motivation is not necessarily reprehensible; much good derives from actions prompted by egoism. Level Two motivators include ethnicity, transactions, leverage, recognition, education, social mobility and social acceptance.

Level One motives are of a higher order. They emanate from inner standards, intellectual and moral security, an innate sense of constructive purpose, a genuine regard for the welfare of others. Level One standards apply when the individual has arrived—a state quite beyond financial security. Level One embraces the following forces: *noblesse oblige*, tradition, power, philosophy, freedom and altruism. They might as readily be titled "leadership."

Income

All other things equal, the capacity to give tends to increase at an accelerating[1] rate with increases in current income. This is so because donations are considered discretionary distributions, made from resources that remain after providing for life's necessary expenditures.

The pool available for donations is, of course, much smaller than disposable income (gross income minus taxes) and somewhat less than total discretionary income (disposable income minus necessities such as food, shelter, clothing and the like). Also deducted are expenditures perceived as necessary to maintain a living standard, a notion not necessarily correlated with income.

Life's necessities have a degree of built-in rigidity at their minimum level. For instance, in 1978, Canadian families in the lowest-income group—$6,070 after taxes—spent $3,735 on food and shelter, 62 per cent of their disposable income. The highest-income earners—$36,000 per year—spent $10,000 on the two essentials, only 29 per cent of their disposable income.

This narrowly defined discretionary pool, the surplus income remaining after deducting necessities, tends to increase proportionately more than a given increase in income. That being the case one would expect proportionately larger donations from upper income groups. Income tax considerations aside, the cost (or value or marginal utility) of a donation of $1,000 to a person in the $100,000 income class is of less consequence than a donation of $100 to someone earning only $10,000. The United Way recognizes the principle of declining marginal utility in its guidelines for giving: 0.6 per cent for incomes up to $25,000; one per cent up to $50,000; 1.5 per cent for incomes over $50,000.

Necessary expenditures are defined more subjectively. Vacations, entertainment, golf club dues, savings and investment programs, private summer camps, while not essential for survival may nevertheless be perceived as unavoidable. Because necessary expenditures are subjective and linked to a complex and compelling constellation of social forces, they could well consume most or all of a family's otherwise discretionary net income. In such cases, the expenditures become indispensable and could preempt charitable donations in an individual's value system.

---

[1]Note the distinction between speed and acceleration. An increase in income level from $10,000 to $15,000 to $22,500 is a constant rate of increase of 50 per cent. The accompanying capacity for donations may expand at an accelerating rate—for example, from a level of one to two to five.

Wealth

Net worth adds another dimension to affluence and has the potential to influence one's propensity to donate. Wealth is the balance remaining after subtracting total debts or liabilities from the value of all assets owned. Assets, of course, can be highly liquid and secure, such as savings deposit balances, Canada Savings Bonds, and so on, liquid but more uncertain in value, such as blue chip common stocks, or illiquid, such as pension plans, unlisted securities, real estate, personal property and the like.

An individual can afford to be generous if his net worth is large enough to provide financial security. The magnitude and composition of wealth may also affect the quantity and quality of current income. A positive net worth invested in deposits or marketable securities may generate interest and dividends, adding investment income to the stream of income from employment. The higher the proportion of investment income to total income, the greater may be the perceived sense of security or stability of that income stream. A more secure income flow would tend to enhance the propensity to donate to humanistic causes.

Taxation

Taxation policies affect both the stream of income and the ability to accumulate and retain wealth. Sales taxes, consumption taxes and income taxes constrict the flow of net income. Capital gains taxes, and wealth, inheritance or estate taxes, diminish net worth.

Sales and consumption taxes are levied on expenditures, thus adding to their cost. Their incidence[2] reduces the base from which charitable donations are made. Increases in these taxes, therefore, would tend to inhibit a person's propensity to donate to charity, since ability or capacity would be reduced. Sales or consumption-type taxes account for roughly one-third of total tax revenues in Canada today.

The impact of income taxes is more complex. Donations made to charitable organizations[3] registered with Revenue Canada are expenditures which are deductible in calculating taxable income (to a maximum deduction of

---

[2]Such taxes are called regressive since their incidence (ultimate resting place) tends to be proportionately heavier on low-income families. For example, consider the effect of a seven-per-cent sales tax levied on all consumption expenditures: a family earning $6,000 would consume 100 per cent of its income paying $420 in sales taxes, seven per cent of its income; a family earning $36,000 would consume only 75 per cent of its income and pay $1,890 in sales taxes, representing only 5.25 per cent of its income.

[3]Of which there are some 47,000, embracing all categories of humanistic service.

20 per cent of net income).[4] For the vast majority of Canadians, donations can be considered before-tax expenditures, amounts that give rise to income tax refunds in the amount of the taxpayer's marginal tax rate[5] multiplied by the total amount of donations made.

The following example may clarify how marginal income tax rates reduce the cost of charitable donations to the donor.

Consider two taxpayers living in Ontario.

Willing earns barely enough income to be taxed at the lowest marginal rate—24 per cent of his taxable income. If Willing makes a charitable donation of $100, he would receive a refund of $24, provided income tax had been deducted from his earnings at source. The $100 donation actually cost Willing a net amount of $76, his out-of-pocket cost after deducting the tax refund.

Able earns $55,000, placing him in the highest marginal tax bracket—50 per cent. If Able were to make a $100 donation, his tax refund would be $50, leaving a net cost to him of only $50 for the $100 donation. The cash cost to Able is considerably less than the cost of an equivalent donation to Willing—a perverse twist considering that Able's ability to donate the $100 is many times greater than is Willing's.

Such is the obverse of a progressive[6] tax system. It magnifies the benefits of any tax shield that reduces income just as it extracts an increasing amount on higher incomes—the acceleration effect.

Taxation of wealth functions in a similarly progressive manner, but the tax base on which progressive rates are applied excludes some important exemptions. The most important and, in all provinces except Quebec, the only wealth tax levied is the tax on realized capital gains—the difference between the cost[7] of capital (investment) assets and the proceeds received on their disposition. Net capital gains are added to all other sources of income—from earnings, investments, etc. —and taxed by the same progressive rate table.

---

[4]Defined for all practical purposes as gross income from salaries, investments, etc., less a limited range of minor deductions.

[5]The rate on the last dollar of taxable income.

[6]In contrast to regressive taxation. Both notions will be explored fully in Chapter XII.

[7]Financial sophisticates will appreciate the utility of this simplified treatment of a highly technical and complex subject. While a later discussion becomes somewhat more involved, readers who require precision in tax matters are referred to *Canadian Income Tax Act* and to Arthur Drache, *The Tax Treatment of Charities and Charitable Donations* (Toronto: Richard DeBoo, 1981).

The operative word is net, a deduction of 50 per cent of the gross capital gain is permitted in calculating the amount of income added to the income base for tax purposes. This has the effect of reducing the tax rate on realized capital gains to half the marginal rate that would apply if the gain had been classified as other income—a significant concession. Furthermore, full exemption from tax is granted on gains made on the sale of any principal residence, personal property to the value of $1,000, and so on.

What is the relevance of capital gains taxation to charitable donations? First, the net (taxable) portion of the gain adds to the income base on which the 20 per cent donation exemption applies, effectively adding to one's tax-free capacity to donate.[8] Note that the sting of the progressive tax table is less excruciating on income classified as a capital gain. So too is the reward (in tax savings) it bestows on the taxpayer who donates up to a tithe on those gains.

Second, investments do not have to be sold for cash to be considered realized income for tax purposes. If a taxpayer donates a painting, for which he paid $1,000, to an art gallery at a time when its fair market value is $11,000, the taxpayer is deemed to have realized a capital gain of $10,000, half of which would be taxable at his marginal rate. The gift would add $1,000 to the tax-free donations limit (20 per cent of $5,000) and if the taxpayer had already donated to the limit of 20 per cent of his other income, the art gallery donation could add $2,000[9] to his income tax payable in the year of the donation. Good news and bad news.

Such is the impact of taxation on *inter vivos* donations. What about charitable gifts made at time of death—directions and bequests specified in one's will?

Governments in Canada do not impose a special tax on the value of a deceased's estate[10] *per se*, nor on amounts received by beneficiaries named in

---

[8]For a taxpayer in the highest bracket, a $10,000 gross capital gain would add $5,000 to taxable income which would be subject to $2,500 income tax. The taxpayer could now donate up to $1,000 and reduce his income tax up to $500, as a result of the 20 per cent exemption.

[9]Incremental taxable income: $5,000 taxable capital gain minus $1,000 maximum donation deduction equals $4,000 multiplied by an assumed marginal tax rate of 50 per cent.

[10]Not entirely true. Quebec imposes succession duties on the value of estates transferred to beneficiaries at time of death. Ontario repealed its Succession Duty Act and the Gift Tax Act on April 10, 1979. Treasurer Frank Miller told the Legislature, "I'm satisfied the present combination of other taxes provides government with an adequate return as wealth is accumulated. As of midnight tonight, there will be no succession duty or gift taxation in Ontario." Then in an aside to Gordon Sinclair, Toronto's cherubic, quintessential capitalist, perched proudly in the south balcony, he added, "Gordon, last till midnight. Pardon me, the House Leader has adjusted it to one minute after." (In fact, Mr. Sinclair lasted until 1984.)

the will or direction. The estate is taxed under the Income Tax Act by specifying the value of the estate assets considered to be income for tax purposes in the year of death. In essence, the taxable amount is 50 per cent of the total capital gains deemed to be realized by the taxpayer as if he had disposed of all his assets at fair market value the instant before he died. As with other capital gains, the taxpayer could reduce the taxable portion of these gains by making charitable donations up to the 20 per cent limit. Gifts beyond that figure provide no shield from income tax payable on the estate's taxable value.

There is one further income tax provision that has had widespread historic relevance to the topic of charitable donations—the $100 standard deduction permitted in calculating taxable income up to 1984. Taxpayers were given the option either of itemizing each charitable donation they claimed (to the 20 per cent limit) or of deducting a flat $100 from their income for the year. Since the alternative was optional, one can assume that taxpayers donating less than $100 opted for the standard deduction and thereby derived a cash benefit to the extent of their marginal tax rate multiplied by the difference between their actual donations and $100. With the withdrawal of this provision in 1984, deductions for donations will be permitted only to the extent of actual payments.

To summarize the impact of taxation on one's ability to donate to humanistic causes: First, regressive taxes such as sales and consumption taxes, constituting about one-third of total tax levies, act to reduce the pool of income potentially available for gifts and donations because governments do not recognize donations as a deduction from the base on which the tax is levied.

Second, progressive taxes, of which income taxes (roughly 40 per cent of government revenues) are by far the most important example, do *not* in themselves reduce the pool of funds otherwise available for donations because they can be avoided by making charitable donations to a maximum of 20 per cent of net income. Beyond that level of giving, income taxation does reduce the available pool by the amount of the progressive income tax rates on the incremental income.

Third, because income taxes can be reduced by making charitable donations, and upper-income taxpayers pay higher rates of tax than do lower-income individuals, the true cost of donations is less for upper-income classes than for lower-income groups.

Ability or capacity to donate from current income or accumulated wealth is partly an objective, measurable value but mostly a subjective, highly personal perception. One individual with a modest income and no wealth may nonetheless consider himself or herself as having a surplus beyond personal needs and thus possessing the capacity to make donations. Another may feel financially strapped on an income of $100,000. To each of us, perception is reality.

But even possessing the ability to give does not cause the act to take place. That requires a motivating stimulus. We consider first those motives that originate largely outside our person, Level Two motives.

Ethnicity

Chapter IV has already demonstrated the link between ethnic origin and generosity in the context of the social and cultural activities of the various immigrant groups that comprise Canada's cultural collage.

Kinship is a compelling force, family ties mean something, country is important. Knowledge sharpens the sense of responsibility, obligation, duty. Blood is thicker than water. Generosity to others would tend first to be narrowly focused within the kin and ethnic group, then over time—perhaps generations—would tend to expand to a broader definition of community to coincide with extended involvement and wider social acceptance.

The degree of one's generosity may also be influenced by ethnic roots. A new Canadian brought up in a country with Stage IV humanistic traditions, whose social and cultural contacts are confined to kin or members of the same ethnic group, is quite likely to retain old-country attitudes and behavior. If promiscuous giving was not a way of life in the old home, it may not become a lifestyle in the new. The opposite, of course, could also apply— old habits of widespread generosity could easily and readily be transplanted to the new environment.

Transactions

Sir John A. Macdonald: "A man must have a weakness, a certain kind of sweetness be it soothing to the spirit or the flesh. Offer this one cash, offer that one a degree, a medal or whatever is his whim: though he may sneer at booty he will stoutly do his duty if he knows there's something in it for him."[11]

---

[11]From *Louis Riel*, Music Drama in Three Acts, libretto by Mavor Moore, music by Harry Somers, commissioned by the Floyd S. Chalmers Foundation (Act 1, Scene 3). The world premiere took place in Washington during Canada's centennial year, 1967.

Quid pro quo—something in return. It was recognized as a force of human nature long before ancient Romans coined the phrase. In donating money, the notion emerges in many guises: trading for equivalent economic, political or psychic advantage, exchanges that resemble insurance coverage, donations to assuage feelings of guilt or fear.

In Calgary, actress June Lockhart and Mayor Ralph Klein pose for pictures behind a bouquet of daffodils to launch the Canadian Cancer Society's $200,000 annual fund-raising campaign. In Portage la Prairie, Phil Carpenter of the Portage Fire Department pours at the Annual Heart Fund Coffee Party that raises $435. In Brantford, Wayne Gretzky presents a cheque for $99,000 to the Canadian National Institute for the Blind[12] at the superstar's Celebrity Tennis Classic that attracted international beauties, including model Cheryl Tiegs. In Toronto, Health Minister Larry Grossman negotiates an obstacle course in the Cougar Superteams Competition at the CNE Tower to raise funds for the Muscular Dystrophy Association, gaining the association and the minister 77 square inches of space in *The Globe and Mail*. Pleasant experiences. Fair exchanges. The only acceptable form of influence peddling.

Insurance payments, in the context of charitable giving, could be made for past or future coverage. Grateful to his *alma mater* for a superior education, one person sends money to perpetuate the institution's strength and pre-eminence for the next generation. Another may donate heavily to cancer research, conscious of the fact that the disease claimed the lives of maternal ancestors. Yet another gives to aid the poor to cleanse a troubled conscience.

Quid pro quo is regarded by many as a potent stimulus to charitable giving. For example, "Give and Take" has been chosen as the slogan for a grassroots campaign to force amendments to the Income Tax Act, making donations less costly to lower-income taxpayers, thus providing them with an incentive to give more. The movement[13] is backed by an informal coalition

---

[12]According to tournament director Zig Misiak, the presentation was a symbolic gesture to reflect a rounded-off estimate of the tournament's gross. Based on the previous year's net results, the CNIB was likely to receive about $20,000, still a substantial contribution stemming from the initiative of No. 99.

[13]"Give and Take" is orchestrated by The National Voluntary Organization Committee in Ottawa. A variant theme promoted by the Harvard Business School is titled "Gaining by Giving." The Ottawa

(Cont'd)

of some 120 national charitable organizations, including the United and Anglican Churches of Canada.

Leverage

According to professional fund raisers, the bulk of the big money that changes hands each year in charitable-fund drives across Canada does so because of the influence possessed by the canvasser over the donor. Businessmen and politicians call it leverage.

Here is a synopsis of how it works—a paraphrase from interviews with two experienced fund raisers. Leverage implies that the canvasser possesses knowledge or power that in some way can be used for the advancement or punishment of the donor, or that he has a favor he can call in. Often the reward is economic—an industrialist fund raiser agrees to call on his company's lead banker for an appropriate donation. It may also be psychic—the seductive suggestion of a coveted social invitation proffered to an upwardly mobile, but sadly middle-class, lawyer in return for his pledge. Or the canvasser may simply be turning the table on a friend who tapped him in an earlier campaign.

The methods used range from the most refined and low-key suggestions to eyeball ultimatums bordering on extortion. Leverage need not be applied so crudely to be effective. A fund drive publishes a list of lead donors whose actions are respected and emulated in the community. A corporation agrees to match employee charitable donations dollar for dollar. However, leverage works.

Recognition

Psychologists tell us that recognition for accomplishment is necessary to gain and retain self-esteem. Properly given, it is both a reward and an incentive. The author needs recognition for her creativity, the homemaker for her harmonious family, the industrialist for his deal, the farmer for his extraordinary yield, the donor for his gift. "It is quite clear," said Cicero, "that most people are generous in their gifts not so much by natural inclination as by reason of the lure of honor. They simply want to be seen as beneficent."

---

proposal recommended two major changes to the federal Income Tax Act: eliminating the standard deduction of $100, and introducing a 50-per-cent tax *credit* to replace the present dollar-for-dollar deductibility against income for actual donations made. The federal government accepted half the proposal in the 1983 spring budget by eliminating the standard deduction.

Modern fund raisers ignore that principle at the risk of their campaign objective. And so gratitude and honor is dispensed, in good taste and in bad.

Reflect briefly on this list of only eight different forms and forums of recognition for donations past, present and future.

Consider first the effectiveness of the letter of gratitude, thanks and appreciation. The mimeographed postcard is better than no acknowledgement, the form letter better than a postcard, one individually typed better yet, and an intimate, hand-written note the best of all.

Listing donor names in newspaper advertisements, playbills, annual reports and the like. Names can appear alphabetically in groups of descending order of monetary importance, but delicately, with no identification of the breaking points (Benefactors, Patrons, Members), in categories with the range of monetary value shown in the group heading, or (are we strong enough?) a list of names and the actual value of the contribution ranked in descending order of size.

Formal press announcement with portrait and copy. These are usually proclamations of impending or current fund drives by a humanistic organization. The focal point of the announcement is a portrait of one or more distinguished persons who are named as volunteer leaders in the financial campaign, a word or two of biographical significance, a paragraph on the organization, the purpose of the fund and the financial goal. Placing of the advertisement is key. Local campaigns may appear on any well-read page in the local newspaper. Campaigns of regional interest would appear in a vehicle of suitable coverage. Campaigns of national significance—e.g., Bishop's College School, United Jewish Appeal, York University Fund—would appear in *The Globe and Mail*, preferably in Report on Business since the picture would be noticed by friends and associates of the volunteer.

The unwritten message implied in the formal press announcement is, "Please notice our organization is raising money; we are grateful to these distinguished men and women for the donation they have already made to the fund, and they look forward to the privilege of meeting you soon to explain our needs and objectives more fully." Recognition and notice of motion.

The donor register or permanent record. This is a more lasting version of the published list of donors. It may be a leather-bound, calligraphic listing of donors on parchment pages placed in the board room, a brass plaque inscribed with the donor's name attached to a theatre seat, a wall of bricks in the foyer of an auditorium, each engraved with the name of a donor contributing at a minimum level, or a brass-bronze Tree of Life[14] where leaves are named for donors from $1,000 to $10,000, base-stones from $10,000 to $100,000, and rocks for more than $100,000.

Naming of rooms, wings and public buildings. A contribution may be large enough, and gratitude deep enough, to encourage the beneficiary organization to attribute more space to the donor's beneficence—an operating room, a classroom wing or a library building. At times the offer is completely spontaneous, in gratitude after the donation has been deposited. Sometimes it is offered as *quid pro quo* to encourage the donor. Rarely, it is made a formal, specific condition of giving that must be accepted before the donation is made.

A mention on the social page. Although it is a custom that has faded noticeably in this generation, some newspapers still retain a social editor to record faithfully the activities of the socially prominent. Perhaps the difficulty today is determining who they are. The articles must be read by somebody. *The Globe and Mail*, for instance, has published Zena Cherry daily for 20 years and allotted an average of 30 column-inches including photographs for each article in 1982. Ms. Cherry mentioned charity, philanthropy, fund raising, volunteer service, or a similar theme, in almost half these articles, even including it in one-fifth of her column titles.[15]

Honorary degrees. As Dr. D. Carlton Williams, former president and vice-chancellor of The University of Western Ontario, expresses it, "In a society where, except for military honors, public recognition in the form of

---

[14]Planted in a wall at the Tillsonburg District Memorial Hospital in 1981. According to Board Chairman Mrs. Geno Francolini, when people saw the type of recognition they would receive, it gave them the incentive to give more. In fact, many are now upgrading their pledge to move from a listing in the memorial register to a leaf.

[15]Throughout the year, July 1981 through June 1982, Zena Cherry provided Canadians with a record of weddings, receptions, birthday *fêtes*, political fund-raising parties and charitable extravaganzas attended by Canada's beautiful people, jet-set elite—whatever. Nor did she limit her functions to Canadian geography. In July 1981, she attended the wedding of the Prince of Wales and Lady Diana Spencer, keeping those at home informed on proceedings, i.e., who was invited, who had parties and who attended. In the winter, Ms. Cherry jetted down to Antigua with "The Canadian Exiles" for winter fun in the sun. Her column could be viewed as a daily social supplement to a Canadian *Who's Who* with lists of names, titles, and occupations of people who are viewed by Ms. Cherry as socially interesting. Of the 262 articles clipped, the average length was 625 words and the size ranged from 24 to 48 column inches. Of the 118 articles in which philanthropy or its theme was mentioned, 66 included a reminder that February is Heart Month, or mentioned a volunteer fund-raising event after a name listed, etc.

awards is sparse and titles non-existent, the honorary degree is one of the most important honorifics we have, second only to the recently established Order of Canada.''[16] Honorary degrees are listed here not to suggest that they are for sale—that topic is examined in Book Two—but to establish their pre-eminent place in recognizing mankind's contribution to society.

The anonymous donor. The anonymous donor? Most contribution lists make reference to gifts from sources who request anonymity. Obviously someone, or some group, knows the donor's identity but is committed not to reveal it. How then does the appellation bring recognition? To some, a gift is more special if it is made quietly, without fanfare or public acclaim. The donor's pleasure is in his or her knowledge of the good deed, not in wider expressions of recognition and gratitude. To others the condition is pragmatic. Public disclosure heightens awareness, raises expectations, makes one vulnerable to the next appeal—puts one's name on The List. And, grotesque as it may seem, the anonymous gift is regarded by some as the supreme act of self-indulgence; the most subtle, sophisticated, exclusive form of recognition that exists. The people who matter will know....

Education

Formal education is probably a neutral force, or more likely plays an ambivalent role, in the donations decision. The majority of the population educated to the compulsory level would receive little if any formal instruction in the humanistic needs of society and the role of the individual in financing those needs. Religious instruction *per se* is not taught in public schools (although it may be in private schools) nor would moral philosophy or ethical instruction be part of the formal core curriculum. Public and secondary education probably would not reform established humanistic values and the student's perception of duty for their delivery. Such is also likely true for those taking advanced technical training in community colleges or commercial schools.

University education may engender two opposing attitudes toward humanistic service in general and its financing in particular. With more education should come a greater appreciation of the human condition, man's needs and aspirations in the fields of health, welfare and culture. One's ap-

---

[16]From *They Passed This Way*, edited by Robert N. Shervill, published by The University of Western Ontario, centennial year 1978. Vesting the Order of Canada was a centennial gift by the federal government to the people of Canada.

preciation for arts and letters may be enhanced, which may lead to an awareness of financial needs and a favorable disposition to donate to cultural and
educational organizations. Higher education generally is associated with
upscale occupations—professionals, management, white-collar—which in
turn are associated with high incomes. Peer-group pressure within these occupations may influence the donations decision, either positively or
negatively.

Education itself may foster attitudes unfavorable to private-sector financing. The study of political philosophies such as socialism and communism
may influence one to accept the principles underlying Stage IV financing—
complete state responsibility. Educated people are more outspoken, more
analytical, more critical. They may question high fund-raising and administrative costs, use and misuse of funds, the relevance of the organization to
society, and so on.

Social mobility

Canada is a socially stratified society, perhaps less rigid than England, more
so than Japan. Sociologists refer to lower, middle and upper classes—then
subdivide the middle class into a lower and upper segment. One can move
horizontally within a class, as when a change of position or occupation does
not significantly alter one's income, prestige or status. Or vertically, which
results in an upward (or downward) change in absolute or relative rank—a
job promotion, marriage to a person of higher status, a move to a better
neighborhood.

In a closed or caste society, social status is predetermined on the basis of
race, sex, age, ethnicity, family background. In an open society, status is
earned by individual performance—skills, knowledge, education. Most societies, Canada included, are mixtures of each. Social mobility is reflected
in changes in occupation, income, wealth, power, prestige—changes
marked enough to effect a change in social class.

To some, the allure of upward social mobility is a compelling attraction.
To others, social positioning is of little consequence. It is the socially mobile
segment that may respond generously to charitable appeals provided the vehicle through which the contribution takes place satisfies a social style. An
established member of an upper class invites an acquaintance and his wife
to join his table at the annual $500-a-couple Beaux Arts Ball; one is invited
to be co-chairman of a high-profile, university fund drive, to share work and
honors with a socially prestigious community leader. The attraction may be

even greater if the linkage automatically gains publicity on the social page or on the list of benefactors, so one could be seen more widely in the right company.

Social acceptance

Even when one has achieved the desired social station, donations to particular charities may be regarded as essential to maintain social acceptance within the peer group, which may be formed along social, work, recreation, religious or artistic lines.

If one's peers are members of (or even attend!) a particular Roman Catholic or Anglican parish, or Jewish congregation, this constitutes a powerful incentive to do likewise. With membership would come a perceived financial obligation to contribute according to acceptable norms. For example, one's friends meet weekly to knit for the Christmas bazaar at the hospital. Or the social group may decide to patronize an emerging theatre troupe with a pledge and monthly *aprés théâtre* supper parties, so one conforms in order to belong. Powerful social motivations channeled into good causes.

Level Two motives range from the subtle to the obvious. They apply equally to rich and poor, capitalist and socialist, and raise money for all four categories of humanistic service from culture to welfare, education to health care. On a continuum of values ranging from altruistic to egoistic, they would tend to cluster at the right. There is a major element of self-interest contained in them all.

But it would be erroneous to conclude that all donations flow from the stimulus of a single motivating influence or, indeed, a set of influences from within the same level. The process is much more complex. We delve deeper and turn our attention now to Level One motives, those considered more selfless, thoughtful and noble.

Noblesse oblige

Although the expression has become proverbial it is not ancient. Duc de Levis first used the phrase as the title of a chapter in his book *Maximes, preceptes et reflexions*, published in Paris in 1825. Conduct befitting one's rank. Reminiscent of the code of chivalry? *Bushido*? St. Luke's reminder to those to whom much is given? Sadly, its use today evokes anger, suspicion, cynicism. The word implies condescension, conjuring an image of wealthy persons magnanimously opening their hoards to the less fortunate. Aristocratic arrogance.[17]

Unfortunate that the conduct of some men who equate possessions with privilege have debased a noble expression of privileged man's duty to mankind. The spirit of *noblesse oblige* applies to the professional hockey player who expresses "some responsibility to put something back into society,"[18] as equally as it describes the duty of those of high social status. It refers to the most enduring and endearing qualities of the true leader in whatever activity he engages. "The beginning of leadership," asserts Field Marshal The Viscount Montgomery of Alamein, "is a battle for the hearts and minds of men."

Tradition

Family tradition speaks to imparting to the family a life philosophy based on cherished values and fitting behavior. Like *noblesse oblige*, the expression often triggers unattractive imagery. In the minds of some, tradition recalls aristocratic duty, the haughty, disdainful conduct of the superior to the inferior.

Nonsense. The notion has as much relevance to families of humble origins and modest economic means as to those with aristocratic family trees and generations of great wealth.

In the context of this discussion family tradition refers to an attitude and behavior rooted in intelligent, responsible, long-term values, a realistic knowledge of one's capabilities and capacity. Responsibility for community. It is a notion more expansive than the local geographic area: actions that bespeak good manners, that recognize and respect the dignity of others; be-

---

[17]Such as this patronizing comment by the U.S. industrialist Andrew Carnegie in *Gospel of Wealth*: "The man of wealth becoming a trustee for his poorer brethren, bringing to their service his superior wisdom, his superior ability to administer, doing for them better than they could or would for themselves."

[18]New York Ranger Barry Beck from Vancouver, describing his work with wayward kids to sportswriter Arv Olson of the *Vancouver Sun*. Or the maturity of young Neil Peart, drummer and lyricist with the group Rush, in explaining his mixed feelings about doing a United Way benefit concert at Maple Leaf Gardens: "One likes to do a nice thing, but it is kind of embarrassing getting this attention and trying to explain it. We've done charity things before but always in private. This time, it's being treated like a big thing. It shouldn't be forgotten that everyone else is coming along, including the Gardens and the unions, and aren't getting any credit. It's the basic atavistic individualism that must not be forgotten, and that individual action is the root of all we do, including giving. We're giving because we enjoy giving."

havior worthy of the standards of those who preceded and a fitting example to those who follow. A tradition of sharing; a family that gives gifts, not makes donations.

Gifts made in the spirit of these traditions carry a special, lasting, multiplying quality. Because family tradition draws on the most intimate, compelling emotions, its power to influence both the quantity and quality of charitable donations should not be underestimated.

Power

Without question, a word that commands attention. Nothing has obsessed man and preoccupied men's minds more than the subject of power, its acquisition, its use and its abuse—with the possible exception of sex. It has been studied from every conceivable angle. Niccolo Machiavelli wrote *The Prince* in 1513, a book considered by some to be the definitive treatise on manipulative power, and advised, "He ought to pay attention to all these groups, mingle with them from time to time, and give them an example of his humanity and munificence, always upholding, however, the majesty of his dignity, which must never be allowed to fail in anything whatever."

Scholars have added other dimensions. Philosopher Friedrich Nietzsche in the late 19th century argued that the will of the conquering superman makes its own right. Pre-Second-World-War psychologist Alfred Adler suggested that power is the prime determinant of human personality, thus challenging Sigmund Freud's assertion that mankind preferred sex. Economist Adolph Berle dissected power into seven elements and examined its application in the economic, political, judicial and international spheres. And now Canadian author Peter Newman treats the subject in an entertaining vein as he writes about the Canadian establishment, the acquisitors, etc.

Power as applied to charitable giving is much more circumscribed in its application. The reference is to its use, by those who possess it, to effect positive humanistic action, to mobilize economic and political resources to relieve poverty, abolish ignorance, reduce bigotry, minimize suffering, enrich lives.

Moral philosophy, religion, humanism

"It is the duty of every confirmed person, after due preparation, to contribute regularly of his substance, as God shall prosper him, to the maintenance of the worship of God and the spread of the Gospel."

Anglicans read that injunction on the first and third Sundays of each month as they prepare for the service of holy communion. The message is similar throughout the Christian church: Blessed is he that considereth the poor and needy...bring an offering and come into His courts...it is more blessed to give than to receive....

For those who miss the written message there often is an oblique (or pointed) oral reminder from the pulpit that God loves a cheerful giver and that people have been known to burn in Hell for disobedience.[19] No rest for the wicked; the offering is collected in *open* plates passed from hand to hand, up and down the pews, gathering contributions in envelopes from the regulars, cash from the transients. Meanwhile, in the parish hall, the children learn parables that heighten their empathy, their sensitivity to others, their sense of responsibility and Christian duty. They, too, are encouraged to contribute some small share of their weekly allowance to support the work of their church—a coin in the mite box.

No force in society is more pervasive and powerful than religion in shaping man's philosophy, his feelings and behavior to mankind, his moral conscience, his benevolence. The Judeo-Christian philosophy is a *good* philosophy, remarkably unaltered after thousands of years, the governor of civilized behavior. Much money is raised in the name of the church. Today most is used for the maintenance of church fabric and for congregational activities. A relatively small proportion is spent in outreach, mission activities and on community services that extend the good works beyond parish boundaries—an inversion of the proportions of church expenditures in the Stage II society of Canada's foundation years.

Religious families are likely also to be generous families in causes unrelated to church affairs. And religious philosophy extends beyond the tithing of one's income. The Protestant tradition of personal service has added an incalculable resource to the humanistic delivery system in this country. Yet, one need not subscribe to a religious sect to embrace a moral philosophy, to practice humanism. Atheists and agnostics whose philosophy stems more from Mill than Moses may nonetheless have a keen sense of compassion and a generous disposition.

But not all religious vibrations are positive to philanthropy today; not all Christians and Jews are moved to generosity by a strong religious or moral philosophy. Many Canadians are only nominally attached to a formal religious denomination—baptised at birth, confirmed during adolescence, but

---

[19]Indeed, the Evangelical sects often use highly colorful imagery in interpreting the Gospel, and employ what some consider to be aggressive methods of raising funds.

otherwise uncommitted and unmoved by formal Christian philosophy. Some Christians may be repelled by the obvious opulence and grandeur of church architecture and dilute or refuse contributions because of the apparent contradiction between need and duty. Others hesitate because of the church's diminishing involvement in social welfare and humanistic programs.

But without doubt one would expect a strong correlation between the degree of religious commitment and the level of financial generosity to humanistic organizations.

Freedom

It was Somerset Maugham who said, "If a nation values anything more than freedom, it will lose its freedom; and the irony of it is that if it is comfort or money that it values more, it will lose that too." He may as well have substituted security for comfort to capture the contemporary challenge in financing the good life.

As Canada has moved more firmly into Stage IV, the nature of humanistic service has changed from a private good to a public good, from a valued, earned privilege to a common universal right. Is that not progress? Surely a nation that produces goods and services in such abundance ought to guarantee its citizens a share of that wealth, a healthy, comfortable lifestyle. But what is the nation? Who guarantees whom? How much is enough?

In earlier stages of the delivery of humanistic service, the answer was clearly the individual or clusters of individuals mobilizing their resources to provide for specific needs which were precise, definitive and immediate. There was broad, personal participation in the financing process, even though a large part of it could be considered voluntary.

Today, governments have taken over the role of identifying needs and norms in all categories of humanistic service: of planning for their provision, of collecting money for their implementation and maintenance, of monitoring their quality and quantity. Provincial health councils plan and coordinate health care, federal task forces assess cultural needs and recommend new directions. Understandable, since governments hold the purse strings and politicians are held accountable for public expenditures.

But deep in the minds of many Canadians lingers a healthy suspicion that concentration of power *has* the potential to stifle freedom of action, that educational institutions *can* be used for political propaganda, that dependence saps vitality. And so, many Canadians contribute money and time to hospitals, schools, girls' and boys' clubs, research institutes and cultural organizations, in order to retain a voice in setting policy, to ensure that quality of service is not compromised for political expediency, to preserve individual freedom.

Level One motives. Hardly the exciting stuff of contemporary bestsellers. They compare to Level Two as saving compares to spending—dull, conservative, even suspect; not showy, interesting, expansive. Both are essential to fiscal health. But saving must precede spending.

Such is the mental process of making donations, of giving gifts. In analyzing the detail we have exposed identifying impulses, but in doing so have torn apart things which belong together. Life's experiences are hardly so disjointed. Motives intertwine to prompt actions which are clearly diffuse in origin. Some gifts we make at Level One, some donations at Level Two. We move across levels at various stages of chronological life, economic and social well-being, and personal maturity.

Yet this is a useful conceptual model, and one is advised to analyze, before attempting to synthesize. We are almost prepared to test the validity of our hypotheses on hard, objective data, to test the usefulness and practicality of the theoretical framework in explaining contemporary donation behavior. But we have one more concept to scrutinize—a motive some consider the most worthy of all.

VI

Altruism

Altruism. Regard for others. Where ego seeks his own gain regardless of that of others, alter freely sacrifices his own interests in their favor. Where ego forms an attachment to another person as a means of strength for himself, alter's motives are pure. Where ego measures correspondent equivalence, alter eschews comparison. Where ego pursues self-interest to emptiness, alter approaches personal fulfillment. The standard of perfection in human behavior. Fundamental, familiar, mysterious, elusive.

Altruism finds expression beyond donating money to humanistic organizations, the giving of gifts. It encompasses gracious behavior in everyday life, how one regards and acts to family, friends, associates, neighbors, strangers, enemies—good manners. Altruistic behavior ultimately attains a state of mutuality which recognizes that alter and ego are inseparable elements, each being essential to the other's welfare, a partnership founded on respect, dignity, equality, harmony. Sharing to make others strong.

Ethics, the science of duty, has attracted man from the earliest days of recorded philosophical thought. Plato's dialogues of ethical behavior, duty, are still regarded as classics in identifying man's impulses for good and just behavior. Yet Plato did not speak of altruism. That notion evolved from the teachings of Jesus and the writings of the moral philosophers starting in the

17th century.[1] Millions of words have since been written on the subject, many calling forth admiration for both substance and form.

Perhaps the most beautiful elucidation of the essence of altruism is contained in a compact, lucid set of notes delivered as eight Ely Lectures in 1918 at the Union Theological Seminary in New York by George Herbert Palmer, professor of Ethics at Harvard. Professor Palmer's words, no more than 25,000, capture the spirit of altruism with clarity and extraordinary refinement. He spoke of the wholesome behavior of the altruistic man and reproduced a passage from the Eighth Discourse of Cardinal Newman's *Idea of a University* to portray the agreeable blending of all three varieties of altruism: manners, giving and mutuality.

The Cardinal describes a gentleman, but he might as easily be speaking of a gentlewoman. His thoughts and words cannot be improved.

> The true gentleman carefully avoids whatever may cause a jar or a jolt in the minds of those with whom he is cast: all clashing of opinion or collision of feeling, all restraint or suspicion or gloom or resentment, his great concern being to make every one at their ease and at home. He has his eyes on all his company: he is tender toward the bashful, gentle toward the distant, and merciful toward the absurd. He can recollect to whom he is speaking. He guards against unseasonable allusions or topics which may irritate. He is seldom prominent in conversation and never wearisome. He makes light of favors while he does them, and seems to be receiving when he is conferring. He never speaks of himself except when compelled, never defends himself by a mere retort; he has no ears for slander or gossip, is scrupulous in imputing motives to those who interfere with him, and interprets everything for the best. He is never mean or little in his disputes, never takes unfair advantage, never mistakes personalities or sharp sayings for arguments, or insinuates evil which he dare not say out. From a long-sighted prudence he observes the maxim of the ancient sage, that we should ever conduct ourselves toward our enemy as if he were one day to be our friend. He has too much sense to be affronted at insults, he is too well employed

---

[1] The notion of altruism has been with us for as long as one was willing to put other before self. It would appear that the word "altruism" was coined c. 1856 and is attributed to Auguste Comte (1798-1857), a French philosopher. Its root was probably the Latin *alter* (other). Comte, a disciple of David Hume and Immanuel Kant, is regarded as the father of modern sociology, a term he also invented. A fascinating theorist, he exemplified our notions of the egoism/altruism continuum. "Comte was a rather sombre, ungrateful, self-centred and egocentric personality but he compensated for this by his zeal for the welfare of humanity...."

to remember injuries, and too indulgent to bear malice. He is patient, forbearing, and resigned on philosophical principles: he submits to pain because it is inevitable, to bereavement because it is irreparable, and to death because it is destiny. If he engages in controversy of any kind, his disciplined intellect preserves him from the blundering discourtesy of better, perhaps, but less educated minds who, like blunt weapons, tear and hack instead of cutting clean, who mistake the point in argument, waste their strength on trifles, misconceive the adversary, and leave the question more involved than they found it.

Cardinal Newman conceived his ideal gentleman in 1852. What would he write today? The concept of morality and standards of ethical behavior change over time, reflecting in large measure the theories advanced by contemporary philosophers. In retrospect the diverging forces of altruism and egoism have undergone significant shifts in emphasis.

The Greeks conceived the notion of intellectual freedom and duty, and idealized a just and good society. During Roman rule, Christian morality evolved from the harsh justice of an eye for an eye to the more gentle persuasion of a God personified as a loving and forgiving being. Then, for the next thousand years during mankind's darkest age, the church suppressed individual ethical expression, repressed free will, and exalted eternal life, provided one conformed to church doctrine—a paradox, because the church was the prime force in the delivery of humanistic service.

Man regained his individuality and intellectual curiosity during the Renaissance, allowing him from that point on to explore freely the concepts of good and evil, selflessness and selfishness. Much of the early and enduring moral philosophy was written in Great Britain, some in France and Germany. A cadre of intellectuals espoused a new idealism about the possible good that mankind could achieve.

But first there were the moral skeptics. Thomas Hobbes (1588-1679) argued that in his natural state man is a brutal and self-seeking creature, an egoist, and that altruism is not a part of man's natural character.

For no man giveth, but with the intention of good to himself, because gift is voluntary; and of all voluntary acts the object is to every man his own good, of which if men see they shall be frustrated, there will be no beginning of benevolence or trust nor consequently of mutual help nor reconciliation of one man to another, and therefore they are to remain still in the condition of war.

Bernard de Mandeville (1670-1733), a Dutch physician who moved to London and became famous in England for his satirical and philosophical works, agreed. De Mandeville believed that men are motivated by vice and selfishness. Although men condemn the vices which give them their uneasy prosperity and comfort, "nevertheless material civilization is the product of vices gratified, *not* the work of virtue." All human actions are motivated by some self-interest such as desire for comfort or praise or pride. While the motives are egoistic, the results of the action are often beneficial and agreeable to man, producing the comforts of civilization. More hospitals, asserted de Mandeville, have been built by vanity than by virtue. Vintage Level-Two philanthropy.

Au contraire, argued his contemporary, John Locke (1632-1704), the first of the empirical idealists. Man is naturally good, and a reasonable social creature. He has the capacity and, indeed, the moral obligation to be altruistic.

> Every one, as he is bound to preserve himself and not to quit his station wilfully, so by the like reason, when his own preservation comes not in competition, ought he, as much as he can, to preserve the rest of mankind, and may not, unless it be to do justice to an offender, take away or impair the life, or what tends to the preservation of the life, the liberty, health, limb, or goods of another.

Jean-Jacques Rousseau (1712-1778), a Frenchman who wandered throughout Europe most of his life, expanded on Locke's theories. Man in his natural state is happy and good, it is natural to feel altruistic toward one's fellow man. Once basic needs are fulfilled, man feels natural pity for those in less fortunate circumstances. Rousseau argued that the ideal society progressed from emphasis on the individual to emphasis on the community. Together, the group works for the common goal of survival. Altruism is a natural state. But as society grows more complex it becomes increasingly self-interested, viz., 18th-century Europe. Society replaced natural order with an artificial intellectual order; society created greed and selfishness. Rousseau believed that freedom is necessary for the existence of natural man, when man loses his freedom he loses his humanity. It is only the free man who can realize the true goodness naturally inherent in mankind.

David Hume (1711-1776) added that ethical behavior is based on two principles: agreeableness and usefulness. Man is reasonable, but reason is always a slave to the passions. Sentiment is dominant in moral decisions. Reason is secondary and used for justification. Nothing can bestow more merit on any human creature than the sentiment of benevolence. And part of that merit arises from its tendency to promote the interests of our species and to bestow happiness on human society.

Most people recognize Adam Smith (1723-1790) as the modern world's first economist. Few appreciate that Smith was first a moral philosopher[2] who argued that man's moral decisions are based on a natural sympathy with other men: an act of altruism generates a good feeling for both giver and receiver. Before Smith gave the world the invisible hand that guides individual competitive economic activity into a general improvement of society, he bequeathed man an inner voice that judges his actions with others by generating a sentiment of moral approval or disapproval.

The last of the great idealists was Immanuel Kant (1724-1804), a German intellectual who asserted that no action can be absolutely good without the existence of a good will—no Machiavellian twist. Further, the good will, if it is absolute, will be characterized by a disposition to do good, one's duty, a natural part of human nature. Altruism, therefore, is not only good but a duty of mankind which is a universal law of nature.

Idealistic philosophy, the notion of innate altruism, was in vogue for almost 200 years. Then Jeremy Bentham (1748-1832), the first published ethical hedonist, challenged the world with his philosophy of utilitarianism. One hundred and eighty degrees. Man's nature is pleasure seeking. Man wishes to maximize pleasure and minimize pain; society should be founded on the principle of the greatest happiness for the greatest number. But altruism is still an agreeable action, according to Bentham, since it is influential in minimizing pain and providing happiness.

John Stuart Mill (1806-1873) published his enduring essay on personal freedom in 1859. *On Liberty* argued that every man has the right and freedom to do anything he desires as long as he does not infringe upon the rights of others. The social obligation of man is the principle of utilitarianism. Mill recognized two causes for human unhappiness: selfishness and lack of mental cultivation. The paradox of utilitarianism is that it naturally leads to selfishness. Mill felt that man must realize his social dependence and obligations through education and legislation. For Mill, altruism would be an obligation in a utilitarian society.

Utilitarianism was the natural forerunner of existentialism, a viewpoint that described the ineffable nature of the world and the volition of man. God is dead, declared Friedrich Nietzsche (1844-1900) from Germany in *Also Sprach Zarathustra*. Indeed, echoed a receptive atheistic audience, tired of or withdrawn from traditional religious philosophy. Nietzsche asserted that

[2]Smith wrote *An Inquiry into the Nature and Causes of the Wealth of Nations* in 1776 when he was 53 years old. He wrote his *Theory of Sentiments* at the more romantic age of 28.

modern man must live by the principle of the overman or superman, that man alone controls his life and destiny, and the only standard is the one he makes for himself.

Nietzsche's followers, the modern French philosophers Jean-Paul Sartre and Albert Camus, retained his theme but were a trifle more compromising. "Man is nothing else but that which he makes of himself," declared Sartre. Man determines the world alone, there is no God or other determinant except mankind. Man is totally free and responsible for his actions, but this burden of responsibility makes it a terrible freedom. There is no moral obligation for man except his own humanity. Camus went further. He suggested that man could avoid the moral emptiness of existentialism through humanism. Creeping altruism?

The German and French schools stimulated a wave of post-Second-World-War North American pop-philosophy, variations of the utilitarian-existential theme. Modern egoists have been variously described as the "me" generation, the acquisitors, and so on. The western world has now endured 200 years of egoistic philosophy to balance the idealistic altruism of the previous two centuries.

We cannot abandon altruism without a word on the contribution of modern psychologists. In his book *Altruism, Socialization and Society*, J. Philippe Rushton[3] views altruism as an essential ingredient for the development and, indeed, the survival of our society. In a very carefully documented thesis, Rushton draws on a growing professional literature to illustrate how pervasive is altruism in human society and how man responds to altruistic reinforcement. "Rather than being a selfish and aggressive species as is so often depicted," Rushton begins, "we might better be characterized as helpful, cooperative, empathic, loving, kind and considerate."

How did, or do, humans become altruistic? Is the sentiment innate or learned? Biological or sociological? Rushton summarizes the psychological literature to support a biological connection—genetics, natural selection, survival of the fittest.

Darwin's theories of natural selection postulate that genetic endowments that occur by chance and increase the "fitness" of individuals are more likely to be handed down in genes to offspring than genetic characteristics

---

[3] My colleague, J. Philippe Rushton, a professor of psychology at The University of Western Ontario, has pursued an active and productive research interest in the field of altruism since graduating with a Ph.D. from the London School of Economics and Political Science in 1973.

that also occur by chance but decrease fitness. In animals, altruism manifests itself in parental care, mutual defence, rescue behavior, cooperation in hunting, food sharing and empathy. As man moved from the hunter (nomadic) to the hunter-gatherer (semi-nomadic) to the agrarian (stationary) some 10,000 years ago, the need for cooperation and consideration for others superseded aggression and selfishness. One cooperated or one died out. The fit survived.

Here is Rushton's hypothesis:

We might speculate that in order to survive, humans had to repress their immediate desires to gratify their own individuality. They had to integrate their behavior with that of their society. Along with cooperation might well have come group loyalty, altruism and a range of related phenomena.

With the increasing complexity of social organization would have come the social rules necessary to keep under control the individual's personal drives and emotions concerning jealousy, fear, sex, aggression and food. Indeed, such rules were actually able to suppress such powerful urges as sex. Thus, humans became religious, obedient to rules, and capable of abstract theorizing about their nature and the society of which they were a part. Humans had created a society in which they were interdependent on others. They had created a society in which *altruism*, in the widest sense of that term (i.e., regard for others) was a *sine qua non* of existence. Altruism and society both arose out of evolutionary necessity, as much as did any killer instincts.

Rushton favors social-learning theories over the biological hypothesis, although the latter is undergoing intensive examination by research psychologists. Rushton describes the altruistic personality: studies done with children suggest that altruism increases with age; females may be slightly more altruistic than males; altruists behave consistently more honestly, persistently, and with greater self-control; they are likely to have an integrated personality, strong feelings of personal efficacy, well being and "integrity."

According to Rushton, one can learn to be altruistic. If children are reinforced for behaving generously, their generosity will increase. Most social behavior is learned by observation. Children emulate generous behavior in others; on the other hand, if they have seen another person behaving selfishly, they will become more selfish themselves. Attractive role models have more impact than unattractive; successful people are more imitated than unsuccessful. Rushton believes the family is the primary socializer and underscores the importance of parental love (nurturance). Children learn appropriate rules of behavior in their early years.

Not surprisingly, perhaps, Rushton sees much societal behavior that is antagonistic to altruism. As divorce increases, the family has become a less effective socializer with the potential of producing under-socialized children. The mass media, especially television, often reinforce anti-social behavior through ubiquitous scenes of violence, force and abuse. The educational system in North America delicately ignores moral instruction so as not to offend religious freedom, and often produces young adults with no standards against which to judge ethical behavior.

Confusing, complicated, contradictory. Yet it is all relevant to understanding the process of donating, of giving, of serving. We have avoided the urgent, pointed questions posed in the Prologue. The digression was necessary. A process so complex as recognizing humanistic service cannot be described with a few tables and graphs; nor can the motives for its financing be analyzed simply by processing data rigorously through conventional formulae and equations. All that is necessary—but much more was required. The framework for analysis is now in place. We have drawn together common strains from an extraordinarily diverse set of disciplines into a surprisingly cohesive, consistent and recurring theme.

Mankind has an innate desire to grow, to achieve, to enjoy the fruits of the good life. As he prospers, man takes more for granted; specialization causes his withdrawal from active participation in providing for his family's health care, education or cultural growth. His concern and care for his fellow man becomes more remote, a function more efficiently performed by the professionals. He becomes more self-centred, more selfish; yet he is also selfless and often generous. Modern man suffers humanistic ambivalence, the classical tug of war between the forces of egoism and altruism.

Our questions can now be phrased more precisely. We can select data that are relevant and discard the rest with some confidence.

Book Two

...much is required

The billion-dollar touch

How to expand or even sustain revenues? That question preoccupies finance committees and boards of directors of humanistic organizations from St. John's to Victoria as the humanistic sector charts its financial course through a decade of austerity. The mood of fiscal conservatism, fashionable in the western world in the mid-eighties, has reinforced management's plea for spending restraint in hospitals, universities, art galleries and the like.

But the struggle to balance budgets continues. The main provider—government—is a courteous listener to budget appeals but, even if it is willing to increase the flow, it simply does not have the money. Recessions devastate tax revenues; government borrowing is increasingly expensive and is not as popular as it used to be. More and more frequently, governments are unsympathetic to demands for more humanistic spending. Politicians sense the mood of the public—economy—and reflect it first in speeches, next in behavior and finally in policies.

In the west today, voices call for a return to the private sector, most strongly in the United States. President Reagan wistfully asks individual and corporate America to fill the void of resources in the humanistic sector left by the forced withdrawal of funds by federal, state and local governments.

Former Prime Minister Pierre Trudeau, Ontario Education Minister Bette Stephenson—even would-be politicians—have eulogized the valued role of the volunteer in Canada's social and economic fabric. More than one federal and provincial ministry is actively formulating policies to support, encourage, even prod the private sector into action.

Are Canadians ready to respond? Let us examine some facts.

CHAPTER **VII**

Families, households and individuals

Canadian families, households and individuals donated $2 billion in cash to humanistic organizations in 1980. Give or take a few dollars, donations averaged $80 per person, $300 per family,[1] that year. It is a sizable sum. It exceeded the entire tax revenue of the Province of Manitoba, equalled the total cost of education in the four Atlantic provinces, and was only slightly less than sales of the T. Eaton Co. It was 10 times larger than the amount contributed by corporations, 20 times that given by foundations. But it was a small fraction of total humanistic expenditures of more than $70 billion in 1980, most of which was paid by governments; it was an even smaller fraction when compared with the family incomes from which the contributions were made, incomes that averaged $25,000 that year. And voluntary donations are in decline.

The decline does not show in donation aggregates; existing sketchy information suggests a year-to-year growth in total nominal dollars. It *does* show when family donations are deflated to real per-capita terms and when total donations are compared with total humanistic expenditures over time, with total family income, or other measures of capacity to give.

---

[1]The terms "family" and "household" are used interchangeably in this discussion. The latter concept may indeed be an increasing lifestyle; four per cent of the respondents to our national survey of Canadians in 1982 checked "live in" arrangements as their marital status. The expression wasn't even acknowledged in the 1976 census.

Our generation of Canadians is relatively less generous than the last. Why? This chapter, and the next, examines the evidence that documents the decline, and analyzes various factors that determine the level of individual generosity. Since all donations, whether made by families, corporations or foundations, are based on decisions made by individuals, the conclusions are fundamental to the discussion that follows.

It is only in recent years that the topics of charitable donations, fund raising, volunteerism and the humanistic sector have aroused even mild interest. Canadian literature is almost devoid of listings under any of those topical headings. For the most part, statistics on giving are sketchy, incomplete or non-existent.

The best sources of national data derive from the statistical summary of all personal income tax returns published annually by Revenue Canada, and the decennial survey of family income and expenditure habits of Canadians, published occasionally by Statistics Canada. Because these statistics are tabulated and published for a wide range of purposes, both studies have major defects as sources of data for rigorous analysis of personal donations and the underlying factors that motivate people to give.

The taxation data, for example, list only those donations claimed as deductions for income tax purposes. Because tax laws concerning the deductibility of charitable donations have changed periodically since the end of the Second World War, the annual series is discontinuous. Annual comprehensive data for all donations made and claimed by Canadians are complete for 1946 through 1956. No donation statistics were reported for the years 1957 through 1960. Since 1961, the report tabulated only those donations claimed by taxpayers provided the amount exceeded $100 per taxpayer. Since an optional standard claim of $100 was introduced in 1957, no listing has since been required for donation claims of less than $100 per taxpayer.

So, while the amount reported by Revenue Canada is an accurate reflection of the total donations *claimed* for tax exemption in Canada, it understates the total amount of donations *made* by Canadians in each year since 1961.[2] Furthermore, tax returns are filed by individuals, not families, and

---

[2]On the other hand, there is evidence to suggest that the charitable donation claims reported by Revenue Canada may be an inaccurate and inflated reflection of actual donations made for the years up to the late 1960s. This results from donations claims in the Province of Quebec. In 1956, for example, Quebec filed 925,000 tax returns, approximately 24 per cent of all returns filed in Canada. On the other hand, the charitable donation claims from the Province of Quebec represented 59 per cent of the total claims of all Canadians. The claim per taxpayer in Quebec was $188 versus $39 for the rest of Canada.
(Cont'd)

it is impossible to merge the donations of a household or family unit or, indeed, to disaggregate the published statistics and to match donation patterns with various family characteristics.

The periodic family income and expenditure surveys compensate for some of the tax return deficiencies in reporting gifts and contributions. The amounts reported are family aggregates, and the most recent survey in 1978 separates donations made to religious organizations, other charitable organizations, money gifts and contributions to persons outside the spending unit (both inside and outside Canada), and the value of non-money gifts such as flowers, clothing, toys.

But the data are reported in broad aggregates by geographic region and income class only, impossible to disaggregate or analyze by the various social, economic, demographic and psychological factors presumed to influence the level of family charitable donations. Furthermore, the studies are published irregularly—until recently, roughly 10 years apart—so trends are difficult to establish.

My earlier work, *Financing Humanistic Service*, published in 1975, drew together what sketchy data did exist on charitable donations and supplemented the federal statistics with a small survey of the donation behavior of individuals gleaned from personal interviews and voluntary written questionnaires. On the strength of the analysis of available data from 1946 to 1970, I concluded that personal donations were in decline in Canada in real per capita terms. The evidence supporting that conclusion was reasonably convincing, but I could offer very little to explain why.

In the decade since that research was undertaken, much more interest has been shown in the subject of philanthropy in Canada and fund raising in particular. Individuals and organizations operating in both the non-profit

---

On March 21, 1961, *The Globe and Mail* published an article entitled, "Quebec clergy protests probe of tax claims" in which it stated "it has been estimated that the federal government could recover an amount as high as $75 million in the Province of Quebec as a result of closer examination of parish books...." The article spoke of "...income tax frauds by means of charity receipts." This sensitive issue was debated vigorously in the House of Commons for the next three years. In one diplomatic exchange in the House of June 22, 1964, Mr. McIlraith suggested, "There has been some question whether or not these claims for charitable donations were made due to a misunderstanding of the law or whether in fact the amount of money claimed as having been donated to charities was actually so donated."

By 1968, donation claims from Quebec had dropped dramatically to $43 million from $168 million in 1956. With still roughly 25 per cent of all Canadian taxpayers, Quebec donation claims dropped to 18 per cent of total Canadian claims. This represented $24 per taxpayer in 1968 in Quebec compared with $40 per taxpayer for the rest of Canada, a differential that has continued to this date.

and for-profit sectors have emerged "to meet the needs of the staffs and volunteers of charities and their professional advisors who are finding old methods of management and fund raising inadequate...."[3]

One of the first Canadians to devote his entire career first to fund raising and latterly to the gathering and disseminating of information on philanthropy is Allan Arlett of Toronto. A slight, bespectacled, intense and immensely helpful man, Arlett is executive director of the Canadian Centre for Philanthropy, which he and a small core of volunteer directors[4] founded in 1980 to encourage philanthropy through increased financial and voluntary support.

Although the field is rapidly becoming crowded with players, Arlett must be regarded as the coach of professional and volunteer fund raisers in this country. The man himself is ubiquitous—speeches, seminars, TV interviews, consultations, fund-raising promotions. And his Centre is a blizzard of activity—provider of a hotline-telephone and mail reference service, reference library, custom computer service; publisher of *The Philanthropist*, *The Canadian Directory to Foundations and Granting Agencies*, *Monthly Memo*, annual reports on giving in Canada; organizer of national conferences, workshops and seminars.

As well as from the Centre, helpful Canadian data on religious donations are published by the National Council of the Churches of Christ in the U.S.A., for example. But it, too, estimates donation aggregates, not linking the gift with a specific family for more penetrating analysis.

To begin to understand the donation decision-making process of individuals and families, we need facts and opinions drawn from individual family units, data that could be dissected, processed, analyzed, merged and synthesized into a plausible story. Anyone remotely acquainted with survey research is aware of the formidable problems and realistic limitations associated with the process: the phrasing of appropriate questions, design and testing of questionnaires, sample selection, distribution, collection, response bias, tabulation, processing, interpretation.

Canada's eight million household units are spread thinly over five vastly different regions. It is difficult and expensive to collect accurate data from a

---

[3]Preliminary Program, Third Annual Canadian National Conference on Philanthropy, November 9-12, 1982, Ontario Institute of Studies in Education, Toronto.

[4]John M. Hodgson, Q.C., chairman, Blake, Cassels, Graydon; C. Arthur Bond, The Physician's Services Incorporated Foundation; Ian Morrison, Canadian Association for Adult Education; Laurence C. Murray, Thorne Riddell.

truly representative sample of all Canadians. Indeed, even Statistics Canada with the professional and financial resources at its command refrains from conducting special-purpose family data surveys until the need is demonstrable and urgent. A national survey of donation habits?

Lacking such data, an investigator has had two alternatives. One is to design, test, revise, re-test and refine the perfect questionnaire, proselytize the need for a study, then wait until the survey could be conducted with scientific precision. The other is to set more modest goals: ask a relatively small sample of Canadian families a series of very personal questions about their donations of money and time to humanistic causes, and invite them to express their feelings on the process of voluntary fund raising.

For this study, I chose the second alternative because it made sense three years ago, as it still does today. The donation model outlined in Chapter V was still in its embryonic state, many of the motives were difficult if not impossible to quantify, and much had to be learned about people's reaction to probing for such highly personal, intimate information. So little is known about the motives for donating money, the initial steps surely would be helpful to understanding.

Much of the material reported in this chapter derives from a national survey of 1,060 Canadian families (households) my team conducted in the early months of 1982 for the year 1981. The questionnaire contained 31 questions, covered four letter-sized pages and was distributed and collected by a corps of volunteers in each of Canada's 10 provinces. We invited participation from all major occupational groups in the community, as well as from retirees. It was a large and demanding organizational challenge and I acknowledge and commend the generosity and dedication of the dozens of volunteers who participated in the project.[5] They withstood a barrage of questions and criticisms from skeptical and reluctant respondents, and the all-too-frequent prodding of an anxious project director, but they delivered one completed questionnaire for every four they distributed—an extraordinarily high response rate.

The sample is biased. Few surveys are not. The Maritimes and Ontario are over-represented; Quebec and British Columbia, under-represented.

---

[5]The key organizer in each of the sampling locations across the country was as follows: Ralph D. More, St. John's, Nfld.; W.P. MacDougall, Charlottetown, P.E.I.; James J. White, Halifax, N.S.; Cheryl Dorion, Saint John, N.B.; Michel Gratton, Montreal, Que.; Professor Jacques Prefontaine, Sherbrooke, Que.; Rod Potter, Cobourg, Ont.; P. Ann Tomlinson, Port Hope, Ont.; Frank Bagatto, Sarnia, Ont.; Jack H. Eakins, Strathroy, Ont.; Claude Wilson, Winnipeg, Man.; R. Scott Rowand, Saskatoon, Sask.; Lyle F. Dunkley, Calgary, Alta.; Jack Range, Vancouver, B.C.

The level of educational attainment is much higher than the population as a whole. Roman Catholics are under-represented; Anglicans and United Church adherents, over-represented. Professionals and managers in the sample account for more than twice the proportion of that occupational grouping in the total work force; blue-collar workers, less than half. And Canadians with Anglo-Saxon heritage are over-sampled while Canadians of French origin are under-sampled. Average reported income and wealth are correspondingly higher than the Canadian norm. As a result, total sample averages do not reflect the responses of the average Canadian family in 1981.

We suspect also that respondents were biased toward generosity. Completing the questionnaire, probably a 15-minute exercise, was in itself an act of altruism, a voluntary, unrewarded gesture. The same generous nature likely would be reflected in family habits of voluntary donations. But even allowing for that self-selection bias, we suspect that many respondents overstated or, more politely, rounded up the amounts they claimed to donate to charitable organizations, even though the questionnaire was anonymous and confidential.[6]

For instance, the participation rates—those families donating more than $100 in 1981—were substantially higher for sample families compared with known participation rates from taxation data, even adjusting for increases resulting from family merging and the one-year lag. This was noticeable at all income levels, across occupation groups, and so on. Furthermore, from write-in comments, we know that some respondents listed donations as $100 while admitting that "what I give and what I claim for taxes are two different things."

So be it. The sample bias will not hamper the thrust of this analysis nor inhibit the nature of the conclusions we are able to draw. To the hard, objective, statistical facts, and the data from the questionnaires, we have added softer information from a decade of formal and informal discussions with fund raisers, fund givers and fund receivers, and a year's clippings from seven daily newspapers across Canada.[7] To it all, we have brought a degree

---

[6]This was, and remains, a curious and revealing phenomenon. In literally hundreds of formal and informal interviews with Canadians in all walks of life, I have encountered only a handful who admitted candidly that they donated nothing to charitable organizations. Most implied that they considered themselves generous, expressed some obligation to contribute to good causes, or some similar sentiment. Yet when one matches the quality of that response with donation participation rates as shown in taxation statistics, the discrepancy is too wide to be caused by chance alone.

[7]Halifax *Chronicle-Herald*, *Le Devoir*, *Globe and Mail*, London *Free Press*, Portage la Prairie *Daily Graphic*, Calgary *Herald* and Vancouver *Sun*.

of personal concern for and involvement in the issues, and a generous infusion of common sense in drawing conclusions and personal observations.

The first, and indisputable, conclusion is that personal donations are in
decline.[8]

The decline had not begun as early as the outbreak of the Second World
War when Canada was still at Stage III delivery of humanistic service, and
was not even in place by the mid-1950s as welfare services expanded more
deeply into Stage IV. It probably began during the sixties as education—
then health care and culture—gained the attention of the public sector and
has accelerated in the seventies and eighties as Canada moves inexorably towards Stage IV in all sectors of humanistic service.

FAMILY DONATIONS

	Donations per family (real dollars) $	Donations/ family income Percentage
1937	49.11	0.012
1947	65.96	0.012
1957	86.01	0.013
1969	85.83	0.010
1978	75.67	0.007

Source: Derived from Family Expenditure Series, Statistics Canada.

In national aggregate terms, the 1980 total of $2 billion[9] is the only au-
thoritative estimate of total individual donations in Canada since 1956 when

[8]A conclusion apparently not shared by the Department of Finance in Ottawa. An internal document
dated June 1984 prepared by the Tax Policy and Legislation Branch concludes that "none of the data
sources supply any convincing evidence of any decline in the real giving per individual." The paper
dismisses Statistics Canada data which show a decline in real donations per family since 1957 as "not
statistically, significantly different."

[9]This is the first comprehensive analysis of the financial statements of registered Canadian charitable
organizations undertaken by Statistics Canada, and it is immensely helpful as a benchmark for veri-
fication of other donations estimates. For instance, in 1980 charitable donation claims by all Canadian
taxpayers amounted to $1.05 billion, 50 per cent of the total reported as received by charitable orga-
nizations. On this basis, 50 per cent of personal donations are made without claims for tax benefit,
providing us with a yield ratio of two—that is to say, total donations equal two times the amount claimed
for income tax purposes.

total donation claims reached $284 million.[10] We are therefore unable to verify by comparable statistics, over time, the trends suggested in the decennial family income estimates. For the 11 consecutive years 1946 through 1956, for which comprehensive donations claims are available, the conclusions are consistent—per capita donations in constant dollars increased from $11 in 1946 to $26 in 1956.

How did aggregate personal donations respond to swings in the business cycle during that early post-war period? Were donations sensitive to downturns in the economy? Or was total Canadian generosity unaffected by economic recessions that reduced personal incomes? There were two business cycles during the 11-year period ended in 1956—strong economic growth from the end of the war until the recession of 1951, a brief recovery, then another recession in 1953-54.

The year-to-year growth pattern of aggregate personal donations exhibited some interesting characteristics over those economic cycles. From 1946 to 1949, total individual donations were virtually stable at $135 million in real terms, no doubt feeling the effects of pent-up post-war personal consumption. For the next seven years there was strong annual growth in total real donations, reaching highs of 22 per cent in 1952 and 1956, a low of nine per cent in 1955.

Total real donations grew as strongly during the recessions of 1951 and 1953-54 as they did in the remaining years of economic growth, suggesting no synchronous relationship between cyclical economic declines and charitable donations in those years. Donations were unaffected by recessionary contractions in national incomes. Unfortunately, the relationship could not be observed during the recessions of 1957-58, 1960-61, 1974-75, 1979-80 and 1981-82, in order to lend more confidence to the conclusion.[11]

The trend that *is* observable over the past two decades is the sharp drop-off in both numbers and proportions of Canadians claiming deductions for charitable donations on their income tax returns—claims of over $100. In 1961, the first year that donations over $100 were tabulated, some 1.5 million Canadians made claims for tax exemption—25 per cent of all taxpayers.

---

[10]The figures are not directly comparable. The 1980 estimate is derived from an analysis of the revenues of all charitable organizations. The 1956 estimate is based on total claims for charitable donations by all Canadian taxpayers.

[11]There was strong growth in real donations claimed by taxpayers during the 1974-75 recession. Recall, however, that the series from 1961 onward is the sum of donation claims of $100 and greater.

By 1970, the number of claimants had dropped to 1.1 million—12 per cent of the total. In 1979, the number rose to 1.4 million—still 100,000 fewer Canadians than 18 years earlier and now representing only nine per cent of all Canadians filing tax returns. It rose once again in 1980 to 1.5 million, roughly 10 per cent of all taxpayers, back to the same number of claimants as 20 years earlier but a much smaller proportion of all taxpayers. About the same number claimed donations as were unemployed in the early 1980s.

That is a steep decline, but it understates the severity. The $100 donations minimum was not adjusted for the inflation of the past two decades. Had it been indexed, the equivalent donation cut-off would have been raised to $280 in 1980, eliminating a substantial proportion of the 1.5 million claimants.[12] For instance, the 1981 sample indicated that roughly one-third of all families donating more than $100 gave between $101 and $250. An indexed standard deduction would have eliminated perhaps half-a-million claimants in 1980, reducing the number to one million Canadians, one-third less than the number who claimed in 1961.

Part of the explanation for the drop-off can perhaps be explained by the realignment of donation claims in Quebec that took place in the 1960s. But, discounting that, the decline spread across all income, occupation, sex and regional classifications. One is struck, for instance, by the sharp (and, to some, alarming) drop in donations by upper-income Canadians, $50,000 and over, precisely the segment with the greatest capacity to give. Less than half these individuals (49 per cent) claimed donations in 1980, down from 51 per cent in 1979 and 78 per cent in 1970. The tendency held true for doctors, lawyers and investors, as well as salaried employees.

That then was the background and milieu for personal charitable giving in Canada at the beginning of the 1980s.

The national family survey for 1981 took a snapshot of the donation decision-making process for that one year. Before we table the prints, one further word on the overall characteristics of the sample families. The questionnaire was completed by the principal income earner in the family, almost one-third of whom were female. The biases toward upper-income, occupation and social status have already been noted and will cause no dif-

---

[12]Perhaps it would be preferable to express the inflationary impact on the real decline in value of the $100 standard deduction in lieu of donations, now claimed by 90 per cent of Canadian taxpayers. The equivalent inflation-adjusted deduction would have been less than $35 in 1980, barely the price of a good dinner for two.

ficulty, since sample size in the relevant categories in this discussion is large enough to establish relative relationships across categories.

As a point of reference for the ensuing discussion, the average total donations reported per family was $517 for 1981, representing 1.4 per cent of total family income, which averaged $35,900.[13] (Fifty-four per cent reported two or more incomes per family.) The distribution of donations was as follows: church—$287 (56 per cent), United Way—$36 (seven per cent), health-related—$56 (11 per cent), education-related—$50 (10 per cent), welfare-related—$29 (six per cent), culture-related—$17 (three per cent), all other categories—$42 (eight per cent). All but 12 per cent of families donated some amount. Forty-three per cent donated $100 or less. The distribution follows.

FAMILY DONATIONS, 1981
BY SIZE OF DONATION

Donations amount $	Families donating Percentage
0	12
1—49	7
50—99	7
100	17
101—250	18
251—500	18
501—999	9
1,000 +	12
	100

It is important to distinguish between the amount of donations and the degree or quality of the generosity. One family could donate a large amount but if the donation represented a small proportion of family income, it could be said to be relatively less generous than another family whose gift was small, but represented a larger share of income. Thus we refer to the quantity and quality of generosity. What proportion of family income did the respondents donate to charitable organizations?

[13]This compares with an average income for all Canadian families of $29,900 in 1981.

FAMILY DONATIONS, 1981
BY SHARE OF INCOME

Percentage of family income	Families donating Percentage
0	12
Up to 0.5	29
0.5— 1.0	24
1.0— 2.5	21
2.5— 5.0	7
5.0—10.0	4
10.0—20.0	2
Above 20.0	1
	100

The average family received 11 donations requests in 1981. Counting all donations to the church as one, they made five donations that year: half of them made between one and three; eight per cent made more than 10. They rejected six donations requests, although 28 per cent claimed to have turned no one down. The average family worked as a volunteer for 1.1 community organizations but 41 per cent worked for none (one per cent for more than five). They contributed an average of 77 hours of voluntary service, ranging from zero (41 per cent) to more than 250 (seven per cent).

By region, the vital statistics are as follows:

FAMILY DONATIONS BY REGION, 1981

	Atlantic	Quebec	Ontario	Prairies	B.C.
Families making donations—%	90	82	90	86	86
Family donations					
Religious	$195	$153	$296	$517	$338
Non-religious	185	124	212	332	291
TOTAL	380	277	508	849	629
Percentage of income	(1.2)	(0.9)	(1.6)	(1.5)	(1.6)
Personal service					
Hours	69	63	87	60	119
Organizations	1.0	1.0	1.2	1.2	1.3

This pattern, relatively high donations in the Prairie Provinces and British Columbia, lower in the Atlantic Provinces, and lowest of all in Quebec, is consistent with distributions based on taxation data for recent years.

And, finally, by broad occupational category:

FAMILY DONATIONS BY OCCUPATION OF PRINCIPAL WAGE EARNER, 1981

	Profes-sional	White Collar	Blue Collar	Retired
Donating more than $100	69%	47%	40%	76%
Family donations				
Religious	$447	$175	$136	$391
Non-religious	309	148	139	235
Total	$756	$323	$275	$626
Percentage of income	1.3	1.1	1.1	3.0
Personal service				
Hours	77	61	83	190
Organizations	1.3	0.9	0.9	1.6

This distribution also confirms the rankings based on an analysis of donations claimed for income tax purposes by various occupational groups in 1980. The five highest participating occupational classifications, taxpayers claiming $100 or more in donations, were all professional groups: self-employed accountants, doctors, dentists, lawyers and engineers. The lowest participators: unclassified occupation, the armed forces, unclassified employees, employees of business enterprises and fishermen.

So much for the overview. We can now examine much more carefully the factors identified earlier as influencing the level of charitable donations by individuals.

First, what role does ability to give—income level, family wealth and taxation—play in determining the quantity and quality of individual charitable donations?

Income

> I feel I have more than my share of income and good health.
> > Halifax engineer
> > Income—$37,500
> > Donations—$700

Too many people asking for money in a time when money is very tight in my family.

> Saskatoon laborer
> Income—$37,500
> Donations—NIL

Any way it is viewed, the income of Canadians is higher in the eighties than it was in the fifties, sixties or even seventies[14]—family or per capita, nominal or real, gross or disposable, before or after hidden taxes. Canadians enjoy economic prosperity surpassed by only a handful of nations in the world. We have earned and are enjoying the rewards of our industry, productivity and good fortune. That those rewards are unequally distributed across the population is a reality in all societies—capitalist, socialist or mixed. Anyway, the government looks after the needy among us from our taxes. And the more affluent families donate generously to good causes when they are asked. Do we?

	Lowest quintile	Middle quintile	Highest quintile
Disposable income:	$5,600	$14,700	$28,800
Non-religious donations:	$ 11	$ 26	$ 71
As percentage of income:	0.2	0.2	0.2

Those figures are for 1978. A decade earlier, upper-quintile families made non-religious donations equal to 0.5 per cent of income, more than twice the recent level. When religious donations are added to the total, the pattern is even more revealing. The lowest quintile donated 1.2 per cent of its income in 1978, compared with only half that proportion for all other quintile groups. The distribution across income classes was the same in 1969, but at a higher level of generosity, 1.7 per cent for quintile one, about one per cent for each of the remaining quintiles.

It follows from that distribution that the absolute burden of charitable donations is not distributed equally across population income-quintiles. The highest fifth of the population contributed 36 per cent of donations in 1978, the middle fifth gave 17 per cent, and the lowest gave 11 per cent. To have shared the burden equally, of course, each quintile should have carried 20 per cent of the total.

---

[14]Family income increased by about 24 per cent in the 1971-81 period, but 23 points of that increase occurred in the first half of the decade. The increase from 1976 to 1981 averaged $72 per family, about enough for a new pair of good shoes.

It is sometimes difficult to grasp the significance of the concept of equality or inequality. Inequality across classes is often conveniently measured by developing an index to show the degree of spread from perfect equality (where each 20 per cent segment received 20 per cent of the item being measured) to extreme inequality (where one of the five segments received it all). Perfect equality would measure zero on the index, the most extreme inequality would measure 160. On such an index, Canadian donation inequality measures 37.

How can that index be interpreted? (We shall resist, for the time being, making comparisons between the generosity of Canadians and other nationalities.) At first glance, an index of 37 when the range is from 0 to 160 must be considered a reasonably equal distribution of the absolute burden. But should the absolute burden of donations fall equally on upper and lower income groups? Isn't income (i.e., ability to give) distributed unequally? Of course it is—an inequality index of 47 for gross family income, 42 for disposable (after-tax) income. We find a higher degree of income inequality than donations inequality. The comparison provides succinct confirmation that the burden of total donations rests more heavily on lower income groups than their income proportion alone would suggest.

And so, we add to our earlier observations. The rich give the most money, the poor are relatively the most generous, and most Canadian income classes give the same proportion of their income to charitable organizations.

A similar pattern is evident in the national family survey for 1981.

FAMILY DONATIONS
BY SELECTED INCOME CLASSES, 1981

	Income class		
	$ 7,000–10,000	$15,000–25,000	Over $50,000
Donating more than $100	21%	43%	82%
Family donations			
Religious	$ 102	$ 188	$ 831
Non-religious	50	98	597
Total	$ 152	$ 286	$ 1,428
Percentage of income	1.8	1.4	1.6
Hours of personal service	107	81	76

Recalling our earlier discussion, where we argued that capacity for making donations increases relatively faster than given increases in income,[15] we might expect an increasing allocation of rising income going to donations. That expectation would be supported by the general principle of declining marginal utility, that the satisfaction or value to a person of spending or consuming additional units tends to decline in importance as spending or consumption increases.

It is apparent that Canadians regard other types of expenditures to be of a higher priority than donations in allocating their incremental disposable income. Spending that once was regarded as discretionary becomes necessary: a second car, a better stereo, heated pool, private school education, the condominium in Florida. Even saving in its many forms (stocks, bonds, RRSPs, etc.) may crowd out donations in the scale of allocative priorities.

That we must infer. What we can demonstrate with more confidence is the tendency for families to donate less as the number of dependent children increases—or, expressed another way, as the need for family consumption increases.

But first we must make a further technical detour to explain an important statistical technique, one that will recur throughout this discussion—multiple regression analysis. Most people use the notion of simple linear regression in everyday affairs: we observe that a family earning $20,000 donates $180; another family earning $30,000 donates $320, and another earning $40,000 donates $390. We conclude that donations are perfectly correlated with income—a coefficient of one.

But what if we also observe that the head of the first family has a primary school education and is only mildly religious, that the head of the second is a high school graduate and reasonably faithful to his religion, and that the head of the third is a college graduate and intensely religious. Assume also that both education and religion have some influence on donations behavior. All three variables move consistently with donations levels, but what is the relative importance of each in explaining the total change?

Multiple regression is a method of developing an equation which relates one variable (in this case donations) to one or more other independent or explanatory variables (in this case income, education and religion—motives developed in our donations model) so that the resulting combination of explanatory variables produces the smallest error between the historic, actual values and those estimated by the regression equation.

---

[15]Expenditures on necessities consume a decreasing proportion of income as one moves up the income scale.

In effect, the equation shows the contribution of each separate independent variable introduced, holding all other independent variables constant. Thus, we can estimate the separate contribution of income, education and religious commitment, provided we have enough observations or cases in the sample; we are able to quantify the different variables appropriately, and so on.

Multiple regression is a well-accepted tool of econometric analysis. And like any statistical technique, it has definite limitations. We shall report the results of our exhaustive regression analysis from time to time throughout this discussion but rely on them only when the results are consistently strong and statistically significant.

Regression equations often confirmed a negative relationship between family donations and the number of dependent children in the family unit. That is, donations declined as the number of dependent children increased. It held for models that predicted total family donations,[16] donations to the church and to the United Way. It was also strongly significant in a model that predicted the quality (or cost) of total family donations and donations to the church, quality expressed as the percentage of donations to total income. The result implies that the pool of income available for donations is sensitive to the size of the dependent family—that charity does indeed begin at home.

We can now draw some conclusions about the relationship of income and personal donations. First, family gross real income has increased significantly in the past generation, as has disposable income and discretionary income (income minus taxes and expenditures for what traditionally have been regarded as the necessities of life). Therefore, ability to give, as measured by family income, has expanded over time.

Second, while the pool of family income *potentially* available for donations has increased, the amount donated to charitable organizations has declined in both absolute and relative terms. Other personal expenditures have become more satisfying, more necessary, to families and individuals than gifts to humanistic institutions. The *perceived* pool of family funds available for donations presumably has not expanded. Or families consciously have decided against donating from the expanded pool.

Third, the level of generosity, as measured against family income, has declined sharply in the past two decades.

---

[16]In this formulation, family donations decreased by $90 for each additional dependent child. The coefficient for children was not statistically significant in the models of non-religious donations, but it had the correct sign.

Fourth, the size of family donations increases with income class.

Fifth, the proportion of family income allocated to donations is roughly the same across all income classes, except the lowest-income earners who donate a much higher proportion of their income,[17] primarily to religious organizations.

Sixth, within income classes the burden of donations falls unequally—some families are very generous donors, many give nothing.

Wealth

A lot of the people that inherited large sums of money are very sympathetic, but they never give anything away. I've found that out. I've watched them pretty carefully. Members of the second generation have a complex; they're ashamed of something. They're sometimes socialist, because they couldn't do it on their own, so they're trying to justify it. But they never give any of their own money away.

Bud McDougald, deceased
Toronto multi-millionaire[18]

The need does exist and we have a very good lifestyle. I feel that by making our donation ($200) we may have helped others, and we can afford it.

Winnipeg, net worth $22,500

The average Canadian family had a net worth of just under $50,000 in 1977: cash, investments, personal effects, equity in homes, businesses and the like. Considering inflation alone, that figure would be much higher today. In fact, our sample of Canadian families—albeit more prosperous than average—declared an average net worth of $130,000 in 1981: $25,000 in liquid assets such as cash, bank and savings deposits and certificates, bonds and stocks; $135,000 in all other assets such as the market value of homes, cottages, automobiles, pension plans; minus $30,000 in debts including mortgages, bank loans and charge-account balances.

Wealth tends to be distributed less equally than income—its coefficient of inequality was 49 in 1977 compared with 42 for income. Do those to whom

---

[17]The distinction between the absolute quantity of family donations and quality of giving, as measured in relation to income, is confirmed by our regression models. Family income level was a significant predictive variable in quantity models, explaining both religious and non-religious donations. It was *not* significant in quality models explaining the proportion of family income donated, meaning that income level was not a good predictor of proportionate generosity.

[18]As quoted by Peter C. Newman, *The Canadian Establishment* (Toronto: McClelland and Stewart, Bantam Books, 1975).

more wealth is given obey St. Paul's injunction? The evidence is mixed. It is necessary to distinguish between net worth represented by the value of real estate and other non-liquid assets, and wealth invested in bank deposits and marketable securities. We have found no systematic relationship between the size of non-liquid asset holdings and either the absolute or relative level of donations.

The same was true for the size of total family liabilities—families with large debts were neither more nor less generous than families with no debt. True, the amount of family donations tends to rise with the size of gross non-liquid asset holdings. But when the influence of other factors is removed—variables such as debt which tend to be closely related to net worth—there does not appear to be any significant connection between the size of donations and the value of fixed-asset holdings.

One's generosity tends not to be influenced by the nominal value of homes or personal possessions. Not altogether surprising, since most families probably are not conscious of growing wealth when it is represented in possessions which are used every day. Furthermore, that type of wealth usually has no cash return—one cannot measure its impact on monthly cash flows. In fact, it may be an increasing cash burden. It is probably ignored in assessing capacity to give.

Not so with liquid wealth. Donations, both religious and non-religious, tend to rise systematically with the size of family liquid-asset holdings. For instance, those with low holdings of liquid assets—up to $30,000—donated about one per cent of income; the middle group—$30,000 to $100,000—donated roughly two per cent; the highest group, closer to four per cent. That strong relationship between size of family donations and size of liquid-asset holdings was consistent and highly significant in explaining the absolute as well as relative size of total family donations, and particularly strong in predicting both the size and proportion of income allocated to non-religious appeals.[19]

We tend, surely, to feel more secure, more munificent, as our liquid portfolio grows. We recognize a growing capacity to give and tend to share the fruits of that growth through charitable donations, do we not? The bad news is that most Canadians do not have a portfolio of liquid assets or, if they do, it is of modest size,[20] and of negligible influence on the donation decision.

---

[19]Interestingly, liquid-asset holdings were not significant in models predicting donations to religious causes. This is explored fully in the next chapter.

[20]Six per cent of the national sample reported no liquid assets in 1981, 50 per cent reported between $1-10,000, and less than five per cent reported more than $100,000.

Taxation

My taxes are too damned high ($40,000). The government squanders it away on social programs of questionable benefit. I think that's enough of a donation.

> Port Hope physician
> Donations—$250

I would like to see a tax system so everyone would contribute to charitable appeals.

> Vancouver retiree
> Donations—$700

I think that I can afford to give more because I know what the taxing is. Tax laws are good for me. When it was 62 and 38 my generosity wasn't costing me very much. Would I give without the tax incentive? I might do some, but I don't know that I would do as much. In a sense it's like pre-paying your income tax.

> Toronto lawyer
> Donations—8% of income

I donate funds but do not ask for tax receipts.

> Port Hope recreation director
> Donations—$200

Giving makes a person feel as a part of the community, as well as a useful man.

> Winnipeg office worker
> Donations—$586

These sentiments, apparently in conflict, reveal the complexity, indeed the confusion, over the role of taxes in the donation decision process. In order to clarify, it is helpful to recall the historical evolution of financing humanistic service in Canada.

In Stages I and II, the period up to the early years of the 20th century, when individuals paid privately for humanistic service and made donations for services beyond their personal needs, public financing was much simpler than it is today. Governments did not intervene in the financing process by taxing the population so as to insure that the burden of financing humanistic care would be spread equitably throughout society. The process was voluntary. Adam Smith's inner voice and invisible hand combined to motivate and discipline individual action to achieve the collective social goal.

Indeed it is remarkable that until 1917—three years into the First World War—Canada's war effort, the largest humanistic endeavor undertaken by

Canadians to that time,[21] was financed largely through voluntary contributions to the Red Cross and the Patriotic Fund, not by taxes imposed on the population. Perhaps it was inevitable, human nature, that as the needs grew larger, the demands greater, and voluntary effort more strenuous, a growing number of Canadians would attempt to avoid participating, and understandable why the proponents of the Income War Tax Act often centred the debate in the House of Commons on the inequity of a system that would allow some who possessed ample means to escape from paying their fair share of a national obligation.

And so income taxes were imposed, first at a modest rate that was the same across classes; a proportional, not progressive, tax. Now the burden of financing the public welfare was seen to be distributed fairly throughout the population, every Canadian would contribute according to his means. What about those Canadians who paid their taxes and also made voluntary contributions to the Red Cross, Salvation Army, hospitals and other organizations serving the humanistic needs of Canadians? Should these contributions not be treated as if they were tax payments, and therefore deducted in full from the new income tax (a tax credit)?

The debates surrounding the imposition of the Income War Tax Act, some 65 years ago, highlight the core of the dilemma concerning taxation and donations that continues to this day.

A. K. Maclean summarized the arguments for a tax credit during second reading of the bill in committee. "I have had many representations that patriotic contributions would suffer very much if the contributors were not given credit for their contributions upon the tax and not upon the assessment.... If the tax results in a substantial diminution of the contributions to the fund, we shall create a burden which the state must take up." To prevent a heavy reduction in voluntary contributions "they ought to be applied in reduction of the tax."

No, replied the government, such liberal treatment would be tantamount to the government paying the entire cost of the donor's gift and it would deny the donor the merit he derived from financial sacrifice. It would work against the spirit of voluntary giving (not to mention what it would do to tax

---

[21]By June 1917 Canadians had contributed $40 million voluntarily to the war funds. Total federal expenditures for all purposes in 1913, the year immediately preceding the First World War, amounted to $112 million.

revenues). Instead, donations to recognized charities were allowed as deductions from gross income in arriving at the amount upon which the tax rate would apply.

Until 1929 there was no limit to the allowable donation deduction but that year it was capped at 10 per cent of income, allowing those who were more generous than that level to have the pleasure and pain that is derived from making a truly generous gift. It was the Canadian compromise. Voluntary donations would cost the donor something, but the government would subsidize part of the cost by recognizing the income deduction.

The principles governing donation deductibility established in the inaugural edition of the Income Tax Act have remained essentially unaltered to this date. A one-year carry-over of non-charitable donations was introduced in 1957, as was the $100 standard deduction in lieu of donation claims; the 10 per cent maximum was raised to 20 per cent in 1972; the carry-forward was extended to five years in 1982; the $100 standard deduction was removed effective in 1984.

Revenues earned through the new income war-tax gradually were diverted to permanent public commitments to humanistic service. The government declared humanistic service a public good, at first tacitly, then explicitly. As Canada moved through Stage III and well into Stage IV financing, the proportion of funds derived from voluntary donations has, of course, diminished to a relatively small proportion of the total financial requirement—in the order of three per cent over all. Taxes levied by all three tiers of government distribute the main burden involuntarily across the total population in a manner intended to be equitable to all.

In recent years, a growing proportion of government revenues has been derived from income taxes, as opposed to sales or consumption taxes. For example, income taxes represented roughly a quarter of total federal revenues as recently as 1966 but now account for more than 40 per cent. Since income taxes are levied at progressive rates—rates that increase with rising incomes—they tend to rest proportionately more heavily on upper-income than lower-income Canadians, an incidence that many view as fair since it recognizes the principle of taxing more heavily those whose ability to pay is greatest.

As humanistic service has become more entrenched in Stage IV and as more of the tax burden has been shifted to the most visible form of taxation, income tax, there has developed a growing linkage between the size of one's tax bill and the degree to which one perceives oneself as having fulfilled a commitment to contribute to the welfare of *others*. Taxes are a direct and valid substitution for voluntary donations and no appeal, whether at Level One or Level Two, will encourage this group to give.

The fact that income-after-tax has expanded or that public benefits have increased for all citizens, including those with high income, has little relevance in this thought progression: the visibly expanded tax burden represents total exoneration from further consideration of public responsibility. For them there is no reason, no motivation, to do more.

Indeed, many are irritated and resentful of the size of the forced contribution they are presently making. The Port Hope physician whose $40,000 in taxes was "enough of a donation" expresses their sentiment. This is classic Stage IV philosophy—the government is responsible. Judging from taxation statistics, people in this group must represent a growing proportion of Canadian society.

While some non-donors are philosophically opposed to voluntary donations, some members of that group no doubt could be motivated to donate, but only on condition that the donation be deducted in full against the taxes they would otherwise pay to the government—in other words, provided the donation was cost-free to the donor. If there was no additional cost, simply a redirection of taxes into a charity of the donor's choice, no doubt some could be persuaded to make the transfer. Donations of this type could clearly be described as Level Two transactions. They could hardly be viewed as gifts in the classical sense.

Another group views taxes as necessary for a civilized society. But they accept a personal responsibility to contribute beyond their legal obligation for the maintenance and enhancement of humanistic care. They are motivated by either Level One or Level Two forces and accept that the donation will have a cost beyond their tax burden. Some, such as the Toronto lawyer who was quoted at the beginning of this discussion, are fully aware of the additional after-tax cost but make donations because they are moved by external (Level Two) or inner (Level One) motives. As explored later, tax policies *may* influence the size of donations made by this group.

A final group, represented by the Port Hope recreation director and the Winnipeg office worker, contribute out of a sense of community responsibility or personal commitment. Level One motives. It is doubtful if they seriously consider the tax implications of their gifts. And improbable that income tax incentives would alter their donation behavior.

The income tax treatment of charitable donations complicates the understanding of one's ability to give money to charity, and may influence the size of the donation, but it does not in itself cause a positive or negative donation decision. When tax rates decline, we do not automatically seek out new charitable causes or increase the size of our ongoing donation to organizations in order to pass on the tax savings. Nor do we necessarily cut back on donations when income tax rates increase. We require a stimulus to give, whether it stems from Level Two or Level One motives, forces which may well be powerful enough to override consideration of the cost of the donation in monetary terms.

Tax policies, however, can play an important role in facilitating a positive and generous response for those who do donate. Tax treatment of charitable donations can be supportive and provide an incentive for generous giving, or act as an impediment in the decision-making process, to inhibit generosity.

This is true because in all but a small minority of cases a charitable donation costs the donor something. Donating $200 to the United Way, for example, requires one to write a cheque for that amount. Tax policies *may* redistribute part of the cost of the donation away from the donor to other Canadian taxpayers who do not make charitable donations. The process can be viewed as an equation where the costs of a donation equal the value or benefit of the gift to the receiving organization.

THE DONATION EQUATION

Donor cost			*equals*	Donee benefit
Donor share (100% to 50%)	plus	Non-donor subsidy (0% to 50%)		Value of donation (100%)

First, assume that donations are not tax deductible. The $200 donation to the United Way costs the donor $200 which equals the value of the donation to the beneficiary. Next, assume that donations are deductible against income for tax purposes, and the donor's marginal tax rate is 24 per cent, the lowest marginal rate in Ontario, reached when taxable income exceeds $2,000. The government effectively subsidizes the donation to the extent of $48, reducing the donor's share of the cost to $152. The United Way still receives the total donation of $200.

For the most heavily taxed donor (a 50 per cent rate reached at $53,000 of taxable income), the cost is split equally at $100 for both the donor and the government. But government subsidies deplete revenue that is replaced by effectively shifting the lost taxes from the donor who is given the tax exemption to taxpayers not qualifying for the reduction, the non-donor. The shifting can be horizontal, to non-donors in the same income category, or vertical, to non-donors in upper or lower-income groups.

Recall that about 90 per cent of Canadian taxpayers did not itemize and claim donations for tax exemptions during the years when the standard deduction of $100 was available to all taxpayers. For this group, the cost of making donations was equal to 100 per cent of the value of the donation—no subsidy.[22]

For most of the remaining 10 per cent of taxpayers, those claiming donations up to 20 per cent of income, the cost to the donor ranges from a high of 100 per cent for the lowest-income classes with no taxable income to 50 per cent for the highest-income earners. For these people, the subsidy for the United Way donation, for example, ranges from zero for lower-income taxpayers to $100 for those who pay the highest tax rates.

To a very small proportion of taxpayers who donate more than 20 per cent of their income, the cost to the donor of donations in excess of the 20 per cent limit is 100 per cent of their value. Revenue Canada does not publish the proportion of taxpayers claiming donations beyond the 20 per cent limit, but it would be significantly less than one per cent—the proportion was barely more than one per cent for the 1981 national sample of families known to be biased toward generous donors.

The 20 per cent limitation can be waived provided the taxpayer has what is affectionately called a Queen's Receipt. The Income Tax Act permits the full deduction from income for gifts to the Queen in the name of the federal or provincial governments, a deduction that can be spread over five years if desired. Cash gifts to Canada or the provinces qualify for Queen's Receipts.

And effective with the proclaiming of the Cultural Property Export and Import Act in 1977, an increasing number of non-cash gifts also have qualified for full deduction. The Cultural Property Act recognizes the desirability of retaining in Canada art objects and cultural property that reflect Canada's national heritage. To prevent such objects from being lost to Canadians through their sale abroad, provision is now made for a Cultural Property Export Review Board to establish a fair value "of objects of outstanding significance and national importance." Once approved, the Re-

---

[22]On the other hand, by claiming the blanket income deduction of $100 they receive a cash tax-benefit of from zero (if they paid no tax) to $50 (if they were taxed at the highest marginal rate). Since the standard deduction was unrelated to demonstrated donations participation, it can be ignored in this discussion. Furthermore, the standard deduction was withdrawn in 1984.

view Board issues a Cultural Property Income Tax certificate which, in the case of objects donated to a designated Canadian institution,[23] acts as the equivalent of a Queen's Receipt for income tax purposes.

Gifts that qualify under these cultural and heritage provisions are deductible against income for the full, certified value of the asset. Furthermore, the donor is exempt from any tax on capital gains that may have resulted in the disposition of the property.[24] Since the 20 per cent limitation does not apply, it is possible to reduce the donor's share of the cost of even large gifts to 50 per cent—effectively shifting half their cost.

For instance, assume a taxpayer with an income of $150,000 donated a cultural object having an approved value of $50,000 to a museum in Canada. The object had an original cost of $10,000. The full value of the donation could be deducted from income-reducing taxes by $25,000. No capital gain need be reported on the disposal—a positive cash flow in exchange for disposing of assets that often are non-liquid.

A relatively small number of donations are made via this route, but those that do qualify tend to be large—an average of $33,000 in 1982.[25] Certification is not automatic. The Review Board, under the chairmanship of R. Fraser Elliott, Q.C.,[26] met four times in 1982, considered 282 new applications for certification, rejected 11, and issued 271 tax certificates with a total value of $9 million. Two hundred and thirty-three of these certificates, with a value of $7.5 million, represented the value of cultural property donated to designated institutions. The remainder were for objects sold.

Anyone can immediately appreciate the attraction of Queen's Receipts for those interested primarily in tax-avoidance programs, just as one can ap-

---

[23]In 1982, there were 146 designated institutions and public authorities authorized to collect and preserve cultural property under the Cultural Property Act.

[24]In the case of certified cultural property that is sold, not donated, to a designated institution, the certificate exempts the seller from tax on taxable capital gains arising on its disposition.

[25]One family participating in the program is the Loebs of Toronto. Jules and Fay Loeb were pictured in the Toronto *Star* on December 27, 1982, showing University of Toronto President James Ham the Canadian art collection that the Loebs plan to donate to the university under the cultural property provisions over the following 10 years. The 200 works of art, which span three centuries, were estimated to be worth $6 million by a Loeb spokesman, an estimate dismissed as "ridiculous" by Robert Welsh, head of U. of T.'s fine art department. If it were valued at $6 million for tax purposes, the maximum potential tax saving would be $300,000 per year over the decade—shifting that much to nondonating taxpayers. The gift was not announced without controversy. Because the paintings will stay in the Loebs' Rosedale home, which will be used for teaching purposes, some neighbors expressed concern that increased traffic might threaten the residential ambiance of the neighborhood.

[26]Of Stikeman, Elliott, a Toronto law firm respected for its expertise in tax matters.

plaud the goal of preserving Canada's national heritage. Success of the program ultimately will rest on the fairness of the valuations placed on cultural property by the Review Board—a responsibility of heroic proportions. If the public perceives the program as a scheme for rich Canadians to avoid paying taxes that otherwise should be paid, then a potentially worthy program will be discredited. Great care must be taken to ensure that the program not be abused, that certificates be issued only for genuine, authentic cultural treasures, that market values be established in a fair and defensible manner, and that the process and awards be reported to the public in whose name the concessions and possessions were made. Anything short of full public disclosure, after the fact, will invite speculation of abuse and sow the seeds of public cynicism.[27]

As the tax law now stands, a minority of Canadians who are claiming-donors shift part of the cost of their donations to the non-contributing majority. But the shift takes place only if a donation is made. And the donation still costs the donor something, even after the subsidy. The absolute cost of an equivalent donation is less for a rich than a poor Canadian, since the subsidy to the rich taxpayer is greater. "Give and Take" would equalize the cash cost by allowing all income groups to deduct 50 per cent of their donations directly from taxes, making the subsidy equal across all income classes.

Since under this proposal there would be no change in the amount of the subsidy to upper-income Canadians, they would likely be indifferent to "Give and Take."[28] The sponsors expect that increasing the subsidy to lower-income classes would provide an incentive for them to increase donations, half the cost of which would be shifted to non-donating taxpayers.

Others argue for even more generous subsidies. Floyd S. Chalmers, former editor of *The Financial Post* and a prominent patron of the arts in Canada, would extend the benefit of the Queen's Receipt to anyone donat-

---

[27]The Federal Department of Communications issues an annual report of activities under the Cultural Property Export and Import Act. It contains valuable information on the process and activities of the Review Board. Unfortunately, it does not contain a tabulation of the cultural objects certified during the year, together with their appraised value for tax purposes.

[28]Of more significance to high-income donors was the reduction of marginal tax rates that took effect in 1982. The highest marginal rate dropped from about 65 per cent to 50 per cent, a change that has effectively reduced the subsidy as much as 15 percentage points on donations made by all taxpayers earning more than $53,000. Those donors who adjust the amount of their donations to an equivalent after-tax level might be expected to reduce the total amount of their giving. For example, a person who donated $10,000 in 1981 with a cost of $3,500 and a subsidy of $6,500 might reduce his donations to $7,000 in order to keep his expected cost at the same level ($3,500 plus the reduced subsidy of $3,500).

ing property and stocks to cultural organizations, or cash and property to foundations, and exempt the donor from any tax on capital gains that might result through valuing the property at fair market value.

According to Chalmers, ''I know of definite cases where these provisions would lead to very large gifts or bequests from well-to-do individuals anxious to give generous assistance to the arts and cultural life of Canada.'' The implication is that the potential donor is less anxious to give generous support to the arts without the tax incentive—an interesting insight.

A similar suggestion was made by Arthur Gelber, Q.C., in a submission to the Federal Cultural Policy Review Committee in March 1981. Gelber would not restrict the full deduction to donations to arts organizations but expand it to foundations devoted to any philanthropic, humanistic concern. He urged also that an appropriate mechanism be established to accept donations from the private sector, issue tax receipts, and then distribute the donations directly to qualified and deserving artists.

The proposals, the permutations and the possibilities are limitless. Each would shift part of the cost of the gift from the donor on the assumption that he or she would respond more generously to donation requests.

Do tax incentives work to stimulate generosity? Economists have attempted to approximate the magnitude of the effects of more liberalized tax treatment of charitable donations. Various studies in Canada and the United States demonstrate an historical response-ratio of from 0.6 to 1.2 of the change in ''price'' of donations (price measured as the percentage of the donor's share of the cost). Thus, a 10 per cent drop in the donor's share of the cost would be expected to yield from six to 12 per cent more in total donations for the whole economy, all things equal. Conversely, an increase in the donor's cost, such as occurred for high-income taxpayers whose marginal tax rates were reduced in 1982, would be expected to reduce donations by a similar ratio.

The estimates are based on highly sophisticated regression models and, particularly in the case of the Canadian studies,[29] model only the association

---

[29]See ''Economic Determinants of Individual Charitable Donations'' by R.D. Hood, S.A. Martin and L.S. Osberg in *Canadian Journal of Economics*, November 1977. That study estimated the price elasticity of Canadian donations in the region of 0.86, based on donation claims for the years 1968 through 1973. It also confirmed a negative time trend.

More recently, economics scholars revived an interest in charity, philanthropy and the process of giving. In the vanguard of this ''new economics of charity'' are A. Seldon, Gordon Tullock, Gary Becker, Thomas Ireland, David Johnson, Russell Roberts *et al.* in the U.S. and Cooper and Culyer in

(Cont'd)

of economic variables (the ability variables identified earlier: income, wealth and taxation) with historic donation behavior, using data expressed in highly aggregated form. But was the demonstrated association *caused* by the economic factors, or by Level Two or Level One stimuli that are not measured in the model? And what about those Canadians who make gifts without first measuring their economic cost?

As implied in the quotation from the lawyer that opened this discussion of taxation, some people are conscious of tax-shifting and take it into account in their donation decisions. To them, making donations is a way of diverting taxes, that otherwise would be paid to the government, into a cause of the donor's choosing—not the government's. The donation still costs the donor more than the taxes that are diverted, the donor's share of the cost, but presumably the benefits to the donor for making the donation are greater than or at least equal to the cost.

Donor benefit		*Donor cost*
Level Two rewards plus Level One rewards	$\geq$	Donor share

If the value of *quid pro quo*, or of benefits such as recognition or social acceptance, can be equated with the total value of the donation received and acknowledged by the donee, it would be reasonable to conclude that tax incentives might be employed by a donor to maximize his total benefits. If $1.00 buys $2.00 of benefit, the advantage is decidedly with the donor. A tax incentive that gave the donor even more leverage must surely have some potential synergistic appeal.

But how many people are as calculating when making donation decisions? One would expect that those making large donations would be most

---

Britain. They give short shrift to existing literature on altruism generated by sociologists, psychologists and other academic specialists. Seldon, for example, proclaims, "The new economic counterrevolution has liberated the noblest instincts of man...from its sociological confusion and shown it to be rational behavior that can be analyzed by micro-economics.... Economic analysis can help giving to be efficient...." (See *Journal of Social, Political and Economic Studies*, vol. 8, No. 1, Spring 1983).

The focus of the new economics, like the old, is rather narrow. It hypothesizes a "charity market" and assumes rational behavior by an economic man. We regard such a view of altruism as altogether too simplistic and inhibiting as a comprehensive framework for discussion.

likely to respond to the tax incentive. Yet almost two-thirds of the families who donated more than $1,000 in the 1981 sample had incomes of less than $50,000, where tax subsidies are lower. Almost half had assets of less than $100,000. Among the most generous donors, those donating more than 10 per cent of their income, more than 70 per cent had family incomes of less than $50,000; one-third had incomes between $15,000 and $25,000. And very few respondents who took the trouble to record their feelings towards charitable appeals, either positive or negative, mentioned taxation specifically or even government policies generally as having any major influence on their philanthropic thinking or actions.[30]

Income, wealth, taxation. Each, no doubt, influences the size of donations made by some donors. But apart from the obvious conclusion that large donations must stem from a large capacity to donate, there is little evidence to link generosity automatically and proportionately to expanded capacity.[31]

What then are the forces that motivate a positive decision?

[30]Less than two per cent of respondents claimed that their generosity was influenced directly or indirectly by government policies. A similar percentage cited taxation policies as affecting their feelings towards charitable appeals, split almost equally between those with negative and positive feelings towards tax levels and their influence on donations.

[31]Confirmed emphatically in regression models. Income was a highly significant variable in equations predicting the total dollars donated both to religious and non-religious organizations. It was *not* significant in quality models showing the percentage of generosity.

CHAPTER **VIII**

Motives

No period of history has ever been great or ever can be that does not act on some sort of high, idealistic motives, and idealism in our time has been shoved aside, and we are paying the penalty for it.

Alfred North Whitehead (1861-1947)
British philosopher/mathematician

That which moves the will. Motives turn good intentions into deeds, ambivalence into action. No donation is made without them. But is it necessary for the donor's motives to be on Level One—the idealism that Whitehead asserts is the *sine qua non* of a great society? Does a nation have to be great to get the job done? Money is money. Why question one's motives for giving? Doesn't the end justify the means? If the cause is worthy, isn't the motive for contributing to it an irrelevant, even impertinent consideration? And who is to presume to judge the quality of another's motives?

This is indeed sensitive territory. Yet we need not impugn another's motives to understand them. And without understanding we are unable to judge the degree to which there is opportunity for change, for growth, for betterment.

This chapter focuses on the 13 motives identified earlier as having an influence on the donation decision. It probes their importance, the degree to which they affect the decision to donate and determine the size of the contribution. The discussion concludes in the next chapter with an examination of fund raising: how the professionals, and amateurs, conduct fund-raising campaigns to identify and collect the millions—billions—of dollars donated each year.

First, the Level Two motives, those that emanate outside the individual or that can be linked with biological or social forces.

Ethnicity

> Simplement, que je n'y crois pas. La charité commence chez soi, avec sa famille. On prend soin de sa famille avant tout.
>
> Sherbrooke journalist
> Donations—nil[1]

> I have a family to support in India who are not eligible for tax deductions.
>
> Sarnia engineer
> Donations—unspecified

> On paie deja beaucoup d'impôt pour les bien-être et autres et ce sont les citoyens les moins productif. De plus ils sont ingrat, demande de plus en plus, ne respecte ni les lois ni les gens ou la propriété.
>
> Sherbrooke policeman
> Donations—$100[1]

The historical accident now referred to as the French Fact has left a legacy that continues to shape the donations behavior of our French-Canadian brethren. It is difficult to separate the ethnic from the geographic because much of the enduring influence of New France is confined to the Province of Quebec and, to a lesser extent, New Brunswick.

From the time of the aristocratic welfare state, the Roman Catholic Church assumed almost total control over the administration of humanistic institutions: hospitals, schools, orphanages, and so on. They were professionally managed by religious orders with little opportunity for personal involvement, or commitment, on the part of the people. French Canadians

---

[1]"Simply that I don't believe in them. Charity begins at home with your family. You take care of your family before anything else."

"We already pay a lot of income tax for the welfare people and others and they are the ones who are less productive. In addition, they are selfish, demand more and more, respect neither laws, people nor belongings."

grew up with little tradition of belonging to voluntary organizations. Voluntary work was largely the outlet of the middle class, and French Canadians were mostly farmers or laborers who could not afford the luxury of free time. Many were literally unable to donate money to charitable causes, and the structure of Quebec society exerted little social pressure to contribute. Family ties were strong. Supporting members of the extended family was seen as enough of a charitable contribution.

That thinking still exists today. Michel Roquet, campaign coordinator for Centraide, Montreal's United Way, claims that "the problem in the francophone sector is that they still believe the (Roman Catholic) Church takes care of everything, even though no one goes any more or gives it any money."

Indeed, Quebecers are less generous to religious organizations than Canadians in other regions of the country, but the discrepancy also exists for non-religious donations. Understandably. The infrastructure of non-religious humanistic organizations in La Belle Province is decidedly less sophisticated than elsewhere. For instance, in 1980 Ontario residents could choose to support more than 6,600 non-religious voluntary organizations— 0.8 per 1,000 of population. In Quebec, there were 0.4 organizations per 1,000—half the number. Perhaps then it is understandable why the level of per capita contributions to hospitals, health and educational institutions is sharply lower in Quebec than in Ontario.[2]

But Quebec is not all francophone and all francophone Canadians do not live there. Is the pattern similar for those Canadians with French heritage? Yes, based on the 1981 sample of families. Francophone families on average contributed 0.9 per cent of their income, one-third less than the Canadian average. Religious donations were sharply lower for francophones, but the reduction was also marginally apparent in non-religious donations.

If the French Canadians have retained old habits, is the Anglo-Saxon tradition of voluntary involvement, introduced by the British settlers, still in evidence? It may well have weakened somewhat. Anglo-Saxons donated an average of 1.6 per cent of income in 1981, only slightly more than the average for the whole sample. Neither were they appreciably more generous with the time they contributed in volunteer service, and they joined about the same number of organizations. Anglo-Saxons did not appear systematically more generous than non-Anglo-Saxons in regression models predicting the

---

[2]This conclusion is readily apparent from examination of donation aggregates. The variable for Quebec residents was weakly significant in the regression model for non-religious donations.

size of family donations. However, in a model predicting the proportion of income donated to the church, Anglo-Saxons did register as more generous—a positive coefficient that was statistically significant.

The evidence is spotty for Canadians of other ethnic origins, first because of sample bias and, second, because the sample size for these groups is so small. There is evidence that Canadians with south-European roots tended to be noticeably less generous, 0.5 per cent of income. Those with north and east-European and Asian roots reported roughly the same levels of generosity as the average for the sample.

Those not born in Canada reported much lower donations than native-born Canadians—1.1 per cent of income compared with 1.5 per cent. But the difference was entirely in reduced religious donations. The proportion of income allocated to reported non-religious contributions was the same. Had support to family abroad been reported as a donation, non-religious contributions may well have been higher for foreign-born Canadians.

In Chapter IV, I described the marked degree to which the many ethnic strains that comprise the Canadian population have retained a decidedly distinct identity, rather than merging and blending into a uniquely Canadian character, a pattern I described as a collage rather than a mosaic. I went on to argue that ethnic origin could be a strong, positive force in channeling donations into causes closely identified with one's cultural group. But because of the retention of sharp ethnic distinctions within Canada's collage, new Canadians may be slower to accept financial responsibility for supporting broadly based community causes.[3]

My data can neither prove nor disprove this hypothesis since the respondents were not asked to identify or give a description of the donee. Nor was I able to test whether immigrants from Stage IV countries demonstrated less voluntary generosity than those from countries with earlier stages of financing. These are interesting questions, and profoundly important in planning financing policies and fund-raising strategies, since the ethnic mixture in Canada continues to diffuse the English/French dominance. The research should be undertaken.

On the basis of the evidence, such as it is today, we conclude that ethnicity is indeed a potentially strong motive for giving, or not giving. So strong in fact that it would likely override concerns of tax deductibility for those impelled to contribute and outweigh the potential appeal of tax incentives as

---

[3]How long does it take for new Canadians, regardless of income class, to be asked to join fund-raising committees such as the United Way? To appear on a list of Art Patrons?

an inducement for expanded generosity for those not so moved.

Transaction

Political potential!

> Ontario MPP
> Donations—$2,000

We almost lost our son in a brain tumor operation.

> Port Hope welder
> Donations—$551

Someday you may be on the receiving end.

> Newfoundland X-ray technician
> Donations—$300

Whether it is in gratitude, in payment for services rendered, or an investment for the future, the donor gives money to charitable organizations because he or she has received, or expects to receive, an equivalent return.

One obvious type of transaction takes place when celebrities or political figures lend their presence to a gala event and exchange their appeal (in attracting people to an auction, fund-raising dinner, or what-have-you) for publicity and contacts. We clipped 26 newspaper articles documenting this type of charitable transaction, ranging from a $250-a-head production of *Evita* in aid of Mount Sinai Hospital, to a $175-per-person gala evening to honor Karen Kain, Canada's prima ballerina, raising funds for the Kidney Foundation of Canada.

Whatever the motive, politicians in particular are generous in support of charitable organizations. A sampling of 25 members of Parliament determined that they donated an average of $2,300 in 1981, almost four per cent of their income which averaged $58,000.[4] One-third went to their churches and the rest was spread around rather equally, cultural organizations receiving the largest share at 18 per cent. Another sample of 29 members of the Legislature of Ontario confirmed the findings. This group donated an average of $1,300, about three per cent of their income which averaged

---

[4]At a marginal tax rate of 50 per cent, the M.P. was out of pocket less than $1,200 for the $2,300 in donations. Like other high-income taxpayers, M.P.s receive the maximum donation subsidy. Referring back to the cost-benefit equation, charitable donations by politicians can produce benefits in exposure, recognition and goodwill, potentially equal to many times their out-of-pocket cost. In addition, the donations may return Level One rewards, making the total package of benefits an attractive transaction.

$44,000. Two-thirds gave more than 10 donations, again with amounts distributed prudently—one-third to the church and one-fifth to unspecified causes not classified under the four conventional categories of humanistic service. It was not exactly a tithe.

And possibly not as punishing as one might have assumed from the comments of London, Ont., politicians in July 1981, soon after passage of the controversial pay bill for federal members of Parliament. ''You don't know my expenses,'' lamented Charlie Turner, M.P. for London East, to reporter Don Gibb of the *London Free Press*. ''A donation to this and to that. We're the first ones they hit. I go to a church bazaar. They meet you with a bunch of tickets and before you get out of there, it's 25 bucks. Some weeks I give over $200 away to charities, the unseen things you guys don't know about. I'd be far better off to have stayed on the railroad.'' His colleague Garnet Bloomfield from London-Middlesex agrees, ''You certainly have your hand in your pocket more than the ordinary person.''

Indeed. Political families are two or three times as generous as the average Canadian family.

Less obvious are those who consciously or otherwise give money to their alma mater in gratitude for their education and the privileges it brings, those who are grateful to a hospital or a particular surgeon for a health care experience that was decidedly satisfactory, and many like the Newfoundland X-ray technician who appreciate the vagaries of good fortune and consider donations as something close to buying insurance.

How often are donations motivated by equivalent exchanges and how powerful is the influence? We have already demonstrated the response by politicians. Although we didn't ask the question directly, the write-ins on our questionnaires provide some useful insights. We classified about five per cent of the respondents as giving for reasons that could be roughly described as insurance motives, or other exchanges for equivalent gain.[5] Their level of giving was about 1.5 per cent, only slightly above average. Provided the appeal is personalized and touches a sensitive chord, *quid pro quo* can be persuasive. And since the nature of a transaction is the careful calculation of equivalent costs and benefits, those who donate for transactional motives

---

[5]The small number of identified respondents does not necessarily indicate the proportion of donors who gave for transactional motives. The motive was inferred from write-in comments probing the respondent's positive or negative feelings towards charitable appeals. Indeed, our suspicion is that the proportion is relatively high, when one adds together all categories of transactions.

would likely also be those who would respond to enriched tax incentives to stimulate donations.

Leverage

As we shall see in the next chapter, leverage is one of the most important tactics employed by professional fund raisers in extracting money from those with ample capacity to give. A donor might not acknowledge leverage as an influence since to do so could admit to a certain character weakness, unflattering to one's self-image. Since there is unlikely to be a reader who has not observed leverage in action—whether as leverer or leveree—we shall simply assert that leverage works, and not question for a moment that it is properly classified as a Level Two motive.

Recognition

> Self-approval depends on public recognition and acclaim, and the quality of this approval has undergone important changes in its own right. The good opinion of friends and neighbors, which formerly informed a man that he had lived a useful life, rested on appreciation of his accomplishments. Today men seek the kind of approval that applauds not their actions but their personal attributes...they want to be envied rather than respected.
>
>   Christopher Lasch, *The Culture of Narcissism*

If Lasch's assessment is correct, it helps to explain why both donors and donees take pains to ensure that donations are given appropriate public recognition. Recognition is intended to make the donor feel good, to single him or her out as special, different or better. It is accomplished by publicizing the donors' names, entertaining them at special dinners or receptions, keeping in touch with them, keeping them informed, adding them to the list of "special names."

In Halifax, donors to the Bill Lynch Fund to aid the handicapped in Nova Scotia are listed, along with the size of their contribution, daily in the *Halifax Chronicle-Herald*. In Vancouver, Agnes Watts, a 92-year-old widow, is honored by the Variety Club for her gift of $250,000 to the Children's Hospital with fanfare and a plaque bearing her name displayed in the children's garden. Across Canada, donors who pledge money to the various TV fundraising telethons are rewarded with instant recognition by a video-display of their names and amounts.[6]

---

[6] Cost-free personal publicity (narcissism?) may well be the sole motive behind many of these pledges. Fund raisers estimate that roughly one-third of the amount pledged on TV telethons is not collected.

The Shaw Festival in Niagara-on-the-Lake offers more tangible recognition for donations—seven categories according to size of contribution. They scale benefits according to the category of membership, each member receiving all the privileges of the lower groups plus one or two added perquisites intended to entice them to upgrade their membership.

For instance, moving from an Annual Member ($25-$99), who receives a tax receipt and membership card, to a Supporting Member ($100-$249) purchases a listing in the Shaw Festival Souvenir Program (if you wish) and a full-color Shaw Festival poster. For $5,000, a Benefactor gets an invitation for two to two opening-night performances and board of directors' pre-performance dinner receptions, *and* an invitation for two to the President's Party, a gala private evening for corporate and individual benefactors, the Shaw Festival board of directors, executive staff and key members of the acting company.[7]

Fund raisers also obtain rewards. Howard Lowe receives Ontario's medal for good citizenship for his work in organizing fund-raising campaigns for medical research. Thomas Bell, chairman of Abitibi-Price Inc., is named Philanthropist of the Year by the National Society for Fund-Raising Executives ''more for his ability to extract money from others for a good cause than for giving his money away.''

Recognition can be ephemeral or lasting, perfunctory or thoughtful, consumable or permanent, bizarre or elegant. Perhaps nothing can match the honorary degree for combining at once all the elements of recognition dear to the hearts of mortal men: reward for accomplishment, exclusivity, dignity, ceremony, permanence. It even carries a title, perhaps more used by doctors *honoris causa* than by those who earn it in course of study. For the man who has everything but the privilege of calling himself doctor, an LL.D. holds a certain attraction.

Can honorary doctorates be bought with well-placed gifts? The thought has crossed the minds of more than one member of the public. Senator Henry D. Hicks, former president of Dalhousie University, relates this amusing anecdote:

[7]The Shaw promotion started in December 1982. After two months, Mrs. Merinelli, in charge of Shaw memberships, indicated a ''positive'' response to the program. She placed a conservative estimate of 3,000 new members from the promotion. At an average of $100 per member (author's estimate), it could yield $300,000 in new money. Shaw's 1982 budget totalled $4 million with memberships providing $200,000.

Shortly after I came to Dalhousie, a leading Nova Scotia businessman asked me at a dinner about the basis of awarding an honorary degree.

"Are you interested in an honorary degree? Then you should give Dalhousie University $100,000."

"Do you mean that you would give me an honorary degree if I gave you $100,000?"

"No."

"What if I gave you $100,000 and you did not give me an honorary degree?"

"Then you should give me another $100,000, and another, and eventually the Dalhousie Senate would recognize that your interest in post-secondary education deserved the awarding of an honorary degree."

Hicks was intrigued enough by the subject that he undertook an analysis of donations made to Dalhousie by the 225 honorary degree recipients over the two decades from 1961 to 1981. Two-thirds of the honorary graduates donated nothing to Dalhousie over that period. The 81 who did donate gave a total of $537,000, an average of $6,600 per donor in amounts ranging from $20 to $100,000.

But even the most cynical would concede that many honorary degrees are awarded purely on merit. To beloved teachers, famous alumni, great Canadians, world leaders. Hicks grouped the graduates into three categories according to the extent to which the award was, in his judgment, related to financial contributions or expectations: yes, 6; no, 206; maybe, 13. "Frankly," says Hicks, "I am surprised that so few of our degrees can be related, either wholly or in part, to financial contributions or expectations. Indeed, I may have erred on the side of 'contributing' to the awarding of degrees when, in fact, honorary degrees would have been tendered whether or not financial contributions were involved."

Of the six with definite linkage, three gave amounts ranging from $3,000 to $43,000, three gave nothing in their own names. One of the latter was president of a foundation which has provided more than $2 million in gifts to Dalhousie. Lady Beaverbrook's friendship with Dalhousie and interest in post-secondary education was so genuine that none would seriously question the motive for the degree. Another was the chief executor and trustee of a sizable estate out of which $30 million was left to Dalhousie. After 20 years, nothing but gratitude has been received from the third. Of the 13 with possible linkage, only two have not donated to the university. The average gift was $25,000, ranging from $100 to $100,000.

Dalhousie's record could hardly be considered scandalous. What about McGill? University of Toronto? The University of Western Ontario?

Professor Robert E. Bell of McGill University could identify only four names out of 263 as among the substantial donors to McGill. "Condemn me as naive, but I believe these donors are genuinely altruistic in most cases."[8] J.A. Sword, former president of University of Toronto, could identify only six (out of 200). "The question of public recognition, prestige and esteem associated with the award of Toronto honorary degrees has probably not changed over the 20 years. There are relatively few declinations from those selected for recognition and they are usually on grounds of high principle."

The University of Western Ontario awarded 115 honorary degrees during the tenure of President D. Carlton Williams. Only 10 or 11 recipients could be regarded as rich. "Half of these have contributed generously of their time, serving this and other universities, but few have directly contributed substantially to Western. If the university should regard the honorary degree as a reward for money raising, it is not doing this job very effectively!"

Perhaps not, yet such impeccable behavior may well prove inadvertently to be the most effective single attribute to attract large donations in anticipation of recognition. Idealism, high standards, quality—these have always held compelling influence over human behavior. Degrees from institutions renowned for their uncompromising standards have always retained their attraction to those who aspire to excellence.

Few would question the exchange of recognition for a donation provided the values were roughly equivalent. Perceptual inequities arise when the equation becomes obviously imbalanced. For instance, recognition usually is based on the size of the donation, not the degree of sacrifice. If a family earning $15,000 per year donates $200 out of a sense of personal gratitude to a local hospital-fund drive, the after-tax cost of $140 hurts it much more than a $1,000 donation from a family earning $100,000.

Yet the larger gift may attract more attention, derive more 'perks' than the smaller. Not only is the degree of sacrifice ignored in most cases, some ask

---

[8]According to Bell, "The naming of buildings is a different matter. For one thing, honorary degrees are awarded by the academic senate at McGill, accounting for the relative purity of the list. Buildings are named by the board of governors, which might be expected to be a little more worldly, but in practice differs little. Buildings or sections thereof are usually named for deceased persons or occasionally for persons who have definitely left the university community. The donors are usually the families (or sometimes the corporation or foundation) of the deceased person, and they can be quite insistent about getting the name on the building as a memorial...."

why the rich taxpayer should derive personal benefit from the public tax subsidy which in this case amounted to $500, more than the total value of the smaller gift.

Inequity may also be perceived when the sum of the benefits derived is noticeably greater than the cost of the donation to the donor, when in some way the benefits are undeserved. It may well be this perceived imbalance that lay behind the prolonged and intense public criticism of the naming of Roy Thomson Hall in Toronto in 1982. The family of the late Lord Thomson of Fleet contributed $4.5 million to the building fund, roughly 10 per cent of the cost of the world-class music hall. Yet many critics voiced the opinion that the gift itself was insufficient justification for conferring the privilege of public immortality on the donor.[9]

But recognition does have its costs.[10] Generous donors make The List of Special Names, those singled out for advanced, personalized and sometimes aggressive calls during every major fund drive. Fund raisers build expectations of the size of donation that is acceptable, based on the size of

---

[9]Financing of Roy Thomson Hall is a classic example of flawless fund raising from all elements of the public and private sector. Private donations from corporations, foundations and individuals provided the first $12.5 million. This was leveraged more than twice by contributions from Wintario, $10 million; the federal government, $9 million; Metro Toronto, $5 million; the Province of Ontario, $2.5 million—a total budget of $39 million. The Thomson gift came in December 1981 when the hall and its financing were virtually complete. The terms were $900,000 cash and $900,000 each year for four years to provide a fund for extras and for a small reserve. The published record of reaction to the donation was overwhelmingly negative: "A vulgar attempt to purchase a monument;" "a comparative pittance;" "My God! You've got to be kidding;" "Cut-rate immortality;" "We music lovers donated money, too, and probably at a higher percentage of our earnings." There were some kind words: "Generous contribution to the Canadian arts;" "Bravo." The reaction voiced a public perception of inequality between the cost to the Thomson family and the benefits they derived from the donation. The benefits in prestige and recognition were indeed generous. Arthur Erickson's creation, now Roy Thomson's namesake, would remain a striking landmark in Canada's premier city, would become known world-wide.

The cost to the Thomson family? Assuming the donation qualified as a tax deduction, from either the Thomson corporation or individuals, each $900,000 payment would carry a potential tax saving of up to $450,000. And since instalments two through five would be delayed, their present value after tax, discounting at 18 per cent, roughly the rate on four-year money in early 1982, would be $1.3 million—a total cost of about $1.8 million. The critics felt this was too little to pay for the value of the psychic income which the Thomson family would derive for many generations from its linkage with the world-class music hall. By way of comparison, the Masseys donated $150,000 to finance 100 per cent of the cost of construction of the original hall in 1894. Coincidentally, that gift would have amounted to $1.8 million in 1982 dollars.

[10]"One has to pay for honors," observed Emmett Cardinal Carter at a civic reception at the time of his installation as bishop of Toronto. The Cardinal's allusion was non-financial, but the sentiment has broad applicability.

previous donations, and sometimes exert extraordinary pressure to exact an even larger pledge. And if their appeal is sensitive, subtle and titillating enough, the prospect's ego often guarantees that the expanded expectations are fulfilled.

Education

It is always difficult to separate the influence of education from a variety of other closely related factors—income, wealth, occupation and so on. Furthermore, in Book One I argued that education itself may be an ambivalent force in the donation decision; more education need not necessarily add to one's desire to donate. Viewing education as a single variable with donations may imply a positive relationship—that increased donations follow higher levels of education.

FAMILY DONATIONS BY LEVEL OF EDUCATION, 1981

	Elementary	High school	Post-college	Graduate
Donating more than $100	47%	50%	57%	68%
Family donations				
Religious	$159	$197	$371	$417
Non-religious	128	149	214	402
Total	$287	$346	$585	$819
Percentage of income	1.1	1.2	1.4	1.9
Hours of personal service	107	69	73	94
Number of organizations	0.9	0.9	1.2	1.6

Regression equations failed to confirm any significant positive association between education and the amount of donations, either religious or non-religious, despite the apparent correlation demonstrated above. The same was true for the number of hours contributed in voluntary service. Presumably other factors also associated with donations and education are the more important influences.

Education was barely significant in the regression model which predicted the quality of religious donations—the percentage of income donated to the church. There was a slight tendency for those with higher education to donate a higher proportion of their income to the church, holding all other influences constant.[11] The relationship was not significant in quality models predicting non-religious donations. Such a finding—that higher education is not necessarily linked to more generosity—has implications for fund-raising appeals by educational establishments, as we shall discover in the next chapter.

Lifestyle

> I often gave out of a sense of guilt or embarrassment when my income was substantially lower. Now that my income is adequate, I am experiencing social pressure rather than a need to give.
>
> Sarnia administrator
> Donations—$60

"Lifestyle" is the contemporary catchword to embrace one's occupation, marital status, residence, mobility, degree of community and social involvement, and so on. It is hard to study, next to impossible to quantify. Therefore its influence on donation behavior is difficult to demonstrate with hard quantitative evidence. Instead, we shall table the information that does relate to understanding lifestyle influences and draw conclusions that seem warranted.

Perhaps more than anything else, living styles reflect the characteristics of one's chronological age. Does one's age, by itself, affect donation behavior? Do men and women mellow with the years, become more generous, more expansive? Is altruism programmed in the genes that govern aging?

The literature on altruism implies a positive relationship. Psychological experiments show, for example, that altruism can be learned, that older children exhibit more generous behavior than younger. Can those experimental findings be extrapolated to adults to predict their donations behavior? Does the progression continue and reflect in accelerating donations as adults get older? We think not, although the raw data suggest otherwise.

The proportion of income donated does increase with advancing years—a trend that held for both religious and non-religious donations. Total family donations also increase with age until about age 55, when the absolute

---

[11]The relationship was weak—at the 10 per cent level of significance.

FAMILY DONATIONS BY AGE OF HEAD, 1981

	School years	Demanding years: 25-44	Established years: 45-64	Senior years
Donating more than $100	41%	53%	83%	74%
Family donations				
Religious	$ 62	$267	$433	$ 312
Non-religious	51	197	333	185
Total	$113	$464	$766	$497
Percentage of income	0.6	1.2	2.2	2.4
Hours of personal service	63	70	84	185

level begins to decline. Much of the above pattern must be attributed to the life-cycle of one's ability to give. Family income was lowest for those under 25 years of age, but advanced sharply during the demanding years, reaching a peak of $46,000 between ages 35-44.

This 20-year age grouping reported the highest proportion of multi-income families of all four categories, 58 per cent. Average family income declined throughout the established years (as did the proportion of families reporting multi-incomes) and averaged $20,000 for those over age 65, a level roughly equivalent to the younger age group.

Liquid wealth, on the other hand, rose progressively with age, reaching a peak of more than $50,000 for those over age 65. The declining capacity to give caused by declining income tends to be offset to some extent by expanded capacity resulting from higher liquid asset holdings, and because fewer dependent children were attached to families of the elderly.[12]

The main explanation, however, lies in the incidence of the most powerful donation motive across various age groups. The degree of one's religious commitment, as we shall see later, is the single most influential determinant of donation generosity and varies progressively with age across our sample families.

[12]The average number of dependent children peaked at 1.9 for families in the 35-44 age group. It declined steadily to 0.1 for those 65 and over.

Those aged 65 and over, for instance, indicated a degree of religious commitment 50 per cent stronger than the average level of the under-age-35 group. Residential mobility, a factor inversely related to donation levels, was sharply higher in the younger population groups (those under 35 reported five times the number of residential moves than those 55 and over). And commitment to humanistic organizations in the community—which carries a positive association with donations—was much higher among the older age segments (families in the over-65 age group belonged to twice the number of organizations claimed by the groups under 35).

When the influence of these motivating forces was removed from total family donation patterns, our regression analysis could not identify any significant association for age by itself, either in the amount of money donated or the degree of family generosity.

That finding is important. Demographic predictions all confirm an accelerating rate of growth in the proportion of population aged 65 and over. Unless Canada's youth begin soon to procreate at more enthusiastic levels, one Canadian in five will be a senior in the year 2020. If the habits, attitudes and actions of the younger population are carried thoughout life (perhaps a moot assumption), it would portend that the expanded pool of future elderly may not exhibit the same high degree of generosity as the present. At the very least, it poses a challenge for private fund raising.

None of our attempts to demonstrate a relationship between a person's occupation and family donations in regression models indicated any significant association. That finding implies that generous impulses are not necessarily stimulated nor suppressed by one's occupational status whether professional-managerial, white collar, blue collar or retired.

Retirees,[13] for instance, contributed at the relatively generous rate of three per cent of income. But when donations are adjusted for ability to give and for the measurable influence of Level Two and Level One motives for giving, there was no measurable association for retirement status by itself.

Perhaps surprisingly, there was very little difference in the level of generosity between white-collar and blue-collar workers. Each gave at the level of 1.0 per cent of income with precisely the same proportions to religious and non-religious organizations.

Labor tended to be more spontaneous in its giving; blue-collar families pre-planned 55 per cent of average family donations, compared with 71 per

---

[13]Almost, but not quite the same group as seniors, discussed earlier.

cent for white-collar families. Both groups joined the same number of organizations, but blue-collar families contributed more hours in personal service to the community, 83 hours versus 61 for white collar. Blue-collar families had slightly lower family income and liquid-asset holdings, but much higher net worth than white-collar families, $13,000 more on average.

Professional-managerial groups do give more, but their income and liquid wealth provide them with much greater capacity to give. I am struck, however, with the consistency of the placement of self-employed professionals such as accountants, lawyers, doctors and dentists in an annual listing of occupations ranked according to the proportion claiming donations for tax purposes.* While the proportion claiming donations is only about 50 per cent for professional groups, it has remained reasonably constant in recent years. Whereas among upper-income taxpayers generally, those earning more than $50,000, the proportion claiming donations has dropped sharply, almost 30 percentage points from 1970 to 1980.

There may well be a large element of enlightened self-interest associated with donations by self-employed professionals. Since many professions discourage or prohibit members from advertising for clients, donations and association with fund-raising campaigns, community organizations, and so on are a convenient and dignified way for professionals to keep in touch with potential clients—a socially acceptable form of business promotion until it becomes obvious and aggressive.[14]

Enlightened self-interest or not, families who joined organizations were more generous than those who did not, and the generosity rose proportionately with the number of groups they belonged to. The relationship was strongly significant in regression models estimating both the amount and proportion of income donated to non-religious organizations, and in a model predicting the percentage of income donated to the church. Membership implies commitment, makes one directly accessible to information and education on financial needs, first to be contacted on fund drives. The linkage is strong and vitally important to those responsible for creating a fund-raising strategy.

---

*See the appendix for a listing of major occupational groupings in Canada ranked in order of generosity.

[14]Chartered accountants, in particular, are conscious of the potential for business promotion that results from fund raising and voluntary work. Some of the major firms have a strictly regulated allocation of community service. A senior partner in one leading accounting firm told me that all partners and senior staff are expected to volunteer an appropriate amount of time to a carefully selected group of community organizations with potential for contacts.

Does the structure of the family group influence donation behavior? There were 38 respondents who classified themselves as separated, 39 as having a live-in arrangement, together comprising about eight per cent of the total sample. These lifestyles are not unique to the 1980s but their rapid growth and social acceptance are a contemporary phenomenon. While both groups reported family incomes lower than average, their reported donations were sharply below those who were married, widowed, divorced or single. Those who were separated donated $211, about 0.9 per cent of income, half of which went to their church. The live-ins donated $118, roughly 0.4 per cent of income, and averaged only $8.00 in donations to the church.[15] Neither group was generous in contributing time to serve community organizations.

If non-conventional household lifestyles—arrangements that subdue personal commitment—continue to gain acceptance and expand as a proportion of the total population, the trend could seriously erode the proportion who donate and the total amount of money raised in this manner.

Perhaps the forces for continued, even accelerated, dismemberment of the conventional family-for-life are already firmly established in Canada. A study released by Statistics Canada in 1983 detailed an alarming rate of increase in the number of divorces throughout the country, an increase of 500 per cent from 1968 to 1981. Today, four marriages in 10 probably will end in divorce.

The corollary to these statistics is the sharp rise in single-parent families, a group that has grown from 425,000 to 637,000 households over the decade of the seventies, a 50 per cent increase. Statistics Canada expects that the single-parent family will outnumber the traditional, nuclear, two-parent family within the next 20 years. These lifestyle statistics have sparked the usual lively social debate with pessimists outnumbering optimists in their assessment of the overall social implications. From the perspective of this inquiry, we can only view the trend as potentially threatening to the flow of personal charitable donations as family cohesion gives way to less formal, more complex household lifestyles.

---

[15]While the variance in amounts and proportion of income donated is readily observable across the various classifications of marital status, the difference could not be confirmed in regression models which attempted to contrast the donation behavior of separated and live-ins from all other classifications.

Our analysis indicates that it would make little difference whether the head of these households was male or female, insofar as sex might be expected to influence the level of generosity.[16] If women are more empathic, more altruistic than men, as some have suggested, we were unable to confirm the tendency in their donation behavior. The influence of sex in our regression models was not significant in a statistical sense.

The location of one's residence, whether in an urban or rural environment, would appear not to influence the level of family generosity. Rural families donated the same proportion of income to non-religious causes as did urban-based families, and regression equations revealed no significant relationship between place of residence and either the amount or proportion of donations. Rural families (in our sample, comprised mainly of commuters) did donate proportionately less to the church, reported higher average incomes and net worth, but in virtually every other comparison were remarkably close in profile to their urban cousins.

On the other hand, there is some suggestion that mobility—measured by the number of occupational changes and the number of changes of residence over a 10-year span—has a negative influence on family donations. There was a barely significant negative relationship between the total number of changes of residence and occupation and the proportion of family income donated to the church. Once roots are disturbed and commitments broken, the mobile family perhaps is less inclined to re-establish a financial commitment. Or, alternatively, families that tend to be mobile may possess characteristics that mark them as less generous than their more settled neighbors.

Other factors, of course, determine lifestyles generally and in turn influence family generosity—friends, business associates, television, radio, newspapers. The evidence is not encouraging for expanded donations.

Almost three per cent of families specified that their level of generosity was influenced primarily by friends; they donated at a level equal to half the average for all families. Those who were influenced by business associates were more generous but still gave below average. And those families, roughly four per cent, claiming that the media exerted the primary influence on their

---

[16]On the other hand, there was a marked difference in the distribution of donations by males and females. Almost 85 per cent of total donations by families with female-principal income earners went to the church, compared with 57 per cent for families with male-principal income earners. This might imply a relative reduction in non-religious donations as more women enter the work force and progress into upper-income classes.

generosity reported the lowest level of donations of all three categories, 0.6 per cent of income.

Do TV, radio and the printed media contain messages that encourage self-indulgence, that discredit commitment and generosity? Rushton and others claim that the mass media, particularly TV, have become a most powerful socializing force, effectively crowding out the influence of family as society's most important socializing institution. As TV continually depicts scenes of violence and the macho message, as it openly portrays sexual promiscuity and non-family liaisons, it may well be reinforcing selfish attitudes that discourage voluntary donations. A sobering conclusion.

Level Two motives for giving tend to be unsteady, changeable, less reliable factors in the complex array of forces that impel the donation decision. The evidence shows them to be difficult to measure and, if measurable, statistically less significant than ability variables in predicting family donation levels.[17] How important then are Level One motives in the decision process?

Noblesse oblige tradition

> It is the duty and privilege of Canadian citizens to support the community, locally and nationally, to the best of each individual's ability.
> Port Hope auto dealer
> Donations—$5,000

There are still those in Canada today who live their lives with a deep sense of personal responsibility, duty, for community. Such an obligation transcends the authority of governments, without implying arrogance or condescension. The responsibility reaches beyond the financial contribution of taxes and the payment of legal levies. There is a certain wholesome humility associated with the true spirit of *noblesse oblige*, a recognition that genuine affection, respect and admiration for leadership is given voluntarily by the community—that it is indeed a privilege to be chosen to serve and to be able to contribute to the larger community.

Families that expressed these sentiments were generous families, in both absolute and relative terms. Their income and wealth was higher, and they contributed an average of 2.4 per cent to humanistic causes. They made an average of 11 donations, twice the sample average, and turned down five,

---

[17]The T statistics for Level Two variables significant at the 10 per cent level or better averaged 5.25. The T statistics for the significant ability variables averaged 26.

one less than average. They supported twice the number of community organizations with twice the number of hours of personal service. These families lived in all five regions of the country and represented all occupation
groups, including blue collar. They tended to be highly educated; 80 per
cent were over age 35. They expressed a strong commitment to their religion, twice the average level of the sample.

In total, they represented less than three per cent of the families.

Power

> True adherents of the Calgary Establishment...have virtually no inter-
> ests except their business pursuits. They take little part in civic affairs,
> charitable organizations, service clubs, or trade groups.
> Peter C. Newman, author

After four best-selling books, scores of prime-time TV episodes, and literally millions of words in magazines and newspaper articles, we might expect
the Canadian public to lose its fascination with "The Establishment." Not
so. Newman's "tentative exploration of its members' essences, flaws, values, strengths and motives" has unearthed a mother-lode of curiosity for
ever-more-intimate detail about the lives of the rich and powerful.

The power Newman describes is "real" power—economic, social and
political power. Political power does not necessarily entail holding public office; it usually means influence over politicians. Socially, Newman's establishment sets the standards of acceptability in morals, manners and taste.
Their economic control is as vast and encompassing as it is rigid. However
one may sniff at the vulgarity of the topic, the books' undisputed popularity
and unchallenged authenticity make them useful reflections of contemporary standards and values.

Our interest in this cult is confined to the insights it gives us into the de-
ployment of this power to the advancement of community—philanthropy
in its broadest sense. We analyzed two of Newman's books for references to
philanthropy, charitable works, personal service and the like. In neither
were the subjects given much priority.

In the 551 pages in *The Canadian Establishment* (Toronto: McClelland and
Stewart, 1975), Newman makes only 26 references that are directly or even
obliquely related,[18] e.g., "As teenagers, they came out at one of the three

---

[18]Nine of the 26 references are relegated to footnotes.

balls—St. Andrews, the Hunt Club, or the Charity." Three of the citations
deal with the raising of money for private boys' schools, e.g., "Graduates
(operating genuine Old Boys' networks) seem to have little trouble raising
money for college capital drives."

Some of the 24 references in *The Acquisitors* (Toronto: McClelland and
Stewart, 1981) reveal an antagonism, not merely indifference, to community involvement. Alberta financier Peter Pocklington says, "All this altruism has got to stop. I hate altruism. Hate it. It's destroying us." About
Toronto's Reichmanns, "The brothers...don't head charity drives—in fact
they seem to perform none of the social obligations or token niceties that
foster most businessmen's reputations. Yet they are widely praised and
admired."

Few of Newman's references to philanthropy are flattering to the subject.
He is particularly harsh on western money, and the "New Rich" in particular. "Old Money" fares somewhat better. "The Old Rich are constantly
attempting to lever their surplus funds into subtle venues such as collecting
Napoleonic toy soldiers...or purchasing hedges against mortality through
enlightened philanthropy." Some references, but they are the minority, indicate the quality of interest associated with the involvement or donation.
Of "Chunky" Woodward, "His loyalty to Woodward's is shared only by
his dedication to the B.C. Heart Foundation."

On the whole, the subjects of philanthropy and community responsibility occupy a trivial aspect of the lives of Newman's establishment. Fewer
than 20 of the hundreds of personalities Newman analyzed were depicted as
men for whom philanthropy and personal service constituted important dimensions of their lives. Possibly there was little more to mention. Possibly
Newman neglected to print more examples of charitable work and the role
it plays in the lives of the powerful. It hardly makes for breath-taking prose.[19]

But if Newman does reflect his subjects' "essences, flaws and values,"
then there is taking place in this country a fundamental shift in attitudes towards the attractive outlets for power and influence by those who possess
vast economic resources.

---

[19]Newman concedes to this author that the omission was a "flaw in the books," a flaw not because he
depicts his subjects as preoccupied with self, but because he did not report the evidence and his analysis of this dimension of their lives. Indeed, explained Newman, many of his subjects proudly recited
a litany of board, committee and commission memberships but "with a few noteworthy exceptions
such as the Koerners in Vancouver, the Richardsons in Winnipeg, Floyd Chalmers in Toronto," their
involvement was a "ritualistic endeavor" which in Newman's judgment stemmed more from social
one-upsmanship ("My board is better than your board") than from "a genuine philanthropic
impulse."

That conclusion is consistent with statistical evidence that shows a sharp decline in generosity by upper-income Canadian families. Is it a temporary phenomenon? Will the new generation in time tire of self-indulgence and eventually turn its interest and resources to constructive community purposes? Or is the pattern of social values and personal rewards more permanently altered? We shall return to this discussion in later chapters.

Religion, moral philosophy, humanism

We are thankful for all we have and we believe that it is in giving that we receive so many blessings.

Winnipeg machinist
Donations—$3,500

More money is donated by individuals to religious organizations than is raised through donations from all sources by all other charitable organizations combined—more than $1.3 billion in 1980. It is not surprising that the degree of one's religious commitment is the strongest single motive for giving money to the church. What is not widely known, but of profound importance in this inquiry, is that the same force, degree of religious commitment, also is the most consistent and powerful motive associated with donations to non-religious organizations.[20] Religion is a topic that deserves careful exploration.

Sample families were asked to specify two separate dimensions of their religious affiliation. First, their religious denomination: Roman Catholic, United, Anglican, other Protestant, Jewish, Buddhist, Hindu or Moslem, other denominations not specified or no religion. Second, the degree of their religious commitment: strong religious ties, frequent religious attendance, infrequent religious attendance, or no religious ties. The donations of families classified by religious denomination, in descending order of total generosity, were as follows.

---

[20]Regression coefficients for a variable measuring degree of religious commitment in models predicting both dollars and proportion of income donated to the church were extraordinarily significant—T statistics of 66 and 138 respectively. The religious commitment coefficient for non-religious donations was significant at the one per cent level in the quality model, at the five per cent level in the quantity model.

FAMILY DONATIONS BY RELIGIOUS DENOMINATION, 1981

| | *Proportion of income donated* | | |
	Religious	*Non-religious*	*Total*
Denominations not elsewhere listed*	3.2	0.5	3.7
Other Protestant**	2.2	0.7	2.7
Jewish***	0.7	1.5	2.2
Anglican	0.5	0.7	1.2
United Church	0.6	0.5	1.1
Roman Catholic	0.5	0.6	1.1
No religion	0.1	0.3	0.4

*Would include many smaller sects such as Mormon, Buddhist, Hindu, Moslem, etc., 42 replies.
**Presbyterian, Lutheran, Baptist, Evangelical sects, etc.
***Based on four replies only.

It is obvious from the table that the main-line denominations were relatively the least generous in religious donations, whereas Presbyterians, Lutherans, Baptists and the various Evangelical sects donated a significantly higher proportion of their income to the church.

This tendency was confirmed in models predicting the amount and proportion of family income donated to the church. Roman Catholic, Anglican and United Church affiliation consistently showed a significantly negative coefficient compared with other denominations in quality models, whereas families with other Protestant affiliations registered as significantly more generous to their church in both absolute and relative terms. The sample from the Jewish community was too small to register a reliable statistical reading.

Not only do the established denominations receive relatively less in donations from their members, the three largest (Roman Catholic, United Church, Anglican), which together claimed 73 per cent of the total Canadian population in the 1981 census, are in secular decline.[21]

The decline may not show in the numbers of nominally registered Roman Catholics because confirmed Roman Catholics do not lightly renounce their

[21]Ironically, we know the least about the denomination with the largest membership—the Roman Catholics. Unlike the United and Anglican Churches, which are structured in a national hierarchy, Roman Catholic dioceses in Canada report not to a national office but to the Vatican.

faith, and their membership rolls have been swelled by new immigrants, the majority of whom belonged to the mother-church in their homeland. It does show in church attendance which has declined consistently in the Roman Catholic community across Canada from 87 per cent weekly in 1957 to 48 per cent in 1982. It shows also in per capita donations, which in the Diocese of London, Ont., for instance, declined in real terms from $25 per year in 1970 to $19 in 1980.

The United Church also has felt the pinch. Canada's largest Protestant denomination dropped from a growth rate of 21 per cent in the decade ended in 1956 to a membership loss of 12 per cent for the 10 years ended in 1976. Coupled with the loss of membership has been a decline in generosity by the committed. In terms of real purchasing power, those who gave $100 in 1970 to the United Church Mission and Service fund, the fund which finances the national and international work of the church, were giving $85 in 1980. "The national United Church is in deep financial trouble," claims Patricia Clarke in the United Church *Observer*. "It has been spending more than its members give for a decade."

The Anglican Church, too, has lost members, although at a slightly lesser rate than the United Church. Total per capita revenue in real terms has actually grown from $66 in 1969 to $86 in 1979, reflecting increased investment income and enhanced cash flow from a church population that is aging.

Both major Protestant churches have acknowledged the deterioration of their revenue bases, and have taken bold steps to reverse their members' declining propensity to give. The Anglican Church conceived and launched Anglicans in Missions (AIM) in 1982, a one-shot program to raise $40 million from its members over a three-year period, later extended to five years, funds that would be used for beefed-up pensions for retired ministers, for new church development, and for training, programs and services. The United Church launched Ventures in Mission (VIM) about a year later, for the same monetary goal and for roughly the same over-all purposes. Not surprising, since both churches retained Community Counselling Service Co. Inc. of New York as their professional fund-raising consultants at a cost for fees and expenses that translated into eight per cent and nine per cent of their respective objectives.[22]

---

[22]Perhaps the most controversial fiscal decisions ever taken by the two national governing bodies. Apart from considerations of timing ("Canada is experiencing one of the most profound economic reces-
(Cont'd)

The programs were designed to raise the sights of Anglicans and United Church members, to challenge them to permanently higher levels of giving. Will they work? As might be expected, the national offices are bullish. But pessimists point to a Gallup Poll conducted in 1982 which revealed that 46 per cent of Canadians believe the influence of religion on Canadian life is decreasing (compared with only 28 per cent who thought so in 1957).[23]

While the religious mainstream languishes, the smaller, often tiny, sects are enjoying vigorous growth and, presumably, relative prosperity. For instance, the Lutheran Council in Canada grew 10 per cent from 1966 to 1976, the Jehovah's Witnesses, 53 per cent, and the Pentecostal Assemblies of Canada, 169 per cent.

But nothing can match the swirl of attention that surrounds a purely nuclear phenomenon—the television evangelist. A segment of the North American population has long been fascinated and influenced by the great Christian evangelists; many Bible-Belt Americans would recognize the name of Elmer Gantry more readily than Jesse James. Television now provides a powerful pulpit from which an ambitious preacher can reach a congregation of millions across the country and, increasingly, across countries.

And color TV with its show-biz accoutrements can enhance their charisma. M.G. 'Pat' Robertson, who founded the Christian Broadcasting Network (CBN) in Portsmouth, Virginia, in 1960 with an investment of $70, now hosts a talk show, "The 700 Club," viewed by a vast audience in North America. In 1981, 600,000 viewers mailed more than $67 million in tax-free donations to the Club. Television evangelist Rex Humbard, working out of head offices in Akron, Ohio, beams his ministry across the United States and into Canada where he has built a dedicated following. Humbard raises $20 million each year in donations, but won't disclose the amount that comes from Canadians.

Canada, too, has its cadre of local and national hard-sell religious personalities. Pastor Maureen Gagliardi regularly packs to overflowing the 1,200 seat Glad Tidings Temple in Vancouver and raised $2 million in a single day in 1978 for a second 2,000-seat auditorium. Her no-nonsense gospel, from

---

sions since the Great Depression''), the lack of sharp program definition (''vague'') and that the program concentrated more on money than spiritual matters, members mostly criticized the high-pressure salesmanship employed by high-priced outsiders. The Anglican Diocese of Huron, for example, agreed to pay Community Counselling Services a fee amounting to $212,000 for 237 days of consulting services, a per diem which staggered many parishioners.

[23]Optimists point to responses to the corollary question—33 per cent saw the influence of religion increasing in 1982, up from 12 per cent in 1968.

capital punishment to global ecumenism, leaves no room for compromise. A tithe still means one-tenth and she won't give a congregant his membership card unless the church first receives a minimum 10 per cent of his annual income. Rev. Robert Taylor, leader of the First Community Church of Canada, hosts the Robert M. Taylor Special, broadcast from Armstrong, B.C., every Sunday on BCTV. It is one of three B.C.-based television Christian ministries broadcast in the Vancouver area. At the end of the program, an appeal urges viewers to write to Taylor at his Armstrong address and make a financial contribution to his ministry.

Canada's premier prime-time evangelist must be Rev. David Mainse,[24] host, star and driving force behind "100 Huntley Street," beamed from that address in Toronto mid-town to 26 independent stations across Canada, six affiliates of the Ontario-based Global Television Network, six U.S. stations, and two U.S. satellites. Mainse's umbrella organization, Christian Communications Inc., embraces three other related activities: Christian Multilingual Programming, Circle Square Television for Youth, and Circle Square Ranch, a summer camp ministering to youth. Mainse himself is an extraordinary personality. Tall, good-looking, bright, intuitive, sincere, he fits television like a glove and could easily command a salary five times the amount he draws from CCI were he to head an advertising agency or consumer-oriented business corporation.

Like his evangelical brethren, Mainse is not ashamed to ask his audiences for money, from subtle requests to tearful pleas. And they respond. CCI collected $10 million in donations from 60,000 listeners and supporters of its several programs in 1981, twice the 1979 level. The growth rate slowed by 1982, forcing a cutback in the program length of "100 Huntley Street" and staff layoffs. But even fiscal adversity is turned into a fund-raising theme, lending a sense of urgency and even more drama to the systematic appeals for funds.[25]

Critics of TV evangelism abound. The press is not overly supportive, labelling the operations slick and gimmicky and charging that the programs prey on low-income, infirm and uneducated viewers who have little to do

---

[24]Mainse, who was born in Ottawa in 1936, is an ordained Pentecostal pastor.

[25]In April 1983 Rex Humbard captured a front-page headline in the Toronto *Star* when he wrote Canadian supporters asking for $50 each, fast, in order to save his organization from imminent financial collapse. *The Globe and Mail* reports that followers of Oral Roberts have donated more than $5 million for cancer research since the evangelist told them he had God's promise to cure the disease.

each day but watch television.[26] Critics deplore the pressure tactics employed in fund raising, the heavy reliance on computer banks to store, sort and purify lists of prospective donors, the use of high-speed word processors to prepare what purport to be intimate, personally written fund-raising letters at the rate of 250 per hour.

As one might expect, the main-line churches have closed ranks in condemning the constant appeals for money through the electronic media. The Interchurch Communion, representing the Roman Catholic, United, Anglican, Lutheran and Presbyterian churches of Canada, and the Baptist churches of Ontario and Quebec, urged the Canadian Radio-Television and Telecommunications Commission to provide protection for the "victims." The Canadian Jewish Congress joined the Christian establishment in this foray. Rabbi Jordan Pearlson urged the CRTC to control not only the type of TV soliciting but the kind of follow-up mail the viewer gets. He said once a person is on a mailing list, solicitations never stop.

To an observer, the energetic fund-raising methods employed by TV evangelists do indeed make the efforts of established Christian churches appear sporadic, low-key, offhand or even anemic. Most congregations have given up on the annual eyeball-to-eyeball, every-member canvass, relying now on mail-based appeals. Families are urged to accept envelopes for their weekly offerings, and perhaps to sign a non-binding pledge signifying their annual commitment.

Jews are much better organized and decidedly the most effective fund raisers of any established denomination. They raise funds at four levels: the synagogue, The United Jewish Appeal (both local and national), miscellaneous construction appeals and Israel bond appeals.

The local synagogue establishes an annual family due, sufficient to cover the operating expenses of the temple. Amounts may range from $200 to $1,000 per year, but once set are assessed equally on all members. The average membership due in 1982 was about $450 per family.[27] Synagogue dues may represent only between five and 10 per cent of total family donations

---

[26]Our attempts to build a reliable profile of the studio audience at 100 Huntley Street in 1982 were unsuccessful, despite the genuine cooperation of David Mainse and his staff. Our rather unscientific impression, however, is that that particular show may have an audience that does not deviate from any random sample of Canadian adults.

[27]That compares with family religious donations of $180 for Roman Catholics and $170 for Anglicans and United Church families in our sample. Families belonging to other Protestant denominations gave more than $600 to their churches.

(religious donations represented more than 50 per cent of total donations of Protestants).

Construction appeals are targeted at the most generous donors and are timed so as not to conflict with the United Jewish Appeal or sales of Israeli bonds. The latter two appeals are perhaps more ethnic than religious, but the target groups are almost identical. UJA is the Jewish community's United Way and operates in Toronto, Montreal and Winnipeg with a national theme. Funds are used to provide social services for the Jewish community otherwise provided by Christian service groups or governments. Slightly more than 40 per cent of the funds support Jews in Israel. Israeli bonds are issued by the Government of Israel, pay three per cent interest and are cashable only within Israel. Rarely are the bonds redeemed.

Jews rely very much on peer pressure to raise funds for these charitable appeals. Full-time professionals organize the UJA, breaking the community first into broad divisions and further into narrow occupational groups. Every Jew is visited annually by two carefully chosen volunteer canvassers active in the potential donor's profession or business, and briefed with a three-year history of previous gifts, outstanding balances due, and other comments of particular interest: a promotion, an important new client, a legacy, etc. Fund raisers often convene meetings of an homogeneous group of business or professional people where the campaign is discussed candidly and individual donations are requested openly.

High pressure? Certainly. Effective? Per family total giving among Jews in our very small sample was nine times the amount given by the average sample family.[28] Others place the amount at much higher levels.

But one need not have a formal religious affiliation to possess a strong moral philosophy and generous disposition. How generous are Canadians who claim no formal religious affiliation? Just under six per cent of our sample families claimed no religious affiliation and they were by far the least generous group. Their total family donations amounted to only 0.4 per cent of income. Almost all was donated to non-religious causes. (They were also the richest group, apart from the small sample of Jewish respondents, with incomes and wealth twice the level of families with formal church ties).

Our second probing of the influence of religion on family donations measured the *degree* of commitment to their stated religion. One can belong to a church, but is one committed? The findings are perhaps the most important insight into people's motives for giving.

---

[28]There were only four Jewish families in the sample, making the results statistically unreliable.

FAMILY DONATIONS BY DEGREE OF RELIGIOUS COMMITMENT, 1981

	Strong religious ties	Frequent attendance	Infrequent attendance	No religious ties
Donating more than $100	88%	69%	45%	37%
Family donations				
Religious	$1,105	$264	$ 84	$ 21
Non-religious	378	133	202	189
Total	$1,483	$397	$286	$210
Percentage of income	4.3	1.3	0.8	0.5
Hours of personal service	118	94	63	50

Those families claiming strong religious ties, 20 per cent of the sample, were the most generous givers in both absolute and relative terms, not only in donations to support their church, *but in donations to non-religious causes as well.* They also joined more humanistic organizations and contributed the largest number of hours of personal service to their community. Generosity declined systematically with the decrease in a family's stated religious commitment.

Families claiming no religious ties (including some who claimed nominal affiliation with a religious sect) were decidedly the least generous in both dollars and time. In a statistical sense the conclusion was most significant. The variable for religious commitment registered as the most powerful of any in the model, whether in predicting the absolute or relative level of family donations.[29]

Furthermore, families who specified that their religion was the most important influence on their generosity were almost three times as generous as those identifying other primary influences. Families with strong religious ties demonstrate the highest level of generosity to their community. Not

---

[29]The T statistics were significant at the one percentage level in models predicting the dollars donated to the church, the percentage of income donated to the church and the percentage donated to non-religious organizations. The coefficient for dollars donated to non-church causes was significant at the five per cent level.

only do they give to their church, but they also are the most generous contributors to non-religious causes. The linkage is strong, consistent and profoundly relevant.

If charitable donations come primarily from families with strong religious ties, and if it is true that the influence of the church on the lives of Canadians has diminished over the past number of decades, then it is understandable why donations have suffered a secular decline. As fewer Canadians maintain strong religious ties, these non-adherents forego their church's formal indoctrination to a religious-moral philosophy that emphasizes responsibility, compassion and sacrifice, and they avoid the weekly reminder that they should give generously of their substance.

Nor would it appear that the religious non-committed substitute alternative education in moral philosophy that might prompt them to demonstrate generosity in donation behavior. According to the Rev. Dr. David B. Barrett, author of the authoritative *World Christian Encyclopedia*, the proportion of non-religious and atheists in the world population has grown from 0.2 per cent in 1900 to 20.8 per cent in 1980, a trend that coincides roughly with the movement of society from the early stages of financing of humanistic service to a level approaching Stage IV in most countries of the western world.

Those who have turned for intellectual guidance to political or moral philosophers, rather than priests and clergy, have been more impressed with the compelling and seductive social logic of Marx and Engels than with the responsible, if romantic, capitalism of Horatio Alger, Jr.—with the ego-reinforcement of Camus's existentialism than the ego-suppression championed in the Bible. Whatever. The post-war environment in Canada as elsewhere has not nurtured formal religion with its emphasis on self-sacrifice and giving.

What of the future? Will the decline in religious commitment continue? Will the decline further suppress charitable donations? Optimists can draw some comfort from Dr. Barrett's prediction that the proportion of non-religious and atheists in the population will remain stable between now and the year 2000. Pessimists bemoan that the moral damage already has been done.

That combination of circumstance, the dilution of religious influence accompanied by no substitution of moral or ethical education, poses the most serious affront to those committed to a strong private involvement in humanistic affairs. It is most assuredly the main cause of decline in donations, probably the reason why volunteers are increasingly scarce, and most likely at the root of a wide range of personal actions that exhibit lack of commitment—to marriage, family, community, responsible government. Ego is in.

But an egoistic society is an unattractive society. Preoccupation with self-interest may advance some individuals but it weakens the community, the nation. Surely Canada will regress in stature if Canadians lose sight of our larger personal duty. If training in morality and ethics, altruism, no longer is acquired through the conventional socializing institutions—the church, the home—then it must be taught in the schools. Psychologists have shown that altruism can be learned, not through a three-day seminar for top management held in some exclusive training centre but through disciplined, repetitive, intelligent instruction begun in early years and reinforced throughout adolescence.

The study of ethics could begin in kindergarten, with the simplest of anecdotes relevant to that age group, progress each year through a widening range of more complex issues drawn from contemporary settings, and culminate in high school with a study of classical ethical concepts contained in the Bible, the writings of Confucius and Plato, and a few of the more durable moral philosophers of the past few hundred years.

It would require that grade-school and high-school curricula be revised, that qualified teachers be recruited, others retrained, in order to render competent instruction. It would mean also that the next generation of Canadians would enter university or the working world with a common perception of ethical issues, equipped with a common vocabulary and analytical arsenal capable of weighing the consequences of alternative actions and unwilling to accept behavior, in themselves and others, that compromised their personal standards.

Freedom

> I feel that government supplies too many items on which we become dependent, and in so doing we lose our freedom. Pay our own way and we control our destiny.
>
> Cobourg lawyer
> Donations—$1,000

Thirty-nine families, just under four per cent, took the trouble to write in comments, such as the one above, which revealed their concern for the dominance of government in supplying needs, which recognized that a growing dependence on government carries with it a diminution of free choice and personal freedom. Not surprisingly, these families were proportionately twice as generous as the average family in the sample. But it is interesting that such a small proportion recognized the trade-off and its cost.

Altruism

Roughly one-third of the families completing our questionnaire expressed sentiments that indicated a general concern for the welfare of others, a caring instinct, the pleasure derived from the giving of gifts, or their *need* to give. One family in three. What is equally interesting is that the level of generosity of these families was exactly the same as the average family in the sample. The altruistic motive may be the noblest of all. But it would not appear to prompt a noticeably higher level of giving than other forces.

Of the six forces grouped under the category of Level One motives, only one, religious influence, was able to be quantified and measured in our statistical modelling.[30] Yet it consistently emerged as the strongest of 24 different variables drawn from all categories and introduced to measure their influence on the level of family donations.

The statistical models were helpful in analyzing the questionnaire data and in identifying and separating the important variables from those of lesser importance in explaining the decision-making process. But, statistically, the models predicted only a small proportion, in most cases less than one-third, of the actual value of donations reported by sample families. We have tempered the statistical evidence with common sense. The process of deciding whether or not to donate and, if so, how much and to whom, is complex and dynamic. Notwithstanding, the foregoing discussion has narrowed the range of factors that are most important in the decision process.

Are the motives for giving, those identified above, equally influential in directing donations to all four categories of humanistic service—health care, education, welfare and cultural institutions? Recall from Chapter I that total Canadian donations from all sources in 1980 were distributed as follows:

Religious organizations	59%
Welfare	13%
Education	11%
Health care	10%
Culture	7%

---

[30]One additional variable tested in the regression models was the percentage of total family donations that were planned in advance. Are people who plan their donation expenditures more generous than those who tend to give more spontaneously? In none of the models was "percentage of donations planned in advance" significant.

The distribution of donations reported by sample Canadian families for 1981 was as follows:

Church	56%
United Way	7%
Health-related	11%
Education-related	10%
Welfare-related	5%
Cultural-related	3%
Other	8%

Donations gathered by the United Way are redistributed primarily to health and welfare-related organizations. When that adjustment is made, the sample distribution is reasonably close to the known national pattern.

First, donations to the church
Our regression models identified the following factors significantly associated with the *amount* of family donations made to the church. They are listed in descending order of significance: degree of religious commitment; level of family income; number of dependent children; affiliation with other Protestant denominations. The following factors were significant in a model predicting the *proportion* of family income donated to the church, that is, the degree of sacrifice: degree of religious commitment; religious affiliation (a bonus for other Protestant denominations, a handicap for Roman Catholics, Anglicans and United Church adherents); number of dependent children; number of community organizations served; Anglo-Saxon racial origin; degree of residential and occupational mobility; level of education.

The results are as interesting for the variables that did not register as significant as for those that did. The level of family wealth, for instance, was not significantly associated with either the absolute or proportionate size of family religious donations. The size of family income had no measurable influence on the proportion it donated to the church.

Religious influence may be in decline in Canada, but Canadians still direct more than $1 billion each year for its maintenance. Perhaps half that amount, $500 million, would be tax-deductible, eligible for a government subsidy that could exceed $200 million, depending on the donors' marginal tax rates.

Should governments subsidize the church, an institution actively and regularly supported by a minority of the population?[31] In Sweden, the model Stage IV society, donations are *not* tax-deductible, including donations to churches. Instead, a separate income tax ranging from 0.5 to 1.0 per cent of income is levied on all taxpayers for church support and maintenance. It is a question we shall return to in the final chapter.

Second, donations to the United Way

Our regression model identified 11 variables that were significant determinants of the size of family contributions in 1981: the percentage of donations planned in advance; the value of family net fixed assets; the level of family income; residence in Quebec (a handicap); Canadian birth; the number of dependent children; degree of religious commitment;[32] age; number of community organizations served; retirement status (a negative factor). The model predicting donations to the United Way was particularly efficient—it predicted about 40 per cent of the actual level of 1981 family donations. It is a topic of major importance and one we shall return to in the next chapter.

Third, donations to health-related organizations—hospitals, research institutes, and the like

The most significant factors identified with donations to health-related organizations were: size of family income; handicap points for Roman Catholics, main-line Protestants or those with no church affiliation; value of liquid assets; number of community organizations served. Health-care institutions, primarily hospitals and research institutes, collected over $300 million in donations in 1980, a very sizable sum. But it shrinks in relative importance, to a level of one per cent, when related to total expenditures for health care which reached almost $20 billion in Canada that year.

What a significant shift in hospital financing! A century ago, during the golden age of philanthropy, it was not uncommon for hospitals to finance

---

[31]Indeed, it has been suggested to this author that members of some religious denominations use the provisions of the Income Tax Act to gain a subsidy on tuition fees paid to a religious organization for private grade-school education for their children. In certain circumstances, a portion of tuition fees paid to institutions that operate in a dual capacity, providing both secular (academic) and religious education, may be considered a charitable donation for tax purposes. Interested readers are directed to Information Circular Number 75-23 published by Revenue Canada.

[32]Strangely, donations to the United Way varied inversely with the degree of religious commitment.

most of the cost of operations from charitable donations.[33] For instance, in 1879, donations supplied 55 per cent of the revenues of the Toronto General Hospital, 100 per cent for the Hotel Dieu in Kingston. A decade later, donations provided Brockville General Hospital with two-thirds of its total revenues. Even in the early post-Second-World-War period, donations were an important source of hospital funds.

Universal health-care schemes have taken the pressure off hospitals to seek private funding for operating purposes. Management emphasis has shifted from a concern for revenue generation to the expenditure column, with less regard for the bottom line, which largely is considered the concern of provincial health ministers. With the exception of intermittent capital campaigns, health-care institutions largely have become passive fund raisers, accepting donations from appreciative patients and friends. But until recently they have been poorly informed and largely ill-equipped to raise serious funds on an aggressive, sustained basis.[34]

Indeed, it will be a formidable challenge to reverse widespread public apathy towards the financial plight of the health-care sector, to broaden the base of donors beyond the core of upper-income, wealthy, community-spirited families which our analysis shows characterize the present donor pool.

The federal and provincial governments are deeply committed to the notion of universal health care, freely accessible to all citizens regardless of economic circumstances. Widespread, aggressive and sustained public appeals for funds by hospitals would most certainly challenge and ultimately undermine the fundamental principle of universality. They are likely to be viewed by governments as disguised user-fees, which many regard as unfairly burdensome on lower-income Canadians. Nor are they likely to meet with overwhelming financial success in the present climate.

St. Joseph's Hospital in London experimented in 1979 with a carefully worded, pointed appeal for donations from patients to assist the hospital in offsetting a sizable budget deficit. Discharged patients were given a letter written by the hospital's executive director, telling them that there was a $12-per-day discrepancy between the cost of operating a hospital bed and

[33]The *ad hoc* Ontario provincial subsidy to hospitals at that time amounted to 20 cents per patient-day, plus some extra accommodation for extras. In 1983, the cost per hospital patient-day was more than $300 in Ontario, financed almost entirely by the provincial and federal governments.

[34]Toronto's Hospital for Sick Children is an extraordinary exception. Its foundation has a portfolio of more than $60 million which supplies a substantial and reliable flow of funds to that venerable institution.

the per diem revenue from the Minister of Health. They were invited to send a contribution to the hospital if they felt they wanted to help. In all, the hospital received 271 donations from 4,700 discharged patients for a total of $15,000. It also elicited a prompt response from Ontario Health Minister Dennis Timbrell who expressed "concern about your decision to solicit donations from your patients to meet an anticipated operating deficit."

There may be other reasons why the general public is largely unsympathetic and unresponsive. Hospitals and the health-care professionals who work there—doctors, nurses, technicians—are seen to be highly paid and relatively well off compared with other groups in society. An appeal for funds by a hospital, for instance, may be seen by some to further reward a group that already has a privileged position in the economic reward system. Strikes by nurses and pressure tactics by doctors do little to enhance their position as respected, humble professionals whose mission is service before financial gain.

Dr. Lionel Reese, president of the Ontario Medical Association in 1982, during the tense period of negotiation with the Province of Ontario over the medical fee schedule, put it bluntly: "People work for three reasons—prestige, job satisfaction and income. Whether we like it or not, our society equates relative merit with dollars. Even though you are held in high esteem and your work is satisfying, if monetary income is being eroded, you don't feel good."

Somehow a widening spectrum of the public no longer views a doctor or nurse as a self-sacrificing humanitarian whose noble work deserves generous financial support. Envy, yes. Respect and prestige, perhaps. But if hospitals are to succeed in attracting significant donations on a sustaining basis from a broad public base, they must be careful to explain that the funds will be used not to reinforce the incomes of an already prosperous minority but to permit the institution to undertake life-saving activities not now supported by government grants.

The case for enhanced donations to the health-care sector is weakened further when one examines the record more carefully. Only half the doctors and surgeons in Canada make meaningful charitable donations, more than $100 per year, although their average income in 1980 was more than $60,000. The record for nurses and other health-care professionals is even less encouraging. Unless the institution appealing for funds itself establishes a record of generosity, it is understandable why some—no, many—feel no pang of conscience in saying no.

Fourth, donations to educational institutions—universities, private schools

Regression equations isolated the following characteristics as significantly associated with families who made education-related donations: size of family income; occupation as a professional; less the handicap adjustments for membership in various religious sects—in short, the characteristics consistent with university alumni/ae, from whom most donations derive.

Donations to educational establishments in 1980 totalled $250 million, which represented about one-and-a-half per cent of total expenditures on education. The bulk of educational donations go to universities and to a handful of private schools. Public schools at the primary or secondary level do not solicit donations and rarely receive revenue, other than municipal and provincial government grants, even though donations to public schools could qualify for tax deduction by the donor. Few donations are received by community colleges or CEGEPs. Since most donors to educational institutions are upper-income individuals, or businesses taxed at the maximum marginal corporate tax rate, the government subsidy to the donors' gifts would be large—likely over $100 million in 1980.

In many respects, university professors are vulnerable to the same potential criticism as health-care professionals in their record of giving. Their average income was $25,000 in 1980, five places below doctors and surgeons. Yet only one in four donated more than $100.

Compared with their U.S. counterparts, Canadian universities do not derive significant financial support from alumni gifts. It is really only since 1980, for instance, that the University of Western Ontario began seriously to solicit alumni gifts through sophisticated fund-raising campaigns and the appointment of development officers. Their efforts have met with considerable success as total alumni giving amounted to $1 million in 1982. However, analysis by the university for 1980 revealed that only eight per cent of Western's 72,000 living alumni made gifts to the university since the start of the Foundation Western campaign in 1979. In 1980, Queen's University in Kingston, conceded by some as having the most spirited and loyal alumni bodies in the country, reported a positive response ratio of 35 per cent from alumni whose year of graduation was prior to 1950, 25 per cent for those graduating in the decade of the 1950s, and seven per cent for graduates of the 1970s.

Despite the energetic efforts of university alumni and development officers, it may be some time before alumni participation rates in financial campaigns swing up. The bulge of university enrolment occurred in the 1960s, a decade of turbulence, cynicism and alienation on campuses across the country. The graduates of the sixties were a different breed from those of the prior or subsequent decade. Will the memories of their university experience engender feelings of loyalty, commitment and financial generosity to their alma mater? Probably not.

An analysis of gifts from University of Western Ontario alumni reveals that both the participation rate and size of alumni gifts to the university 15 years after graduation is substantially lower for graduates in the 1960s compared with those in the 1950s. For instance, eight per cent of Western's class of '55 made a financial contribution to Western in 1970, an average gift of $29, but only three per cent of the class of '63 made a gift in 1978, a donation that averaged $30 in nominal terms, but $17 in comparable (1970) dollars.

The largest private donations to Canadian universities do not come from individual alumni, but from corporations and foundations whose motives will be explored in later chapters.

Fifth, donations to welfare organizations

These totalled almost $300 million in 1980, about 1.5 per cent of total welfare expenditures. Much of what is classified as a welfare expenditure represents payments directly from governments to individuals (old age pension, family allowances, etc.). The privately operated welfare organizations depend on donations to a much greater extent than any other category of humanistic service. Organizations backed by the United Way—services for the poor, the unemployed, the elderly, the disabled, the disturbed—do receive government subsidies, but some depend on charitable donations to supply up to a third or more of their revenues. A newly spawned organization, established by compassionate citizens to meet an urgent need in society—a rape crisis centre, for instance—may derive all its funds from private sources until it is able to prove its worth to the relevant government ministry.

Appeals for funds by welfare organizations rely heavily on emotional themes: sympathy; compassion; empathy; perhaps guilt. Donor motives for giving are likely the same today as they were a century ago when Canada was at Stages I and II in the financing of humanistic service, largely Level One motives: altruism; freedom; a strong religious and moral philosophy; family tradition; *noblesse oblige*. By and large they are motives that are difficult to identify in people, next-to-impossible to measure. At least two, religious commitment and family tradition, have been shown to be in decline in Canada. It will come as no surprise therefore that our attempts to quantify the variables that influence donations to welfare organizations were largely unsuccessful. The only significant force that was strongly associated with welfare donations was the family's degree of religious commitment.

Sixth, donations to cultural organizations

This is the smallest of the categories of humanistic service and it received the smallest share of total donations—$160 million in 1980, about five per cent of the total. Like some of the private welfare organizations, cultural institutions depend on private donations to supply a large proportion of funds. Unlike them, cultural appeals emphasize the more pragmatic motives for giving, Level Two motives—recognition, special privileges, social acceptance and so on.

Some people still make cultural donations because they want to improve the quality of life in their community, out of a sense of *noblesse oblige*. But most cultural donors today expect an equivalent return for their contribution. Our attempts to model the relationship between motives and generosity to cultural causes met with limited success. There was a strong positive relationship between size of cultural donation and the number of community organizations the family belonged to. Large donors also had higher incomes, were older and better-educated than those who gave little or nothing.

The following table summarizes this discussion on the motives that prompt family donations to the various categories of humanistic service. Religious and welfare donations are prompted largely by Level One motives, whereas donations to cultural, education or health organizations are more likely prompted by the motives we have categorized as Level Two. The table is useful for planning or analyzing the themes emphasized in fund raising appeals by institutions in the humanistic sector.

MOTIVES EFFECTING POSITIVE DONATION RESPONSES

	Humanistic Sector				
	Religion	*Welfare*	*Health*	*Education*	*Culture*
LEVEL II					
Ethnicity	★	★			★
Transaction	★		★	★	★
Leverage	★	★	★	★	★
Recognition			★	★	★
Education			★	★	★
Social Mobility					★
Social Acceptance					★

MOTIVES EFFECTING POSITIVE DONATION RESPONSES

	Religion	Welfare	Health	Education	Culture
LEVEL I					
Noblesse Oblige		★			
Tradition	★	★			
Power			★	★	
Philosophy	★	★			
Freedom	★			★	★
Altruism	★	★	★		

Humanistic Sector spans Welfare, Health, Education, Culture.

Personal service

During the span of years throughout Canada's golden age of philanthropy, a person's status was enhanced not only by the donations he made but by his record of personal service to the community. One was expected to select a favorite charity, join, contribute money, and serve as a volunteer to advance its cause, perhaps as a director, a fund raiser or a worker. Personal service was a necessary condition for personal advancement.

Is it so today? Is volunteerism a strong socializing force in today's society? Certainly much is written and spoken about the virtues of the voluntary spirit, particularly by politicians in recent years. Canada's Secretary of State is committed to promoting an effective relationship between volunteers and their community organizations, between the voluntary sector and the federal government. At the same time, women have been urged to "seek work that is real"—that is to say, paid employment. "Money is the way society shows that it values what you are doing," says a disillusioned volunteer.

Data that indicate the quantity and quality of voluntary service by Canadians are even less complete than information on family charitable donations. The only comprehensive and reliable Canadian study was conducted by Statistics Canada in 1980.[35] From it we know that 2.7 million Canadians, about 15 per cent of the working-age population, were involved in some unpaid voluntary work over the previous year.

By province, the participation rate ranged from a high of 27 per cent in Saskatchewan to 11 per cent in Quebec. Volunteers tended to be older (over

---

[35]*An overview of volunteer workers in Canada*, February 1980, Statistics Canada, Catalogue 71-530.

25), well-educated, and in the managerial, professional and sales occupations. Volunteers contributed 374 million hours of work during that year, an average of 15 hours per Canadian. Widowed, divorced and separated people individually allocated the most time to voluntary activity. Slightly more women than men were active volunteers.

The largest group of volunteers was involved in social welfare organizations which included fund-raising groups, child care, service clubs and so on. The second most popular choice of volunteers was religious activity which claimed 26 per cent of the volunteers. Educational activities followed with 16 per cent, health with eight per cent and politics with four per cent.

Much of the volunteers' work was administrative, although a sizable proportion involved direct personal service. Inactive volunteers attributed their lack of activity to "no demand for services." The dominant personal reason for not participating in voluntary activity was "not enough time" or "too busy."

It is this survey that supports the view that voluntary effort represents a significant contribution to Canada's economy in general and the humanistic sector in particular. At the minimum wage, the value of voluntary service was $1.3 billion in 1980, slightly more than half the value of cash donations that year. At $7.00 an hour, twice the minimum wage, the value of voluntary service would match the dollars contributed.

Our 1981 family survey portrayed a slightly more active voluntary involvement. Almost 60 per cent of the families claimed to have contributed one or more hours in voluntary service to community organizations in 1981. The distribution was as follows:

**HOURS OF FAMILY
COMMUNITY SERVICE, 1981**

Volunteer hours	Percentage of families
0	41
1-10	8
11-25	8
26-50	10
51-100	14
100-250	12
Over 250	7

Most family voluntary effort was centred in one community organization.

**CONCENTRATION OF FAMILY
COMMUNITY SERVICE, 1981**

Number of organizations served	Percentage of families
0	41
1-2	46
3-5	12
Over 5	1

Adjusting for average family size, and extrapolating to the whole population, this works out to roughly 25 hours of voluntary service per person per year, compared with 15 hours in the Statistics Canada survey of a year earlier. The difference is not statistically significant since both the sample selection and questions asked were different. Both studies do confirm that Canadians engage in substantial voluntary effort with considerable economic value to the country. The average family in our sample contributed 77 hours per year in voluntary service. At the minimum wage, this contribution had a value of $270; at twice the minimum, the value of their voluntary service would exceed the value of their cash donations over the year.

But like cash donations, voluntary effort is skewed unequally throughout the population. Both studies suggest that a high proportion of the adult population is not involved in voluntary public service, perhaps five out of six adults. And there is the *perception* that volunteerism, like cash generosity, is in decline. A Roper survey in 1981 determined that a substantial majority of the U.S. population, ranging from 58 per cent to 72 per cent, perceived that people were less willing to help their neighbors, to volunteer for youth activities or to help elderly parents, than they were 25 years earlier.

In Canada, this perception is reinforced by reports that the local United Way campaign has switched to mail solicitation instead of a door-to-door canvass because volunteers are difficult to find and reluctant to be trained, that the Canadian Red Cross cannot staff its blood-gathering clinics with enough aides who are willing to work for nothing. "Volunteers are a rare commodity," claims Merrideth Berman, head of Red Cross donor recruitment in Ontario. "They are hard to get and hard to hold on to."

In neither country can we confirm that voluntary participation is in decline. Surveys and polls conducted in the United States by reputable organizations in various years since 1965 phrased different questions concerning voluntary activity, so results are not comparable over time. Gallup polls conducted in 1977 and 1981 indicate that between 27 per cent and 29 per cent of U.S. people were engaged in volunteer work—almost twice the level determined by Statistics Canada for the Canadian population.

If it is true that there is a decline in voluntary involvement among the Canadian population in recent decades, it is perhaps understandable. Consider some of the forces working against the volunteer. Whether by choice or out of economic necessity, most adult Canadians work full or part time—54 per cent of our sample families had multiple incomes. People simply don't have time.

The massive infusion of government funds into health-care institutions, education, welfare and even cultural organizations as we have moved towards Stage IV has given the humanistic sector resources to hire professionals trained in specialized services previously supplied by the volunteer, or not provided at all. Labor unions and professional organizations are sensitive about their territorial prerogatives and have effectively prohibited the volunteer from performing work within their jurisdiction. Often the jobs that are left are the ones that are perceived to be insignificant, unchallenging, harmless.

In some cases, volunteer managers feel ill-equipped for the demands of the job—fund raising, for example. And for some, such as a public trustee in a hospital, community college or university, the public demand for higher and higher standards of accountability has forced the conscientious trustee to spend more and more time in discharging his obligation. Tensions often develop between volunteer boards and professional staffs, an atmosphere sometimes leading to acrimonious feuds. Many volunteers are simply fed up with the responsibility of "constantly raising money from an indifferent public for an ungrateful staff of paid professionals."

Anyway, who likes to be labelled a "do-gooder?" Just as one is repulsed by the condescension of the self-styled, superior "man of wealth" ministering ostentatiously to his poor inferiors, thoughtful people are equally repelled by the self-righteous zeal of the professional volunteer. Every community has them—the accountant, housewife, teacher, who is on every community board and committee, and who is just so busy but so generous with his or her time.

Dr. A. Menninger describes the syndrome in *Foundation Work May Be Hazardous to Your Health*:

A high risk of burnout afflicts conscientious people, who are so strongly motivated to provide service to others. They have a much higher need for appreciation and fulfillment than they are often willing to recognize. Most conscientious people, for example, have a terrible time taking a vacation. They feel indispensable. They feel guilty about leaving. They feel they do not deserve to be good to themselves, that personal pleasures are not nearly as important as wanting to help those suffering people or those vital projects. To believe that one is stronger and indispensable is a kind of negative—and it isn't true anyway.

Yet Canada today needs a strong voluntary sector like no time in her history. Our 47,000 humanistic organizations depend on voluntary boards for management and leadership. If they are not able to attract and keep Canada's brightest and best, then most assuredly the managerial leadership will come from the same source as now provides financial dominance—the federal, provincial and local governments.

Furthermore, financial contributions to the humanistic sector from both public and private sources are threatened and constrained. In many cases, properly supervised voluntary effort could well provide services comparable in quality to those now provided by paid professionals.

If fewer Canadians serve as volunteers for community organizations for whatever reason, the loss of association not only deprives the organization of the time and talents of the volunteer but is likely also to diminish the amount of cash donations the former volunteer and his family will make during the year. Recall the very strong relationship between size of family donations and the number of voluntary organizations served by the family. People who are associated with community organizations are the ones most likely to contribute money to advance their cause.[36] The linkage is strong and consistent. But the flow of donations will continue to diminish if society increasingly regards humanistic service as a right, a public good, *their* responsibility, as fewer people share their free time serving others.

The voluntary spirit does require nurturing in Canada. Personal service must be seen to be important to leaders in business, the professions, arts, sciences, labor—service measured not in the number of lines it attracts in

[36]There was an observable relationship between the number of hours contributed by families in voluntary service to community organizations and the number of organizations served per family, a correlation coefficient of .42. However, the linkage between number of organizations and family donations was strongest in multiple-regression models and is the variable used throughout this discussion.

the social column, nor in the number of entries on one's C.V., but recognized as an essential grace of the civilized man.

Let us summarize

Families who are serious givers in Canada are rare. The few who still tithe share one overwhelming characteristic. They are committed Canadians. Committed to their religion, to their family and marriage, to their community.

Most families give little. Many give nothing. Their profile contrasts sharply with the committed minority.

DONOR PROFILE

	Non-donors (n = 121)	Serious donors (n = 31)
Family income	$31,000	$ 47,000
Percentage multi-income families	46	48
Number of dependent children	0.8	1.6
Net worth	$58,000	$182,000
Liquid assets	$16,000	$ 85,000
Family donations	0	$ 7,000
Percentage planned	0	87
Non-religious	0	$ 800
Hours of personal service	43	161
Number of organizations	0.4	2.6
Degree of religious commitment (1)	3.3	1.6
Educational attainment (2)	2.6	2.8
Residential mobility (3)	2.4	1.9

(1) 1 = strong religious ties; 4 = no religious ties
(2) 1 = elementary school; 4 = post-graduate
(3) number of changes in past 10 years

Are there *any* optimistic signs that family charitable donations can be encouraged? That the donor base can be expanded? That the secular trend can be reversed?

Most encouraging is that half the Canadian families in our survey generally felt positive towards charitable appeals. They were the ones who identified motives such as humanism, freedom, religious and moral philosophy—the idealistic motives of Whitehead's great society. These are the families donating cash and time to the enhancement of their communities. The ones who feel some sense of duty and personal obligation.

What about the other half? Most expressed strong negative feelings towards charitable appeals, 28 per cent of the families in our sample. Why?

I am a single mother and I can't afford to give.

Too much of the money donated goes to pay for the cost of administration and doesn't reach the intended people.

I don't like it when people come knocking at my door asking for money.

The government should take total responsibility for these areas.

I don't believe in their causes.

Too many.

Too pushy.

Too bothersome.

The remaining 22 per cent were ambivalent, neutral or confused—"Sure there is a need, but...." An engineer from Halifax expressed their dilemma in eloquent terms:

I feel bad when I do not give. This is negative. Life has enough complications without added stress. I feel bad because I do not give enough—I feel bad if I give too much. I can't win.

Why the ambivalence? The antipathy? Perhaps the answer lies in the way we raise funds for good causes in this country. We turn our attention now to fund raising, an art that is older than Canada itself.

CHAPTER **IX**

Fund raising

One that gave me a great charge was when Charlie Isard was still alive. We were on an organ-fund drive, and we had been fooling around on that drive for two years. Isard called me on the phone and asked me how much we needed to finish. I said that about $500 would clean the thing up. Charlie said, "Come with me and I'll teach you how to raise money." So we called this old guy who was head of Richards Wilcox and we met 15 minutes in advance in the ballroom of the old Hotel London. Charlie said, "Robert, go get me a drink and our friend a drink and yourself a drink and bring them back here." We were standing at the piano and he told me to make them doubles. So I brought the drinks back, and Charlie poured that drink down that old fellow, he was about 75 or so, as fast as I had seen anybody do it before. He said to the old guy, "Do you remember that you said to me that you'd help me out again with the organ fund if we need it?" "Yes." "Well, we've come to the end of our tether and we have to come to you for the last bit of money." So the old guy's glass in his hand starts to shake and he puts it down on the piano. He said, "How much money are you looking for?" Charlie said, "Nothing serious, $2,500." "Twenty-five hundred dollars! There's no goddam way I'm going to give you $2,500!" Charlie said, "You'll do it for the church, won't you?" The man said, "No, I won't do it for the bloody church or anything else. Where's my cheque book?" So he gets out his cheque book and his hands are shaking so bad like he has epilepsy. He wrote out a cheque for $1,500, three times the amount we needed, and he hands it to Charlie and says, ''You know what you can do with that, you can go straight to hell! I won't give you another cent as long as I live.''

Robert Porter
London's indefatigable fund-raising coordinator

Every community in Canada has a clutch of men who are acknowledged to be Master Fund Raisers. Women are not excluded. They just don't have the credentials. MFRs are men with clout, which is to say money. Industrialists. Lawyers. Investors. People return their phone calls, immediately. They are capable of exerting extraordinary leverage on an impressive range of people. They are men of action with an awesome track record.

MFRs share one common passion. They love raising money. Their names and pictures surface regularly as chairmen of the Art Gallery Capital Drive, The University Development Fund, Rebuild the Y Campaign. They become obsessively committed to the causes they serve, and, goddammit, their friends are going to be too! They volunteer countless hours in organizing campaigns and making calls. They are always the first contributors and among the most generous. They are local characters. A folklore builds around their fund-raising prowess. Their friends simultaneously smile and grimace when they recall the size of the cheque they wrote the last time a Master touched them for a donation to his current good cause.

The Masters are gifted amateurs. But they are a dying breed. When they retire as fund raisers, which is to say when they die, they are not replaced.

The fund-raising gurus of the eighties are not volunteers with a compelling commitment to community and an honorary Master's title. They are no-nonsense professionals—Ph.Ds in market research, consumer psychology, persuasive communications. State-of-the-art fund raising for the humanistic sector is sophisticated, calculated, controlled and contrived.

Canada is well entrenched in advanced Stage III financing—the era of the professional gift seeker. For an appropriate fee, professional fund raisers (that is to say profit-making organizations)[1] will raise money for virtually any legal cause. The name of the game is marketing. Stripped to its essentials, selling the donor on a specific charity has become no different from selling

---

[1]Among the more visible fund-raising consultants: Robert Bedard, Robert Bedard Ltd; George Barker, Community Relations Consultants; Gordon Goldie, Gordon Goldie Co. Ltd.; Christopher Lang, Christopher Lang and Associates; John Martin, The Martin Group; Tom Rowe, formerly Community Charitable Counselling Service, more recently with Gordon Goldie.

the housewife on New Improved Oxydol. The key is business problem-solving: research, planning, strategy, organization, execution, control, evaluation.

Successful campaigns conform rigidly to a dozen or so fundamental steps. The allusion to a military campaign is not accidental.

First, the organization must determine its need. The goal cannot be vague and open-ended. It must be clear, precise, real, preferably exciting and capable of being presented in a concise, appealing manner.[2] The need must be translated into attractive imagery and reduced to a reasonable dollar objective. Depending on the goal, the campaign can be styled in a variety of forms: special-event fund raising, new-donor acquisition, renewal and annual giving, project fund raising, capital campaign or deferred giving.

Second is a dispassionate evaluation of resources—the external constituency and internal campaign leadership. Who are the potential donors? Who has a special reason for supporting the campaign? Which of the Level Two and Level One motives are most compelling in this case? Who exert the power in the community? Who can influence others? Where is the money? Who make the economic decisions for business and governments? What is the economic climate? What is the potential size of the donor pool, and who is able to tap it?

The answers to these questions will determine the attributes of the campaign leaders. Someone has to be a chairman who will accept responsibility for meeting or exceeding the campaign objective, who does not countenance failure. It helps if he is committed to the cause. The chairman should be prominent, respected, capable, knowledgeable and well-connected. He should either have political, economic or social leadership, or be able to influence those who have. The chairman should be capable of a substantial gift and should be the first person to make his pledge.[3] The chairman is the Five-Star General of the campaign. He attracts the team of sub-chairmen and canvassers, and is the public spokesman for the campaign. It is he whose reputation will rise or fall with its success or failure. The chairman must possess power and leverage, for it is he who must solicit the large lead gifts.

---

[2] "One of the toughest ones I have ever been involved in was a deficit fund-raising effort for Theatre London."

[3] "I said, 'You can't run a campaign and be campaign chairman unless you give big. I've got to be able to go around and tell them how much money you're going to give.' 'How much do you think I should give?' 'Not less than $100,000.' He dropped his spoon right in his soup, but I got him."

One must appreciate subtle but significant gradations of campaign leadership. A campaign committee often gives top billing to an honorary chairman or patron. H.R.H. Prince Philip would be the most prestigious but the Prince rations his endorsements; the Governor-General would be high on the list; the 10 Lieutenant-Governors would be next, followed by those few Canadians who have gained a position of unquestioned prominence and public affection. The patron, of course, takes no responsibility for the campaign and may or may not contribute financially. Lending his or her name gives the undertaking a legitimacy that has value beyond cash.

The chairman may also appoint a co-chairman or working-chairman, someone who is respected and acceptable, perhaps possessed of less stature and more time than the campaign chairman.[4] The working-chairman, usually also a volunteer, plans the campaign and coordinates the work of the committees. He or she selects and recruits leaders for the various sub-committees—professional groups, national corporations, local corporations, and so on.

The chairman's right arm is the paid staff coordinator—the mercenary. The coordinator has the professional expertise in fund raising, works closely with the campaign leaders, offers suggestions and advice based on knowledge and experience, and is responsible for the day-to-day running of the campaign. In political jargon, the coordinator is the *eminence gris*, the power in the back room.[5]

Third, the core group recruits leaders for the various committees and specialized tasks. These would be trusted, seasoned peers, campaign veterans or promising rookies, capable of recruiting others, of conceiving and executing an effective promotional campaign, of communicating with the media. This group constitutes the campaign cabinet and must be dedicated, enthusiastic, supportive, positive, optimistic.

Fourth, set up the campaign office and establish records and resources. Today this means computer access and word-processing capability. Now is the time the campaign prepares The List: vital statistics on specific donors, individuals who have donated in the past, or who are prime prospects, key corporations and foundations. If it has done its homework, the backroom

[4] "A campaign chairman doesn't necessarily have to be wealthy, but he has to be known, favorably known."

[5] "The chairman thought if you had a paid coordinator, that person raised the money. But that's not the way you do it. You use your coordinator as your right bower to help you."

will have loaded the computer's memory with intimate and powerful intelligence on its donor pool: names, addresses, phone numbers, place of employment, position or occupation, financial data (income, net worth), record of past giving, and other pertinent information such as number of dependent children, community activities.

With appropriate software and word-processing capability, the backroom can quickly retrieve, sort, analyze and print lists of prospects, arranged in an infinite array of categories—new donors, old donors, rich, poor. The word processor can spew out dozens of sincere, personal, intimate letters, reminding donors of the size of their last gift, reinforcing the decision-motives most likely to appeal. The letter would naturally make frequent reference to your name, last name, first name, or nickname if that is what you prefer. It's even capable of signing the campaign chairman's name. It will send you your tax receipt, offer you a sincere word of thanks from the chairman, and wish you Godspeed.

Meanwhile, the computer's central processing unit is tirelessly updating The List based on daily returns—changes of address, occupation, financial status. At regular intervals, it creates a status report, results to date, incomplete calls, follow-up lists for canvassers. And at the end of the campaign, it prepares a complete financial report of the campaign with comparisons with past campaigns and strategies for the future.

But we have jumped ahead of ourselves. It is from the computer lists that the campaign cabinet evaluates the financial potential of prospects. The cabinet assembles all pertinent information on prospective donors, then makes a judgment of their potential for the current campaign as they are assigned to one of three or four categories.

Fifth step. Prepare and print campaign material. These are the visual aids, advertisements, campaign folders, case histories, canvasser instructions, and so on. Creative work and printing can consume a large proportion of a campaign budget, particularly in small campaigns that do not benefit from economies of scale.

Sixth. Determine constituencies and campaign schedule. At this stage, there is a careful matching of the internal resources (leaders and potential canvassers) with the external constituency. Potential donors are meticulously matched with solicitors of the same social and economic strata. If there is to be an imbalance, the solicitor should be the superior—it will flatter the donor. The appropriate solicitation technique is determined, i.e., whether the optimal strategy is one general campaign, or a phased campaign where large gifts are solicited first.

Seventh. Recruit and train canvassers and volunteers. The number and type of volunteer, and the style and method of training, will be determined by the size of the campaign, the level of canvasser experience and the nature of the donor constituency.

Eighth. Solicitation of advance gifts. Before the campaign opens publicly, the chairman makes his personal calls on the donors expected to make the largest gifts. Here is where his personal prestige, leverage and influence goes on the line.

Ninth. With a dozen cheques in hand, representing a quarter or more of the campaign goal, the campaign is given a public kick-off and a schedule of progress meetings is established.

Tenth. General solicitation. The team now goes to work. Personal solicitation is absolutely necessary for securing capital and special donors, for nailing down bequests, and for making deferred-giving arrangements. It is desirable for confirming substantial regular donors, for upgrading annual renewals, for encouraging promising new prospects. Mail solicitation may be acceptable for hooking first-time givers, for systematic annual renewals, for routine donor-upgrading. Direct mail is satisfactory for the general public. The campaign may include special projects and events such as a walka-thon, a telethon, celebrity auction, and the like.

Eleven and Twelve. Celebration. Recognition of and thanks to donors, leaders and volunteers. These are acts of courtesy sometimes overlooked by an exhausted campaign chairman. Most volunteers are sensitive individuals whose reward is knowing that their contribution is valued and appreciated.[6] Furthermore, a sincere thank-you will assure the chairman of a pool of receptive leaders and donors for his next successful campaign.

The Anglicans in Mission campaign of 1982-83 was a model of formula fund raising. AIM was orchestrated at the national level by fund-raising mercenaries, at the diocesan level by mercenaries and clergy, and in the parishes by volunteer lay people. The consultants produced a step-by-step plan which parishes were urged to follow meticulously and without deviation if they wanted to succeed. The campaign plan segregated parish lists into three groups and solicited pledges in three consecutive waves or phases.

In the Forward Phase, the campaign leaders made personal calls on those parishioners financially able to make gifts of $7,500 and up. These were

[6] "I don't think I ever got a thank-you note. No, I'm not bitter about this. If you're doing a fund-raising job, and you've been pushing and pressuring people, they're so bloody glad when the thing is over, to get you off their backs and get out of it."

called "Leadership Gifts," highly publicized to show the parish that its sights were high. Canvassers were urged not to accept a lesser gift. Instructions were explicit: *"The best financial development technique available to the experienced large-gift solicitor is the ability to defer a suggested gift that is below the amount expected.* No single manoeuvre in solicitation strategy is more effective than the solicitor's readiness to suggest with sensitivity and tact that the offered gift is below expectations and then request that the prospect give the matter more careful thought."* Let them squirm; they'll eventually come around.

After a decent interval, the floor for Forward Gifts was dropped to $5,000. Only then, after the big money was in, was the second phase launched. In this Special Phase, parishes were asked to solicit approximately half of their members. "Generally, these will be those members who are regular contributors and who will find it possible to contribute a gift of perhaps $1,500 to $2,000 over a period of five years."

By the end of the Special Phase, the results would indicate whether or not the parish campaign was going to be successful. Then it could be opened up to the General Phase, for the great unwashed. "Here all members who were unable to contribute to the Forward or Special Phases will be asked to give their meaningful and sacrificial gifts of a lesser amount than suggested. It is important that their value be decided only after some indication has been received of the acceptability and success of the Forward Phase."

This is hardball fund raising. And it works. AIM exceeded its national objective in May 1983 without seriously depending on Phase Three giving. The pros were right.[7]

Yet it is a Canadian amateur who holds the Guinness World Record for personally raising the largest amount of money for a charitable cause. In 1977, at age 18, Terry Fox, a native of Port Coquitlam, B.C., lost his right leg to cancer. Three years later, he persuaded the Canadian Cancer Society to endorse his idea of a Marathon of Hope: he would *run* across Canada on one leg—from coast to coast—and raise $100,000 for cancer research. The

---

[7]But they have left some deep scars on Anglican congregations across the land. Consider this letter written in July 1983 to the AIM volunteer coordinator in a small rural parish in the Diocese of Huron, perhaps the diocese with the least enthusiasm for the manner in which AIM was organized. "I agree completely with the principle of AIM but I did not agree with the hiring of a commission agency from the United States to direct the manoeuvre. I believe the carpetbaggers have now left and I wish to write you and pledge ...."

run began in St. John's, Nfld., on April 12, 1980, and halted after 5,342 kilometres near Thunder Bay, Ont., on September 2, 1980, when doctors discovered a reemergence of cancer in Terry's lungs. Terry Fox died on June 28, 1981.

Terry's run failed to attract much media attention on the east coast and in Quebec but by the time he reached Ontario, Terry was a top news item. Hundreds pressed him along the highways, 10,000 turned out to greet him in Toronto, the Prime Minister and sports celebrities endorsed his cause. The run became emotion-charged. The nation was impressed by Terry's determination, youth and courage, and with his dignity and integrity. "I'm not going to make a cent out of this...not now and not later."

By the time of his death, Terry's Marathon of Hope had raised $23 million, including million-dollar gifts from the Provinces of Ontario and British Columbia and $10 million from a CTV telethon hastily organized and aired on September 7, scarcely five days after his poignant capitulation. He swiftly became the most honored young man in Canadian history, the youngest Companion of the Order of Canada, Canadian Press Man of the Year. In an unprecedented break from tradition, Canada Post commemorated a stamp in Terry's honor while he was still alive; only royalty had been so recognized.

Terry Fox will be remembered as a symbol of grace, courage, self-sacrifice. What of his legacy, his endowment? Anniversary marathons were run in September 1981 ($3 million) and September 1982 ($2.3 million). "Each year, the Terry Fox Run has earned less," said Dr. Peter Scholefield, executive director of the National Cancer Institute of Canada, recipient of the proceeds. In June 1983, Scholefield warned that if the institute did not get more money and put a brake on expenditures, there would be nothing left by 1988. The 1983 run raised $3.2 million and CCS officials scheduled a fourth run in 1984, expressing belief that the public had not tired of the event.

And how do professional fund raisers view the exercise? Christopher Lang, Christopher Lang and Associates: "I'll tell you the worst organization and the toughest to deal with is the Cancer Society. They're a bunch of self-serving doctors. I think the way they handled Terry Fox was an absolute bloody tragedy. Nobody ever sat down with the guy. The cancer people wouldn't do it. If you listen to all the machinations of how they handled Terry Fox you'd throw up. It's brutal. They hired a PR firm after to handle all the funds they koshered because they were too embarrassed. They should never have raised that money. They put a great blight on charity in this country because I think they hurt a lot of other organizations. They cut in front of them. They put on a telethon and hurt organizations that already had pledges made. They never gave any consideration for that. They scooped an awful lot of money out and the question is, who plays God?''

Fund raising can be a savage battleground. Each year more and more organizations attack a static pool of donors. Success is reserved for the most imaginative, colorful, even bizarre campaigns—walkathons, jogathons, runathons, canoe-athons, shine-athons, telethons.[8] Anything to grab attention for the cause, to gain those precious few seconds of exposure on local TV news, to add new names to the donor list. Winners have short life cycles. Success is instantly mimicked, the unique becomes commonplace and a fickle public moves on to the latest gimmick.

In the eye of this swirl is the United Way, the sexagenarian fund-raising army engaged each autumn in a nation-wide campaign of community compassion. For 60 days each year (more often now extended to 90), the volunteer canvassers face a hundred communities across the country with an awesome display of organized, precision manoeuvres. For the other 300 days, a much smaller but equally structured team of professional fund raisers, the permanent United Way staff, analyze the past campaign, compare notes through national headquarters in Ottawa, and plan strategy for next year's effort.

When the idea for a federated fund-raising campaign was first introduced in Canada, it made good sense. Not only was it welcomed by the general

---

[8]Weekend fund-raising telethons are the current rage, mimicking the television fund-raising formula pioneered in the United States by Jerry Lewis for Muscular Dystrophy. A cause blocks off 24, 48 or 72 hours of live TV time, sets up a phone bank in the studio, mans it with VIPs and politicians, and parades another series of celebrities through the studio to pitch for donations to the cause. Everyone's time is donated. Well, not everyone's.

The Easter Seal Telethon begun in the late 1970s brought in a record $21 million across the U.S. in 1983. Barrie and Windsor initiated a Canadian version in 1982, the Ontario Easter Seal Telethon, by tapping into the U.S. broadcast and supplementing it with local talent and local phone numbers. The Ontario telethon expanded to 10 centres in 1983, including southwestern Ontario.

Clayton Warmuth, president of the Rotary Club of London, was chief organizer of the 22-hour broadcast over CFPL-TV during the last weekend of March. Warmuth estimates that he, along with about 500 other volunteers, raised $72,000 in pledges during the marathon. How much will Easter Seals net? Unpaid pledges (practical jokers, publicity seekers, ego trippers, emotionally vulnerable— but poor) will shrink the collections by 20-25 per cent. Studio time, telephone charges, mailing and salaries will skim off another $30,000. The net may be $25,000, about one-third of the total pledged, half of which London sends to Easter Seals in Toronto, the franchisor.

Was it worth it? "No, not really," admitted Warmuth 10 days after the event, with $45,000 still to collect, "but it's a great practice run for next year's effort. We plan to raise $200,000 gross next year." Exploitive of crippled children? "Parents and kids were upset because they weren't exploited enough. Next year our priority is to keep kids on the air at all times."

public, who even then was showing signs of irritation with multiple fund-raising appeals, it was also attractive to business since it solved a tough political problem—saying no to a director who requested in-plant canvassing for his favorite charity. Uniting the diverse fund-raising groups into one appeal was efficient and a logical evolution beyond Stage II financing with its fragmented loyalties and destructive competition for funds.

The movement grew. From 36 communities right after the Second World War, to 61 in 1955, to a peak of 124 in 1967. But now it was a more complex entity. In an effort to provide more community coordination, the social planners (spenders) were merged with the fund raisers, professional social workers were united with volunteer solicitors, in an attempt to reconcile the community's social welfare needs with its free-will resources. There were inevitable tensions between the professionals and the amateurs, not unlike the sometimes strained relations between a university senate committed to academic excellence and the board of governors responsible for its fiscal integrity.

Despite the differences, the United Way worked—until the late 1960s. From 1946 to 1969, the United Way posted annual gains in its national receipts. But from 1970 forward to the early 1980s, real-dollar receipts, after adjusting for inflation, have eroded to a level some 20 per cent below the 1969 peak. If compared with the national capacity to give, receipts as a proportion of GNP, United Way giving in the 1980s had dropped to two-thirds of its 1950s level. Community participation shrank to 93 campaigns in 1981.

What went wrong? To answer the question, we compared the 1981 campaign with 1972, both seen through the eyes of campaign chairmen[9] immediately after they had packed it in. The contrast is illuminating; both the differences and similarities. Some features have not changed. The average campaign chairman still is male, a business executive, college-educated and urban. His campaign cabinet remains a team of business and professional males with token female representation and virtually none from organized labor.[10] But his foot soldiers, the volunteer canvassers, still are largely (two-thirds) women.

---

[9]Exhaustive "debriefing questionnaires" were completed by 41 campaign chairmen in 1972 (representing 86 per cent of total dollars collected), and 23 chairmen in 1981 (45 per cent). The questionnaires were similar although not identical.

[10]It would be interesting to document the extent to which the various ethnic minority groups in Canada participate in the United Way, both as to their involvement in the fund-raising hierarchy and their financial participation in United Way disbursements. We do know that the new Canadian families in our 1981 survey donated significantly less to the United Way than did families born in Canada ($22 versus $39).

The differences are significant. Most striking is the shrinkage in size of the volunteer team. The 41 campaigns sampled in 1972 averaged 4,000 volunteer workers each; the average for the 1981 campaigns was half that number. The shrinkage was particularly acute in campaigns in the largest urban centres: Greater Toronto dropped from 40,000 to 2,000 volunteers; Winnipeg from 10,000 to 7,000; Vancouver from 15,000 to 3,000. A.C. Wilton, president of the Brandon, Man., United Way claims, "It is impossible to get volunteers from employee groups." The United Way establishment in B.C.'s Lower Mainland approached six seasoned fund raisers before one agreed to chair the 1982 campaign.[11]

More than half the 1981 campaigns had abandoned door-to-door canvassing in favor of a mail-in. The trend is likely to continue despite the cost of postage. Two of the 10 campaigns that had used canvassers in 1981 planned to switch to mail-in the following year because they were dissatisfied with results. In fact, not one campaign chairman judged their 1981 canvass to be greatly effective, whether door-to-door or mail-in. Many reasons were advanced for discarding the face-to-face canvass: "Housewives find it very discouraging to go door-to-door for small contributions." "It requires one full-time staff person for every 1,200 canvassers." "Cost of kits." "Poor per capita returns." "Don't want to bother neighbors." "Cost of gas." "Dogs."

Even business, which for years provided strong and generous support for the United Way, appears to have dampened its enthusiasm. In 1972, 34 per cent of campaign chairmen rated cooperation from corporations as excellent, five per cent said it was poor; in 1981, the proportions were 25 per cent and 10 per cent. But corporations continued to support the United Way financially. They provided roughly one-third of total receipts in both years, as well as an impressive contribution of loaned executives seconded each year to work full time in campaign administration.

How effective was the 1981 United Way drive across Canada? The 93 campaigns collected more dollars than the previous year—exceeding $100 million for the first time in history. But when inflation was squeezed out, 1981 receipts actually shrank by two per cent.

In 1972, 60 per cent of the campaigns had equalled or exceeded their total financial objective after two months, by November 30, a goal that generally

---

[11]"Today we're not using our young people. The older people will not relinquish their hold...."

included a margin of growth over the inflation rate. In 1981, two of the 23 campaigns in our sample, including Toronto, the nation's largest, had abandoned goal-setting entirely. Of the remainder, less than 30 per cent had reached their objective by the end of the calendar year. Fewer than one in three achieved final receipts that were equal to the previous year in real terms.

Yet despite a milieu that at best could be described as challenging, campaign chairmen in 1981 remained doggedly optimistic and enthusiastic. In retrospect, two-thirds rated the rewards to themselves as greater than they had expected. Most said they would do it again. Allowed one, "This was my third year on the campaign and I've had enough, but probably will come back for more." Bravo!

Brian Crombie, who was commissioned to analyze the 1981 United Way debriefing questionnaires, drew this thoughtful conclusion in his report for this study:

> The United Way is withering. It is not dead as some would make us believe nor will it soon die. In fact, there is a small movement for reform. The establishment of an Inclusivity Committee in Vancouver, a long-range planning committee in London, and the appointment of "Metro's social conscience" as president of Toronto's United Way, are all examples of attempts at reform. Yet it is definitely withering. The United Way campaigns across the nation have consistently not been reaching their goals, growing at less than the inflation rate, and have not been able to fund all of society's needs. Unless the need for change is felt in the United Way and this small band of reformers can effect this change (and perhaps even if it does), the United Way will continue to wither. It will last a decade or maybe even five, yet it will continue to lose funds in real terms, come under competition from other charitable organizations, lose its committed volunteers, and cease to be a relevant part of society. The task of reform will be hard. The United Way is a very large, structured, inflexible institution. Its biggest challenge will be to open its ears to criticisms and then to effect change to answer the criticism.

Canada's champion fund raiser is on the ropes. Fund-raising leadership in the eighties is an unstable liaison between volunteers and mercenaries. The amateurs are committed to the cause and volunteer their time for a constellation of motives ranging from altruistic idealism to ego reinforcement.[12] They work cheek-to-jowl with well-paid mercenaries, men and women who view each new campaign with clinical detachment, who harness science and technology with cool efficiency, who play probabilities and whose decision rule is, "Will it work?"

Many recoil when they learn the per diem fee schedule of professional fund raisers. It is considered un-Canadian for someone to get rich from sacrificial donations made to the church, pledges to crippled children or gifts to cancer research. Yet the same lawyer who is outraged at the size of the fund-raising consultant's fee for the university development drive thinks nothing of charging full tariff for his routine title search on property donated for future campus expansion. The lingering mythology of the eighties is that specialists who serve the public through the humanistic sector do so at a discount—that, certainly, they *should* be paid less than those who do battle in the real world.

Specialists are expensive. Administrators. Brain surgeons. Computer scientists. Dentists. Engineers. Fund raisers. And there is increasing pressure for them to bill their time, rather than donate it. Should an accountant serve as university trustee or be engaged as paid auditor? Should an architect volunteer for the museum property committee, or be retained as building consultant? Should a management consultant serve as a member of a hospital board or teach hospital administration on a paid seminar? Should a communications consultant join the United Way campaign cabinet, or design its fund-raising theme for a fee? Real conflicts. Conflicts of conscience. Conflicts of professional ethics. Economic conflicts.

It is no contest. The mercenaries will overcome. Not only because they produce better results and with greater efficiency than the well-meaning

---

[12]Why on earth *do* people raise money voluntarily? Some because they think it is good for business. ("Anybody who does fund raising to get something out of it financially is out of their minds.") Some because it offers a rare opportunity to rub shoulders with the wealthy and influential, hoping the contact will advance them socially. ("I've seen a number of people try it, thinking they could jump up three strata on the social scale.") Some because they are levered by an Important Person (employer, client). Some because of the influence and prestige it gives them over the people who will spend it. Some because they crave external recognition, and the involvement means a newsclip, success means a testimonial banquet or, dare one hope, an honorary degree. All Level Two motives.

Others raise funds out of a sense of altruism or duty, recognizing their responsibility and perhaps their unique ability to influence others and improve the quality of their community. Level One motives.

And for many more, the motives are mixed.

amateur but because for many talented Canadians today there are more attractive outlets for the volunteers' energy—paid employment, self-improvement, leisure. Methodically, humanistic institutions are adding a new box to the organization chart of their professional staff—fund-raising executive. More often, a former job title remains but the function changes. During a university development campaign, for instance, it is not uncommon for the president to devote half his time over a full year to raising funds. Directors of medical research institutions may be potential Nobel laureates but hospital trustees expect them first to impress foundations and granting agencies at home.

Groups that don't have expertise in-house can choose from a variety of consultants. The Yellow Pages today list a plethora of fund-raising organizations.[13] Toronto boasts 25 entries; Montreal, 14; Edmonton, five. There is even a National Society of Fund-Raising Executives, Canada ("Be a part of the fund-raising network...if eligible, become professionally certified through the NSFRE Certification Program, sit for a 200-question multiple-choice examination...carry the initials CFRE behind your name.")

Indeed, the NSFRE network is expanding rapidly. Membership doubled from January to April 1983, reaching 134 members. Conferences and seminars abound where fund raisers learn the "new technologies in fund raising" and swap intelligence on the latest campaign, the biggest gifts, the most effective new gimmick. If one is to raise money today, one must move with the current. The exercise is calculated and costly. Despite the paradox, the key actors will be shrewd professionals, quietly orchestrating a campaign that engenders spontaneous goodwill and munificence.

Still the mercenaries know they cannot succeed without the amateur front men. And so there will be unresolved conflicts between the amateur and the professional. Conflicts among amateurs and among professionals. And internal conflicts of conscience within both.

---

[13]For-profit fund-raising organizations are a post-war import from the United States where charity has been a serious business for several decades. Canada's three pioneers were listed in the 1955 Toronto Yellow Pages: Jones John Price Co. (Canada) Ltd., National Fund-Raising Services, and Wells Church Fund Raising.

CHAPTER

Corporate philanthropy

I should like it to become more generally recognized that the privilege of carrying on business in our free enterprise country carries with it the strongest moral obligation to maintain a substantial measure of private support of both our welfare institutions and our institutions of higher learning and research...

Hon. Donald M. Fleming
former Minister of Finance

Few trends could so thoroughly undermine the very foundations of our free society as the acceptance by corporate officials of a social responsibility other than to make as much money for their stockholders as possible. One topic...has been the claim that business should contribute to the support of charitable activities and especially to universities. Such giving by corporations is an inappropriate use of corporate funds in a free-enterprise society.

Milton Friedman
Capitalism and Freedom

A critique of corporate philanthropy can be more concise and precise than the rather lengthy analysis of individual and family donation behavior. This is so for three reasons. First, authoritative and comprehensive statistics on corporate charitable donation aggregates have been provided by Statistics Canada on an annual basis since the Second World War. Second, much more has been published on the topic of corporate responsibility and corporate philanthropy. And third, our own research has involved the detailed tracking of donation policies and priorities in many of Canada's largest corporations for a period extending beyond a decade. One can be much more confident, less tentative, in drawing conclusions about corporate philanthropic behavior in Canada than is the case with individuals and families.

Canadian business has a long tradition of corporate philanthropy. Our great retail chains—Eaton's, Simpsons, Woodward's—were founded by men who exhibited a generous public spirit themselves, and instilled the same tradition of service and duty in the succeeding generations.

Timothy Eaton, for instance, was half-a-century ahead of government in assuming cradle-to-grave responsibility for his employees' welfare. It was also he who gave Canada its first Santa Claus Parade in 1905.[1]

The Burton family, who controlled Simpsons for many decades, were particularly respected for their strong commitment to personal service in their community. Charles Luther Burton stressed the enormous value that could be derived from personal participation by businessmen in social service organizations, value both to the individual as well as the community he served.

P.A. Woodward in British Columbia managed the family company for many years while his brother, W.C., fulfilled the family duty to public service. P.A. ("Puggy"), too, eventually turned to philanthropy and in later years distributed much of his money for the good of the people of Vancouver.

Labatt and Molson, Stelco, Sun Life, these and many other old and prestigious Canadian corporations are widely respected to this day for generous financial support to health, education, welfare and cultural causes across the land. In the early years, gifts by the Molson family and the corporation were indistinguishable as to their source. The Molsons were particularly generous to McGill University and Montreal hospitals. Sun Life, for understandable reasons, has invested generous sums in public health and welfare causes, particularly the diseases of later life—cancer, heart and vascular disease. Stelco was and remains a generous donor, especially to education and research, not only in Hamilton but across Canada.

---

[1]Santa fell victim to an Eaton's economy drive in the 1981-82 recession when they discontinued the parade's sponsorship in Toronto.

Canada's early corporations shared one common characteristic: they were owned, controlled and very definitely managed by a single, dominant personality. His values were indelibly inscribed and inexorably intertwined with the values, policies and actions of the corporation he led. Timothy Eaton's sense of gentle *noblesse oblige* became the standard for T. Eaton Company. Personal generosity was reflected in corporate philanthropy.

But time and size have diffused the control of our pioneer entrepreneurs. One-man dominance has yielded to committee consensus; tracing ultimate corporate control through the layers of related ownership blocs is more challenging today than winning at Pac-Man. How has this affected corporate donation decisions? Who determines the amount and direction of corporate philanthropy? What motives lay behind the decision? Whose philosophy predominates in corporate boardrooms—the tunnel vision of Milton Friedman or the moral conservatism of Donald Fleming?

This chapter examines the record of corporate philanthropy in the post-Second-World-War era. The discussion begins by examining the size and direction of aggregate corporate donations over time in order to place in perspective the corporate role in financing the humanistic sector. Next, we explore the contemporary donation record of Canada's 240,000 registered corporations by industry, size, profitability, locus of voting control and so on. Finally we report the results of extensive survey-research conducted over the past decade on a sample of Canada's 500 largest corporations, and compare the performance of these giants with a similar survey drawn from the small-business community in 1981—precisely the sector that political leaders today are relying on to create employment growth and to rekindle our country's economic vitality.

First, the post-war record of the business community. How generous has the corporate sector been in donating its profits voluntarily to humanistic causes? The aggregates are impressive. Corporate tax returns show that donations from all filing corporations grew from $11 million in 1946 to $196 million in 1980, that total donations trebled in the decade of the seventies.

Even when inflation is eliminated, the upward trend is encouraging. Graphing the results reveals the most important characteristic of corporate donation behavior—a consistent and rigid conformity with the business cycle. Canada experienced seven recessions from 1950 through 1983.

Each of these recessions had a noticeable effect on corporate donations. Donations declined moderately in the 1951 recession, which was of moderate intensity, and sharply in the 1953-54 recession, the most severe until the extraordinary contraction of 1981-82. During the recession of 1957-58,

CANADIAN RECESSIONS: DURATION/SEVERITY

Monthly reference dates	Duration (months)	Severity (rank)
June 1951 to December 1951	7	4
June 1953 to June 1954	13	2
February 1957 to January 1958	12	7 (least)
April 1960 to January 1961	10	3
June 1974 to March 1975	10	6
November 1979 to June 1980	8	5
July 1981 to December 1982	18	1 (most)

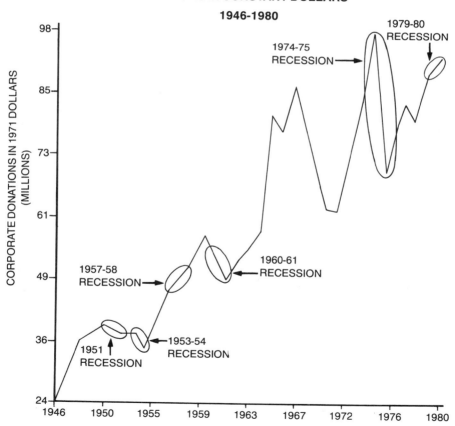

CORPORATE DONATIONS IN CONSTANT DOLLARS
1946-1980

the least severe of the seven, corporate donations did not drop but their rate of growth declined perceptibly. In the 1960-61 recession, the third most severe, corporate donations fell considerably from their 1959 peak.

In the period from February 1961 to May 1974, Canada registered a record-breaking span of 160 months of uninterrupted economic growth. It was also a period when real corporate donations grew rapidly, reaching a post-war peak in 1974. The rug was pulled out in the 1974-75 recession. Corporate donations plummeted in 1975, a drop of $27 million or a 28 per cent reduction from 1974 figures. Growth of donations slowed in 1980 reflecting the impact of the 1979-80 recession.

The statistics are not yet available for the period since 1980, but we can be confident that the contraction in real corporate donations will at least echo the shrinkage in corporate profits in Canada's modern depression. Not so with donations by individuals. Our earlier analysis suggests that while personal donations are in secular decline, they are largely immune to contractions in the economic cycle.

This synchronization of corporate donations and the business cycle is not coincidental, as we shall see later. But it is important to understand, especially for those humanistic organizations who depend on corporate charitable donations for their sustaining revenue. Corporations are not capricious in their donations behavior; they simply have their eye on the bottom line.

As one probes further, there are other interesting characteristics of corporate donation aggregates. First is the observation that they have shrunk in size relative to corporate profits[2] in recent years. In 1946, Canadian corporations contributed 0.86 of their pre-tax profits to charitable organizations. The payout increased to an all-time high of 1.5 per cent of profits in 1958. It has declined ever since, reaching a low of 0.4 to 0.5 per cent in recent years. Why?

The answer lies in changes in attitudes, policies and practices towards charitable donations by decision-makers in separate business entities. But even observing business behavior at the macro-level (the sum of all corporate decisions) reveals some interesting insights. If corporations are an amalgamation of resources—human, physical and financial capital—then

---

[2]Corporate profits, or net income, like family income represents the ability or capacity to give.

one should be able to define the relationship between those three fundamental resources (ability or capacity to donate) and the degree of corporate
generosity.

The most effective modelling of these inter-relationships, resources and
real corporate donations over the 35-year period since the Second World
War is one that relates corporate charitable donations to two independent
variables. First is corporate pre-tax income. Second is an index that com-
bines the influence of both capital and human resources—a capital intensity
ratio (total corporate assets employed by Canadian business divided by total
number of corporate employees). Since the Second World War, and particularly in the decade of the 1970s, the cost of creating one new job in the corporate sector in Canada has risen sharply. In constant dollars it required
$26,000 in corporate assets in 1946 to support each employee. In 1969, it re-
quired $49,000; in 1980, more than $65,000 per employee.

The inter-relationship of employees, capital and profits explains a great
deal about aggregate corporate donation behavior over the past 35 years.

Regression models of donations versus corporate profits and capital intensity showed a high level of confidence in predicting actual corporate donations behavior.[3] If the total post-war period is split between the early post-
war era, 1946 to 1967, and the more recent Trudeau era, 1968 to 1980, the
results are equally significant and even more interesting.

In the early post-war period, aggregate corporate donations were predicted almost entirely by the two variables: level of corporate profits plus a
donations "allowance" related to the average amount of capital required for
the average Canadian employee.[4]

During the more turbulent Trudeau era, the same two variables, profits
and capital intensity, were less highly explanatory, but their relative influence had undergone an interesting change. The level of corporate donations
was still significantly responsive to annual swings in corporate profits in recent years, but the capital-intensity ratio (the value of assets per employee)

---

[3]Using constant dollar data over the 35-year period, $R^2 = 78$ per cent. The capital intensity variable
was significant at the two per cent level, corporate profits at the seven per cent level. In the more rigorous test, first differences on the time series, R^2 equalled 26 per cent; the corporate profit variable was
significant at the one per cent level, the capital intensity variable was not significant.

[4]The profit coefficient was significant at the eight per cent level, capital intensity at the two per cent
level. R^2 equalled 87 per cent. Using first differences on the time series, profits were significant at the
one per cent level, capital intensity was not significant, and R^2 equalled 58 per cent.

had become negatively correlated.[5] That is to say, total corporate donations tended to decrease as the level of assets required per employee increased.

Furthermore, corporate donation behavior had altered. Whereas in the early post-war period corporations rarely pledged long-term charitable commitments, it was not uncommon in the 1970s for a corporation to commit for periods up to five years for major university development campaigns or hospital capital drives. Thus, a significant, built-in annual floor developed under total Canadian corporate donations. Our models covering the 1968-1980 period place this committed floor at roughly $70 million in 1971 dollars.[6]

This implies that a high proportion (about three-quarters) of annual corporate donations, representing previously committed pledges or entrenched annual renewals, has become fixed in nature, essentially uncontractible during business recessions. But since we know that corporate donations *do* contract during recessions, it also suggests that the remainder of the corporate donations budget, the smaller uncommitted portion available for expendable annual renewals or new commitments, is now much more volatile and vulnerable than was the case in the early post-war years.

The implications of the recent relationship are indeed significant. As Canadian corporations generally become increasingly capital-intensive we might expect them to become less philanthropic. The hard internal demands for capital tend to preclude, or at least crowd out, the softer requirements of the humanistic sector.

If one calculates real corporate donations per employee in the post-war period, one observes a sharp cyclical pattern but over-all secular decline, from $14 in 1946 to $13 in 1978 (after reaching a high of $23 in 1949). Over the same period, business employment has shrunk relative to total employment while the non-profit and self-employed sectors have grown from 21 per cent of total employment in 1946 to 49 per cent in 1979. Therefore the relative reduction in business employment makes the decline in donations per

---

[5]The coefficient for capital intensity was negative in both real-dollar and first-difference models although it was not statistically significant (levels of 31 per cent and 24 per cent respectively). The suggestion is strong enough, and the swing from the previous era pronounced enough, to lend credence to the argument of a changed relationship of resources to donations by the business sector. (R^2 equalled 63 per cent in the real-dollar model, 30 per cent in the first-difference model.)

[6]This constant was highly significant in the real-dollar model (two per cent level). Corporate donations in 1980, expressed in 1971 dollars, equalled some $93 million, suggesting a potential contraction of $23 million.

employee even more severe than the above calculations imply.

As business firms make capital/labor trade-offs, favoring investment over employees, their "people presence" in the community tends to decline. If corporations make donations in part to support the communities in which their employees live and work, relatively fewer employees would mean a relatively decreased propensity to give. This would appear to be the case during the 1970s.

While corporations have curtailed their charitable donations relative to net income, the income tax burden on corporations also has steadily declined, from a high of 53 per cent of income in 1946 to about 24 per cent in 1978. Since corporate taxes are used in part by governments to finance humanistic service, corporate indirect financing of the humanistic sector has also declined proportionately. Thus both voluntary and involuntary[7] contributions have shrunk considerably.

When corporate giving is analyzed by industry, the results tend to confirm the earlier conclusions regarding the effects of capital intensity on corporate generosity. Over the period 1976 to 1979, only seven of the 37 industry classifications donated an average of one per cent or more of pre-tax income. These generous industries were knitting mills, clothing manufacturers, textile mills, metal fabricators, leather products, furniture and beverages. As a group they tend to be relatively labor-intensive and thus would have a higher community profile due to their heavy employment. They tend to be older, established businesses, often controlled by a single family with traditional patterns and habits. (The knitting, clothing and textile industries also are heavily controlled by Jewish entrepreneurs, a religious-ethnic group that tends to be very generous).

The least generous industry groupings, the 18 classifications that averaged less than 0.5 per cent donations to pre-tax income, tend to be those with extreme capital intensity; for example, storage, transportation, metal mining, agriculture, petroleum and coal, chemical, communications, public utilities and mineral fuels. Most of these are large, publicly owned or Crown corporations, many are technologically innovative, often exhibiting less traditional patterns and habits. This impersonality, capital intensity and nonconformity makes it more natural, perhaps, for these corporations to participate less in corporate philanthropy than corporations in the seven most generous industries.

---

[7]This applies to corporate income taxes only. Corporations make other tax payments, e.g., royalties, employee health insurance premiums, unemployment insurance contributions, and so on.

Those observations and conclusions are based on national aggregates. Probing behind the aggregates to the donation performance of Canada's 240,000 corporations shows the narrow concentration of corporate philanthropy. According to their tax returns,[8] only 23,000, less than 10 per cent, of all profit-making corporations made charitable donations in 1979, 1978, 1977 or 1973. Corporate philanthropy is therefore even more sharply concentrated than personal or family generosity.

ALL CANADIAN CORPORATIONS, 1979
TOTAL DONATIONS

Corporate net income $	$ millions	Percentage net income	Percentage donating
To 50,000	16	0.6	3.2
50/100,000	11	0.5	13.7
100,000/1 million	56	0.7	34.1
1/30 million	63	0.4	61.9
Over 30 million	49	0.2	75.6
All profit corporations, 1979	195	0.4	9.6

Almost 60 per cent of Canadian corporate donations are made by corporations earning more than $1 million per year, about two per cent of all corporations in the country. The propensity, or tendency, for a corporation to donate increases with the size of its annual profit. Even so, one out of four of Canada's 200 largest profit-making corporations, those earning more than $30 million, donated nothing throughout the 1970s.

Donations as a percentage of pre-tax income tends to decline with increased income. Consequently, larger corporations are *relatively* less generous than smaller ones. Since the burden of income taxation tends to increase with the size of profits (ranging from a low of 20 per cent of pre-tax

---

[8]The data bank for corporate tax return information for 1973, 1977, 1978 and 1979, on which this analysis is based, was generously made available to us at no charge by the Canadian Centre for Philanthropy which obtained it from Revenue Canada. We acknowledge with deep gratitude the cooperation of the Centre generally, and its executive director, Allan Arlett, in particular. The Centre, of course, bears no responsibility for the analysis and conclusions we have drawn from the data.

income to 29 per cent in 1979), the after-tax cost of donations by small-profit corporations is greater than for large-profit companies.

When corporations who donate (the givers) are separated from those who do not (the keepers), we can begin to isolate further characteristics. Corporate givers in all net-income categories paid a higher rate of corporate taxes than did keepers, from a thin differential in the smallest-profit category to a 24-point spread in the largest-profit category.

Much of the difference in the latter category likely results from the donation policies and taxation regulations of large-scale Crown corporations. Some of the major federal Crown corporations pay income taxes in the same manner as privately owned companies: Canadian National Railway Systems, Petro-Canada, Teleglobe Canada. Others do not: Atomic Energy Corporation, Bank of Canada, Export Development Corporation. Provincial Crown corporations, such as Alberta Government Telephones and Ontario Hydro, are income tax-exempt. While a few Crown corporations report that they make corporate contributions to charitable organizations (for example, Air Canada), most of those corresponding with us indicated that their policy was *not* to contribute.[9] These likely account for many of the large-profit keepers identified in the previous matrix.

Keepers tend to be more profitable than givers. They averaged an eight per cent return on assets in 1979 compared with a return of slightly more than six per cent for givers. Some of the differences are striking. For instance, the spread in profitability between keepers and givers was eight percentage points, from 13 per cent to five per cent on assets in corporations with profits between $50,000 and $100,000. In all profit groups, keeper corporations retained for corporate reinvestment a larger share of each $100 they earned before taxes.

	Givers	*Keepers*
Charitable donations	$ 0.57	$ —
Taxes	32.94	19.17
Dividends	26.19	29.16
Residual reinvested	40.30	51.67
Pre-tax income	$100.00	$100.00

[9] "As a Crown corporation fully owned by the Government of Canada, and partially funded by the same, it is our policy not to make charitable donations. It is up to the Government to decide the use it will make of taxpayers' money in respect to charitable donations."

This result is consistent with our earlier findings that showed an inverse relationship between donations and the capital intensity of corporations. It also suggests that a whopping majority of Canadian corporations heed the philosophy of Milton Friedman and stick strictly to business—apparently with profitable results.

Separating the giver corporations from the keepers also permits a more penetrating analysis of the incidence of corporate donations across profit-size categories. Small-giver corporations carry a disproportionately higher share of total corporate philanthropy than their profits would suggest. For instance, while the $1 to $50,000 giver corporations accounted for only 0.24 per cent of total corporate profits in 1979, they contributed eight per cent of all corporate donations. In contrast, large-giver corporations under-contributed relative to their total profits. And corporations controlling 38 per cent of all profits earned in Canada in 1979 contributed nothing.

What is the record of foreign-controlled corporations? The news is both good and bad. Foreign-owned corporations have a higher tendency to give than do Canadian companies—almost half of the 5,600 foreign corporations in 1979 donated something. This compared with a participation rate of less than nine per cent for Canadian corporations. On the other hand, foreign-controlled corporations were relatively less generous in donating from their pre-tax profits. Here is how both distributed $100 of net income in 1979.

	Canadian givers	Foreign givers
Charitable donations	$ 0.80	$ 0.35
Taxes	34.28	31.07
Dividends	29.15	22.05
Reinvested earnings	35.77	46.53
Pre-tax income	$100.00	$100.00

Since much of the foreign ownership of Canadian business lies in U.S. hands, it is useful to examine the record of generosity of corporations in the United States. In virtually every year from 1946 to 1964, Canadian corporate donations (expressed as a percentage of pre-tax profits) were higher than U.S. corporate donations.

For instance, the rate was 0.9 per cent in both countries in 1946. While the Canadian payout grew to a high of 1.5 per cent in 1958 before it began to decline, the U.S. payout declined to a low of 0.6 in 1950 and then increased to 1.1 per cent in 1964. From then to the late 1970s the Canadian corporate payout rate eroded to its 1978 level of 0.4 per cent. In contrast, the payout rate in the United States has remained around one per cent for the past 20 years.

The explanation is not found in differences in the tax treatment for corporate donations in the two countries. Indeed, Canada's upper limit of 20 per cent for corporate-donation deductions is four times more liberal than U.S. tax limits. More likely, the cause is embedded in the velocity of acceleration towards Stage IV financing of the humanistic sector generally in the two countries. In the past two decades, Canada has moved sharply towards state dominance in all categories of humanistic service. Americans, too, have increased the proportion of public-sector funding, but at a slower rate.

The American ethos, from the president on down, is to champion the volunteer, to promote private philanthropy. Since 1927, U.S. presidents have spoken to the nation annually in a United Way charity drive address, a tradition that heightens national attention on charitable organizations. The president's personal tax return that itemizes his own charitable donations is laid open to public scrutiny and criticism.[10] In contrast, Canadian political leadership is somewhat less visible.

That much we can learn from analyzing national aggregates, the dull statistics that summarize the results of the donation decisions of all corporations after the fact. But corporations do not make decisions. Individuals do. To understand why and how corporate donation decisions are made one must identify the decision-makers, probe their methods and motives and document the process.

The corporate donation decision may be made by a single individual/shareholder or by a committee of management. These individual decision-makers bring with them the same values and attitudes towards corporate donations as they do towards their personal affairs. The motives that prompt their individual or family-donation decisions most likely carry over to the

[10]President Reagan's 1982 tax return drew vigorous comment when it was made public. The Reagans donated $15,000 to charities, about two per cent of total income. Although substantially below the tithe, which the president claimed was his tradition, he said his conscience is clear on the amount he gives to charity.

corporate setting. For instance, in the simplest case of a corporation owned and managed by a single shareholder, there would be a mutuality of interest in donations made in the name of the corporation or the name of the individual. The donation decision would be prompted by a combination of what we have described earlier as Level One and Level Two motives.

Because the corporation is a separate entity, the corporate setting complicates the decision process. The owner-manager may segregate in his mind a separate set of motives underlying the corporate-donation decision, the conventional and familiar laundry list of reasons why corporations donate to charitable organizations: to cement employee relations; to enhance its public image; to attract sales or potential employees; to advance technical research; for advertising potential; for political or public leverage.

Essentially each of these objectives is really an extension of the transactional motive we described earlier as Level Two—the definite expectation of something in return. In this case, the ultimate expectation is enhanced profits for the corporation which directly or indirectly benefit the decision-maker. Even if the motive is expressed as corporate good citizenship, or corporate responsibility, its source is not the corporation. It is an individual, or a group of individuals, in the corporation who is moved to make donations for altruistic reasons—the motives we described earlier as Level One. The corporate-donation decision process is simply an extension of the individual-donation decision model described earlier.

Even when ownership and management are separated, the same process is likely to occur although it may be obscured and diluted. Members of donation committees bring with them a set of personal values, susceptibilities and prejudices as well as a posture towards private-sector responsibility for the humanistic sector. In some cases, a committee member may receive personal rewards emanating from a corporate donation. For example, the secretary of the corporate contributions committee, with a passion for ballet, may receive an invitation to an opening-night cast party for the National Ballet whose performance the corporation sponsored. The corporation's CEO may collect a $50,000 marker for the contribution his company made to a hospital fund-raising campaign chaired by his counterpart in another corporation. The chit would be redeemable when the tables turned. A third member believes that government should assume total responsibility for welfare and views the United Way as redundant. A fourth is intimately involved with time and money in support of drug-addiction centres. And so on.

THE CORPORATE DONATION DECISION

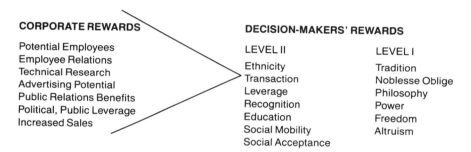

ABILITY

Income
Capital Intensity (Assets/Employees)

MOTIVES

CORPORATE REWARDS

Potential Employees
Employee Relations
Technical Research
Advertising Potential
Public Relations Benefits
Political, Public Leverage
Increased Sales

DECISION-MAKERS' REWARDS

LEVEL II	LEVEL I
Ethnicity	Tradition
Transaction	Noblesse Oblige
Leverage	Philosophy
Recognition	Power
Education	Freedom
Social Mobility	Altruism
Social Acceptance	

Is it realistic to assume that personal motives and feelings are entirely suppressed when one assumes the role of corporate decision-maker? That a generous individual becomes a corporate Scrooge? We think not. Indeed, the evidence we have from the personal and corporate donation record of 92 individuals connected with 60 separate corporations[11] shows an inextricable linkage between the level of personal generosity and the level of donations in the corporation with which they are connected as members of the donation committee. Generous individuals are connected with generous corporations. Keepers with keepers.

Family generosity for the 92 individuals was expressed as the percentage of donations to family income and arrayed on a continuum from low to high.

---

[11]Ninety-two individuals completed a questionnaire concerning their family donation behavior in 1981. They were connected with 60 separate corporations, which also had completed questionnaires, 29 of which were among the list of Canada's 500 largest companies, and 31 of which were selected from the small-business community. Regions represented included Ontario, 61 per cent; the Prairies, 22 per cent; British Columbia, nine per cent; Quebec, nine per cent.

The generosity of the connected corporation was similarly arrayed. Individuals and corporations were broken at the median into two groups, low and high donors. The results were as follows.[12]

Family generosity

		Low	High
Corporate generosity	Low	30	17
	High	16	29

The association is statistically significant. The odds are almost 99 to 1 that the results do not occur by chance alone.

The linkage is crucial to this analysis. It means that the explanations for individual and family-donation behavior described in the previous chapters have direct relevance to the discussion of corporate donations—that the causes for decline in the latter may be found in the causes of decline in the former.

Half of these connected corporations are part of a larger sample of 59 co-operating companies selected for intensive analysis from the list of Canada's 500 mega-corporations, the group that supplies most of the country's corporate-donation dollars. Of the 59 major corporations studied in 1981, nine had participated in a similar survey in 1972, permitting us to track their record of donation policies and actions over a complete decade.

The changes are significant and reveal a great deal about how corporate behavior has responded to the financial crunch on the humanistic sector. The nine corporations are among Canada's largest and would be considered leadership prospects on any fund raiser's national list. Half were foreign-controlled, seven were listed public companies, two privately held. Average sales mushroomed over the decade from below one billion dollars to $3.8 billion, pre-tax income from $109 million to $430 million. Capital investment increased from $80,000 per employee in 1972 to $150,000 in 1981.

---

[12]Corrected chi square: 6.3 with one degree of freedom. Significance: 0.0123.

All nine companies had a well-defined, written donation policy through-out the decade. All administered their donation program through a formal contribution committee, but its average size had ballooned, from four members to 11. The average committee considered 1,500 donation requests in 1981, treble the number of 1972. It granted 860 of these, roughly one out of two. In 1972, the approval ratio was two out of three. It disbursed a total of $2 million in 1981, up from $600,000 in 1972, but its payout ratio dropped from 0.6 to 0.5 per cent of pre-tax income. It had shifted the emphasis of its giving, cutting back on contributions to the United Way, health and edu-cation, and increasing its allotment to cultural causes. It had 52 unpaid pledges outstanding representing a total commitment of $1.5 million or 75 per cent of its annual budget, a slightly less-constrained position than 1972.

That, in microcosm, is how large corporations have reacted to the chari-table fund-raising offensive—with a donation budget that has grown in ab-solute size, but shrunk in relation to corporate income. And by recruiting more members of its staff to screen requests and to decide which would re-ceive corporate support and which would not.

When 50 additional large corporations from across Canada are added to the nine, there emerges a rather more comprehensive profile of the corpo-rate donation decision-making process, circa 1981. The sample group is reasonably representative of Canadian business. It contains old and new companies, public, private and Crown corporations, companies that are Canadian and foreign-controlled, companies with head offices in each re-gion of the country, and with sales throughout Canada, the United States and abroad, and includes all industry classifications, from manufacturing to service. The average sample company was still large—1981 sales of $1.7 billion and pre-tax income of $140 million.

All but four of the 59 companies[13] made charitable donations in 1981, an average of $760,000 or 0.55 per cent of income. In addition, 90 per cent of the companies made donations in kind—time, services or products—that had an average value of $50,000. The sample, therefore, is somewhat biased, more generous, when compared with all large corporations in the country. Donations were distributed as follows: United Way, 18 per cent; health-re-lated, 15 per cent; education-related, 28 per cent; welfare-related, eight per

---

[13]The four non-donors were Crown corporations. Two were provincial utilities, two were federal Crown corporations with pre-tax income of more than $10 million each. None of the four paid income tax.

cent; cultural and community-related causes, 31 per cent.

Each company received an average of 750 donation requests in 1981. They turned down half. Most often the request was rejected because corporate policy specifically excluded that type of organization. Other reasons in order of importance: not enough funds in the budget; a donation had already been made to an organization with parallel services; the organization was located outside the community served by the corporation; lack of Revenue Canada registration number; appeal was not persuasive; lack of financial statements; corporation accepts no new approaches; size of request was too large; too many requests received to handle all professionally. The successful half received a cheque that averaged $2,000, although a fifth received a donation of $100 or less. Unpaid pledges, which averaged 21 per corporation, totalled two-thirds of the 1981 budget. The commitments extended all the way to 1993.

The program was expensive to administer. It cost the corporation one dollar for every $10 it gave away. One-third of the corporations employed a full-time contribution administrator. Three-quarters used a donation committee. Direct costs for administrative salaries, secretaries and the like averaged $40,000; indirect costs of executive time in setting budgets and evaluating requests was another $30,000.

How was the donation budget determined? Two-thirds of the corporations established it as a percentage of expected pre-tax profit, which confirms our earlier findings based on national aggregates. Many companies simply made an arbitrary adjustment to the budget of the prior year. Other budget methods included an inflationary adjustment to the previous year, industry or peer-company comparisons, or a formula based on the number of employees. A few companies established no budget but assessed each request separately, on its own merits.

The single most important influence on the level of corporate generosity was the board chairman or chief executive officer. But only half claimed he was *the* most important. The others? Executives other than the CEO, other corporations, individual board members, philanthropic research institutions such as IDPAR[14] and CBAC, employees, customers or clients. A

[14]The Institute of Donations and Public Affairs Research was incorporated in 1975-76 as a non-profit organization. Its function generally is to provide its members, primarily large-scale corporations, with information and research on the donation activities of corporate donors and to act as a clearing-house for information on donees. Members pay an annual fee to IDPAR ranging from $1,000 to $5,000 based on the size of the corporate donation budget.   (Cont'd)

sprinkling cited government policies, income tax legislation, shareholders and the media as exerting some influence on the extent of corporate generosity.

Why do corporations bother to make donations? The reason most often cited was to demonstrate corporate leadership, followed closely by the personal conviction of the CEO or chairman, altruism, and tradition—Level One motives. Yet barely more than half cited these as the most important motive. As many cited more pragmatic reasons: their public relations value; persuasion from the organization; encouragement from community; employees; customers; shareholders. Some followed the example set by peer corporations. Others gave to offset government intervention, for the tax break or simply out of habit.

What did they hope to gain? The responses illustrate the multiple goals for corporate giving, the coexistence of both Level One and Level Two motives, objectives that are both selfless and selfish, outward and inward-looking. The overwhelming response was to service real community needs on a local, regional and national level, or to the social advancement of health, education, welfare and culture. Yet there were many votes for a positive community image, promotional or advertising value, or expected increased sales. Seven wanted a clear conscience, and two expected nothing.

The donation decision generally involved two or more people. In only 15 per cent of the companies was it made essentially by one person. More than half the companies involved four or more individuals in the process (one company used 12, one 17, and one 40). The composition of this decision-making group is revealing. In only 64 per cent of the companies did the chairman, director, CEO or president become involved in the donation decision. More often it was handled by a vice-president or other executive. One company in six engaged the donation administrative staff actively in the decision process. Two companies involved retired personnel. Only one had a union representative.

The driving force behind IDPAR is Richard A. Hopkinson, Second World War veteran, Oxford graduate, and a pioneer researcher in the field of corporate donations. Hopkinson worked five years, from 1967-1971, with the Conference Board in Canada and the United States, then joined the Brakeley/Ryerson Group until he formed IDPAR in 1975. The core of IDPAR's information and research program stems from his work with the latter organization.

IDPAR has a nine-person board of directors, mostly senior executives with responsibility for their corporate contribution program. Board chairman is Betty Kennedy, O.C., public affairs editor of CFRB Limited, and chairman of the donations committee of Bank of Montreal.

Corporate donation decision-makers are not your average group of Canadians. Our sample shows them to be male-dominated (more than 90 per cent) and older (40 per cent were over age 55). Eight out of 10 had at least one college degree. The same proportion claimed Anglo-Saxon roots. United Church adherents outnumbered Roman Catholics by two to one. The intensity of their religious commitment was close to the national average. They were, of course, prosperous if not rich. Their net worth averaged just under half-a-million dollars. Average holdings of liquid assets were about $200,000. Family income averaged $120,000; only three out of 10 families reported multi-incomes.

Their family donations? They averaged $2,200, roughly 1.9 per cent of income, both measures higher than the Canadian averages shown earlier. Yet the spread was still wide—while six out of 10 donated more than $1,000, one family in six gave less than $100, some gave nothing. Their donation preferences? The church and the United Way each received 25 per cent, the balance was spread around prudently to 10 different organizations. They belonged to an average of two community organizations. One in four families belonged to none. The family contributed about the same number of volunteer hours to community organizations over the year as the average sample family.

This decision-making group followed a well-defined written corporate policy, outlining the analytical procedure, in just over half the companies. One in three claimed to analyze each contribution on the basis of cost versus benefit. Eight companies consulted their peers for advice. And seven had no analytical procedure.

In one out of three multi-plant companies, all donation decisions were made at head office. And one in three companies controlled by a parent organization followed the donation directives of the parent.

The chief executive officer, or chairman of the board, plays an important but by no means exclusive or even dominant role in the donation-decision process. Only one in three claimed that he did or could exercise absolute discretion over the amount and nature of his corporation's donations. Only half were involved in assessing specific requests. More often, his involvement was in setting budget levels or establishing objectives for the contribution program. Only one in eight claimed that he initiated specific requests.

This evidence tempers the conventional wisdom which holds that CEOs are part of an exclusive club of "old boys" who wheel and deal with each other, using corporate money to give and collect markers for each other's favorite charity. Perhaps some still do but, as we shall see in a moment, while many are frequently involved in community affairs, most view it as an obligation associated with top management. Very few consider personal service to be high-status activity. If control of the corporate donation budget ever was considered a valuable "perk" associated with the top job, its currency today has evidently depreciated.

Most CEOs feel that corporate donations would be increased only if the company earned higher profits. A few gave other possible motives: tax incentives; better assurance that the money would be spent effectively; strong personal conviction towards a specific organization; other corporations increased their payout. Their overall assessment of the corporate donation program was highly favorable. On the basis of a cost/benefit evaluation, more than 90 per cent judged it effective in aiding society and worth the time spent. None judged donations to be a waste of corporate resources.

About half the CEOs claimed frequent personal involvement in community organizations. A quarter claimed to contribute a high level of personal service,[15] while a quarter were infrequently involved. The CEO allowed that top management in the company generally was more active than himself in public service.

Corporate policy regarding employee involvement in voluntary service is interesting. Half the CEOs described their policy as one that encourages involvement at all levels, yet does not deem it to be a criterion for promotion. A quarter claimed that it was an important activity so long as it did not interfere with performance. Only one CEO claimed that personal service was an absolutely essential ingredient for achieving a top management position. Ten companies, about one in six, had no corporate policy regarding service.

And how do CEOs evaluate voluntary personal service rendered by their peers to charitable organizations? Two-thirds view it as an obligation associated with top management, two termed it a necessary evil. Fourteen top executives, less than one in four, view personal service as a high-status activity.

---

[15]But when they reported, on a separate questionnaire, the hours they and their family contributed, their involvement was close to the average of all families in our national sample.

THE CORPORATE DONATION PROCESS FLOW

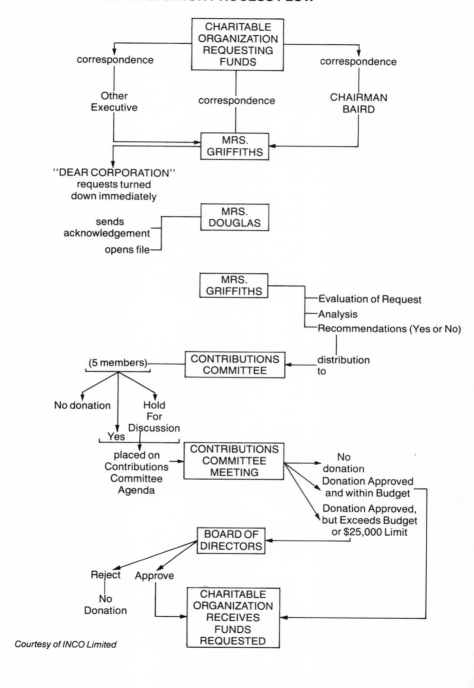

Courtesy of INCO Limited

Donation decision-making in Canada's larger corporations is now in sharper focus. The process is formal, structured, organized and conservative.

Before we address the issues surrounding the role of the business sector generally in the financing process, we need to describe the donation record of the small-business community and of the entrepreneurs who own and manage that vibrant, vigorous and voluble constituency. The 46 small companies[16] we studied were located in Ontario, the Prairie Provinces and British Columbia, but did business in all regions of the country. They averaged 17 employees and sales of slightly more than one million dollars. Their donation record was similar to the smaller-business segment discussed earlier in the context of national aggregates. A smaller proportion of companies donated (in this group the proportion making donations was seven out of 10) but as a group they were proportionately more generous than the corporate giants (donations to pre-tax income averaged 1.3 per cent). They received 33 requests and made seven donations, an approval ratio of one in five. Their preferences differed considerably from large corporations: 22 per cent went to the church; only 12 per cent went to the United Way; only 13 per cent went to education. They tended not to make long-term pledges.

Donation decision-making in the small business sector is very much a one-man function; in only one out of five of the companies did it involve two individuals. It wasn't always the president; a quarter of the companies delegated the decision to a vice-president, manager or member of the staff. Only one company had a written donation policy or even specified an analytical procedure. Five out of six did not set a budget for donations, but assessed each contribution separately. The rest simply made an adjustment to the amount donated the previous year, made peer-company comparisons or targeted for a predetermined proportion of pre-tax income.

Small business donated for many of the same reasons as the large. Most often it was because of the personal conviction, tradition or habit of the president, or out of a spirit of altruism, to demonstrate corporate leadership or to offset government intervention. Next was because of persuasion or encouragement from the soliciting organization, employees, customers, shareholders or the community. About one in four cited the tax break as a reason for giving. Interestingly, they, too, were less hard-nosed in stating what

---

[16]We are grateful to the Canadian Organization for Small Business, and its chairman, Ian C. Kennedy, for cooperating with us in the distribution of the questionnaire to its membership.

they hoped to gain from the donation. By an overwhelming margin, small businessmen cited social advancement, servicing community needs, or nothing, as opposed to increased sales, advertising or public relations value, as their primary goals for giving.

All other aspects of the donation decision in small companies reflect the active or potential influence of the president. He is the one who would increase the budget, provided he held a strong personal conviction towards a specific organization, if he could be persuaded that the money would not be squandered, or if the threat of government intervention seemed near. But the increase would come only if company earnings increased and, to a much lesser extent, if tax incentives were enhanced.

Small-company presidents generally are satisfied that their company contribution activities are worthwhile, but not nearly as unanimously as their counterparts in major corporations. Three out of four judged them to be effective in aiding society and worth the time spent on them. But one in three felt that donations were a waste of company resources. Perhaps the most interesting responses come from those whose companies did not make donations. They turned down an average of 23 requests in 1981. Their reasons? Lack of profits was in first place. Second, "Charitable organizations are not effective; they waste money on administration." Third: "Our goal is to maximize profit." "Too many requests." "Taxes." "Unattractive appeal." "Charities are poorly managed." "Government responsibility." "Owners make donations personally."

The owners of small business do indeed give at home, an average of $1,200 per year, an overall rate of 1.8 per cent of income, just one-tenth of a point under the donation rate of decision-makers attached to large corporations. The spread in their personal generosity is much wider (14 per cent gave nothing, three per cent more than a tithe). Their giving was more spontaneous, less premeditated. Ability to give was lower (average income of $70,000, three out of four with multi-incomes, net worth just under $400,000). As a group they were more youthful (the median age about 40) than their counterparts in the giants, and less conventional than society at large. One in five claimed no religion and those that belonged were not heavily committed.

Their involvement in personal service to their community was almost dead-on the national average. Forty per cent of the families of these owner/managers belonged to no community organizations and contributed no time. And how did they view voluntary personal service to society by their business associates? Most often with cynicism: "a necessary evil," "a hypocritical exercise," "a time-wasting nuisance," "a distasteful association with do-gooders.'' One-third viewed it as an obligation associated with top management. Only 12 per cent, one in eight, considered personal service a high-status activity.

What emerges from this entrepreneurial group is a contradictory pattern of donation behavior not unlike what one might expect from a colorful, diverse, heterogeneous group of individualists. They curse irreverently at the waste in social institutions but support welfare groups and the United Way at home and at the office. They don't budget for donations in their companies, and fewer companies make donations, but as a group they are proportionately three times as generous as major corporations. The donation decision occupies a trivial amount of their time, and many bluster that donations are a waste of company resources, but underneath they are creampuffs. Their company gifts generally are not motivated by the expectation of ultimate financial gain or equivalent return. Many small businesses are generous with their money; they are the ones who elevate the averages. But the overwhelming majority are not.

Even more ominous for those who would see an expanded voluntary participation in the financing of the humanistic sector is the attitude of businessmen towards personal service. For many businessmen, large or small, involvement in community organizations does not have particularly high priority in their allocation of time. Only a small minority regard personal service as high-status activity. Many, particularly those associated with small business, view it with contempt.

Since there is a strong relationship between voluntary involvement and the size of family donations, one can perhaps understand more clearly why the latter has diminished in recent years, why donations will continue to shrink so long as business and social leaders regard personal service with indifference or disdain.

That attitude towards personal involvement has emerged, largely unnoticed, within this generation of Canadians. Consider the contrast in a 30-year period. In the early 1950s, sociologist Aileen D. Ross published widely quoted research findings on the various ways in which participation in philanthropic activity advanced the career of the businessman. She contended that such activity not only was substantial among those who were successful but also was a significant ingredient in the corporations' public relations program.

Compare her views with those of Sidney A. Humphreys, a vice-president of Spencer Stuart Associates, Toronto management consultants. As a professional head-hunter, hired to match top executives with suitable firms,

Humphreys knows contemporary job specifications as well as the characteristics of those he places.

Is involvement in community activities important for a business career?

Ross c. 1950	Humphreys c. 1980
YES. A substantial activity of the successful businessman. It is now essential for most business people to take part in them. An inner circle of important businessmen has gradually come to control the top positions in these campaigns. Indeed, participation has become so essential that many business enterprises now include "training" for these community roles as part of the regular training of their staff. It has been pointed out that philanthropic activity is an exceptionally good way in which to test a man's ability, as the success of any canvasser is clearly marked in terms of dollars and cents. Many corporations realize this and conspicuously use campaign activity to test a promising young man.	NO. Most are not involved, and they give you all kind of reasons, like "I've been transferred around a lot and I haven't had time to get involved…" I think that sometimes if it comes out that the guy is a "do-gooder" there may be the perception that he may be too soft and not tough-minded enough. Or he may be a leader—it depends on what roles he's taking. Sometimes it may be an indication that a person is taking part in these humanistic endeavors perhaps because he's not doing so great at his job, so he finds other diversions. A lot of people, perhaps not everybody, involved in these things are very *nice* people, the cream of the crop in this sense and sometimes people perceive that if he's too nice a guy, he can't manage because he's going to be treating everyone so nice he won't see the forest for the trees and he won't be able to make the hard decisions.

Employers rarely if ever ask for a record of past personal service or list it as a requirement in job specifications for top management positions. The new breed of business-school graduates entering the workforce already senses what Humphreys articulates—service may be perceived as softness.

At the conclusion of a classroom discussion of the donation program of INCO Limited, I asked my students—all MBA candidates or senior undergraduates—which assignment they would prefer if INCO hired them on graduation: membership on the contributions committee, or membership on a task force for improved productivity? All 60 of them chose the second alternative! Their priorities are perhaps understandable and not necessarily linked to 1983 recession psychology. Young people today often are counselled to participate in community affairs because, "It'll look good on your résumé." One more ingredient of the marketing mix in selling oneself.

Chances are today that these new recruits will observe similar behavior in the majority of their business peers and among their management superiors. Odds are that half the members of their employer's board of directors and senior officers claimed the $100 standard deduction for charitable donations for 1983. If personal values are learned from example, Canadian business has already predestined a further contraction of voluntary involvement and financial participation in the succeeding generation of business leaders.

Canadian business voluntary community leadership is far from the level of indifference that seems to prevail in Sweden where a whole generation of management has grown up in the Stage IV philosophy. Carl Erik Hedlund, group manager and managing director of Ahlsell AB, one of Sweden's giant suppliers of construction and installation materials, points to articles in Swedish business journals documenting that those companies where business executives have become involved in politics and community affairs show poor performance. "We keep our nose to the grindstone." Was Mr. Hedlund involved in any community organizations? "Yes, our yacht club, things like that." What about hospitals, universities and the like? "No, there is no power on those boards. No action. They all are political appointees, not really able to do much."

In Canada, voluntary boards still have power that is independent of government, despite the fact that most of the funding comes from the state. It is a Canadian tradition dating back to the days of the British conquest. If that independence is to continue, the boards of humanistic organizations must demonstrate effectiveness and efficiency. These skills are the stock-in-trade of the corporate manager, and leaders in the business sector could make a significant contribution to the country by elevating personal service to a more prestigious plane, encouraging widespread participation, perhaps taking it into account in evaluating candidates for promotion. A written policy that articulated the corporate view towards personal service by labor, junior, intermediate and upper management would dispel any ambiguity in the minds of those who wish to serve, as well as those who don't.

Other trends have potentially disquieting overtones for expanded corporate giving.

First is the movement towards democratization of the donation-decision process in major corporations. In most large companies, the contribution program is managed by a committee, a group which has expanded in size over the past decade. As more people become involved in the corporate donation-decision process, with its norm of group consensus, an individual might tend to advance only the safest proposals, those that would not provoke a hassle with colleagues. Large donations are subjected to tougher and tougher scrutiny by more and more people. In large committees, it is more difficult for fund raisers to learn the points of leverage that would affect a positive committee decision.

It may be that expansion of the donation committee is another factor accounting for the contraction of corporate donations. In the corporations we tracked, there tended to be an inverted relationship between corporate generosity and the number of donation decision-makers.

Number of decision-makers	% Donations to pre-tax income
1	1.31
2	0.66
3	0.71
4	2.33*
5+	0.52

*Four cases only

When power is diffused, bold action may be diluted. Democracy has its price.

Second is the expanding incidence of Crown corporations, at both the federal and provincial levels. Crown corporations accounted for one-half the assets of the 25 largest non-financial corporations in 1978. By 1982, the assets of federal Crown corporations alone exceeded $62 billion spread over a wide range of industries: transportation, communication, energy and resources, finance, insurance, real estate, agriculture, fisheries, culture. Since then a series of federal loan guarantees to sick corporations has made the

Canadian people potential investors in farm machinery, automobiles and others. Provinces, too, have stepped up their investment activities: petroleum, airlines, potash. University of British Columbia professor William Stanbury estimates that federal and provincial Crown corporations now account for between 10-12 per cent of Canada's GNP.

By far the majority of Crown corporations we contacted, at both the federal and provincial levels, operate with a strict policy of not contributing to charitable organizations. Some said they were prohibited from doing so by their corporate bylaws or by specific government direction. Should Canada continue in the direction of expanded public-sector ownership of production resources—a trend considered inevitable by many thoughtful observers—then one could logically expect a further reduction in donations from the corporate sector. To the extent that corporate behavior may influence personal generosity, an historical association already demonstrated, one could anticipate a decreased incentive, a relaxed motivation, in the personal donations of executives and employees associated with these firms.

Third is the unequal, some might term unfair, incidence of charitable donations across the corporate sector. More than 90 per cent of Canadian corporations do not contribute voluntarily. While many of these corporations no doubt are inactive, unproductive, or otherwise not capable of sharing the financial burden, many are. Indeed, as a group, the ones that do not donate control more than one-third of the corporate income in the country and tend to be more profitable than the ones that give. They contribute proportionately less in income taxes. Even among the donors, generosity is concentrated in a relatively small group of major contributors.

Some argue that corporations should assume a greater share of the financial burden of the humanistic sector through expanded donations. This could be accomplished in two ways—extracting more from existing donors, or encouraging (forcing) the non-donors to participate. It is unlikely that corporate donations would increase significantly if taxation incentives were introduced, reducing the after-tax cost of donations to the corporation. We have already demonstrated the overwhelming influence of expected pre-tax profit levels on the size of the donation budget, that donations represent an insignificant proportion of income flows, that few corporate policy-makers consider the tax consequences of charitable donations, and that fewer yet claimed they would likely alter their behavior if tax incentives were enhanced.

Why then should some corporations handicap their shareholders by contributing shareholder income voluntarily, while others, perhaps financially more able, choose not to? If one is generous, shouldn't all be? Why not force the keepers to carry their fair share of responsibility? Legislate a donation payout?

The suggestion is not new. Leon David Crestohl, Member of Parliament for the riding of Cartier-Quebec, advanced a similar proposal in the House of Commons in 1958 when Parliament was debating tax legislation to increase the maximum corporate donation deduction from five to 10 per cent of income. Crestohl wondered whether or not that would give corporations much encouragement or whether "the addition of five per cent would merely widen the margin of deficiency, of neglect or carelessness or avoidance of responsibility." Could not the law "be changed to compel corporations to take full advantage of that exemption? If, for example, a tax were imposed on corporation profits to the extent of five per cent...the revenue from that tax could be...distributed amongst educational and charitable institutions."

Such legislation would have exacted $2 billion from corporations in 1980, more than the total donations collected from all individuals that year and 10 times the amount voluntarily contributed by Canadian corporations. Legislated payouts are appealing on grounds of equity, the ability-to-pay principle. But if contributions are forced, are they donations? Some argue that even today corporate "voluntary" contributions have ceased to be gifts but are blatantly promotional expenditures, and that corporate donors largely are unworthy of receiving the psychic rewards attached to that noble gesture. But legislated gifts? Better to call a tax a tax.

Perhaps wider public awareness of the degree of generosity of Canada's public corporations would be a more appropriate incentive. A number are extraordinarily generous. Many of Canada's giants continued a contributions program of considerable magnitude throughout the severe economic recession of 1981-82, a period when some were suffering multi-million-dollar losses. Yet corporations have been uncharacteristically reluctant to publicize their donation program. An analysis of the published annual reports of 168 Canadian companies for 1981 determines that only 13 corporations mentioned their involvement in charitable activities or donations, or even acknowledged a broad social responsibility. When it was mentioned, the detail of involvement was sketchy. None of the companies listed the dollar amount of their donations in their financial statements. Only two, Bank of Montreal and John Labatt Limited,[17] revealed the dollar amount of donations in the body of their report.

---

[17]Canada's first bank reported total donations of $2.3 million in its 164th year, 0.5 per cent of pre-tax income. It also listed a percentage break-out of the categories of charitable contributions. Labatt donated $1.2 million, 1.7 per cent of its pre-tax income.

There are understandable reasons for this reticence. Some very generous donors refrain from publicity out of a sense of genuine modesty and good taste. More often the reasons are pragmatic. If the dollar amount is shown to the public, it might raise expectations, invite more requests, which would mean having to say no to more solicitors. Publicity might show the corporation in a bad light compared with competitors or peers. With such downside risks, the best strategy is confidentiality.

Indeed, an atmosphere of privacy is often reinforced by those who research or advise corporations on contribution activities. One of the most influential bodies researching donations in the corporate sector, the Institute of Donations and Public Affairs Research in Montreal, surveys Canadian business enterprises yearly, collecting reams of statistics on donation patterns and policies. IDPAR's annual report to members, *Corporate Giving In Canada*, contains a hundred pages of quotations and statistical tables giving every conceivable cross-classification of corporation donations: by size of donor, industry, size and number of donations, type of recipient, purpose of appeal, geographic region, upcoming appeals, and so on.

The report does not reveal the names of corporate donors or other identifying characteristics. In fact, to ensure confidentiality, IDPAR asks the 300-400 cooperating corporations to return their completed questionnaire to a public accounting firm for registration and coding before it is sent to IDPAR for processing. A full report identified by code number is sent to each of IDPAR's 97 members. Cooperating non-members are sent a summary of the study in return for their cooperation. Copies of the summary are available to the public for a nominal charge to encourage interest in giving by corporations and to enlighten the public on the scope of social involvement by the corporate community.

Other participants feel that modesty may be short-sighted on the part of corporations and costly in lost opportunity. Communications experts see a great waste in employee and public relations appeal of a liberal donation program that is shrouded in secrecy. Corporations often support hospitals, cultural events, recreational facilities, and other activities used by employees and their families.

For instance, we are impressed by the scope and range of amenities available in Thompson, Man., a mining town literally carved out of the northern wilderness. Many community organizations in Thompson depended initially on International Nickel for seed money and moral support, the classical ingredients for spawning a company-town mentality. Yet we are equally impressed by the sense of appreciation, loyalty and genuine respect towards INCO voiced by many town leaders, whether or not they were connected with the company.[18] Creating positive employee and community recognition of corporate good deeds requires the most delicate touch and keen sensitivity. Perhaps that is why corporations have been reluctant to try to exploit that source of goodwill.

Business firms can gain positive recognition from important people and peer companies by supporting attractive causes. *The Financial Post* recognized the potential in 1979 when it teamed up with the Council for Business and the Arts in Canada (CBAC) and the Canadian Conference of the Arts (CCA)[19] to sponsor annual awards to Canadian corporations involved in supporting arts organizations. Winners in three major categories—innovative support, community support, sustained support—receive a bronze statuette created by Canadian sculptor William McEacheran at an elegant black-tie dinner party for top-drawer business executives and senior members of arts organizations and their spouses.

The winners in 1982 were American Express Canada Inc. for innovation, Quebec Telephone for community support, and IBM Canada Ltd. for sustained support of the National Ballet of Canada. The awards certainly do translate into good publicity for the winners and those honorably mentioned with full-page photo and story coverage in *The Financial Post*, plus residual mention in other media. But predictably, the exercise is not without its critics, prompting Ed Bovey, former chairman of CBAC, to observe, "It is very difficult to be generous in this country."

To the critics, and there are many, the issue revolves around the overt exploitation of vulnerable but respected arts groups by predatory business whose aim is only to increase sales. To Scott Macrae, of the Vancouver *Sun*, the American Express campaign illustrates the repugnance of the unsanctified merger of business and the arts. In 1982, American Express launched a half-million-dollar advertising campaign featuring TV clips with Peter Ustinov. The campaign theme emphasized that American Express had

---

[18]The same sentiments would appear not to prevail in Sudbury, where INCO has received much bad press. Yet the level of INCO's generosity in Sudbury in the early 1980s was higher on a per capita basis than in Thompson. INCO's presence in Sudbury pre-dates Thompson by more than a generation. For many years, INCO not only was the first donor approached by community groups but often was the only one, meeting their total budget with the company gift. History and tradition like that make it difficult for any corporation to reduce its involvement, regardless of justification.

[19]The CCA is a national, non-profit organization based in Ottawa, and supported by the federal and nine provincial governments. Under president Lister Sinclair, it encourages the development of arts in Canada through its more than 1,400 individual and organizational members.

guaranteed a minimum donation of $25,000 each to the National Ballet School, The National Theatre School and the National Youth Orchestra. During March and April, American Express would donate five cents for each traveller's cheque purchased, one cent for credit card transaction and $2.00 for each card application. (With normal volumes, the months of March and April would yield $50,000 based on the formula. According to spokesman Tom Caden, American Express actually donated $102,000 to the three organizations.)

Columnist Macrae was offended that the public relations hype for the campaign made no attempt to camouflage that "American Express is just riding on the coattails of these organizations." Edwin Cooperman, a company vice-president who proposed the scheme, concluded, "There is no question I'm trying to achieve a double result—to increase my business and to support these groups."

At issue is the perennial chestnut—at what point does financial patronage compromise artistic expression? Ray Conlogue, writing in *The Globe and Mail*, feels that art groups are being taken advantage of in their hard-pressed financial situation. To Conlogue, there is a difference between indirect corporate rewards through donations and direct benefits accruing from the active involvement of the arts group as a marketing tool. "Do we really want arts organizations to be, in effect, pushing one brand of credit cards over another?" It is a thoughtful question.

High-profile corporate donations have other risks. Ronald McDonald House attracted enthusiastic support in Halifax—"The house that love built"—and cynicism in Vancouver—"McDonald's demands its quo for its quid." Volkswagen hit the headlines, usually an ominous sign, in the summer of 1983 by withdrawing its financial support to the Toronto Symphony Orchestra because 80 members of the orchestra had participated in a Sound of Peace Concert in High Park to express their concern and desire for worldwide peace. The auto-maker, which contributed $6,500 to a symphony advertising supplement as well as a $32,000 Porsche for a symphony fundraising auction, judged the action of orchestra members as "political propaganda" on the part of the TSO. Volkswagen Canada policy prohibited donations to organizations engaged in political activities. VW reversed its decision after it became obvious that public sympathy was with the orchestra members.

The episode illustrates how corporate goodwill can turn quickly to ill will and why corporations hesitate to publicize their donations. Someone is bound to be offended, and what corporation needs the bad press? Of course,

the TSO survived the flurry. As will Volkswagen. But the episode illumi-
nates a challenging dilemma, not only for culture but the humanistic sector
generally—how much flirting with business is acceptable? At what point
does a voluntary organization sell out? How does a donee contain the leverage of the donor?

The Ontario Easter Seal Society[20] has had as much experience as any humanistic group in cooperating with business interests in fund-raising ventures. Besides the annual telethon, Easter Seals joined with Vic Tanny's in
1981 to help sell fitness memberships, part of which went to the Easter Seal
campaign. They participated with Pitney Bowes in 1981 and 1982 in a national advertising campaign to "Rent A Little Happiness." Full-page, four-
color ads in *Time*, *Maclean's*, and 10 other publications announced the
challenge: "Order a postage meter now and we'll donate your first month's
rental to Easter Seals." The ad featured the meter, a facsimile of the current
Easter seal, and a photograph of three smiling children whose handicap, if
any, was discreetly masked by the machine.

Pitney Bowes rented in excess of 1,000 machines during the campaign in
1981 and contributed $18,500 to Easter Seals. They ran the campaign again
in 1982, but opted out in 1983 when advertising budgets generally were
scaled back. Norman McKee, Pitney Bowes advertising manager, judged
the campaign an effective corporate image-selling tool. "Nice exposure...corporate presentation by the president at the Easter Seal Telethon." Hard sales results? "Pitney Bowes' (soft-sell) ads will not likely
promote a sale. Hard core, hammering ads produce better results." Any reaction on the campaign? "In 1981, we received five letters and five telephone calls saying that they did not want to support Easter Seals. They were
small companies...if they wanted to give to charity, they would themselves." Did anyone suggest corporate exploitation? "No criticism on
taste...we were conscious beforehand of criticism."

Soft-sell (testimonial type) ads are the first casualties during a recession.
Pitney Bowes' withdrawal in 1983 was a major disappointment to Barry
Baker, director of fund raising for the Ontario Easter Seal Society. Baker
certainly sees no ethical dilemma. "I think that kind of cooperative advertising is tremendous...everybody benefits...a great income-generator,

---

[20]For more than half a century, the various groups supporting crippled children incorporated a reference to the disability in their name. The name change reflects a healthy self-confidence—"we are
not handicapped children."

traffic creator.'' Baker heads a group that extracts $9 million a year in private donations from Canadians—99 per cent of the Ontario Society's annual budget. For Baker, testimonial advertising campaigns and the various spring telethons give Easter Seals an opportunity to project their corporate sponsors ''as the good citizens they are.'' If there is any diffidence about the media marriage of business and charitable organizations, it doesn't exist in Baker's camp.

If fund-raising specialists and marketing consultants have their way, Canada soon will see a plethora of imaginative liaisons between business and the humanistic sector. Christopher Lang summarizes the pitch:

> I have the idea that a lot of corporations don't know what they're doing with their funds. They're bombarded with 200-300 requests. They just take their money and spread it across the water. They get no value, they get no image,[21] certainly no internal motivation because they don't tell their employees about it and it certainly doesn't impact on their sales. We think donations is another vehicle for the promotions budget...the more value they get, the more for the non-profit.

If such promotions become widespread, it may indeed help alleviate some of the short-term financial problems of some humanistic organizations. But it poses significant risks for many others. How closely should a hospital, for instance, be seen as a partner to a brand-name pharmaceutical house? Half of the public today feels generally positive towards charitable appeals by humanistic organizations, still retains a sense of respect, affection and goodwill towards them, still recognizes their special status, still makes donations. Can that goodwill be transferred to the business sector without selling some of it off?

Humanistic financing tied to corporate sales *is* different from corporate gifts, which typically carry no strings. Whether warranted or not, promotional partnerships have the potential for expanding the level of cynicism and indifference towards charitable organizations already widely held, of introducing complicated problems of conflicts of interest for the dependent partner.

On the other hand, closer involvement by business men and women in the affairs of humanistic organizations could have many positive spin-offs, for

---

[21]''I say, 'Look Jim, you run an owner-operated business. You need a profile in this country. Get off your ass!' He legitimately has things to say. 'Why don't you use what you do in the non-profit sector to build the other way?'''

both the organization and the company. While the humanistic sector waits for the corporate overture, it would be well advised to ponder the implications of a theme that was repeated often by a strong minority of corporate leaders and hundreds of individuals across the country. A senior bank spokesman puts it concisely: "Volunteers come and go and the quality of management and/or efficiency changes with the expertise of the individuals, but on the whole I would rate efficiency at well below that of private business." Perhaps there is mending to be done on both sides of the fence line.

For its part in this constructive union, business could demonstrate intelligent and mature leadership by becoming more candid and forthright in the publication of its donation program. Canadian business has much to be proud of. Generous corporations deserve public approbation for contributing to their community beyond the corporate income tax levies. All Canadian companies should publish their humanistic contributions as an integral element of their financial statements in the corporation's annual report to shareholders. The statement of income would show how the corporate stewards allocated total earnings, the extent to which they responded voluntarily by donations, and involuntarily through taxes, to the welfare of the general public.

SPECIMEN INCOME DISTRIBUTION STATEMENT

Net income for the year before taxes	$100,000,000
Distributed as follows:	
Directly for humanistic service	$1,000,000
Provision for corporate income taxes	49,000,000
Dividends to shareholders	25,000,000
Reinvested earnings	25,000,000
	$100,000,000

Public disclosure is the essential first step in determining whether corporations should contribute more, or less, in supporting the requirements of the humanistic sector. Public disclosure would require corporate executives to justify the amount and nature of their corporate donation program, first in their own minds and second to the satisfaction of the publics to whom they report. It would be an enlightening exercise. And painful. Perhaps promotional expenditures would replace donations in some companies, total donations shrink or even disappear in some, expand in others. The sunshine would be refreshing. The debate, wholesome.

Recent history in Canada has shown that corporate fiscal management is competent management. Corporate stewards have managed well the resources entrusted to them. That same expertise must be shared with the humanistic sector if it, too, is to fulfill its mandate effectively.

Crown corporations should make donations like any other corporation. Since less-generous companies tend to have less-generous management, any expansion of the role of Crown corporations in Canada would work against expanded donation behavior on the part of their management. If government policy prohibits donations by Crown corporations, management should work through the chain of command to the power that inhibits corporate involvement. Crown corporations, too, should publish the extent of corporate donations in their annual reports.

Disclosure of the corporate financial commitment to its community would be a quantum step forward in a constructive partnership for mutual benefit. It would require corporate management to learn more about the organizations their company supported. It would insist that the organization demonstrates sound financial planning and management before the gift is made, that the corporate contribution for capital this year does not predestine an operating deficit in future years. There would be monitoring and follow-up of corporate gifts, something that is now rarely done by corporate donors. Gifts would be fewer but larger. Corporate donation budgets would be set less as a target of pre-tax profits, or peer-company comparison, and more on the basis of community needs. Corporate donation disbursements would be less volatile; corporate donations would perhaps become more dependable as a source of sustaining revenue for the donee.

Knowledge would lead to personal involvement which would lead to a transfer of skills which would encourage increased personal financial support which would reinforce expanded corporate support. But the first step is voluntary corporate disclosure, the price for public trust and privileged status.

CHAPTER **XI**

Symbols of excellence

We do not issue Annual Reports and do not wish to
be included in any research your particular group is conducting. I am
sure if there is any information you desire in this direction, you will find
it easy to obtain.

A typical Canadian foundation

A good foundation should be a two-way street where interaction and
communication between itself and society bring rewards for both.

Richard M. Ivey
Richard Ivey Foundation, London

If corporations are taciturn about their donation activities, Canadian foundations are downright clandestine. There probably are close to 1,000 foundations operating in Canada, controlling a billion dollars of assets, roughly
$40 for every living Canadian. They enjoy the privileges of corporate status,
accommodating tax concessions under Section 149 of the Income Tax Act,
and a wide measure of goodwill from the Canadian public.

Yet most retain an attitude of privacy about their affairs that borders on
arrogant concealment. Money held in public trust is viewed as a private resource—"It's our money, not theirs." Canadian foundations generally are
inaccessible to the public, their purposes obscure, their decision-making
process mysterious, and their boards and staff distant and uncommunica-
tive. They have become symbols of secret wealth.

No wonder there has grown a misconception, suspicion and even distrust of foundation activities on the part of responsible Canadians. Critics insinuate a wide range of alleged abuses: foundations hoard their money; they dodge taxes; they are self-dealing, paying exorbitant salaries and fees to family members, lending money to themselves at sweetheart rates, leasing space at outrageous rentals from family members, employing relatives in the summer who are unemployable elsewhere, buying goods and services from family corporations; they donate money to political parties; practice discrimination in their payouts; are vehicles for the idle rich to indulge themselves by supporting their favorite charities which have narrow and parochial interests; they assume a passive posture, making little impact on major problems, showing little leadership, engaging in no communication and cooperation, even among themselves.

The list is endless. Yet because little factual information has been available on foundation affairs, the insinuations can be neither confirmed nor refuted. One gets a glimpse now and then by reading the digest of court cases involving income tax disputes between Her Majesty the Queen and taxpayers involved in foundation activities. The one most frequently cited does little to dispel the suspicions. Antoine Guertin Ltée., a taxpayer incorporated in Quebec in 1946, operated a feed mill as well as several farms in the village of Saint-Pie. Guertin, the founder of the company, also incorporated the Fondation Saint-Pie in 1960 under the Quebec Companies Act and registered it with Revenue Canada. Its object was to support a foreign religious mission, a program that held intense interest for Guertin.

Funds for the Fondation Saint-Pie came largely from employees of Antoine Guertin Ltée., who were paid year-end bonuses. Guertin persuaded these employees to contribute one part of the bonus payment as a charitable donation to the Fondation, for which they were given a tax-deductible receipt, relieving them of income tax on that amount. The Fondation immediately lent the money to Antoine Guertin Ltée., which gave the Fondation a promissory note bearing interest at seven per cent per year. Each year the Fondation received the interest on the notes, it distributed that amount to the Brazilian mission and renewed the notes for the principal.

It repeated the process each year from 1972 to 1977 by which time the capital of the Fondation had reached a half-million dollars, all of which was invested in notes payable to Antoine Guertin Ltée. at seven per cent interest, by then a deeply discounted rate. Revenue Canada challenged the transactions as a sham which conferred a tax-free benefit to the company. But the Crown lost the case in the federal court in 1981, effectively legitimizing all similar arrangements.

Foundations—funds held in trust—are as old as recorded history. Wealthy Greeks and Romans, who wanted their good works and good name perpetuated, often established funds which they entrusted to friends. The trustees agreed to dispose of the income and principal according to the wishes of the donor. The arrangements really were little more than gifts with strings attached, and since ancient laws were loose, and memories short, the funds often were dissipated soon after the donor's death.

Despite difficulties of uncertain succession, man's compulsion for immortality, personal recognition, and family honor has remained a powerful force throughout the ages. Many rich men discover late in life that there is much pleasure to be found in giving money away for agreeable causes. With the invention of the corporation, and legal recognition of the principle of perpetual succession, benefactors realized that they could indeed control their estates from their graves through the vehicle of a corporate charitable foundation.

Foundations flourished in the West, particularly during this century. They thrive in every conceivable political milieu—capitalist, socialist, fascist. The world's largest, Ford Foundation, is relatively new and, of course, is located in the United States. It was formed in 1936 by Henry Ford and his son, Edsel, with an initial gift of $25,000, topped up from time to time by the transfer of Ford Motor Company stock from the automaker's estate. Its investments are now worth $3 billion, a sum of money three times the total assets of all foundations in Canada. Today there are more than 20,000 active foundations in the United States with assets of $40 billion, representing an endowment of $160 per U.S. citizen.

Ironically the world's most prestigious foundation, the Nobel, is located in Sweden, a country in advanced Stage IV financing of humanistic service, and whose government refuses to recognize charitable contributions as deductions from taxable income. The Nobel Foundation's sole activity is the administration and financing of the Nobel Prizes, awarded each year to five citizens of the world who, during the previous year, conferred the greatest benefit on mankind for their work in the fields of physics, chemistry, physiology or medicine, literature and peace. Each laureate receives a Nobel Gold Medal, a Nobel Diploma, a cheque for roughly $200,000, and worldwide honor and prestige that is priceless.[1] It is estimated that Sweden, a

---

[1] Alfred Nobel was born in Stockholm in 1833 of Swedish parents. A restless man of extraordinary talents and catholic interests, he travelled the world throughout his life. Nobel's fortune and the base for his foundation stems from his invention of dynamite. The five prize categories reflect Nobel's favorite disciplines and lifelong passions. The Nobel Prizes, widely recognized as the world's highest civic honors, are awarded at a glittering ceremony in Stockholm's breathtaking *Konsert Huser* on December 10, the anniversary of Alfred Nobel's death in 1896.

country of eight million people, has 50,000 foundations with total assets of $5 billion, more than $600 per Swede. Many are church-related but others exist to advance medicine, research, education and other good causes. Swedish foundations may be set up out of taxed dollars, but the money then enjoys tax exemption and few inhibiting regulations.

Even Argentina, hardly a showcase of Western democracy, condones, if not encourages, family foundations. Who can forget the delightful parody by Tim Rice in *Evita*?[2]

> And the money kept rolling in from every side/
> Eva's pretty hands reached out and they reached wide/
> Now you may feel it should have been a voluntary cause/
> But that's not the point my friends/
> When the money keeps rolling in you don't ask how/
> Think of all the people gonna see some good times now/
> Eva's called the hungry to her—open up the doors!/
> Never been a fund like the Foundation Eva Peron!

Canada's oldest foundation was established by the Massey family in 1918 out of the residual estate (chiefly shares in the family business) of Hart Massey, grandfather of Vincent, the late Governor-General. The corporate objects of the Massey Foundation were made identical with those in Hart Massey's will, enabling his progeny to control a vehicle "of permanent usefulness." The Massey Foundation was the forerunner of the family foundation, which since has become the most popular estate-planning vehicle in the country.

Yet it would take 20 years before John Wilson McConnell, the inscrutable Montreal industrialist, established Canada's second family foundation, now the country's largest and most powerful. In the meantime, in 1921, a prosperous Winnipeg banker by the name of W.F. Alloway, a Winnipeg resident of 51 years, drew a personal cheque for $100,000 payable to the "Winnipeg Foundation." "I owe everything to this community," explained Alloway, "and I feel it should receive some benefit from what I have been able to accumulate." The Winnipeg Foundation became the first community foundation, conceived as an endowment, given freely by diverse citizens and corporations to provide for the needy and for the enrichment of the physical, educational and cultural life of the city and its

---

[2]*Evita*, an opera based on the life story of Eva Peron, 1919-1952. Music by Andrew Lloyd Webber. Lyrics by Tim Rice. Copyright by MCA Records, Inc., California and Ontario.

environs. Community foundations have never really caught on in Canada. It took 13 years before Winnipeg's example was emulated in Vancouver, 33 years in Hamilton, and 60 years in London, Ontario.[3] The total assets of all four today are barely $100 million, mostly represented by the gigantic Vancouver fund, the second largest foundation pool in the country.

It is unfortunate that Canada remains a country without heroes. If they were tolerated, J.W. McConnell most certainly would be in their ranks, warts and all. McConnell was All-Canadian, born on Dominion Day, 1877, in Muskoka, Ont. With no advanced education, he sold coal in Toronto then moved to Montreal at age 23. He married Lily May Griffith when he was 28. At 35, he negotiated control of St. Lawrence Sugar Refineries, dominated the sugar market, then swiftly parlayed his gains through a range of financial manoeuvres in mining, banking, publishing, insurance and transportation. Handsome and smart, McConnell developed two pronounced eccentricities—he became preoccupied with business and obsessed with privacy.[4] He established the McConnell Foundation in 1937 when he was 60 and turned his formidable talents to charity. He soon became Canada's best-known anonymous donor. Today, his foundation has assets of $180 million and ranks among the 50 largest foundations in the world.[5]

Canada entered the 1940s with only three significant foundations. Six more were spawned during that turbulent decade, five by prominent Canadian families—Atkinson, Morrow, McLean, Ivey and Laidlaw—and one by a proud community, Vancouver, B.C.

Joseph E. Atkinson, publisher of the *Star* in Toronto, had the misfortune to time his death during an era when a Liberal federal government collected estate taxes and a Conservative provincial government levied succession duties. He complicated matters further by stipulating in his will that the trustees of The Atkinson Charitable Foundation, which was to receive the

[3]The London Foundation was incorporated in 1954 but lay dormant until reactivated in the fall of 1979 by several civic-minded citizens.

[4]Although he owned four newspapers in Montreal, McConnell's editors were warned never to print his name or photograph. He refused honorary degrees from four universities. In 1949, when McConnell was 72, the Canadian Press news service still had no biographical sketch.

[5]The current president of Canada's No. 1 foundation, responsible for directing annual disbursements of $8 million in grants, is Derek A. Price. The son of John H. and Lorna MacDougall Price of Quebec City, Price married Jill McConnell in 1954, forging a union of two of Canada's important families. He serves currently as chairman of Starlaw Holdings Ltd., a family investment vehicle. Princeton-educated, thoughtful and disciplined, Price illustrates the quality as well as the quantity of power and influence behind Canada's major foundations today.

residue of his fortune, should also be trustees of his estate, which consisted mainly of shares in the *Star*. The legal wrangling over values was a solicitor's dream. When the dust settled, the Atkinson Foundation inherited a respectable sum which has since grown to $20 million.

Atkinson himself was a singularly modest and retiring man. His father, a Newcastle, Ont., miller, had been killed by a train while walking home in 1866 when Joseph was eight months old. His mother, a rigid evangelical Methodist, had considerable influence in shaping his personality and character. The foundation's first grant in 1946 was to Toronto Hospital for Sick Children for research on hearing defects, an impediment Atkinson inherited from his father. The foundation today retains the founder's interest in health care but has branched out considerably to education and general welfare.

The affairs of Richard Green Ivey of London, Ont., were as organized as Atkinson's were haphazard. R.G. followed his father in the practice of law, nurtured a family fortune in paper products, insurance and finance, and enjoyed the good life as a hobby farmer in his rolling estate north of London. Dignified, devout, unpretentious, R.G. supported his community with time, talent and money. He spawned two formidable foundations, the Richard Ivey in 1947 as a vehicle to perpetuate the family name through the male offspring, and the Richard and Jean Ivey Fund 20 years later for the distaff branch. Each has assets of $10 million, enough to provide a significant flow of resources which are deployed thoughtfully and creatively to help enrich life in London and southwestern Ontario.

The uncomplicated decade of the 1950s produced more millionaires than perhaps any other time in Canada's history. A dozen of them immortalized their family names by incorporating foundations which today are worth more than $200 million. Canada's money was still largely concentrated in the East—McLaughlin, Bickell, Bronfman, Greenshields, Lawson, Eaton, Molson. Western money was just becoming visible—Woodward in British Columbia, Muttart in Alberta.

Yet it was a U.S. citizen, the late William H. Donner, who had the distinction of founding what has become Canada's second-largest family foundation, The Donner Canadian. Donner was born in Columbus, Indiana, and made his initial stake by capitalizing on the industrialization that accompanied the discovery of Indiana natural gas. His real money, though, was made in tin and steel. When he was in his eighties, Donner became interested in the pioneering work of Dr. Wilder Penfield, who was then director of the Montreal Neurological Institute. He established the Donner

Canadian Foundation in 1950 and left it a sizable endowment when he died in 1953 at the age of 89. Today Donner Canadian has assets of more than $50 million, is one of the few that can claim a truly national presence and, ironically, is the only major foundation to publish a bilingual annual report.

Perhaps more has been written about Samuel Bronfman and his dynasty than all other Canadian philanthropists combined. How he was born in Brandon, Man., in 1891 of Orthodox Jewish parents, how his business career began in Winnipeg in the hotel, mail order and liquor businesses, how he conceived and developed the Seagram's empire in Montreal, and how his progeny have multiplied his wealth to exponential dimensions. Sam was good to his various communities, particularly, but not exclusively, Jewish causes. He earmarked a few million dollars in 1952 to establish the Samuel and Saidye Bronfman Family Foundation which has grown to about $20 million today, placing it 10th on the list of Canada's largest. For someone who relished being first, Sam may not appreciate the placement.

The 1960s marked a banner decade for foundations with 18 major ones incorporated across Canada, six during Centennial Year alone—Windsor, Beaverbrook (Aitken), Eldee, Dunn, Tanenbaum.

Trust an obstinate Maritimer to leave a biography that is at once the most colorful and yet revealing of the affections and affectations of Canada's grand philanthropists. James Dunn was born in Bathurst, N.B., and trained for law at Dalhousie. Law was but an entry to business and finance. Dunn invested heavily in the Algoma Steel Company in Sault Ste. Marie, Ont., eventually acquired control, and became president and chairman of the board. It placed him well. During the First World War, he arranged the sale of desperately needed nickel from Norway to Great Britain and smelted it in Canada. When the Germans threatened invasion of Norway, he personally supervised the blow-up of the Norwegian mining operation. A grateful king bestowed upon him a baronetcy in 1920 for his services to the Mother Country.

Today, Dunn might be termed a health food nut and a jock.[6] He experimented with many different types of diets—vegetarian, meat, watermelon, wheat germ. He inspected and supervised the preparation of his meals, wherever and whenever—hotels, ships, trains. He exercised regularly and vigorously.

---

[6]Dunn was also often married. His first wife was Gertrude Price, daughter of the Quebec lumber baron; his second was Irene Clarice, the Lady Queensburg (Lord Beaverbrook was best man at that wedding in 1926); his third and last was Marcia Christoforides, whom he married in 1942.

Dunn didn't wait until later in life to demonstrate his philanthropic propensities. As a young lad, James acted as assistant and aide to Gideon Duncan, the town doctor in Bathurst, one of two men who apparently influenced his attitudes and actions profoundly. As soon as Dunn made some real money, he built a hospital for Bathurst and his adolescent friend and mentor. When the hospital burned to the ground years later, Sir James offered the town two dollars for every dollar raised locally on the condition that his second mentor, George Gilbert, be named chairman. The hospital committee said no, his friend was too old. It was a costly decision because Dunn held firm on the terms of the tied grant. His generosity extended beyond Bathurst to other parts of New Brunswick, and in the case of universities, across Canada. At one time or another, he supported eight across the country, endowing chairs at Mount Allison, Dalhousie and Queen's.

His retreat, where Dunn withdrew for absolute privacy and personal pleasure, was his comfortable house, Dayspring, at St. Andrews-by-the-Sea. There, on the shores of Passamaquoddy Bay, in Canada's most agreeable blending of nature and man-made beauty, Dunn would restore, reflect, dream, and conceive his next action.

French-Canadian money, too, was now becoming institutionalized—Lévesque, Bombardier. Jean-Louis Lévesque established his family foundation in 1961 to help celebrate his 50th birthday. The foundation was large enough (now $10 million) to fund major projects, and the founder young enough to stamp his imprimatur on its activities during its first two decades. Lévesque was born in Nouvelle, a small village on the Gaspé Peninsula. He studied the classical liberal arts first in the seminary school, then at St. Dunstan's University in Charlottetown. Lévesque began his career as a banker with the Provincial Bank of Canada but left when he was 26 to become a bond salesman. His talents flourished in the financial world and found expression through his own investment house and two personal holding companies which controlled Industrial Life Insurance Company, Fashion-Craft Ltd., Lallemand Yeast Ltd., and a host of diverse corporations. He loved thoroughbreds. And, like many sports enthusiasts, linked his passion with his portfolio—Blue Bonnets Raceway, Windsor Raceway, Richelieu. His brood mare *Fanfreluche* threw exquisite foals and Lévesque won much acclaim across Canada as owner and breeder of his stable's magnificent offspring.

When he turned his mind to philanthropy, Lévesque operated with the same style and *panache*. He gave his foundation an objective purpose and focused his gifts where he could see the results. He supported heart research in Montreal's renowned Heart Institute because cardiovascular disease strikes one of three Canadians. He gave money to the Miami Heart Institute for similar reasons and in doing so cemented Canada/Miami relations for his family and other Canadian winter expatriates. He supported education in eastern Canada and persuaded Queen's University to name its Centre for Continuing Education after Donald Gordon, the crusty railroader who also had been Lévesque's intimate friend. In 1980 his foundation established the annual *Prix au Mérite*, a mini-Nobel prize to honor a Canadian citizen for leading achievement in nine spheres of action. Although the Fondation Lévesque has national objects, it has confined its grants largely to eastern Canada, particularly Quebec.

A dozen more significant foundations were created during the 1970s: four more Tanenbaums, each now worth $6 million; the Devonian Group (the Harvies of Alberta); Van Dusen; Loblaw; Kahanoff. The largest ones were launched not by families but by special-interest groups who established endowments to support narrowly defined objectives.

Much capital came from the medical community when private insurance plans phased out in favor of medicare. The PSI and Associated Medical Services foundations alone control $50 million of investments devoted exclusively to advancing health care in Ontario. The Hospital for Sick Children spun off its trust-fund portfolio into its own captive foundation in 1972, which since has grown to become the third-largest fund in the country. The "Sick Kids" foundation has become the model for similar captive foundations across the country, which restrict their activities primarily to support a related hospital, university or cultural institution.

What has not caught on in Canada but flourishes in the United States is the corporate or company-sponsored foundation. These are formed to carry out a corporation's contribution program. Funds are donated by the corporation to a captive foundation which, in turn, administers the investment and distributes the grants according to policies consistent with the related corporation's donation goals. The foundation is a natural for corporations operating in highly cyclical industries—mining, forestry, agriculture. Large gifts can be made to the foundation during prosperous years when directors are looking for ways to dispose of obscenely high profits. As the foundation's capital builds, the annual income provides a stable and secure base to continue the corporate donation program throughout the lean years. Despite its attractions, there are probably no more than two dozen company-sponsored foundations in Canada,[7] among the oldest being Canada Packers

Foundation and the Ontario Paper Company Foundation.

Details for that pencil sketch of Canada's foundation fathers, the ones who made the money, were much easier to unearth than hard information on how their contemporary progeny spend it. We wrote the presidents of Canada's top 50 foundations asking for copies of their latest published annual report. The response is revealing. Twelve made no reply whatsoever, including two with assets greater than $10 million. Thirteen wrote letters similar in vein to the quotation which opened this chapter. Eleven sent some descriptive information, confined mainly to their granting policies or scope of interest. Fourteen sent essentially complete reports that included financial statements. Only one of these, the Richard Ivey Foundation, made full disclosure of its total investment portfolio. Of the 15 largest Canadian foundations, seven, with 1979 assets totalling more than $300 million, made no voluntary financial disclosure in an annual report.

Were it not for the initiative of Jeff Andrew, executive director of the Association of Universities and Colleges in Canada during the early 1960s, persistent probing by Allan Arlett in Toronto's Canadian Centre for Philanthropy, and a federal government reporting requirement initiated in 1977, Canadians would know even less about this important national resource. Arlett began studying Canadian foundations as a hobby in the early sixties and volunteered his services to the AUCC to help improve the quality and scope of the first *Guide to Foundations and Granting Agencies* published by the association in 1966. To overcome the reluctance of foundations to complete information questionnaires, Arlett built his early foundation profile by tracking the source and size of gifts received by various charitable foundations across the country. Foundations were given the opportunity to vet their listing before publication but, since Arlett's information was in the public domain, entries were published with or without foundation consent.

Arlett's sideline continued for nine years while he worked as a university development officer in New York. He served as a consultant on the second edition of the *Guide*, then edited the third and subsequent editions. Despite

---

[7] In contrast, company-sponsored foundations flourish in Japan, accounting for virtually all of their estimated 16,000 charitable corporations (*Koekl hojin*). Among the better known names: The Toyota Foundation, 10 billion yen; Mitsubishi Foundation, 5 billion yen; Honda Foundation, 750 million yen. The North American preoccupation with the accumulation of personal wealth appears not to have infected the Japanese character. Tax laws and personal behavior both act to distribute wealth more equitably in Japan, leaving few very rich Japanese families.

errors of omission and commission the *Guide* was an instant best-seller, eagerly devoured by volunteer as well as mercenary fund raisers. The directory is now in its fifth edition and contains vital statistics on hundreds of Canada's identifiable foundations.[8]

The most recent edition has been expanded immeasurably, thanks to a federal income tax regulation introduced in 1977. Commencing that year, all charitable organizations in Canada were required to complete a Public Information Return (T3010) which disclosed the names of foundation officers and core financial data. The required financial detail was sketchy, the forms badly filled out, and copies were available from only one source, Revenue Canada in Ottawa. Arlett used the most recent T3010s to compile his directory, then made copies available to our research team for analysis.

Prior to that reporting requirement, Canada's 40,000 humanistic organizations, handling a sizable proportion of the country's national income, operated with privileged tax status yet were subject to little serious monitoring, auditing or control by Revenue Canada, or indeed any other government department.

Their tax advantages are significant. The key is registration under the Income Tax Act. Once blessed by the Minister of National Revenue, a charity is exempt from tax on any income it earns. It is then able to receive donations that are tax deductible by the donor. As we have seen, deductibility for donations has been a feature of the Income Tax Act from its inception in 1917. At first, the act made no distinction between charitable organizations that actually performed a humanistic service, and a charitable trust or foundation whose sole function was to provide other charities with money for the service.

With interest in foundations picking up, the "feds" introduced a few new rules for charitable trusts and corporations by amending the Income Tax Act in 1951. The next amendments were in 1966, following the church scandals in the province of Quebec. From then on, charities had to register with the Minister, issue receipts that could be verified, and file information returns with Revenue. The filing was perfunctory, but sporadic field audits by the department's staff eliminated the more flagrant abuses of issuing inflated receipts.

---

[8]Arlett gives Jeff Andrew much credit for the *Guide*'s success. "He initiated the first directory and supported me in my subsequent efforts even when foundations wrote letters, sometimes threatening legal action, with regard to the entries we prepared."

More elaborate rules were enacted in 1976. From then on, charities were required to spend certain minimum amounts on charitable activities, not an unreasonable expectation. The disbursement requirement for foundations was set at 90 per cent of their net income; that is, the foundation's total income less reasonable operating expenses. Capital gains earned by a foundation were not classified as income and could be fully retained. For charitable organizations, the doers, it was set at 80 per cent of the gifts they received. Commencing in 1977, all charities were required to file the public information return already referred to.

The disclosure requirement was helpful but tended to raise more questions than it answered. It pointed up, for instance, that disbursement requirements could be satisfied by transferring funds between charities without any of the funds necessarily being devoted to charitable activities. Foundations could reduce or possibly eliminate their required payout by arranging their investments in equity securities and realizing their return by way of capital gains instead of income. Charities were free to redefine their status annually in order to take advantage of the most attractive of the two payout requirements. And foundations were free to engage in the friendly financial transactions already described.

This then was the income tax milieu for foundations in the late 1970s and early 1980s—attractive, supportive, permissive, serene. Until November 12, 1981.

That evening, Finance Minister Allan MacEachen announced the federal government's intention to enact sweeping reforms of the Income Tax Act. He zeroed in particularly on foundations and proposed measures to force larger payouts, to thwart self-dealing in sweetheart loans and investments, to block transfers between charities to avoid payout minimums, and to impose a penalty tax on foundations that were deficient in their annual disbursements. But the *coup de grâce*, the cruelest cut of all: he would require charitable foundations to include the full amount of capital gains in their income subject to the disbursement rules.

The giant came instantly awake. It was one thing to close a few loopholes to prevent self-dealing. But quite another to force foundations to encroach on capital. Within 24 hours, C. Arthur Bond,[9] secretary of a rather loosely

[9]Bond, who is executive director of PSI Foundation, is perhaps the most influential of the small cadre of professional foundation administrators in Canada. Born in Toronto in 1929, Bond completed high school and went to work immediately. He joined PSI in 1949 when the private health plan was first introduced, grew along with it and was secretary-treasurer when it folded into the PSI Foundation in
(Cont'd)

knit and soporific Association of Canadian Foundations, shot off a letter to each of the 72 members proposing a meeting of foundation leaders to discuss the announced changes. He followed it four days later with a written brief to members outlining in detail several key problem areas: static incomes which, in real dollars, would mean considerably less purchasing power on the granting side; the tendency for foundations not to sell winning investments unless they could find a matching loss on another security—investment policy dictated by taxation decree; the tendency to move portfolios into short-term investments exclusively, resulting in incomes that would fluctuate wildly with interest rates.

Bond then moved into high gear. He wrote letters to MacEachen, to R.A. Short, general director of Tax Policy, to his local M.P., and to the Hon. Michael Wilson, Opposition finance critic, explaining his concern for the effect of the capital gains policy. To MacEachen he wrote, "Foundations today are unable to support more than 25 per cent of the requests received from these charities.... At a time of government cutbacks and financial restraint, it is difficult to understand (any) legislation which would reduce even further the money available for the arts, medical research, education, social services, etc. If inflation continues, (these) proposals will spell the death knell of Canadian foundations."

The association also took action to inform university and charity personnel of the likely impact of the tax changes. While foundation personnel continued to contact government officials with informal protests throughout November and early December, a formal brief was being prepared by representatives of approximately 15 foundations, both private and public, as well as from different geographical regions across Canada, to be sent to the Department of Finance before Christmas.

This brief, with full endorsement from the association's membership, acknowledged fully the public right to a reasonable return from the tax-exempt funds of charities but, at the same time, demonstrated that the possible

---

1970. His career took a boost from his part-time studies with the Certified General Accountants Association. Bond won the CGA Gold Medal in the 1959 examinations and was further honored in 1980 when the association elected him a Fellow, a distinction awarded to less than one per cent of their membership. Bond married Anne Urry and has three children. Religion is an important dimension of Bond's life. He calls himself a traditional Anglican who prefers the Book of Common Prayer to the Alternate Rights. Hobbies are reading, roses, cross-country skiing and jazz, particularly Louis Armstrong. His record collection contains a few of the original 78 rpms. Bond allows he has had little diversion since November 1981—60 per cent of his time is spent educating bureaucrats and orchestrating tax legislation through the House of Commons.

abuses of a very few foundations did not reasonably warrant a large-scale restriction on all foundations; indeed, the return to the public in the long run would actually fall off dramatically if the proposed changes were legislated. The brief analyzed each proposed amendment separately and made comments or suggestions where appropriate. It ended with a request that a meeting between the association members and the government take place in the near future.

On January 29, 1982, association representatives and a tax advisor met with government officials in Ottawa. Glenn P. Jenkins, assistant deputy minister, Tax Policy, was to have attended the meeting but was called away. Instead, other officials of the same department attended. The association's intended purpose was to determine why the government had proposed such strong measures, to what extent the government was prepared to back down from these measures and, finally, to determine the magnitude of the so-called abuses that were continually cited by the department.

Bond summarized the events of that meeting in a letter to all association members: "The Finance officials seemed to avoid answering our questions on the magnitude of the abuses and it appeared (that) the Superintendent does not have any hard evidence...." Bond also felt that the support for the capital-gains proposal was very strong while the department may have been prepared to consider alternative payout requirements.

What followed this meeting was a continual stream of formal government contacts by many Canadian foundations but, more importantly, a few well-placed informal calls. The Finance Minister announced his capitulation in a press release on April 21, 1982. He would redefine the original budget proposals. New rules were being proposed as a result of extensive consultations held between the Minister of Finance and members of the various charitable foundations and these consultations had proven "very worthwhile."

The new rules were unveiled in a White Paper on Charities and the Canadian Tax System issued for discussion in May 1983. Conciliatory in tone, the new proposals softened the disbursement requirements considerably. All charities would be required to disburse 80 per cent of the gifts received in the previous year, not including endowments received for long-term investment purposes or other capital receipts. Gifts from a related charity must be disbursed the same year as received.

In addition, and this was the crucial rule for foundations, they must distribute for charitable purposes each year an amount equal to 4.5 per cent of their invested capital. This would eliminate the problem of segregating capital gains from income. Nor would it matter whether the investment was in shares of a public company or preferred accommodation to a relative. To take care of the latter, transactions not entered into at arm's length and called non-qualified investments, the White Paper proposed a penalty tax on all taxpayers who received benefits under those arrangements.*

The association's awesome offensive was the most work it had done since it was conceived a decade earlier. Bond recalls that, in 1971, 15 people connected with 10 or 11 Ontario funds got together informally to exchange views on the status of foundations in Canada. Informal meant just that. No minutes were kept and nothing was done to draw attention to the group for fear that publicity would invite scrutiny, which might lead to pressure to open foundation financial statements to public scrutiny. The informal sessions went well. Regular semi-annual meetings were held until 1974.

That year, the group was expanded to 36 foundations including some from Quebec and western Canada. Although still informal, it had now become an association. Bond wasn't particularly thrilled with the informal status but noted "at least we were all talking." The paranoia over published annual reports was still very much in evidence. Nonetheless, the membership elected Bond as their secretary, each anted up $100 for his paper, postage and incidental costs (the fund lasted until the fall of 1981), and attended one meeting each year for the next four years. The association stopped meeting in 1978 because there wasn't anything to discuss and members lost interest. Even the attack on the 1981 budget was stage-managed without a meeting of the association.

Today, the association lists 85 foundations as members, representing about two-thirds of all Canadian foundation assets. Conspicuous by their absence are all the Tanenbaums, Eldee, Dunn and Lévesque.

Bond allows that when the new rules are finally legislated, he will make a renewed effort to organize yearly meetings. He sees the association's major role as one of educating government bureaucrats about the role of foundations. Some might say they have already made an impressive start.

The bureaucrats unquestionably knew far more about foundation activities than is revealed by an analysis of their public information returns filed in Ottawa since 1977. But even relying on that tenuous data base, we gain important insights into the scope of foundation operations. First is the high degree of concentration of assets. The top 20 control more than half the

---

*Draft legislation spelling out the specific tax changes for foundations and other charities was tabled in the House of Commons in the spring of 1984. It died on the order paper when Parliament was dissolved for the September 4 election.

foundation assets in the country. Ontario still hogs the lion's share, more than half, even though her population is only slightly more than one-third of the total. As a result, other regions are under-represented. Quebec has the widest discrepancy between foundation assets and population—15 versus 27 per cent. The Atlantic Provinces host only about three per cent of the assets, a third of what they should control, based on their populations. Yet when total grants are analyzed, the discrepancy narrows. The income payout is proportionately less in Ontario, British Columbia and the Atlantic Region than asset holdings would suggest. It is greater in Quebec and the Prairie Provinces.

Determining how much foundations disburse is far easier than learning what kind of activities they support. We must rely on information contained in the few annual reports that are available, plus some interpolation and intuition. The majority of the money is given to health-related activities. This is so not only because health care has long been a favorite cause for many families and their foundations—Atkinson, Bickell, Muttart, Ivey, Lévesque, Spencer—but also because three substantial funds, totalling more than $100 million, channel all grants into health. Education, particularly universities, is probably next in popularity. These gifts are not confined to scholarships or bursaries bearing the name of a foundation father, but include good-sized endowments for residences (McConnell), professional schools (Ivey) and faculty clubs (Koerner). Grants for social-welfare causes would rank slightly ahead of arts and culture. Eaton and McLean have been particularly supportive of social development, and many large and small foundations across the land have linked their names and funds with theatres, museums and art galleries.

Environmental causes have become the most recent frontier for foundation funds. The most substantial and impressive program was launched by the Devonian Group of Charitable Foundations in 1973. During the next eight years, that group, representing the Harvie family in Alberta, invested more than $60 million across Canada in the creation of more than a dozen public parks, and in the preservation of historic sites and artifacts unique to the Canadian heritage. Devonian Gardens in Calgary, Ryerson Community Park in Toronto, Maritime Museum of the Atlantic and the Archival Collection in Whitehorse exhibit the good taste and intelligence of the Harvie gifting program.

The genius behind the fortune was Eric Lafferty Harvie who was born in Orillia, Ont., in 1892. When he was 52, Harvie purchased the mineral rights to some acreage southwest of Edmonton and leased three-quarters of a section to Imperial Oil for exploration two years later. That leasehold became the great Leduc strike and was the basis for the massive Harvie fortune. Harvie himself was interested in his community, not only in western Canada which he loved, but at the national level as well—youth, heritage, geography. To a very great extent, the foundation's parkland acquisition and heritage program simply extended the scope of Harvie's personal interests in collecting. Unlike virtually all foundations, the Devonian Group freely encroached on capital to speed the development of its projects. It is still worth about $8 million. And while still prepared to take risks in pioneering ventures that show innovation and imagination, Harvie's son Donald has served notice that its activities will terminate in the foreseeable future.

Granting guidelines for the Devonian Group contain a caveat that has become standard practice across most foundations. Grants will not be made to cover on-going operating costs, annual appeals, deficits, travel costs, scholarships, bursaries, academic leaves, conferences and seminars. Foundations prefer innovation—unique, newsworthy activities. They fund equipment but not its upkeep, a building but not its overhead, a computer but not its software. Their gifts exert tremendous leverage on the finances of the donee. Unwittingly, their generosity often exacerbates an already difficult financial picture. In providing seed money to a teaching hospital to acquire a Nuclear Magnetic Resonance body scanner, very much the cutting-edge of diagnostic technology, the foundation also bequeaths the hospital an obligation to provide a perpetual operating commitment of half-a-million dollars a year. Inevitably, these operating annuities fall back on the state and are one of the reasons why hospital costs, for example, have exploded in recent years.

The leverage extends far beyond the resources of the foundation itself. The top 50 foundations in Canada list a pool of 200 officers who influence every conceivable industry and sector in the country. The Macdonald Stewart Foundation in Montreal, for instance, lists four officers: David M. Stewart, Paul B. Paine, J.K. Finlayson and Léo Lavoie. This quartet holds directorships in no less than 32 corporations including Power Corporation, Royal Bank of Canada, Canadair, Great West Life. As officers, they are directly responsible for allocating millions of dollars annually in foundation grants; as directors, they have potential to determine corporate donation budgets amounting to many millions more. If the handful of 200 foundation leaders decided to support—or ignore—a major humanistic initiative, one could safely predict its outcome.

But are these trustees faithful stewards of the foundation resources entrusted to them? Are Canada's major public-trust funds treated as instruments for personal indulgence and private exploitation? If they are, it is well disguised. An analysis of the public-information forms for 40 of the top 50 foundations[10] in 1980 contains few shocking revelations. It shows, for instance, that these foundations received most of their income from investments. Slightly more than half of total reported income came by way of interest and dividends, about one-third from capital gains. The remaining 12 per cent derived from gifts, most of which represented public contributions to community and special interest foundations.

The disbursements are more interesting. About five per cent of income came off the top for administrative expenses. Sixteen of the 40 foundations claimed expenses for remuneration of officers working directly for the foundation, 10 of whom were paid more than $25,000. Nine listed remuneration to other employees. Thirty-five claimed general administrative costs.[11] Thirty-two per cent of income was held back and reinvested to preserve capital, or used to purchase foundation assets. This represented mainly the capital gains realized by 24 of the 40 foundations, amounts which are excluded in determining disbursement requirements. The remainder, 63 per cent of total income, was disbursed: 34 foundations made gifts to qualified donees (representing 50 per cent of the total income of all 40 foundations);

---

[10]Pin-pointing the top 50 foundations in Canada is a challenging exercise. The public information forms make no distinction between foundations and other charitable organizations. Since there are some 47,000 separate entities filing T3010s, a searcher has difficulty in spotting every foundation from an alphabetical printout of organization names. We have relied on a listing prepared by the Canadian Centre of Philanthropy, whose information on foundations is considered to be the most complete in the country.

[11]Attentive readers will have deduced that a maximum of 25 of the 40 foundations paid administrative salaries. What of the other 15? Were administrative services donated? Likely not in the case of larger foundations. The management of many is contracted to a trust company which not only handles the bookkeeping and grant administration, analysis and recommendations, but in many cases also directs the investment of foundation assets. The appropriate trust and agency fees would be billed to the foundation and shown as general administrative costs on the T3010 public information form. The R. Samuel McLaughlin Foundation, for instance, with assets of $40 million is administered by the E.T. & A. Division of National Trust Company in Toronto. Preston J. Sewell, a National Trust trust officer, acts as correspondence secretary for the McLaughlin and others with crisp, clinical efficiency.

Having another entity bill the foundation for administration relieves the foundation of the need to set up costly payroll services—the tax deduction, unemployment insurance, fringe benefits and the like. It has been suggested to this author that the device also could be used by foundations to stretch further the tax deductibility of donations by a tax-paying entity controlled by the same persons. For instance, a corporation paying the maximum marginal tax rate and contributing the maximum donation limit of 20 per cent of income simply assigns a corporate employee to foundation administration. If the cost of that employee is billed to the foundation, the corporation receives no tax deduction for the salary expense. And since the foundation pays no income tax, the deduction is of no value to it. But if the billing is for a reduced amount, or ignored entirely, the corporation saves the tax on the salary expense buried as a corporate deduction.

eight disbursed money directly on charitable activity (representing three per cent of income); seven foundations made gifts to associated charities (the remaining 10 per cent of total income).

It is the latter category of disbursement, a total of $12 million from all seven foundations, where potential diversion of foundation revenues could occur, and which represents the target of the White Paper reform proposals.

Foundation balance sheets typically are uncomplicated. Assets are invested almost exclusively in securities—notes, bonds, stocks, a few fixed assets. Few show liabilities. But the public information form was poorly designed, making it impossible to determine if investments are carried at cost or market values. However, for the half-dozen that supplied both values, the two amounts were reasonably close over this period.

What, then, of the charge of hoarding assets? Of manipulating investments to convert income into capital gains? Of investing in family businesses? The published data give some indication, but are not detailed enough to answer the questions definitively. They show, for example, that the assets of 38 of Canada's 100 largest foundations that filed usable information returns for the years 1978, 1979 and 1980 grew at the rate of six per cent in 1979 and seven per cent in 1980—hardly keeping even with inflation.

Of the 40 large foundations studied for 1980, 24 of them, 60 per cent, reported capital gains indicating a portfolio which probably contained equity securities. The remainder reported only investment income. These, of course, could have held equities but made no trades that year. Both groups reported investment income that averaged between seven and nine per cent of assets for the years 1978 through 1980. In addition, the equity investors reported annual capital gains in the range of four to five per cent of assets. This would suggest that capital gains are not realized and retained at the expense of income subject to the disbursement requirement.

Stripped to its essential meaning, our largest foundations distributed $53 to charitable causes in 1980 for every $100 they took in, or $63 if gifts to associated charities are thrown in. Expressed another way, the typical large foundation earned an investment return of eight per cent on its assets plus an average of five per cent in capital gains for a total return of 13 per cent. It distributed to charitable causes an amount equal to 7.6 per cent of assets[12] at the minimum and nine per cent at maximum.

If these numbers are anywhere nearly reflective of current realities, the large foundations should have little difficulty in meeting the disbursement

---

[12]The ratio of disbursements to assets was nearly eight per cent in 1978 and 1979.

guidelines set out in the tax reform proposals. Indeed, the 4.5 per cent disbursement minimum may work to contract, not expand, the flow of funds from foundations into humanistic service. But these are, at best, educated guesses about investment performance. Foundation portfolio management, in all but one family foundation, is carefully sequestered so as to render impossible a truly informed critique.

Such is the profile of Canada's large foundations, those with assets of at least $2 million, circa 1980. Although small in number, they control 80 per cent of total foundation dollars. Little can be said about the 900 smaller foundations that make up the total set. One might expect them to exhibit more creativity, less conformity, perhaps less restraint, than their more visible counterparts.

The public will soon know. A revised public information form, effective fully for 1983, demands considerably more information that its predecessor. Sources of revenue must be spelled out in much greater detail, as must expenditures and liabilities. Amounts receivable from founders, officers, directors, members, or to entities related to such persons, must be segregated. Similar detail is required for debts and liabilities. Disbursements must show the name, location, registration number and amount of donation to each recipient charity. Domestic and foreign expenditures must be shown separately. Those charities which operate outside the country, or engage in non-arm's-length transactions, should be prepared to answer probing questions from an inquisitive, skeptical and sometimes hostile public.

So be it. The disclosure requirements are healthy and long overdue. They will do much to dissipate the grotesque preoccupation with secrecy in foundation affairs. The tax exemption on foundation income alone costs the treasury—the Canadian public—$50 million a year. It is the trustees' duty to report on their stewardship of these public funds.

That foundations were forced into public disclosure is an unworthy reflection of the inherent quality of leadership latent within their ranks. No doubt some are rich and idle, some are dilettantes, some manipulate the tax laws for personal gain. But that is the fringe minority. Within the pool of foundation officers is some of the finest talent our country has to offer. Men and women with good minds, strong character, independent thought. Educated. Fiscal conservatives and social liberals, or vice versa. Doers. But with the luxury of time to probe, ponder, reflect, sift and create. Not burdened with routine, beholden to no one. Responsible. Above politics and petty intrigue. Leaders.

When performance is measured against potential, we become conscious of Canada's lost opportunity from this rich national resource. Foundations, singly and in concert, could provide stabilizing, rational leadership for the voluntary private sector. They have or could command the intellectual and financial resources to identify, anticipate and support attention to major societal needs that neither the government nor other social organizations are in a position to provide. Unlike governments, foundations can address the long-range, more difficult and often more controversial but vital questions which face society.

Without relinquishing their individual freedom of action, foundations collectively could set an example of cooperation by coordinating their policies to provide a healthier, better educated, more advanced society. Without engaging in political advocacy, they could consult annually with cabinet ministers in relevant departments to ensure that private initiatives complement rather than collide with public policies. Without denying family roots and traditions, foundations could rekindle the philanthropic zeal of their founders by confronting contemporary challenges that extend their reach.

Foundations could become symbols of excellence, an example to society that the accumulation of wealth is not the end, but merely the beginning, of a life-long mission of usefulness, productivity, compassion, civility. Show Canadians, by action and example, that it is the duty of each to nurture the freedom and growth of Canada. That voluntary effort, personal service, is indeed the highest calling for those who wish to gain self-respect and the esteem of others. That giving can be motivated by nothing more than the knowledge and satisfaction of doing something constructive for others.

Foundations could spawn a new source of intellectual leadership in the country, by elevating foundation administration to a most respected form of public service. At present, there are less than 20 full-time administrators employed by foundations to manage their ongoing affairs. Most are not equipped by education or capacity to tackle the complex issues facing the humanistic sector, and articulate a bold, coherent, feasible design for their solution by the combined efforts of the public and private sector.

Such respected leadership is forthcoming in the United States. Men like McGeorge Bundy,[13] with a distinguished record of public service to his

---

[13]Bundy was born in Boston in 1919, married into the Lowells of Massachusetts, attended Groton, then Yale. He excelled in academics, in oratory and in writing, earning him the nickname "Mahatma" Bundy. Harvard accepted him, without advanced degrees, as a Junior Fellow. Although 4F for bad eyesight, Bundy served as assistant to a Navy admiral during the Second World War. He rejoined Harvard as professor after the war and forged a friendship with Arthur Schlesinger, Jr., an intimate of John F. Kennedy. Although a Republican, Bundy was one of the "Harvard mafia "who followed JFK to the White House during his term.

country, moved easily from academe (Harvard), to government (President Kennedy's special assistant for National Security Affairs) to foundation administration (president of the Ford Foundation), and left a legacy of constructive thought and action that was enriched by every move.

Such a role would require major changes in foundation action. The association would require strengthening and a definition of purpose. A few of the larger foundations would have to assume a national outlook and allocate an increasing portion of foundation resources to a few carefully researched, self-initiated actions national in scope and executed with excellence. More foundation resources would be required for professional staff, perhaps as much as 10 per cent of income, $10 million a year, for the talent to do the job well. The money would be an investment in Canada's future.

All foundations would require a review of their objects and essential purpose to determine what role they could best fulfill in the grand design, what constituency they propose to serve. Some may alter the composition of their boards to accomplish this goal. Association meetings should be open to the public, as should a précis of the summit meetings with governments. It would be a refreshing change of pace from the trivia that fills the airways and pages of our communications media. Who knows, Canadians might discover a new breed of hero, men and women, cast in the mold of Cardinal Newman's model of the gentleman.

Too idealistic? Don't governments exist to assume leadership in public affairs? To define and carry out humanistic programs? They do, and it may well be too late to halt the progress towards total government dominance of the humanistic sector. Yet many feel that the quality of the Canadian way of life would diminish in a Stage IV society, that governments need checks and balances to preserve and protect individual freedoms. Foundations could focus that counterpoint to government ambition and, at the same time, be the conscience of the private sector which reminds us that freedom commands a high price in personal responsibility.

XII

Where the buck stops

Plato once mused, "When there is an income tax, the just man will pay more and the unjust less on the same amount of income." Human nature has changed little in 2,000 years. Today we call the exercise tax planning, tax avoidance, horizontal inequity or tax evasion, depending on one's viewpoint. The objective is identical: to reduce, or avoid, paying one's share of the cost of common services, those amenities that are usually accessible to citizens for their protection, regulation, transportation, welfare, growth and economic stability. Government.

At issue is not government itself. Most acknowledge the need for rules of common order and accept the burden of their cost. The perennial dilemma is how much government? For what common services? Who should pay? What is a fair share? These are complicated, controversial questions and probe far beyond the scope of this inquiry. Yet, in segregating humanistic service, we cannot avoid confronting the principles of public finance. In a society approaching Stage IV, governments *are* the dominant source of funds and we must understand the fundamentals of taxation theory in order to render judgment on future directions.

The facts are relatively simple. Like most large Western states, Canada recognizes three levels of government—federal, provincial and local (municipal). Our original constitution was uncommonly prescient in dividing responsibility and taxation authority between the senior government and the provinces, which in turn controlled the municipalities. At least for the

first 50 years. Because Canada sprawled so clumsily from coast to coast, and
the population was so thinly distributed across her southern boundary, it
was obvious that a central government must be strong enough to forge a
transportation and communication infrastructure that would unite the
country and maintain a common national identity and purpose.

Understandably, the Fathers of Confederation foresaw the heavy financial burden on the nation at large and provided the federal government with
authority to levy the broadest possible taxes in order to discharge its mandate of peace, order and good government. Provinces were permitted to levy
the unpopular direct taxes, those, such as income tax and property tax, that
are readily identified and difficult to disguise. All concerned at the time conceded that that tax base would be sufficient to satisfy the revenue needs of
the provinces which, after all, were charged with peripheral responsibilities
such as the education, health care and general welfare (''charities and elee-
mosynary institutions'') of the population within their jurisdiction.

Of course, no one could foresee the abundance of wealth generated by our
forefathers, the broadening definition of humanistic service and the rising
expectations of the population. Canada moved rapidly through the first
three stages of humanistic development. As the financial burden fell more
heavily on the provinces, there developed constitutional wrangles between
the provinces and the ''feds'' over responsibility and the scope of taxing authority. The debates have been vigorous and at times acrimonious. But the
country has muddled through.

Except that today all levels of government are over-extended. They have
assumed responsibility beyond their financial capacity. Humanistic service
alone consumes 40 per cent of total federal government outflows, half of local government budgets, and more than 60 per cent of provincial expenditures. For well over a decade, the senior levels of government have spent far
more money than they have been prepared to tax, have accumulated sizable
deficits, and are now bumping the upper limits of debt capacity for a nation
with pretensions to financial integrity.

It is not a uniquely Canadian problem. Small comfort. The pain of adjustment is no less severe. Quite the contrary. Since our trading partners are
similarly handicapped, they are unlikely to enhance our prosperity through
expanded exports. Canada's fiscal problems are likely to remain with
Canadians. The fiscal options are limited—continue to accumulate deficits,
increase government revenues, curtail government expenditures.

All these courses will have serious ramifications on financial flows to the
humanistic sector. But we require some common vocabulary before these

implications can be explored—a basic understanding of the underpinnings of taxation theory and the principles of public finance.

The expenditure side is relatively easy. Governments—that is to say politicians—eventually recognize a fundamental truth, that expenditures, which are popular, become constrained by government's willingness to tax the citizenry, always an unpopular action, or to borrow the deficiency, increasingly so.

Revenue, therefore, is the tougher issue. How to tax with the least pain? The best taxes are *indirect* taxes, those whose ultimate burden of payment can be passed on. The initial payer, the point of *impact*, simply *shifts* the burden of the tax to other taxpayers—for example, the federal manufacturer's sales tax which typically is incorporated incognito in the retailer's final price. Shifting can be backward towards the factors of production (read "labor") or their owners (read "shareholders") by a decrease in wages or prices. More likely, in recent years, the shifting has been forward—to consumers by way of increased commodity prices. The point of tax *incidence* occurs when a taxpayer becomes unable to pass on the tax and accepts the ultimate burden.

It is at this point that the economy (read "politicians") feels the *effects* of the tax. Effects are the consequences, ripples, that flow from the initial levy of a tax. Shifting causes the downstream effects of higher prices, decreases in disposable income, and consequential behavioral changes in consumption or savings patterns. Effects can be benign or devastating. Walter Gordon, Prime Minister Pearson's besieged Minister of Finance, discovered belatedly that even a hidden tax can be politically destructive.[1] Taxes work or they don't. Much depends on public perception, "Is the tax fair?"

We are now at the essence of the problem. Who should pay? How much? The first principle is *neutrality*. A tax is said to be neutral if it doesn't interfere with the economic decisions of individuals, such that their decisions remain unchanged in the presence of the tax. A tax is *progressive* if it increases at a rate greater than a proportionate increase in the taxable base, for example, the Canadian personal income tax, structured to increase faster than incomes to around $50,000 where it levels off (the ability-to-pay principle). It is *regressive* if it imposes a smaller proportionate incidence on high-income taxpayers than those with lower incomes, for example, a sales tax levied on food, which typically consumes a greater proportion of the family

---

[1]Finance Minister Walter Gordon's 1963 budget proposed an 11 per cent tax on building materials, a measure that met with stiff political opposition.

income of low-income taxpayers. A *proportional* tax exacts the same percentage of sacrifice across all income classes. Consumption taxes, retail sales taxes and the like thus are labelled regressive; income taxes, progressive. Wealth taxes, corporate taxes, licenses, health insurance fees and a multitude of government levies defy precise classification.

A "good" tax structure is described as one in which the distribution of the tax burden is perceived as *equitable*—that is, everyone is made to pay his "fair share." Taxes can be levied to correct inefficiencies in the private sector, in the case of disruptive monopolies, for instance, and to support fiscal stabilization policies. An equitable tax system should permit efficient and non-arbitrary administration and it should be understandable to the taxpayer. Administration and compliance cost should be as low as is compatible with other objectives.

Contradictory as some of these requirements may seem, they contain the essential criteria against which a tax system may be judged. Fairness, for some, may interfere with the economic decisions of others, but both tests are important to consider. Trade-offs must be made. The nub of the issue is *equity*. If citizens perceive they are paying a fair share, then they are at equilibrium with their economic peers, inferiors and superiors. If not, they resort to practices which reduce their payments, either through tax avoidance transactions which are legal, or through illegal tax evasion schemes.

Horizontal equity requires that "equals should be treated equally," that persons with the same level of well-being before the tax is imposed have a comparable level of well-being after the tax is paid. It requires that all income flows that increase economic well-being—capital gains, inheritances, gifts, windfalls—be treated equally as sources of income subject to tax, that deductions and exemptions not discriminate between equivalent taxpayers.

Vertical equity recognizes the principle of declining marginal utility, that citizens with more income can pay a higher proportion of tax and still be incrementally better off than those with less income. Progressive tax rates tend to equalize the degree of sacrifice across income categories. Extreme vertical equity implies a tax system that leaves all individuals equally well off, that net income after tax be distributed equally throughout the population. Practical vertical equity, in Canada, is a compromise that leaves all groups reasonably satisfied with the degree of after-tax income disparity. It is here, more than anywhere else, where economic and moral issues collide—the twilight zone that is avoided aggressively by economists, politicians and theologians alike.

The theory is relevant to our discussion because governments collectively now direct just over 50 per cent of their disbursements to the humanistic sector. It is a level of spending roughly equal to the total tax revenues now collected by the federal, provincial and municipal governments combined. The remaining expenditures for debt service, defence, transportation, justice and so on are financed from non-tax sources—license fees, royalties, investment income—and borrowing. Therefore, any changes in the revenue mix of governments are likely to be reflected in changes in the level of humanistic expenditures, and vice versa. The imposition of new or increased taxes to close deficits likely will be measured by the public against visible changes in humanistic benefits, and expenditure cuts are most likely to occur there simply because it is the largest expenditure category. The third alternative, continued borrowing to sustain ''unproductive social expenditures,'' already has become unpopular public policy in the neo-conservative era.

Canada's governments use a broad array of taxes to collect their revenues. While no tax is totally regressive or progressive, it is generally conceded that the personal income tax tends to have a progressive incidence on the population; provincial sales taxes tend to regressivity, as do health insurance premiums, real estate taxes and so on. For some taxes, such as the corporate income tax, strong arguments have been advanced to support either classification. Precise allocation is not that important for this discussion. Using even the roughest screen, dividing total tax revenues between personal income tax, with a progressive tendency, and all other taxes which have regressive tendencies, illustrates the fundamental structure of the Canadian tax system.

TAX REVENUES OF ALL GOVERNMENTS
CLASSIFIED BY INCIDENCE, c. 1980

	Federal percentage	Provincial percentage	Local percentage	Total percentage
Progressive tendency				
Personal income tax	47	42	—	39
Regressive tendency				
Lotteries	—	4	—	2
All other taxes	53	54	100	59
Total tax revenues	100	100	100	100
Proportion of total tax revenues collected	48	40	12	100

Personal income taxes have become the single most important source of government revenues. Twenty years ago they were much less important, accounting for 33 per cent of federal tax revenues and only five per cent of provincial. Provincial lotteries, discussed in a few moments, exact a noticeable cash flow from individuals and are shown separately because governments tend to earmark the net profits of lotteries to finance humanistic projects.

With a large proportion of government revenues collected by a progressive tax, one would expect that upper-income taxpayers would pay proportionately more income tax than lower-income Canadians. They do. Families in the lowest-income quintile paid just over one per cent of all income tax in 1978, whereas the highest quintile paid 49 per cent.[2] It can be said, therefore, that upper-income groups bear a higher share of the cost of humanistic benefits. Expressed another way, governments redistribute the income of upper-income Canadians to the benefit of the lower-income classes.

And since the proportion of income tax to total tax revenues has increased over the past decades, we might expect that the degree of income redistribution has improved over time, that is, that lower-income groups should have increased their share of total Canadian income. Not so. The bottom 20 per cent of all Canadian families received only 4.6 per cent of total income-after-tax in 1975, while the top quintile commanded 40.6 per cent. That relatively high degree of inequality has remained almost identical for the past 30 years,[3] despite government efforts at redistribution.

The problem of income distribution has long been a thorny economic/moral issue. We must be careful to confine our discussion to its impact on the financing of the humanistic sector. Consider each of the three sources of funds: public sector from income tax; public sector from regressive taxes; private sector from donations. The lowest quintile contributes little in the way of income taxes, so we can conclude that 40 per cent of the tax burden of the public sector does have a progressive incidence. Although there is no reliable way to distribute the incidence of all the remaining taxes across income categories, one can be confident that it would be distributed much more evenly across the five groups of income earners and probably would show a regressive tendency—that is, the percentage of regressive-type taxes

---

[2]The index of inequality was 69.8, indicating a relatively high degree of inequality in the incidence of the income tax. The index was 77 in the United States, 45 in Japan. Interestingly, in Sweden the index of tax inequality was 68 and disposable income inequality 42, exactly the same as Canada.

[3]The Gini coefficient of Canadian income distribution was 0.3904 in 1951, 0.3679 in 1961, 0.4001 in 1971, and 0.3917 in 1975.

to total income in Quintile One would likely be higher than in Quintile Five.

What about the incidence of the cost of donations, the third financing category? It was reported earlier that low-income families are much more generous than their share of national income would predict. The distribution of total donations by quintile in 1978 was as follows:

**DISTRIBUTION OF FAMILY INCOME AND
DONATIONS BY INCOME CLASS, 1978**

Income quintile	*Family donations percentage*	*Disposable income percentage*
Q1	10.9	6.9
Q2	13.9	13.2
Q3	16.8	18.8
Q4	22.5	24.5
Q5	35.9	36.6
	100.0	100.0

In fact, the degree of sacrifice is more pronounced than this distribution implies. Since donations are tax deductible, they are less costly to upper-income taxpayers. Adjusting family donations for the effect of marginal tax rates shows that Canadians are much more uniformly generous, across income classes, than our U.S. neighbors, where both financial generosity and national income are highly concentrated in upper-income groups. Japan, on the other hand, has the most equal distribution of generosity across income classes. Coincidently, the Japanese also have the most equitable income distribution, either on a before or after-tax basis. Family generosity in Japan has actually increased over the past decade, from 3.4 per cent of income to 3.9 per cent.

**QUINTILE DISTRIBUTION OF THE
AFTER-TAX INCIDENCE[4] OF DONATIONS, c. 1980**

Family income quintile	Canada percentage	United States percentage	Japan percentage
Q1	14	9	13
Q2	15	11	15
Q3	15	16	18
Q4	22	23	21
Q5	34	41	33
Total	100	100	100
Coefficient of inequality of donations	31	48	28
Coefficient of inequality of disposable income	42	55	25

The ratio of donations to GNP has dropped sharply in Canada and to a lesser degree in the United States.[5]

International comparisons of family generosity reveal few consistent themes. One tendency does recur. The level of family generosity declines as nations advance through the four stages of financing of the humanistic sector. Japan and the United States, now in less advanced stages, have the highest levels of family generosity. Canada is somewhat less generous. And Sweden, firmly entrenched in Stage IV, probably has the lowest level of voluntary generosity.[6] Not surprisingly, perhaps, the equality of donations

---

[4]Quintile proportions for family donations before taxes in Canada and the United States were reduced by the estimated marginal tax rate for the quintile group, and a new proportional distribution calculated. No adjustment was made in quintile proportions in Japan since donations generally are not deductible there.

[5]The ratio of donations to GNP in the United States dropped from 1.8 per cent in 1970 to 1.6 per cent in 1980.

[6]Swedish tax authorities do not recognize donations as deductions from taxable income and donations are not shown as an expenditure category in the Swedish survey of family expenditures. Discussion with Swedish officials confirms that while Swedes do support certain charities, such as the Red Cross, the level of family generosity is comparatively low.

across income classes coincides with the equality of income distribution, becoming flatter as incomes become more evenly distributed.

Increased taxation, such as Canadians have experienced since 1960, spawns two distinctly different types of negative reaction. First is the sense that one is being treated unfairly—that other taxpayers in similar economic circumstances somehow pay less tax on their equivalent income. This is the perception of horizontal inequity—someone else is ripping off the system. Someone else may be a small businessman who enjoys tax concessions and incentives, or a neighbor enjoying depletion allowances, RHOSP benefits, hobby farm write-offs or what have you. Second is that everyone's taxes are too high and that the government should encroach less on one's economic life. In this case, there is the perception of both horizontal and vertical inequity.

Canada is feeling the backlash of both reactions. Tax evasion in its many guises—barter, non-reporting of income, padding of expenses—is increasingly prevalent. At the same time has grown a mood of general discontent with the size of government and its costs—a theme that won unprecedented popularity for the federal Progressive Conservatives and their new leader in 1983. Both reactions ultimately exert pressure on the funds available for humanistic services, both involuntary through taxes and voluntary through donations.

While there is indeed a vague public perception of tax inequity, it has not crystalized into predictable and detectible behavior patterns. People have known since 1979,[7] for instance, that the Canadian income tax structure contains 119 separate exemptions, incentives or preferences that permit, indeed encourage, taxpayers to reduce their taxable income by undertaking certain transactions considered desirable public policy: deducting charitable donations; deferring the tax on RRSP contributions; enjoying a tax credit for political contributions; claiming the small-business deduction; deducting medicare expenses; excluding gambling gains from income.

Roger Smith estimates that these tax expenditures cost the federal and provincial governments up to $9 billion in 1975 or an amount equal to one-half to two-thirds of federal income tax levies. The benefits of those tax expenditures are not equally distributed throughout the population. Most, such as the benefits from MURBs, Canadian feature films, research and development ventures, accrue to upper-income taxpayers only. Most salaried

[7]Roger S. Smith, *Tax Expenditures: An Examination of Tax Incentives and Tax Preferences in the Canadian Federal Income Tax System* (Toronto: The Canadian Tax Foundation, 1979).

employees are unable to qualify. The concessions, therefore, become in-equitable, both vertically and horizontally.

Ironically, when the federal government proposed a major tax reform in the November 1981 budget, a reform that would have made the incidence of federal and provincial income tax significantly more equitable, both within income classes (horizontal equity) and across income classes (verti-cal equity),[8] it met hysterical opposition across the country. Indeed, it de-stroyed Finance Minister Allan MacEachen, tumbling him from a position of power, authority and respect. Since then, budgets at both the federal and provincial levels have tended to be conservative, safe, and have tampered little with the revenue side for fear of arousing taxpayer antipathy. The B.C. government's 1983 budget, which slashed spending on the humanistic sec-tor, aroused considerable controversy. But by concentrating on expendi-tures, rather than revenues, governments are able to target the affected groups and contain the direct impact to an isolated minority.

Expenditure cuts on humanistic services may be the least politically pain-ful option for reducing uncontrolled deficits. If so, the problems of deficits will be shifted to hospitals, universities, schools, welfare and cultural or-ganizations, causing them either to cut costs, reduce services or look else-where for funds. Such action would force an even greater reliance on donations to meet revenue needs.

The prospect of increasing government revenues through taxes and other levies cannot be dismissed peremptorily, especially as the economy shows signs of sustained recovery. Governments have shown much ingenuity in designing revenue schemes that work. Perhaps the most ingenious new tax in recent memory is the introduction of lotteries. Sales of lottery tickets across the country in 1981 withdrew more than one billion dollars pain-lessly from an eager population, more than half as much as they donated to all charities combined. Net lottery profits of $400 million were directed mainly to the humanistic sector, either through tied grants or direct alloca-tions to community projects. Sweepstakes are successful because they tap two of mankind's fundamental emotions—his gambling instinct and his greed.

Surprising as it may be for young people who have grown up with a tele-vision blasting ''Play the Provincial!'' and ''With Wintario we all win!'' and ''What's your favorite number?'' lotteries were illegal in Canada until 1970.

---

[8]Table 4.2 in the MacEachen budget showed that, in most income brackets, there would be more gain-ers than losers from the proposed changes in tax expenditures and cuts in marginal tax rates.

Now they are a way of life. A lottery transaction offers individuals an often hard-to-resist chance to win millions in return for a ticket purchase costing a few dollars. Lotteries in Canada are voluntary, support good works and appear to be fun—especially for the winners. Yet complaints calling for their demise abound. Charges range from moral decay to economic unfairness, from political corruption to social instability. What is the harm in supporting lotteries? Why the controversy?

Evidence of lotteries dates back to ancient Rome, but they got their big start in medieval Europe. Elizabethans used them to finance public works—ports, harbors and the like. Colonial Americans used them to help finance the War of Independence. In Canada, lotteries were illegal under the Criminal Code from Confederation until 1969.

This is not to say that lotteries were not a popular form of illegal entertainment. In fact, lotteries were used often by service organizations to raise funds for worthwhile causes. Army and Navy veterans in the 1920s, for instance, raised tens of thousands of dollars for welfare organizations through lotteries and sweepstakes. Authorities looked the other way rather than prosecute groups who were breaking the law for such noble purposes.

Efforts to legalize lotteries began half a century ago. In 1931, Bill E in the Canadian Senate proposed a sweepstake system to raise revenue for hospitals hard hit by the Great Depression. Private and municipal funding had dried up. The Hospital Sweepstakes would be national in scope and carried on with the consent of the attorney-general of each province. The bill reached second reading, but was rejected after the committee report. Apparently the moral implications of legalized gambling posed too much of a political gamble for the senators. Interestingly, the arguments used in 1931 to defeat the bill are identical, even to the word, to those advanced today by opponents of the lottery.

Proposals to legalize lotteries resurfaced from time to time during the 1960s, but nothing much was done until 1968 when the mayor of Montreal, Jean Drapeau, initiated the *"Taxe Volontaire"* to help wipe out the lingering debt of Expo 67. *Taxe Volontaire* was a lottery, but called a tax, to get around the Criminal Code. The disguise didn't work and the courts ruled it illegal. Drapeau shifted his tactics. He lobbied the federal government for reform of the Criminal Code, succeeded in having it amended in 1969, and paved the way for Loto-Québec in 1970, the first government-run lottery corporation in Canada.

Manitoba followed in 1971, other western provinces in 1974, Ontario in 1975 and the Atlantic Provinces in 1976. A national lottery, the Olympic, was started in 1974 to raise revenue for the Olympic Games to be held in Montreal in 1976. After the Games, it was renamed Loto-Canada and the proceeds used to support fitness and amateur sport. Loto-Canada helped finance the Commonwealth Games staged in Edmonton in 1978, for example. Then, with a stroke of uncharacteristic decisiveness, the Progressive Conservative government of Joe Clark vacated federal participation in lotteries in 1979 by selling federal rights to the provinces for a payment of $24 million annually indexed, of course, to inflation.

When the Liberals regained power from the Conservatives in 1980, rumors resurfaced that the "feds" would propose a new national sports lottery in which participants would predict scores of major sporting events—NHL, CFL, major-league baseball. The Canadian Sports Pool actually was launched by the federal government in Spring 1984 as the vehicle for funding a $200-million federal commitment to the 1988 Winter Olympics. The provinces, not surprisingly, regarded the move as an intrusion into their lottery domain and mounted a counter-attack by dissuading retailers from selling the sports tickets. By late summer of 1984, the sports pool had lost millions of dollars. It was mercifully scrapped by Fitness and Amateur Sports Minister Otto Jelinek within days of his appointment to the new Conservative cabinet of the Mulroney government.

Today, there are six government-operated lottery corporations in Canada: Atlantic Lottery Corporation; Loto-Québec; Ontario Lottery Corporation; Western Canada Lottery Foundation; the Interprovincial Lottery Corporation, a joint undertaking of the provinces; Loto-Canada, which has kept a skeleton staff in exile. With over a billion dollars of sales, it is difficult to argue that lotteries are not popular. The statistics are most impressive. Loto-Québec presents this player profile: 75 per cent of all Quebecers 18 or over purchased one or more lottery tickets during 1981; males and females participate equally as lottery players; more than 50 per cent of the university-educated and more than 65 per cent of Quebecers earning over $30,000 purchase lottery tickets. Asserts Loto-Québec, "(Our) principal clientele is the vast middle class, not the under-privileged classes."

An Ontario Gallup Poll provides further insights: 87 per cent of Ontario households bought Wintario lottery tickets in the late 1970s; participation was almost as high among the professional and executive classes as it was among blue-collar workers; participation by income class ranged from a low of 77 per cent for those earning less than $10,000, increased to a peak of 93 per cent in the $15,000-$20,000 group, and fell back to 87 per cent for those earning more than $20,000.

The average amount spent per person, per year, on lotteries ranged from a high of $51 in Quebec, to $38 in Ontario, $23 in the western provinces, to a low of $18 in Atlantic Canada. This means that a family of four in Quebec would spend $200 per year on lotteries, in Ontario, $150. Kevin Mc-Laughlin, writing in *Canadian Taxation* in 1979, argues that despite the fact that the purchase of a lottery ticket is a voluntary act, the lottery is a form of taxation because governments retain about 40 per cent of the selling price, and have a monopoly over ticket sales. He argues further that the tax is highly regressive and shows that the incidence of the lottery tax is much more severe on low-income Canadians (0.9 per cent on families earning less than $6,000) than high-income families (0.1 per cent on those in the $15,000-plus group). Lottery officials concede the entertainment value of lotteries, and that people buy tickets because they want to win a prize, but reject the taxation label because a lottery is not a mandatory payment.

The label matters little, particularly when participation is so pervasive throughout the population. Governments use the proceeds as they do other taxes and levies, so if it looks like a tax, and is used as a tax, then probably it is a tax. More to the point are the moral issues. Religious groups, particularly the United Church,[9] argue that the lottery is a form of gambling, the Bible condemns gambling, and the continuation, sanction and promotion of lotteries by government contributes to the social and moral decay of society, indeed, that it is blasphemy.

The anti-lottery group's most eloquent spokesman is Professor D. McCormack Smyth of York University. The charges are heavy: lotteries encourage selfish behavior and promote greed; promote a belief in luck and chance rather than hard work; promote winning at the expense of others; dry up the wells of charity because as lotteries increase personal generosity decreases; widen the gap between the rich and the poor by creating millionaires. There's more: gambling, like alcohol and drugs, becomes a compulsion for some and lotteries help spread this social disease; where there is gambling there is crime and eventually organized crime; lotteries use deceptive advertising techniques—ads that are slick, sophisticated and expensive. . . .[10] In case that list of indictments isn't enough, the critics toss in the

---

[9]Supported by the Baptists, the Salvation Army and the Christian Reform Church.

[10]At least one statistician charges that lotteries may be unfair to the participants. After studying the odds of winning in certain lotteries, Prof. David R. Bellhouse of the University of Western Ontario contends that "a number of lotteries in Canada currently are unfair games of chance." The 1978-79 Provincial, for instance, offered "inequality in the chances of winning the second prize. By choosing certain numbers, a player could increase his chances of winning by 20 per cent." Big deal. The odds dropped to one in a million from 1.2 in a million. (David R. Bellhouse, *Fair Is Fair: New Rules for Canadian Lotteries*, Canadian Public Policy.)

charge of political abuse—they allege that certain Tory ridings in Ontario receive a proportionately larger share of Ontario Lottery profits than their Opposition counterparts. Shame!

What self-respecting charity would accept money that is so morally tainted? What kind of Canadian would engage in such decadence? According to Pat Mackay, spokesman for the now-defunct Ontario Charities Lottery Group, "Charities need money more than ever and raising it by lottery is the most efficient way. You just can't raise the kind of money we do in bake sales or charity balls." Presumably any blood on the lottery dollar has been laundered effectively as it passes through a government lottery corporation. For Miss Penelope (the tremulous aspirant in Lottario commercials) and millions and millions of Canadians from coast to coast, the ticket offers a chance to be a winner, to feel the tingle of excitement as the numbers are drawn, to escape into a fantasy world, to dream a life of riches and power. And, oh yes, if part of one's money happens to find its way to a hospital or a disabled treatment centre, that's all right too.

Lotteries, no doubt, are here to stay. Governments would find it difficult to give up the revenue. But they are not an efficient form of taxation. With the cost of promotion, administration and prizes skimming off 60 per cent of the gross, they make Canada Post look good by comparison. The $400 million of lottery profits could be raised simply by tacking half a point on to the income tax marginal rate schedule, at virtually no incremental collection cost and with less regressivity. Trouble is, the taxpayer would notice and would not be amused. Better to pay twice the amount and purchase a piece of a dream.

More practically, lotteries could not raise more than a small fraction of the cost of supporting the humanistic sector. What is required to satisfy the voracious appetite for funds is the broadest possible base of taxation of the three levels of government. Paradoxically, Canada has reached a record level of national spending on humanistic service precisely at a time when national production has stagnated and the population has become resentful of the level of taxation imposed to support public services. Indeed, the major challenge to governments in the 1980s will be to resist a withdrawal of the national commitment to a high level of humanistic expenditure—the essential ingredients of the good life now universally available to all Canadians. In our zeal to purge the public sector and humanistic sector of sinecures, waste and inefficiency, we must not reduce the quality, quantity and accessibility of service.[11]

---

[11]Russell Roberts (*Journal of Political Economy*, vol. 92, No. 1, February, 1984) develops an elegant model of private charity and public transfers in the United States and predicts that "private charity

(Cont'd)

Canada now spends roughly one-third of national income on the four classes of humanistic service. Governments must be resolute in their determination to sustain our national commitment at that level. They must reaffirm that Canadians will not be satisfied with a lower standard of health care, less educational opportunity, a less-secure level of public welfare and fewer, less-varied forms of cultural expression.

The present system of financing will not ensure that commitment. It will fail because individual Canadians are now ignorant or only remotely aware of the cost of humanistic service and how their taxes relate to its delivery. Most Canadians sense that they are not getting what they pay for with their taxes, that they are shouldering an inequitable share of the burden. It is true of low-income, middle-income and high-income taxpayers. It is a perception that will require change in taxation policies, then widespread public education before it is dispelled. And it will be dispelled only when individual Canadians in all circumstances see that they are treated equitably and accept a personal responsibility for, involvement in and commitment to the institutions that deliver humanistic services in their community.

Government, which after all is where the buck stops, must assume the leadership in this renaissance of personal commitment. What this inquiry has shown, more than anything else, is that individual generosity increases with community commitment. A committed society will see to it that its hospitals have sufficient funds to sustain high-quality care, that its children have a challenging, fulfilling educational experience, that society's casualties are cared for with understanding and dignity, that all Canadians develop pride in our unique contribution to cultural expression.

How can politicians enhance this individual, personal commitment? Rhetoric that heaps flattery on the volunteer is insufficient; indeed, political pandering to citizens who participate out of genuine conviction is both demeaning and nauseating. What is required is a rethinking of the balance of financial responsibility between the state and individual members of society, a recognition that humanistic benefits are not distributed equally among all citizens, that some will benefit more from training and education, others will use health-care facilities to a greater extent, and so on.

---

will not increase when governments cut welfare spending.'' Such a conclusion is likely equally valid for Canada.

In short, individual benefits and individual burden must be linked more consciously in the minds of Canadians. Financial responsibility must be redistributed so that it is perceived to be, and indeed is, more equitable than at present.

In the field of education, for instance, governments could recognize that post-secondary education is not, and never will be, accessible to all members of society—some for lack of desire, most for lack of ability. Elementary and secondary education, which is obligatory for all members of the population, is quite properly considered a public good and equally properly financed out of general tax revenues. We cannot doubt that society at large benefits from the superior productivity, advanced technology and artistic enrichment that flows from those who are educated in Canada's universities and community colleges.

But just as surely, the minority of Canadians privileged to gain higher education reap significant personal benefits that enrich their lives, both aesthetically and financially. Who knows what proportion of the cost of higher education is a public good and what share is legitimately personal? The present ratio of financing, 85:15, clearly is a bargain for Canadian university students. The ratio of 43:57, proposed by Professor Stephen Peitchinis of the University of Calgary in a thoughtful critique of the financing of higher education, perhaps is too extreme to be tolerated or implemented.

A reasonable goal, with a target for full implementation by 1990, is a ratio of 67:33. Under this proposal, the state would underwrite two-thirds of the budgets of universities and community colleges, realistic budgets which demonstrated a sensible operating plan. Each institution would then establish the pricing of its service, tuition, so as to cover the remaining third, a price that could be reduced by the amount of donations the institution could attract from alumni and friends. Invoices for student fees should indicate the value of the state subsidy for that student's education that year, as well as the tuition fee payable by the student. Such a system would make the student body and alumni much more inquisitive about university and community college financing, more attuned to the problems of depreciating plant and equipment, more critical of the misallocation of funds.

But would not the higher tuition fees place an insurmountable entry barrier to students with capacity to learn but not to pay? No. The system could be made much more accessible than it is at present. With provincial cooperation, the federal government could establish the Canadian Youth Endowment Fund, a gigantic investment trust created to direct public money into Canada's most precious resource, its brightest and best, the educated young who will be the leaders of their generation. The sole purpose of the Canadian Youth Endowment Fund would be to lend money to all Canadians who have gained admission to a university or community college and would otherwise be prevented from attending because of financial circumstances. The great universities of the world provide similar assistance. It is the policy of Harvard University, for example, to choose applicants without knowledge of their financial circumstances. Once accepted to Harvard, a student is assured of financial assistance to complete his or her program.

The Canadian Youth Endowment Fund would derive its capital from federal borrowing—the most attractive borrowing rate in the country. The loans, and all assistance would be in the form of loans, would be made at the same federal borrowing rate, recognizing the high quality of the investment. Repayment terms could be amortized over long periods but the same strict collection policies would apply to debtors as pertain in the private sector. Bad debts should be no more prevalent than a similar portfolio in a bank or trust company. Microchip data-processing technology would keep administrative costs low.

The fund could be a recognized charitable institution, able to issue tax-deductible receipts. It could be promoted as the most prestigious humanistic cause in the country and attract voluntary gifts, donations and bequests that would build a capital base whose investment income eventually could be used to reduce the lending rates charged. Far from leaving a stigma on those who borrow from the fund, membership would connote a singular honor, that one has been chosen by one's country as a worthy investment in her future—one of society's privileged minority in whom will be entrusted the country's leadership.

The Canadian Youth Endowment Fund must be a federal institution, despite the constitutional amendments necessary for its creation and operation. It must provide equal opportunity for each qualified Canadian whether living in Newfoundland or British Columbia, Quebec or Saskatchewan. Students would view their higher educational options on a national scale, tailoring their programs much more closely to their interests. The intermingling of Canadians from across the country would break down parochial attitudes which inhibit growth, tolerance and understanding. That in itself would be an enriching education.

For their part, universities should be free to establish their individual fee schedules. Students in medicine, business, law, engineering and other professional schools should shoulder a proportionately larger share of the costs to recognize their superior earning capacity. The classics, theology, anthropology and other more abstruse departments should be subsidized to recognize and protect their absolutely essential role in a liberal education.

It would mean that universities would engage their alumni in a lifelong relationship of commitment. Undergraduates would be made aware of the extent of community resources diverted to their benefit, understand that by receiving a once-in-a-lifetime privilege, they accept a lifelong obligation. Universities and community colleges soon would learn if their place in society was secure. The marketplace would have a stronger, yet not dominant, voice in the allocation of educational resources. It would be a sensible recognition of contemporary realities. It should also increase the level of personal donations to education as closer ties were developed between the university and her alumni/ae. Most importantly, the non-participants—the majority of Canadians—would be assured that the burden of higher education was distributed more equitably throughout the population.

Financing health care, which along with education consumes about nine per cent of national income, also requires reform. The architect of health insurance in Canada, the Rt. Hon. Mackenzie King,[12] never envisaged state dominance of health care. "Health insurance," said King, "is a means employed in most industrial countries to bring about a wider measure of social justice, without, on the one hand, disturbing the institution of private property and its advantages to the community or, on the other, imperilling the thrift and industry of individuals."

Canadians now enjoy health care that is universally accessible and, in all but a few provinces that charge health-care insurance premiums, totally financed from general revenues. A much greater attempt must be made to relate family benefits to family burden. Charging user fees for health benefits is perverse, if one accepts the principle of universal access. But charging families and individuals a reasonable yearly premium for insurance against health catastrophes not only is good business, but reinforces the notion of personal responsibility. A 50-50 split between state responsibility for a healthy populace and individual responsibility to share in the cost of health-care delivery would not be an unreasonable distribution of relative benefits.

---

[12]King's vision of social insurance, which he equated with health insurance in one form or another, was published in 1918 in a volume entitled *Industry and Humanity: Some Principles Underlying Industrial Reconstruction*. It puts forth his social philosophy with concision and clarity.

This would mean that health insurance premiums would increase from their present levels—20 per cent of the cost of health care in Ontario, for instance—to 50 per cent of estimated medical and hospital costs, and would be introduced in provinces where they do not now apply. The burden of the premium would tend to fall regressively on the population,[13] perhaps not an unreasonable distribution of this essential element of personal welfare. A statement of the cost of health-care services actually used by each family over the past year should be mailed annually, as a reminder of the value of this irreplaceable public service.

Hospitals and medical research institutes, like universities and community colleges, should be encouraged to increase their flow of private donations to augment revenues from public sources. While private donations may not reach significant proportions of total health-care budgets, each institution should seek to define its constituency, fashion an effective communication mechanism, and undertake the responsibility to explain its problems, accomplishments and needs to the public it serves. For their part, provincial governments should recognize that revenue from donations or endowments represents discretionary funds of the institution, over and above the operational allowances from the health ministry.

The federal government should abandon the principle of universality in welfare payments. Social welfare now consumes about 12 per cent of national income. Only a small part of the billions of dollars that are labelled welfare expenditures represents transfers from the fit, able and productive members of society to those who temporarily or permanently require assistance from the state. Much of what is labelled welfare is nothing more than an unnecessary redistribution of income among families who require no income supplement in order to sustain a decent standard of living. Old age security payments, family allowances and Canada Pension Plan payments alone cost the federal treasury more than $13 billion in 1983—an average of $500 per living Canadian, many of whom could manage well without the money. The administrative costs are mind-boggling.

It is illuminating to reflect on how distorted has become the public notion of state responsibility for social welfare or social insurance. Mackenzie King, generally conceded to be the fountainhead of Canada's social insurance mentality and Liberal Party social philosophy, no doubt is deriving wry

---

[13]Subject to the safety valve that exempts very low income families and perhaps seniors from paying premiums.

amusement at the preposterous extremes to which his sound principles have been stretched in the name of justice and equity.

> Workmen's compensation, sickness and invalidity insurance, widows' pensions, maternity and infant benefits, recognize wherein personal relationships in industry have changed, and where as a consequence of new conditions permanent handicaps arise. The social legislation of which these measures are an expression rejects, as unworthy, the thought that men and women voluntarily incur accident, sickness, disease, enfeebled health, or dependence in distress, any more than they willingly seek enslavement of any kind. It recognizes the difficulty of differentiating between industrial accident and occupational disease, and between disease occasioned by occupation or its environments and illness otherwise contracted, also the impossibility of dissociating from economic conditions the social waste caused by excessive and preventable illness. It sees that debt binds health as it binds freedom, that sickness represents the most frequent factor of individual destitution, and that it is in painful crises that handicaps for the whole of life are oftenest imposed. To save the spirit of men from being crushed is quite as important as to prevent their bodies from being broken or infected. Many a man's spirit fails when, through no fault of his own, or of his family, efficiency is permanently impaired through accident, or savings become exhausted by unemployment or sickness, or where a new life in the home suggests an additional burden instead of joy. Much invalidity and penury is due to lack of character and thrift, but much also is evidence of want of effective social control. What society fails effectively to prevent, society is in some measure under obligation to mend.

King wrote those words in his philosophical manifesto published in 1918 and was so proud of them that he read them into Hansard on March 26, 1926, during debate on the Old Age Pension Bill. ''I am proud,'' said King, ''to be able to stand here tonight and to join with others in giving permanent expression in the legislature of our country to the ideas and the purposes that are therein expressed.''

That social philosophy did not envisage a ludicrous labyrinth of contradictory fiscal legislation where the most well-to-do members of society are taxed heavily by one federal department, then given a monthly refund in the form of family allowances by another.

Indeed, family allowances, when they were introduced by the King Government in 1944, were paid only to lower-income Canadians who truly needed additional cash flow to survive with dignity. Universality crept in first as an administrative convenience, then quickly spread when politicians discovered its political potential.

Today in the microchip era, social allowances are easily targeted to those who require the state support system. All that is required is political statesmanship. The federal government could begin by eliminating family allowance payments for the upper quintile of the population and transfer that wealth, $240 million,[14] to the neediest members of society, the lowest quintile. Reform of family allowances, as a beginning, would demonstrate a resolve to reduce government to its fundamental purpose—to provide social services that are essential for a strong, dignified society, not to create and perpetuate a system which accentuates inequality and whining dependence.

Governments, at all levels, should recognize that the welfare sub-sector must never become totally state-dominated and professionally managed so as to exclude the services of the volunteer. More than any other class of humanistic service, welfare service calls upon mankind's deepest sense of caring, compassion and selflessness. Welfare institutions offer the vehicle through which these decent human qualities can be expressed. For this reason, the United Way should not be permitted to atrophy. All governments in Canada should recognize the value of the United Way and give Canada leadership to that end. Leaders in government could speak and act as if the United Way counts for much that is good in our society. Governments could accept that they have a duty to take over the funding of some established programs, now dependent on the United Way for resources.

Just as foundations represent a rich financial resource, the United Way coalesces society's human resources. Governments should take United Way leaders into their confidence, as they should foundation leaders. Such liaison should explore which programs deserve significant public support and which are best left for private dominance. The pool of potential donation funds for welfare causes should always be the largest of any of the four classifications of humanistic service. The motives for giving to welfare organizations should be mainly on Level One—highly altruistic. Welfare donations should be the least affected by economic cycles. The voluntary flow probably will not be responsive to income tax incentives or disincentives.

---

[14]Family allowance income of $400 million paid to the upper quintile nets to $240 million after deducting income taxes estimated at 40 per cent at the margin.

Canadians are fond of the put-down, particularly if the butt of the jab is another Canadian. We bemoan an absence of national identity, our lack of distinctive Canadian food and of unique cultural and artistic expressions. Yet, if we reflect briefly on the artistic progress the country has achieved in only the past 30 years, we must be favorably impressed. First-class and in some cases world-class theatre is regularly available from coast to coast. Two or three ballet companies easily can claim international stature. An expanding core of writers and poets is creating a Canadian library that at once is distinctive, readable and professionally respectable. Canadian actors and actresses excel on the fast track in Hollywood or London.

Without realizing it, Canada no longer is an adolescent in cultural affairs. Yet, it is doubtful if we would be where we are today were it not for the steady, conservative, disciplined plodding of the CBC, the National Film Board, Canada Council, the provincial arts councils and other public entities, and for the magnificent work of the Council for Business and the Arts in Canada and other private concerns in mobilizing business and personal resources behind artistic causes.

Indeed, the very success of the past formula may lead us unwittingly to assume that more is better, that if public funding of 50 per cent is good, 75 per cent would be better, and 100 per cent best. It is a logic that must be rejected. Cultural institutions should *never* accept government funding that exceeds 49 per cent of their revenues. The state should *never* have the dominant voice in cultural expression in the country. Only then can art legitimately retain its independence, its irreverence, its freedom to expose our strengths and our weaknesses for better or for worse. Similarly, culture should resist the temptation to depend too heavily on business for financial support. At some point, artistic expression will offend corporate goals and the weaker partner will concede.

Such a policy imposes rigid standards for cultural institutions. They must work vigorously at cultivating community support in the form of voluntary involvement and seek significant financial donations to augment ticket revenues. But, isn't that the purpose of cultural institutions, to engage and reflect society?

At the same time, the federal government and the provinces should rethink multicultural policies. Without denying their ethnic heritage, Canadian immigrants should be encouraged to integrate quickly into a Canadian mosaic, not to accentuate the Canadian collage of a hundred discrete ethnic streams which could tend to divide Canadian society. Commitment to the new community, not preoccupation with the old, should be the theme of multicultural initiatives. By such encouragement, new Canadians may be more inclined to expand their scope of generosity and participation in broadly based community organizations, to integrate more readily into the many facets of Canadian life.

Should the state enrich the income tax incentives for private donations by offering expanded deductions from income, or by substituting tax credits? Judging from the present propensity to donate, which tends to be proportional across income classes despite a declining after-tax cost of donations to upper-income taxpayers, and recalling the earlier analysis of personal motives, many of which appear insensitive to changes in economic ability, it is quite likely that, at best, the net increase in donation flows would be disappointingly small. At worst, enriched tax incentives would not contract donation flows. The lost tax revenue caused by the larger donor subsidy would be shifted to taxpayers not claiming donations, perhaps in itself a mild form of social justice. Donation tax credits, the 50 per cent credit widely promoted in 1982 and 1983 for instance, are more vertically equitable than expanded (say, 125 per cent) deductions from income, and would accomplish a secondary purpose, a modest redistribution of income into the hands of generous Canadians earning low incomes.

But the personal donation tax credit should be set at 60 per cent, not 50. Unless the credit provides a greater after-tax benefit than it does at present, there will be no incentive for upper-income Canadians who donate to increase their donations. The more generous credit would restore some of the tax benefit enjoyed by upper-income families before the highest marginal tax rates were reduced from 60-plus per cent to 50 per cent in 1982. And, after all, a very large proportion of donation dollars do come from a relatively small number of upper-income Canadians.

Equity. Responsibility. Commitment. These three themes connect all the suggestions advanced for consideration by governments in this chapter and, indeed, scattered throughout this study. Implicit in them all is the underlying assumption that Canadians wish to preserve a modicum of individual responsibility for those special services that mark a civilized society. Canadians can be a committed people, given leadership that exhibits commitment to worthy goals. But neither widespread responsibility nor commitment will flourish unless the public perceives a widespread fairness, equity, in the distribution of the fruits of our national wealth and in the burden of paying for the common necessities and public amenities. Equity, like excellence, shall remain always an elusive ideal, impossible of achievement, but eternally worthy of pursuit.

The humanistic sector in Canada will find the finances it deserves. The funds will flow ultimately from individuals, forcefully through taxes or freely through donations. The amount and proportion not only will reflect but will be reflected in the character and values of the people.

Epilogue

The air around Minaki Lodge was bracing on the third Sunday in June 1990. And fresh and pure, causing one rookie M.P. to quip, "My lungs can't take this after Hamilton." It was the day before the first meeting of the newly announced Cabinet of the government which Canadians had swept into office 13 days earlier. There was no disputing the size of the majority—204 seats from all 10 provinces. What was vigorously debated on all sides, however, was whether Canadians had voted the old party resoundingly out of office, or a new government emphatically in.

To the 30 politicians at Minaki the question was irrelevant. They were now, and for the foreseeable future would be, the most powerful group in the country. Twenty-eight million Canadians had entrusted the government of the country to their party, and the Prime Minister had chosen them for the inner circle. The Minaki retreat, scheduled to last three days, was called to crystalize government policies. Decisions reached would provide the basis for the Speech from the Throne and determine the thrust of the federal budget which the new Prime Minister had promised to introduce within 100 days.

Item One on the agenda read, "Established Programs Financing: Policies regarding federal financing of health care, education, welfare and culture."

EPF had remained a provocative issue throughout the 1980s. For more than a decade the provinces and the federal government had been unable to agree on an appropriate formula to distribute the financial burden of the broad array of social programs that now consumed 25 per cent of Canada's national income. The federal government had argued that the provinces should shoulder more of the burden, the provinces contended that the "feds" should finance a greater share since they had the broader tax base, and both agreed that the private sector—individuals and corporations— should be much more willing to support universities, hospitals, welfare agencies and the like, voluntarily through gifts, donations and personal assistance.

Cabinet briefing documents reviewed highlights of the past decade as they related to the financing issue:

...total spending on humanistic services has receded from its peak of 32 per cent of national income in 1983 to about 25 per cent today. The shift in emphasis, particularly at the federal level, stems from the Canadian commitment in 1987 to join the United States in an all-out effort to conquer outer space for military defence. Canada's allocation to defence and the space program—now about 10 per cent of national income—has preempted expenditures on humanistic services. It should be noted that when the trade-off occurred, there were few strong advocates for a continued high level of state support for social pro- grams if that meant restricted spending for defence;

...the personal income tax continues to provide the largest source of federal revenues. The Income Tax Act is widely criticized as being im- possibly complex, unfair and perverse. The new incentives and exclu- sions introduced in the 1980s have brought the number of so-called tax expenditures to 150. Prosecutions for tax evasion have increased 500 per cent over the decade;

...three debt-ridden universities are expected to close by the end of this year, bringing the total to 13 over the decade. Most are small, having been established in the 1960s, and never were able to attract significant financial support from their alumni/ae. One of this year's closings is the same university that offered two honorary degrees for tender to a select group of potential donors in 1986, hoping to endow two faculty chairs. The practice is not uncommon in the United States, dating back to the early eighties, but is only moderately successful here;

...the practice of government-appointed hospital boards is now in place in all provinces. Despite this measure of control, more than half the hospitals in Canada recorded an operating deficit in 1989. The provinces contend that control was necessary because voluntary boards just were not effective in containing the cost of hospital care;

...since the United Way was dissolved in 1988 in all but 20 small centres, the provinces now control virtually all the organizations and agencies administering health and welfare services. There are some extraordinary exceptions—The Salvation Army, Red Cross, Heart, Cancer and a handful of organizations whose appeal is intimate, emotional and powerful. Their perceived ability to attract funds directly was behind their decision to begin withdrawing from the United Way years earlier. Their prediction was accurate;

...the entry of religious organizations into the educational field continues to accelerate. Most denominations now offer primary-school classes in secular/religious instruction; some are considering adding high-school classes. The activity has found a productive use for church buildings increasingly under-utilized for Sunday worship. The tax advantages for upper-income parents are attractive since much of the tuition fee is deductible as a charitable donation. A wide variety of new sects have been registered in recent years, the most important being the Church of Atheology which now claims membership of eight per cent of Canadians from coast to coast;

...federal and provincial income tax concessions to religious donors are substantial, topping $2 billion for the first time in 1989. Most of this benefits the upper quintile of income earners, reflecting the profile of church membership making charitable donations. Observers attribute the shift to church fund-raising policies which concentrate on the large gift;

...the balance of the income tax concessions for personal donations to humanistic organizations also favor the large dollar-giver. The successful fund-raising groups, and some are remarkably successful, have perfected the art to an impressive degree. Lists of known and targeted prospective donors are compiled and stored in microcomputers (PCs) together with a surprisingly accurate and comprehensive dossier of relevant data on each family—characteristics that are known to influence the amount they donate: past history of giving; liquid wealth; income; community involvement; susceptibility to flattery; religious commitment; etc. Safeguarding these lists from thievery by other fund raisers is a major preoccupation, particularly since 1987 when computer students at McGill were convicted of stealing McGill's list and selling it to five Montreal hospital and art groups for a total of $50,000;

...income tax concessions for charitable donations by corporations are relatively modest; only one in 30 claimed deductions in 1989. With the sharp growth of Crown corporations since 1985, less than half the largest corporations in the country contribute voluntarily. Consideration might be given to withdrawing the deductibility for corporate donations, although the revenue pick-up would be modest;

...some of the provinces want a stepped-up federal commitment to health care, one that would...

As the Prime Minister digested the briefing documents prior to tomorrow's opening session with his Cabinet colleagues, he reflected on his options. Fortunately, he had spelled out very little detail about his vision for Canada, and had made few election promises during the campaign. Within reasonable limits, therefore, he was free to introduce bold initiatives to restore the country's fiscal health and to rekindle the imagination, excitement and sense of constructive purpose of the Canadian people. The Prime Minister relished the challenge.

Still, he mused, I wonder if we could have done anything different a decade ago that would have altered the progression to nearly total dependence on the state?

Appendices

312

Appendix A

**CANADIAN EXPENDITURES ON HUMANISTIC SERVICE
EXPRESSED AS A PROPORTION OF NATIONAL INCOME
1937, 1947, 1957, 1969, 1978**

	Percentage of national income				
Humanistic expenditure	1937	1947	1957	1969	1978
Health care	5.1	3.7	5.1	4.9	8.7
Education	4.3	3.4	4.6	10.1	9.0
Social welfare	6.3	4.7	5.3	7.2	11.8
Culture, recreation, religion	1.7	1.4	1.6	1.8	2.2
Total	17.4	13.2	16.6	24.0	31.7
National income at factor cost (millions)	$3,900	$12,300	$25,400	$60,500	$179,000

Source: Derived from National Income and Expenditure Accounts Series: Family Income and
Expenditure Series; Corporation Taxation Statistics Series: Statistics Canada.

Appendix B

**SOURCES OF FUNDS FOR HUMANISTIC SERVICE
EXPRESSED AS A PROPORTION OF NATIONAL INCOME
1937, 1947, 1957, 1969, 1978**

Source of funds	*Percentage of national income*				
	1937	1947	1957	1969	1978
Public sector	9.0	8.3	11.3	18.9	27.9
Private sector					
Individual expenditures	7.3	4.0	4.3	4.2	3.1
Individual donations	1.1	0.8	0.9	0.8	0.6
Corporate donations	0.1	0.2	0.1	0.1	0.1
Total private	8.5	5.0	5.3	5.1	3.8
Total	17.5	13.3	16.6	24.0	31.7
National income at factor cost (millions)	$3,900	$12,300	$25,400	$60,500	$179,000

Source: Derived from National Income and Expenditure Accounts Series; Family Income and Expenditure Series: Corporation Taxation Statistics Series: Statistics Canada.

Appendix C

**AMOUNTS SPENT BY LOCAL, PROVINCIAL AND
FEDERAL GOVERNMENTS, CORPORATIONS, INDIVIDUALS
AND FOUNDATIONS ON HEALTH, EDUCATION,
WELFARE AND CULTURAL SERVICES IN CANADA, 1980**
(Humanistic matrix)

Source of funds	*Humanistic service provided ($ billions)*				
	Health	Education	Welfare	Culture*	Total
Local governments	1.41	11.05	.78	1.61	14.86
Provincial governments	14.21	5.99	4.87	.75	25.82
Federal governments	.38	.72	19.44	.54	21.07
Total public sector	16.00	17.76	25.09	2.90	61.75
Individual expenditures	3.37	1.02	1.57	.65	6.61
Individual donations	.18	.11	.18	1.46	1.93
Corporate donations	.03	.12	.08	.03	.26
Foundation grants	.03	.02	.03	.02	.10
Total private sector	3.61	1.27	1.86	2.16	8.90
Total all sources	19.61	19.03	26.95	5.06	70.65

*Including recreation and religion

Source: Derived from National Income and Expenditure Accounts, Family Income and
Expenditure, and Selected Financial Statistics of Charitable Organizations: Statistics
Canada.

Appendix D

DONATION CLAIMS BY VARIOUS OCCUPATIONAL GROUPS

(ranked in order of gross income, average donations claimed, percentage of donations to income, and percentage claiming donations, 1980)

Occupation group	Proportion of total	Average income	Average donations claimed		Percentage donations to income		Percentage claiming donations	
				Rank		Rank		Rank
1. Doctors and surgeons	0.19	$62,273	$778	(1)	1.2	(5)	51.9	(2)
2. Dentists	0.05	55,328	725	(2)	1.3	(4)	49.1	(3)
3. Lawyers and notaries	0.11	45,921	641	(4)	1.4	(3)	47.1	(4)
4. Accountants	0.06	39,317	674	(3)	1.7	(1)	52.1	(1)
5. Engineers and architects	0.03	36,477	333	(5)	0.9	(8)	35.6	(5)
6. Teachers and professors	2.12	24,632	172	(9)	0.7	(11)	23.9	(7)
7. Federal government employees	2.48	19,362	75	(13)	0.4	(14)	14.0	(14)
8. Provincial government employees	3.60	18,973	75	(13)	0.4	(14)	13.5	(15)
9. Armed Forces	0.55	18,193	34	(17)	0.2	(18)	6.2	(22)
10. Other professionals	0.26	17,851	209	(6)	1.2	(5)	22.6	(8)
11. Investors	6.69	16,560	172	(9)	1.0	(7)	20.8	(9)
12. Municipal government employees	3.66	16,286	63	(14)	0.4	(14)	11.2	(18)
13. Property owners	0.72	15,370	199	(7)	1.3	(4)	19.8	(11)
14. Employees of business enterprises	48.61	15,140	52	(16)	0.3	(15)	9.3	(20)
15. Salesmen	0.23	14,306	116	(10)	0.8	(9)	16.3	(13)
16. Institutional employees	5.44	14,075	82	(12)	0.6	(12)	13.0	(16)
17. Farmers	1.87	13,265	194	(8)	1.5	(2)	25.6	(6)
18. Business proprietors	3.39	12,049	90	(11)	0.7	(10)	19.9	(10)
19. Fishermen	0.27	10,795	47	(18)	0.4	(13)	9.8	(19)
20. Entertainers and artists	0.12	9,188	53	(15)	0.6	(12)	11.7	(17)
21. Unclassified employees	2.44	8,632	28	(19)	0.3	(16)	6.3	(21)
22. Pensioners	6.32	8,323	90	(11)	1.1	(6)	19.2	(12)
23. Unclassified	10.75	2,193	6	(20)	0.3	(17)	1.6	(23)
TOTAL CANADA	100.00	$13,716	$ 71		0.5		11.3	

Source: Derived from Taxation Statistics 1980; Statistics Canada.

Appendix to Chapters VII and VIII

FAMILY DONATION REGRESSION MODELS

Two measures of family donations were specified as dependent variables in regression models: family donations expressed in dollars (quantity model) and family donations expressed as a percentage of family income (quality model).

Family donations were separated into two categories: total religious donations and total non-religious donations.

Twenty-four independent variables were formulated to measure various decision variables specified in the Family Donation Decision Model outlined in Chapter V. The independent variables were as follows:

Ability variables (5)

INC1	Income (continuous)
CHILDREN	Number of children (continuous)
LIQ1	Liquid assets (continuous)
ASSET1	Other assets (continuous)
DEBT1	Liabilities (continuous)

Level Two variables (13)

ANGLO	Anglo-Saxon (1,0)
QUEBEC	Quebec (1,0)
BORNCAN	Born in Canada (1,0)
EDUC	Education (4 levels)
AGE	Age (6 levels)
SEX	Sex (1,0)
PROF	Professional (1,0)
WHITCOLL	White collar (1,0)
BLUECOLL	Blue collar (1,0)
RETIRED	Retired (1,0)
RES	Residence (1,0)
MOBIND	Mobility index (continuous) (sum of residence and occupational changes over past 10 years)
NORGS	Number of organizations (continuous)

Level One variables (6)

RELCOMM	Religious commitment (4 levels)
CATHOLIC	Roman Catholic (1,0)
UNITANGL	United Church or Anglican (1,0)
PROT	Other Protestant (1,0)
NORELIG	No religion (1,0)
PERCPLAN	Percentage planned (0 to 100%)

FAMILY RELIGIOUS DONATIONS   N = 699

	Quantity model	*Quality model*
	T statistic	
Ability variables		
INC1	24.14***	
CHILDREN	[−] 6.38***	[−] 7.54***
LIQ1		
ASSET1		
DEBT1		
Level Two		
ANGLO		4.65**
QUEBEC		
BORNCAN		
EDUC		2.80*
AGE		
SEX		
PROF		
WHITCOLL		
BLUECOLL		
RETIRED		
RES		
MOBIND		[−] 3.41*
NORGS		4.93**
Level One		
RELCOMM	66.15***	138.06***
CATHOLIC		[−] 9.12***
UNITANGL		[−] 5.38**
PROT	5.32**	5.00**
NOREL		
PERCPLAN		
R²	.23	.34
F statistic	8.84	16.42

All B coefficients were positive except where indicated [−].

Level of significance for T statistics: *** 1%
                                                                    ** 5%
                                                                    * 10%
                                                                    blank not significant

FAMILY NON-RELIGIOUS DONATIONS N = 699

	Quantity model	Quality model
	T statistic	
Ability variables		
INC1	41.20***	
CHILDREN	33.57***	46.17***
LIQ1		
ASSET1		
DEBT1		
Level Two		
ANGLO		[−] 2.83*
QUEBEC		
BORNCAN		
EDUC		
AGE		
SEX		
PROF		
WHITCOLL		
BLUECOLL		
RETIRED		
RES		
MOBIND		
NORGS	8.18***	17.33***
Level One		
RELCOMM	4.95**	8.29***
CATHOLIC	[−] 6.98***	[−] 5.10**
UNITANGL	[−] 7.61***	[−] 6.08**
PROT	[−] 3.03*	
NOREL	[−] 4.51**	
PERCPLAN		
R²	.22	.22
F statistic	9.47	8.49

All B coefficients were positive except where indicated [−].
Level of significance for T statistics: *** 1%
** 5%
* 10%
blank not significant

Index

Level One, 104, 122, 156, 182, 241
Level Two, 104, 122, 156, 165, 236, 241
Leverage, 104, 112, 170
Lévesque, Georges-Henri, 79, 80
Lifestyle, 97, 176, 180
Live-in arrangement, 180
Locke, John, 126
Lotteries, 291-295
Lower Canada, 60, 61, 62, 65
Loyal and Patriotic Society of Upper Canada, 62
Luther, Martin, 47
Lutherans, 92, 95

Macdonald, Sir John A., 66
Marx, Karl, 53, 193
Massey, Hart, 70, 263
Massey, Vincent, 79, 80
McGill University, 4-8, 173
Medicare, 75-77
Mercenary fund raiser, 222
Methodists, 93
Middle Ages, 46, 47, 50
Mill, John Stuart, 53, 127
Mobility, 99, 100, 181
Mosaic, 100
Motives, 103-122, 164
    corporate, 237
Multicultural policies, 303
Multiculturalism, 86
Multiple regression analysis, 149, 150

National Society of Fund-Raising Executives, 223
New France, 56-59
Newman, Cardinal, 124, 125
Newman, Peter C., 119, 183, 184
Nietzsche, Friedrich, 127, 128
Noblesse oblige, 67, 104, 117, 182

Ontario Charity Aid Act, 67

Palmer, George Herbert, 124
Patriotic Fund, 154
Pearson, Lester B., 28, 77
Personal service, 179, 203-205, 248
Philanthropy, 53
    corporate, 224
    Golden Age of, 66, 82, 98
Philosophy, moral, 104, 119, 185
Plato, 42, 44, 123, 282
Polis, 42
Poor Laws, 49
Power, 104, 119, 183
Presbyterianism, 93, 95

Protestants, 47, 90-93

Quebec, 56-59, 70, 73, 84, 166
Queen's Receipt, 158, 159
Quid pro quo, 111, 162, 169

Recessions, Canadian, 227
Recognition, 104, 112, 170
Reformation, 47
Religion, 88-95, 119, 185-194
Renaissance, 48
Responsibility, 304
Roman Catholic, 90, 95, 186
    Catholic Church, 47, 58, 60, 90
Roman Empire, 45, 46
Rousseau, Jean-Jacques, 126
Rushton, J. Philippe, 128, 129
Ryerson, Egerton, 64

St. Laurent, Louis, 28, 79
Sartre, Jean-Paul, 128
Shaftesbury, Lord, 53
Small business, 245-247
Smith, Adam, 53, 127
Social Credit Party, 72
Social acceptance, 104, 117
    -learning theory, 129
    mobility, 104, 116, 181
    welfare, 75
Stage I, 25, 26, 35, 36, 39, 46, 53, 59, 82, 153
    II, 25, 26, 39, 46, 59, 82, 120, 153
    III, 25, 26, 54, 66, 69, 82
    IV, 25, 27, 35, 46, 47, 53, 54, 55, 56, 59, 82, 86, 121, 155, 249
Sweden, 46, 48, 52, 54, 289
Sweepstakes, 291

Tax effects, 284
    equity, 285
    impact, 284
    incentives, 161, 162
    incidence, 284
    neutrality, 284
    progressive, 284
    proportional, 285
    reform, 291
    regressive, 284
    revenues of all governments, 286
    shifting, 284
Taxation, 103, 106-110, 153-163
Tied gifts, 257
Tithe, 58, 91
Transaction, 104, 110-111, 168
Trudeau, Pierre Elliott, 28, 77, 80, 82, 133
Tuition fees, see education

Union Gas Limited, xv
Union Nationale, 73
United Church, 93, 95, 186
United States, 234, 235, 289
United Way, 69, 105, 197, 218-221, 302
  of Lower Mainland, 8
Universality, 300
University, 78, 96, 200
  fees, 297
  of King's College, 65
  of Toronto, 65, 173
  of Western Ontario, The, xiv, xv, 173
Upper Canada, 61, 62, 64, 65

Vertical equity, 285
Volunteerism, 69, 70, 204-207

Wealth, 99, 103, 106, 151, 152
  liquid, 152, 177
Welfare services, 15-16, 21, 22, 25, 28-29, 32-33
Woodsworth, J.S., 72

YMCA, 67